The War of Succession in Spain 1700–15

The War of Succession in Spain 1700–15

Henry Kamen

Indiana University Press
Bloomington · London

Published in Canada by Fitzhenry & Whiteside, Limited, Don Mills, Ontario

Library of Congress catalog card number: 75-85088

Standard Book Number: 253-19025-8

Printed in Great Britain

Contents

APPENDICES

Tables

DIAGRAMS

Abbreviations used in footnotes

Paris archives

AE Corr. Pol. (Esp.)	Archives du Ministère des Affaires Etrangères, section Correspondance Politique (Espagne).
AE Mém. et Doc. (Esp.)	*Ibid.*, section Mémoires et Documents (Espagne).
AN	Archives Nationales.
AN Aff. Etr.	*Ibid.*, section Affaires Etrangères.
BN	Bibliothèque Nationale, section des manuscrits.
Guerre	Dépôt Général de la Guerre, Vincennes.

Spanish archives

AGI	Archivo General de Indias, Seville.
AGS	Archivo General de Simancas.
AHN	Archivo Histórico Nacional, Madrid.
B Nac	Biblioteca Nacional, Madrid, sección de manuscritos.
BRAH	Biblioteca de la Real Academia de la Historia, Madrid.

BUV   Biblioteca de la Universidad de Valencia.

Hacienda   Archivo del Ministerio de Hacienda, Madrid.

British libraries

BM   British Museum, manuscript room.

NLS   National Library of Scotland.

Foreword

The scope of this book requires a few words of explanation. My researches began as an inquiry into French policy in Spain during the War of the Spanish Succession. From this I was led into an examination of Spain itself. The theme which helped to unify both these approaches was the study of the finances of the Spanish monarchy, round which most of my chapters have been built. If this has helped to make the book more coherent, it has not contributed to its structural unity, for these pages certainly do not offer a satisfactory or comprehensive survey of Spain during the War of Succession. In the case of Aragon, I have made no archival study of the origins and course of the rebellion during the war. In several other respects, there are serious gaps in my account, largely because the documentation for the period is often inadequate, so that the book is very much an introductory study. As such, however, it is the first analytical work to be published on what may well be thought of as the 'dark ages' in modern Spanish historiography, that is the years 1665 to 1746, a period of which we still remain colossally ignorant. Perhaps the most notable omission in this book is any treatment of Catalonia. I have deliberately omitted this area, firstly because other historians have made the study of Catalonia during the war their task, secondly because Castilian financial control over the principality begins only after 1715, when my study ends.

My debts are many, both to those friends and historians who gave me the benefit of their advice, as well as to the many archivists in France and Spain who introduced me patiently to the often elusive documentation for my subject. Mrs Menna Prestwich was the first to encourage me in my research, and supervised most of the work before its presentation for a doctorate at Oxford. Mr Raymond Carr, now Warden of St Antony's College, Oxford, supervised the doctorate in its later stages, and has never failed to help generously at all times. In common with other historians of Spain, I owe much to the scholarship and personal kindness of Professor Fernand Braudel. Monsieur Pierre Vilar and Professor Pierre Chaunu were generous both with their advice and encouragement.

My research was made possible initially by the kindness of St Antony's College, Oxford, which granted me a scholarship for three years and allowed me to benefit from that hospitality which has made it a unique international centre of learning. Dr John Lynch was kind enough to look through the text, and made several valuable suggestions. My wife typed the whole book, impeccably, in the middle of a hectic summer.

University of Warwick

Prologue: the Spanish Succession

On 7 November 1659, the same day as the Treaty of the Pyrenees which brought hostilities to an end between France and Spain, it was solemnly agreed to unite in marriage the French king and the Infanta Maria Teresa, eldest daughter of Philip IV of Spain. The contracts of peace and marriage were ratified by Louis XIV on 24 November in Toulouse, and on 1 December Philip reciprocated in Madrid. On 2 June the following year Maria Teresa renounced for herself and her descendants any right to succeed to the Spanish crown; a second renunciation made by her the same day declared that she forewent all her rights of succession in return for the payment of a dowry of half a million gold crowns. This dowry, according to the original marriage treaty, was to be paid within a period of eighteen months from the marriage: a third was payable at the time of marriage, another at the end of the year, and a final third six months later. On 6 June 1660 Louis swore to observe the treaty and the renunciations, and three days later he married his bride at Bayonne.

At no time did Louis or his advisers ever take the renunciations seriously. From the first they had looked on the marriage as a means to the eventual unification of the two crowns, despite the specific terms of the testament of Philip IV, which excluded Maria Teresa and her descendants from the succession. The new ambassador to Madrid, the archbishop of Embrun, was instructed in 1661 to sound the opinions of Spaniards. In August that year he reported back to Louis that the secretary of Don Luis de Haro, the Spanish prime minister, had confided to him that he considered the renunciations invalid. Louis was not surprised. Don Luis himself, he wrote to the archbishop, had said much the same to the late Cardinal Mazarin.[1] On this note of hope the French

[1] M. Mignet, *Négociations relatives à la Succession d'Espagne sous Louis XIV* (4 vols) Paris, 1835–42, vol. 1, p. 74.

king proceeded to put into effect his campaign to assure the throne of Spain to a descendant of his newly acquired wife.

The subsequent policy of France towards the Spanish succession became the primary issue in European war and diplomacy. Confident though he might often be of eventual success, Louis took no chances. Bribery in Madrid, diplomatic pressure in foreign courts, and military aggression in specific disputed areas, came to form the barbs of his three-pronged attack on the succession question. The initial – and justifiable – excuse was that the dowry of Maria Teresa had never been paid, and that this automatically made the renunciations invalid. Yet the marriage treaties had never made payment of the dowry an explicit condition of renunciation. Moreover, Louis himself betrayed what importance he attached to the money by ordering the archbishop of Embrun in November 1661 to suspend all demands for payment, since the recent death of the Spanish heir left the succession momentarily vacant. Only when a new son and heir was born on 6 November did Louis decide to resume his demands.

Failing complete possession of the monarchy, Louis had to agree to partial possession. The diplomatic method was to come to an agreement with the other interested parties, above all the Austrian Habsburgs. A partition treaty, agreed upon secretly on 19 January 1668 with the Emperor Leopold I, provided for a division of the monarchy if the sickly child king Charles II were to have no heir: the emperor would get Spain, the Indies, and the Italian territories; the rest would go to France. Unfortunately for the signatories of this predatory treaty, Charles II lingered on from apoplectic, moribund childhood into apoplectic, moribund adulthood, and the political interests of other European powers had inevitably to be considered. The result was a series of partition treaties which satisfied no one and outraged public opinion in Spain. Distrust of France made the emperor approach the maritime powers for their support, and in 1689 England and the United Provinces, both now under the command of William III of Orange, guaranteed Leopold possession of the Spanish monarchy in the event of Charles II dying without issue. Not only had the emperor now extracted varying support from the principal European powers, he was also assured within Spain of substantial influence since the marriage in 1689 of Maria Ana of Neuburg to Charles II.

The maritime powers now became the arbiters between the conflicting interests of France and Austria. At this point Louis decided to safeguard peace as well as the interests of France. After the peace at Rijswijk in 1697 he gravitated towards William 111 and persuaded him and Heinsius to agree to a general partition of the Spanish monarchy. The treaty was signed in September–October 1698. By it the electoral prince of Bavaria (chosen by a testament of Charles 11 in September 1696 as sole heir) would receive Spain and its empire outside Europe, leaving Milan to the Archduke Charles of Austria, and the Sicilies, some Italian possessions and Biscay to the French. This agreement, known conflictingly as either the First or the Second Partition Treaty, was indignantly repudiated in Spain, and its terms soon lapsed when news came in February 1699 of the sudden death of the Bavarian prince.

The final Partition Treaty, agreed upon again between France and the maritime powers, was signed in March 1700 without the participation of the emperor. By this, France added Lorraine to its previous spoils, and the duke of Lorraine was to receive Milan or Savoy; all the rest was to go to the imperial candidate, the Archduke Charles. Louis could congratulate himself on a solution that was generous to Austria. The Spanish court saw things differently. The last years of the reign had witnessed feverish diplomatic activity in Madrid on the part of representatives of the German and French governments. In 1697 the imperial ambassador, Harrach, had taken up residence in Madrid, and a year later the French envoy, Harcourt, arrived in the capital. Both these diplomats were well aware that partition was completely unacceptable to the Spaniards, and that one or the other of the contending parties must take all. By the summer of 1698 Harcourt had virtually assured victory for the French cause, but his ill health did not allow him to remain in Spain to see the triumph. He returned to France in May 1700, after the last Partition Treaty, and his place was taken by the marquis de Blécourt.

Despite the partition treaties, Spanish opinion rallied to a French succession. Charles 11, influenced by his wife, favoured the Austrian archduke, but the anti-German sentiment at court ruled this out as a workable solution. When the council of state met in Madrid in June 1700 their voting was almost unanimously in favour of a French candidate. The papacy in July 1700 also came to the conclusion that a French succession was the most desirable, because least prejudicial to peace.[2] With all concerned in reaching a decision, the uppermost consideration was how to prevent the dismemberment of the Spanish empire. Eventually, on 2 October 1700 Charles 11 drew up a testament which left the entire monarchy to Philip, duke of Anjou, the grandson of Louis xiv. A month later, on 1 November, the last and unhappiest of the Spanish Habsburgs died.

Would Louis accept the testament or would he adhere to the terms of the Partition Treaty? His final decision to accept the will can be regarded as a sincere desire to choose the more peaceful and defensible of two alternatives.[3] With the causes of the War of Succession we are here not directly concerned. It is important only to emphasise that the war came about because of circumstances not entirely within Louis' power to control. The maritime powers were prepared for war long before French blunders gave them an excuse for hostilities. By the end of 1701 the principal European powers had rallied to a Grand Alliance. France was left with the sole support of the elector of Cologne and his brother the elector of Bavaria (governor since 1691 of the Spanish Netherlands). The duke of Savoy, Victor Amadeus 11, whose daughter was subsequently to marry the new French king of Spain, allied with France by the Treaty of Turin in April 1701; six months later, in October, he joined the emperor. Portugal signed the Treaty of Lisbon with France in June 1701: in 1703 the efforts of the English envoy Methuen took it into the Allied camp. France and Spain were left almost alone against the combined forces of the rest of Europe. In May 1702 the maritime powers declared war on Louis xiv and the War of Succession had begun.

Within Spain the relief at finding a solution to the succession was equalled by a widespread satisfaction at the passing of the House of Austria. The corruption, incompetence and economic crises that had distinguished the reign of Charles 11, and the predominance at court of Germans who brought the Habsburgs into disrepute, were factors that worked more than anything else to build up a Francophile party in Madrid. The last act of the old

---

[2] Arsène Legrelle, *La Diplomatie française et la Succession d'Espagne* (4 vols), Paris, 1888–92, vol. 3, pp. 367–74.

[3] Such at least is the very plausible argument of Louis André, *Louis XIV et L'Europe*, Paris, 1950, pp. 295–303.

dynasty was played out in the palace at Madrid, where the king had just died. Ministers from all the European courts gathered outside the royal bedchamber to hear the terms of the will of Charles II.

At length the folding doors being thrown open, the duke of Abrantes appeared, and a general silence ensued to hear the nomination. Near the door stood the two ministers of France and Austria, Blécourt and Harrach. Blécourt advanced with the confidence of a man who expected a declaration in his favour; but the Spaniard, casting on him a look of indifference, advanced to Harrach and embraced him with a fervour which announced the most joyful tidings. Maliciously prolonging his compliment, and repeating his embrace, he said, 'Sir, it is with the greatest pleasure – Sir, it is with the greatest satisfaction – for my whole life – I take my leave of the most illustrious House of Austria!'[4]

[4] William Coxe, *Memoirs of the Kings of Spain of the House of Bourbon . . . 1700 to 1788* (5 vols), London, 1815, vol. 1, pp. 85–6.

PART ONE

The Government and the War

1 The War of Succession

'The history of the war of the Spanish Succession is not the internal history of Spain'.[1] The European dynastic struggle, in other words, had little immediate relevance to events within the peninsula, and we can safely leave aside any discussion of it, in order to concentrate on the internal history of Spain. The campaigns of the war in Spain have not so far received the treatment they deserve from a military historian, although the available sources are legion. The purpose of the following pages is not to make good this deficiency, but merely to give an outline of the military background against which the events with which we are concerned took place. The whole reign of Philip v was profoundly affected by developments which originated in the war: for the first time in Spanish history since the Moorish invasions, foreign troops controlled vast stretches of the country and Spanish *tercios* fought a defensive war on their own soil. The situation was not to be repeated for another hundred years.

Philip v, then a young man of seventeen, entered Madrid as king on 18 February 1701. Fifteen months later, in May 1702, the powers of the Grand Alliance, led by England and the United Provinces, declared war on France and Spain. When Portugal subsequently defected to the side of the Allies in 1703, the Bourbon dynasty in Spain was left to rely exclusively and solely on French aid against the combined intervention by land and sea of English, Dutch, German and Portuguese forces. The Allied campaigns were a joint effort, not always happily organised or led because of the differing aims and methods, which soon became very obvious grounds for dissension. The English and Dutch were committed to intervention principally because of their concern for the future of the Indies trade, and their first military

[1] Arsène Legrelle, *La Diplomatie française et la Succession d'Espagne*, vol. 3, p. 332.

operation – an attack on Cadiz – betrayed the interests of the maritime powers in controlling the traffic to America. Portugal, won
over by the Methuen Treaty in the summer of 1703, was attracted
not only by British trade offers but also by the opportunity to
redress the political preponderance of Castile in the peninsula.
The empire, outmanoeuvered in the diplomacy of the succession,
refused to consider that the Habsburg day was over in Spain, and
intervened solely to impose on the Spanish people another
Austrian ruler in the shape of the Archduke Charles, son of the
Emperor Leopold 1. The archduke was solemnly crowned king
of Spain at Vienna on 12 September 1703. It was in his name for a
decade thereafter that Allied forces struggled fruitlessly to impose
their will on the population of the peninsula.[2]

The western Mediterranean formed a single strategic unit, and
it was to the Bourbon interest to maintain the adherence of the
Italian states to the Spanish crown. Philip was consequently prevailed upon to visit his Italian possessions in 1702. This, as we
shall see, was to prove to be a serious error of judgment, and few
benefits were gained from it. During his stay in Italy war broke
out, and the first campaigns fought by the young king were
indecisive but not unsatisfactory ones in the state of Milan,
against the forces commanded by Prince Eugene of Savoy. In
Spain, which is our present concern, hostilities were opened by
the dispatch of a powerful Allied expeditionary force with instructions to seize Cadiz, or, failing that, any other suitable port.
The Dutch and English ships, fifty in number, were commanded
by Sir George Rooke, and had on board a landing force of about
fourteen thousand men, under the duke of Ormond. In July this
navy invested Cadiz and by the end of the month had landed all
its troops. But the capture of Puerto Santa María led to scenes of
plunder and sacrilege which disgusted the native Spaniards and
alienated Catholic supporters of the Austrian party, notably Prince
George of Hesse-Darmstadt, a former viceroy of Catalonia. In
addition the fierce resistance from a rather poorly garrisoned
Cadiz made its capture impossible, and sea conditions made ship

---

[2] Unless otherwise noted, the following account of the war is based largely on
Arthur Parnell, *The War of the Succession in Spain during the reign of Queen Anne 1702–
1711*, London, 1905 (first published 1888), and on V. Bacallar y Sanna, Marqués de
San Felipe, *Comentarios de la guerra de España e historia de su rey Felipe V, el Animoso*,
Madrid, 1957 edn.

manoeuvres hazardous. Facing certain failure, Rooke reembarked
the troops and set sail at the end of August.

The failure at Cadiz was soon forgotten at news that the
Spanish silver fleet, due from America under the escort of the
French admiral Chateaurenaud, had arrived off the coast of
Galicia. The English had already sent out a fleet under Admiral
Sir Cloudesley Shovel to attack the galleons, and Rooke was at the
same time informed of the situation. The latter instantly sailed to
Vigo Bay, where the silver fleet had taken shelter, and proceeded
to land Ormond's troops. In an engagement between the Allied
and French ships on 23 September, most of the Franco-Spanish
fleet was destroyed, many prizes taken, and much merchandise
sent to the bottom.[3] Shovel arrived four days later to help clear
up what was left. In terms of bullion the incident was not a disaster for the Spanish crown. The real disaster, as San Felipe
observes, was that the traders of Cadiz suffered a bitter blow to
their commerce; and, above all, that the destruction of the Spanish
fleet deprived the king of vessels to carry on the Indies trade, so
that he was to some extent obliged to rely on French shipping for
the maintenance as well as the protection of the *carrera de Indias*.[4]

Philip returned to Spain at the end of 1702 and entered his
capital again towards the end of January 1703. The years 1702 and
1703 saw no hostilities within Spain, so that some effort of reorganisation was made during this respite. A general conscription
order was issued on 3 March 1703, ordering the recruitment of
more *tercios*. The task of building up a properly equipped fighting
force was far from easy, yet an effort was made by Jean Orry,[5]
who seems to have had very little success indeed. The recovery of
the Spanish military machine during the war was so slow a process that its beginnings, even its progress, cannot be described
with any certainty. It was fortunate that Philip could rely on the
intervention of his grandfather. In February 1704 the first French
troops crossed the Spanish border on their way into the peninsula. They were commanded by the marquis de Puységur, later a
marshal of France, and by the duke of Berwick. Their numbers
were made up of twenty infantry battalions, six cavalry regiments

---

[3] For a detailed discussion of the Vigo disaster, see Henry Kamen, 'The Destruction of the Spanish Silver Fleet at Vigo in 1702', *Bulletin of the Institute of Historical
Research*, Nov. 1966, pp. 165–73.

[4] San Felipe, *Comentarios*, p. 50.

[5] For Orry, see below, p. 46.

and two of dragoons. On 16 February, after a splendid entry into Madrid, Berwick was appointed captain general of the Franco-Spanish armies in the peninsula. He was the first and greatest of several distinguished French generals whose victories were to preserve the Bourbon succession.

Meanwhile the Archduke Charles had at the beginning of January 1704 paid a visit to Queen Anne at Windsor, in his new role as Charles III of Spain. On 24 February the Allied candidate was accompanied towards Lisbon by an enormous fleet commanded by Rooke. The Habsburg king arrived at Lisbon on 7 March, and with the disembarkation of the armies the campaigns of the war began to be seriously deliberated. This year witnessed conflict principally on the Spanish–Portuguese border, but there were naval battles of serious consequence to the Spanish crown. The war was now well under way.

Philip decided to lead his army in person. On 4 March 1704 he left Madrid in the direction of the Portuguese frontier. The Franco-Spanish force under Berwick and the king consisted of eighteen thousand infantry and eight thousand cavalry,[6] and this force was first directed against the Portuguese garrison at Salvatierra, which fell in the middle of May. Bourbon strategy aimed at the capture of Lisbon. Berwick and the king were to advance down the right bank of the Tagus to Villa Velha, the Principe de Tserclaes Tilly was to follow the other bank and take Portalegre, Don Francisco de Ronquillo was to invade Beira, the north was to be invaded by the duque de Hijar, and from the south the governor of Andalucia, the marqués de Villadarias, was to take the rest of Portugal. The king presided personally over the capture of Castel-Branco, while Tserclaes, by his capture of Portalegre, consolidated the possession of the whole province of Alemtejo. Lisbon itself was threatened, but bad supplies and unfamiliar terrain began to hamper the efforts of Berwick, and the onset of summer made it uncomfortably hot to press the advantage. The royal army was left on a defensive footing and Philip returned home, entering Madrid on 16 July.

The Allies made excellent use of this respite. Early in May the fleet under Rooke left Lisbon. It included thirty English and nineteen Dutch ships, besides some smaller vessels, and a landing force of some 2,400 men. Supreme command over this force was

6 San Felipe's figures.

in the hands of Prince George of Hesse-Darmstadt. The ships sailed in the direction of Nice, and attempted on their way to attack Barcelona, where their weak efforts were beaten off by the viceroy, Don Francisco de Velasco. On resuming the voyage in early June, it was discovered that the main French fleet under the comte de Toulouse and Admiral d'Estrées was off Toulon, whereupon Rooke returned towards the Portuguese coast, where he was joined by Shovel with twenty-three ships of the line. For most of June and July the Allied fleet remained cruising on the Atlantic side of the Straits of Gibraltar, with the intention of attacking Cadiz once more. Finally it was proposed by Darmstadt that an attempt be made on Gibraltar.

On 1 August Rooke took up positions in the bay of Gibraltar. That afternoon the forces disembarked and cut off communications between Gibraltar and the mainland by occupying the isthmus. Despite his tiny garrison and poor defences, the governor of the city rejected a call to surrender. The Allied ships on the morning of 2 August thereupon drew up in the bay, preparatory to an attack. Early in the morning of 3 August they began their bombardment. By the evening the governor agreed to capitulate, terms were agreed, and three days grace was given. On 6 August Darmstadt occupied the city in the name of Charles III, though effective possession remained with the English.

The same month saw the biggest naval engagement of the war. This was the battle of Málaga. The comte de Toulouse with the French fleet was known to be in the vicinity of Gibraltar, so Rooke kept his fleet ready for defence, and in the middle of August he was joined by Shovel. On 23 August Toulouse was sighted off Málaga, and an engagement became inevitable. On the morning of Sunday, the 24th, the two navies took up battle positions. On each side the principal naval forces of the countries involved had been committed, making the outcome a matter of supreme importance. The French fleet, under Toulouse and D'Estrées, consisted in all of ninety-six vessels. On the Allied side there were over sixty-eight vessels, commanded by Admirals Shovel and Rooke, Vice-Admiral Sir John Leake, and two Dutch admirals. The battle, which began in mid-morning, lasted for thirteen hours and wreaked severe damage to both sides. Though not a single ship on either side was taken or totally destroyed, numerous vessels were seriously incapacitated, several captains and admirals were killed, many other senior officers (including Toulouse himself) were wounded, and the casualties on both sides ran into thousands. The indecisive result of the struggle made both parties unwilling to prolong the conflict, and next morning they steered away from each other. The remainder of the Peninsular War saw no further naval engagements of importance, and the respective navies were employed principally in giving support to land campaigns.

Attention now shifted back to the Portuguese expeditions. The Allies had decided to use Portugal as their base for the invasion of Spain. By spring 1704 the total Allied commitment in Portugal was about 20,300 foot and 700 horse. The English detachments were commanded by the duke of Schomberg, second son of a famous namesake.[7] The commanders-in-chief of the Portuguese and Allied forces were two Portuguese generals – the conde de las Galveas and the marqués Das Minas. Their campaigns in early 1704 were purely defensive ones against the highly successful Bourbon forces. When Berwick retired in July, however, some readjustments for the autumn campaign were carried out. Schomberg was recalled to England and replaced by an eminent French exile, Henry de Ruvigny, earl of Galway, who joined the Allied forces late in August. Das Minas was meanwhile made supreme commander of the troops. These changes on one side were accompanied by one on the other. News of the fall of Gibraltar in August had made the authorities in Madrid concerned about the safety of Andalucia, and Berwick had been asked to divert his troops to the south. Aware of the Allied build-up across the Portuguese border, he had refused to move. Consequently he was recalled to France and a new commander was sent in his place. This was Marshal de Tessé, who arrived in Madrid on 10 November. Berwick, suitably rewarded with the Golden Fleece, returned to France.

Tessé's first task was to recover Gibraltar. In February 1705 he arrived before Gibraltar and began measures to recover a fortress whose loss had seriously wounded Spanish prestige. By April, however, attempts to recover the town had failed and the idea of a blockade seemed impractical; at the end of the month the

---

[7] It will be recalled that the great marshal, one of Louis xiv's best generals, was exiled from France because of his religion, by the Revocation of the Edict of Nantes.

Bourbon troops raised the siege and marched north. The case of Gibraltar is of some significance. As was to happen subsequently with whole provinces of the monarchy, resistance to the Allies had collapsed because of inadequate means of defence, whereas resistance to the Bourbons often succeeded because the Allies took care to garrison and equip places they had overrun. The parlous defences of Spain, rather than the desire of the people to embrace the cause of Charles III, explained a great deal of the success of the Allies.

The first half of 1705 saw little military activity outside the Gibraltar area. In the summer the Allies in Portugal tried to consolidate an invasion of Spain by laying siege to Badajoz, but Tessé came up to defend the city and when the Allies resumed the siege in October after the summer season, they were forced by the French general to retreat towards Portugal. Allied successes in 1705 were made possible only by sea operations. The well-known separatism of the Catalans, and the contacts maintained with several of their leaders by Darmstadt (their last Habsburg viceroy), influenced the English government to send an invasion fleet to the Mediterranean coastline of the peninsula. An expeditionary force for Catalonia was formed. At its head (since Darmstadt was a Catholic and ineligible for office under the English crown) was placed the controversial earl of Peterborough, the naval contingent being commanded by Sir Cloudesley Shovel. On 24 July 1705 the whole force set sail from Lisbon, with the Archduke Charles on board. At Gibraltar on 4 August more troops were embarked, and six days later the fleet put in at the port of Altea in Valencia. Altea joined the Allies, and this began the movement of civil disturbance in Valencia, which we shall examine in detail in a later chapter. On 22 August the fleet anchored off Barcelona.

At Altea the Allies had put ashore an exiled Valencian soldier, Juan Bautista Basset y Ramos, together with a small force of Spanish troops. While Basset continued to raise Valencia for Charles III, the Allies were besieging Barcelona. This twin pincer movement was completely successful. On 9 October Barcelona capitulated to Charles III and two months later, on 16 December, Basset entered Valencia city in his sovereign's name. By the end of the year the provinces of Catalonia and Valencia were largely in Allied hands. The unpopular viceroy of Catalonia, Francisco de Velasco, was hurried on board the English ships when an anti-Bourbon riot broke out in the streets of Barcelona. The rapid subjection of the eastern provinces was, to the Allies, proof of the readiness of Spaniards to accept a Habsburg monarch. The reality was not as simple as this, and events were to show how sanguine Allied hopes had been.

By the end of 1705, however, the cause of Philip v was seriously threatened. The subsequent year saw comparable disasters. Tessé left Extremadura for Madrid in November 1705, and arrived in Saragossa at the end of December. The campaign he was commissioned to carry into effect involved the recapture of Barcelona. Philip came with the army in order to stress the great importance of the objective. On 12 March the king arrived at Tessé's camp at Caspe. The army then took the route through Cervera and Igualada. On 3 April Tessé and Philip arrived before Barcelona. Two days before that the French fleet from Toulon, commanded by Toulouse, had dropped anchor outside Barcelona. On 6 April the attack on the fortress of Montjuich began.

In spite of the time, money and materials spent on the siege, it was a signal failure. What saved Barcelona was the arrival on 7 May of an Allied relief fleet with armed reinforcements. That same day the French ships withdrew quietly, and on the night of 11 May Tessé also struck camp and withdrew north towards Perpignan in France. The presence of Allied forces in Aragon made it necessary for Philip to retire through France and return to Spain through Navarre. On 6 June the king was back in Madrid. By then his cause in Castile had received a crushing blow.

The diversion of most Bourbon resources to the siege of Barcelona had seriously exposed the rest of the peninsula. With Allied troops under Das Minas massing on the Portuguese border, it became imperative to open a second front. In February 1706, accordingly, Louis xiv created Berwick a marshal of France and sent him to Spain to conduct the campaign against the Portuguese. At the beginning of April the Allies crossed the border, but Berwick was unable to prevent them breaking through successfully to capture Alcántara, on the Tagus. For the next few weeks, Berwick was obliged to stand by helplessly while the Allies, superior in numbers and in equipment, pushed successfully through Castile. On 28 April Plasencia fell, on 26 May

Ciudad Rodrigo, on 7 June Salamanca. Madrid was now threatened. On 20 June the queen, the court and all the organs of government left the capital and retired to Burgos in the north. Philip stayed to join Berwick's force, but instead of offering battle to the now depleted Portuguese they withdrew to Alcalá de Henares on 25 June and allowed Galway and Das Minas to enter Madrid on 27 June.

The fall of Madrid was a hollow victory for Das Minas. Charles III was proclaimed king, the disaffected queen dowager (widow of Charles II) sent her submission from Toledo, and several nobles joined the Habsburg cause. But in Madrid, as in most of Castile, the people refused to accept the foreign troops as their masters, and so long as a junction could not be effected with the troops in Aragon, or adequate garrisons placed in Castile, the conquests remained illusory. At the time, however, enthusiasm ran high. On 29 June an Allied force had taken Saragossa. This meant that the four chief cities of Spain were now in the hands of Charles III. It only remained for the invaders to consolidate their gains. Galway and the Portuguese waited beyond Madrid for Charles to arrive. The delay allowed Louis to send an extra detachment of horse and foot through Navarre to join Berwick: the two forces met at Xidrueque, and by their junction sealed the fate of the triumphant Allies.

Charles III entered Saragossa on 15 July and stayed in the Aragonese capital till the 24th. On the latter date he left the city and made his way to the Allied camp at Guadalajara, where he arrived on 6 August. His troops reinforced Galway's numbers, but already inroads had been made on their conquests, and a month later, on 4 October, Philip v reentered Madrid without difficulty.

In the eastern half of the peninsula the Allies were still impregnable. The fortress of Alicante, on the Valencian coast, was reduced by them on 8 August 1706, and on the 9th the Bourbon garrison under Colonel Mahony was allowed to march out. But in Castile the position was not so favourable. Communications between the Allied army and Portugal had been broken by the fall of Madrid, and Galway and Das Minas had of necessity to rely on the bases of the Levant coast. Accordingly a retreat towards Valencia was ordered. The army crossed the Tagus at Duennas and marched towards Valverde on the River Júcar. At

Vélez on 17 September they were met by some English troops that had captured Requena (2 July) and the fortress of Cuenca (11 August) during their march westwards. Galway pushed on over the Júcar and then crossed the River Gabriel on 25 September. All this while Berwick had been harassing the rear of the Allied army, but failed to prevent them crossing into Valencia. On 1 October the archduke entered Valencia city and made it his capital for the next five months.

The Bourbon cause improved rapidly after this Allied retreat. The last months of the year saw the turn of the tide. On 8 October a detachment was sent out by Berwick to recapture Cuenca; the task was fulfilled after only two days' resistance. On 11 October the city of Orihuela was retaken by Spanish troops commanded in part by the embattled bishop of Murcia, Luis Belluga. On 21 October the duke of Berwick entered the town of Elche, and about a month later, in November, he also captured the city of Cartagena. By these successes the Castilian territories together with Murcia and the extreme south of Valencia returned to the Bourbon obedience and were used as winter quarters for the royal armies. Aragon was still largely under Allied control, but in Extremadura the marqués de Bay had recaptured Alcántara in December.

The strategy now adopted by the Allies in Valencia, and one which went against the wishes of the English generals and government, was to divide up the available forces and defend gains already made. In accordance with this decision, Charles left Valencia in early March and went to Barcelona, taking a number of Dutch and Catalan troops with him. Galway and Das Minas were left behind to defend Valencia.

Louis xiv had in the meantime decided to send another commander to Spain in the shape of his nephew, the duc d'Orléans. Orléans arrived in Madrid on 10 April 1707, and was immediately made supreme commander of the Bourbon armies. Berwick avoided encountering Galway before the reinforcements brought by Orléans could arrive, but the issue was forced by the wish of Das Minas and Galway to prevent a meeting between the two French commanders.[8] On 25 April the opposing armies met on the plains before the town of Almansa. The Franco-Spanish

---

[8] According to Berwick's own account, the French reinforcements had already joined him, and Orléans alone had delayed in Madrid.

forces (including one Irish regiment) amounted to somewhat over twenty-five thousand men, whereas the Allied army was much smaller, consisting of Portuguese, English, Dutch, Huguenot, and German troops to a total of fifteen thousand or more men. The battle, which began early in the afternoon and went on for two hours, resulted in the total defeat of Galway's forces. The number of casualties and prisoners on the Allied side has been estimated at half their army. Berwick's total losses were not far short of this number, at about five thousand men. Orléans came up the day after the victory, too late to share its glory. The importance of Almansa, as the one decisive battle of the Peninsular War, is beyond dispute. By it Valencia was permanently won back for Philip, the principal Allied army was shattered, vital moral initiative was regained, and the archduke was compelled to rely solely on the resources of his Catalan supporters. By Almansa the marshal duke of Berwick saved the Bourbon succession.

The task of recovering Spain was yet to be done. Subsequent months witnessed a series of wearying sieges throughout Valencia and on the borders of Aragon and Catalonia. Valencia city was recaptured on 8 May. Orléans now split forces with Berwick and made northwards to reconquer Aragon. Within Valencia the town of Játiva (whose history we shall examine later) was reduced by the commander D'Asfeld in June. Meanwhile Orléans had successfully retaken Saragossa, which he entered on 26 May. Most of Valencia and Aragon had now returned to the Bourbon allegiance. Pressure was thereupon applied to the borders of Catalonia. After the summer break, Orléans united his forces to those of Berwick and undertook the siege of the important fortress of Lérida. The city fell on 14 October, but the garrison in the citadel kept up resistance for another month, capitulating only on 14 November. Meanwhile in Castile the city of Ciudad Rodrigo had been recovered from the Portuguese on 4 October. The year 1707 ended with the Bourbons on a victorious offensive.

The following year witnessed the departure of the two principal French commanders. Berwick received a recall order from Louis XIV, who needed his services elsewhere, and the duke therefore left Valencia on 16 January, arriving on 25 February at Saragossa. His conduct after this was odd, as he appears to have left Spain in March without bothering to inform the Spanish crown – nominally his employer – of his impending departure. Orléans alone was left to attempt the siege of Tortosa. At about this time senior changes occurred in the Allied command. An imperial marshal, von Stahremberg, took over the supreme charge in Spain, and Stanhope (the English envoy to Charles III) replaced Galway at the head of the English troops. Their first concern was to relieve the pressure on Tortosa, but the foreign troops arrived from Italy too late. On 11 July 1708 Tortosa capitulated to the Bourbon army. Other successes marked the Bourbon campaign in Valencia. On 17 November the town and port of Denia fell to Spanish troops, and on 7 December the town of Alicante fell to D'Asfeld, though its garrison continued to hold out. In the autumn of this year Orléans returned to France.

Allied failures on land in 1708 were compensated for at sea by the capture of Minorca in September by land and naval forces escorted by Admiral Sir John Leake, who was now commander of Mediterranean operations. A further, and psychologically serious, setback to the Spanish cause occurred on 3 April this year, when the African fort of Masalquivir fell into the hands of Muslim forces, its garrison being carried off into slavery.

1709 everywhere was a year of disaster. The bad harvest of 1708 promised difficulties ahead for the victualling of troops, and the exceptionally cold winter of 1708–9 made matters worse. 'There had not in mortal memory been a year as cold as this', wrote San Felipe.[9] The thaw led to floods accompanied by excessively heavy spring rains. A few successes occurred in the spring campaign. On 19 April the English garrison of Alicante finally capitulated and was allowed to march out free to the ships in the bay. On 7 May the marqués de Bay won an important victory at the Portuguese border over the main body of Allied troops stationed there. The battle was fought at the River Cayo, by the plain of Gudina, and resulted in considerable losses for both the English and Portuguese.

The rest of the year witnessed no major encounter. For Spain the principal concern was Louis XIV's desire to withdraw his troops from the peninsula in an effort to placate the Allies. The French point of view was not appreciated in Spain and at court the indignation on hearing of Louis's decision was immense. Anti-French sentiment among the Spanish troops led to the

9 *Comentarios*, p. 167.

exchange of blows and even bloodshed. Unwilling to leave his grandson totally without aid, Louis ordered a few battalions to stay in the peninsula and also maintained the French garrisons in key forts such as Pamplona, Fuentarrabia and the ports of Biscay; all other troops were recalled to France. General Bezons, then the chief French commander, was ordered back, and in July D'Asfeld left Valencia for France. Spanish generals now assumed the supreme commands. With the departure of the ambassador Amelot from Madrid on 2 September, the last link connecting Philip to his grandfather was severed.

The fears of France and the hopes of the Allies hung on the conduct of the Spanish troops. The campaign of spring 1710 was conducted principally in Aragon, where the marqués de Villadarias, formerly commander in Andalucia, was placed at the head of the royal forces. On 3 May Philip left Madrid to join this army. Unfortunately, the summer was not a successful one for the Spaniards. After facing each other near Lérida for two months, on 27 July the opposing armies joined battle near Almenara, on the River Noguera. In the ensuing conflict the Allied forces were victorious, and Philip withdrew towards Lérida. The battle of Almenara was only a limited engagement, but it was enough to depress Bourbon hopes. Philip immediately replaced Villadarias by the marqués de Bay, who arrived on 15 August from Extremadura. Under the latter general, the royalist forces withdrew to Saragossa and camped outside the city. It was here that the pursuing Allies under Stahremberg caught up with them. At 8 a.m. on 20 August battle was once again joined. The Bourbon army on this occasion numbered under twenty thousand men, all Spaniards, while the slightly superior Allied army of over twenty-three thousand was a mixed force, as usual, but included nearly fourteen thousand Germans. The defeat at Almenara was repeated, this time with a vengeance. By early afternoon the Spaniards were in full retreat, having suffered about three thousand casualties and lost about four thousand as prisoners. On 21 August the archduke entered Saragossa and stayed there for five days; most of Aragon now returned to Allied control. Philip withdrew to Castile, but clearly his tenure of the crown was once again insecure. The Allies had reached Calatayud by 4 September. It was decided to evacuate the capital as in 1706. On 9 September the royal family left Madrid and arrived at Valladolid on the 16th. Twelve days later, on the 28th, Charles III entered Madrid, a week after his forces had taken possession of the capital.

Louis could hardly fail to intervene at this point. The peace terms proposed by England were totally unacceptable, and the most urgent problem now was to remedy the error of having deserted Spain. On 28 August the duc de Vendôme left Paris in order to put himself at the head of the troops in Spain. French soldiers and supplies once more flowed into Spain. On 17 September Vendôme and his fellow general the duc de Noailles arrived at Valladolid to confer with Philip v. It was decided to let Bay hold Extremadura against the Portuguese while Vendôme held the centre of the peninsula and Noailles went to Roussillon to attack Catalonia from the north.

Stahremberg meanwhile considered it inadvisable to seek winter-quarters in the hostile territories of Castile, and it was consequently decided to retire to Catalonia. The Allied position was made difficult not merely by the obvious hostility of the people of Madrid but, more threateningly, by the fact that Vendôme had an army of over twenty-five thousand encamped at Talavera de la Reina. Charles III left to journey eastwards, and reached Barcelona on 15 December. Stahremberg delayed in the rear, living off the country wherever possible. At the end of November the Allies began to retreat towards Aragon. On 3 December Philip returned to Madrid.

The retreating Allied army moved in national detachments, and of these the English under Stanhope formed the rearguard. On the night of 6 December Stanhope arrived at the town of Brihuega and took up quarters there. Believing that Vendôme was still some distance away, Stanhope delayed in the town for a couple of days. This allowed a forward detachment from the Bourbon army to reach Brihuega in the afternoon of the 8th. By that evening Vendôme had surrounded the town with troops and artillery. Next morning the French marshal called on the English to surrender. When they refused, orders were given to storm the town. At 6 p.m. Stanhope ordered a general surrender. The English had lost (according to English figures) three hundred dead, three hundred wounded, and 1,936 taken prisoners. Among the latter were Stanhope himself, and other officers who were later to distinguish themselves.[10]

---

[10] Stanhope was kept prisoner for two years.

Stahremberg hurried back from Cifuentes when he heard of the siege at Brihuega. On 9 December he took up a position nearby at Villaviciosa, quite unaware of Stanhope's surrender. On the morning of the 10th Vendôme was joined by the rest of his army and took up positions against the Allies. Against his twenty thousand or so men were ranged about fourteen thousand under the German general.[11] The engagement began in the early afternoon and continued till nightfall. Conflicting versions of the battle do not affect the fact that it was a Bourbon victory. Stahremberg retreated swiftly through Aragon and reached Barcelona on 6 January. The pursuing Bourbon troops recaptured Aragon and its cities as they went. At Villaviciosa Vendôme had permanently saved the cause of Philip v. The desultory campaigns of the next year or two did nothing to alter the supremacy of the Bourbons in Castile and Aragon.

Meanwhile Noailles had been preparing his campaign in Roussillon. Despite the wintry conditions, on 15 December the French forces laid siege to the important fortress of Gerona. The surrender of the city on 25 January 1711 opened the way for the capture of the plain of Vich and the Valle de Aran. Vendôme in the meantime held to a base in Cervera. The Allies were now reduced to the area enclosed by Igualada, Tarragona and Barcelona. Everywhere else in peninsular Spain the Bourbon cause was triumphant. But the well-defended Catalan triangle, supported from the sea, proved extremely difficult to reduce, and the generals had perforce to wait on events elsewhere in Europe.

Peace was made inevitable by two circumstances. In 1710 a Tory ministry, committed to end the war, had come into power in England; and in April 1711 the Emperor Joseph died, leaving the imperial crown to his brother the Archduke Charles. Military actions in Spain now hung on decisions reached in European diplomatic circles. On 27 September 1711 the new emperor, Charles vi, left Barcelona for the last time on an English ship. The peninsular crown was put by for a more accessible prize. A month after this, the English government extended peace feelers to France, and in February 1712 a peace conference between the maritime powers and the French opened at Utrecht. That summer, on 10 June, Vendôme died in Valencia from apoplexy brought

---

[11] San Felipe, probably erroneously, estimates the royal army as being a third smaller than that of the Allies.

on by a meal. His sudden death was a severe blow to the Spaniards, but the approach of peace was soon to perfect the work he had so brilliantly carried on.

In August 1712 hostilities between England, the United Provinces, France and Spain were suspended, and on 11 April 1713 the Treaty of Utrecht was formally concluded. By its terms Spain and the Indies were formally guaranteed to Philip v, who was, however, required to renounce his right of succession to the French throne. For the rest, Utrecht was fundamentally an English peace, and England emerged with all the honours. From France the English received several territorial concessions in America, and a recognition of the Hanoverian dynasty. From Spain they received the Asiento for the slave trade to America (March 1713), and the formal possession of Gibraltar and Minorca (by treaty on 13 July 1713). The Spanish territorial losses in Europe were humiliating but not politically or economically disadvantageous. The Spanish Netherlands were given to the empire, Sicily to Savoy. Peace was made with the Dutch in June 1714, and with Portugal seven months later in February 1715. Meanwhile the emperor continued to struggle for his rights, so callously abandoned by the maritime powers. On 13 September 1714 the unhappy Catalans, deserted by their English allies, surrendered Barcelona to Bourbon troops. In the same month France and the empire confirmed the Peace Treaty of Rastatt which they had signed with each other on 6 March. Rastatt was a totally different matter from Utrecht: the latter had received Philip v's approval, but the former he refused to accept. By it the French handed over to the empire all Spain's Italian possessions, including Naples, Sardinia, and Milan. With Minorca and Gibraltar in English hands, and Italy under Austrian control, Spain found itself deprived at one blow of its control of the western Mediterranean. Utrecht and Rastatt opened a new era in Spanish history. Relieved of the deadweight of its possessions in northern Europe, the monarchy could now devote its resources to internal rejuvenation. At the same time the desire to redress the loss of Italy led to a new aggressive policy in the Mediterranean, so that the forty-five years of Philip's reign witnessed no more than ten years of peace.

2   Spain in Decline

One of the last great servants of the Habsburg dynasty, the duque de Escalona, marqués de Villena, who had served the crown in both Spain and Italy, turned in relief on the death of Charles II to the powerful resources of France. Writing in November 1700 to greet Louis' acceptance of the Spanish throne for his grandson, he painted for him a mournful picture of what the monarchy had now been reduced to:

> The present state of the realm is the saddest in the world, for the feeble government of the last few kings, and the base adulation of servants and ministers, have produced a horrible disorder in affairs: justice is abandoned, policy neglected, resources sold, religion distorted, the nobility demoralised, the people oppressed, power decayed, and love and respect for the crown lost.[1]

Such sentiments from the pen of a grandee are more eloquent than a score of testimonies to the demoralisation produced among Spaniards by the atmosphere of decay and decline that haunted the last decades of the old dynasty. Yet the decay, real as it was, produced its own exaggerations and myths. Contemporary civil servants, anxious to ingratiate themselves with the new dynasty, painted the preceding reign in the most sombre colours possible and greeted in their new king a long-sought saviour. Later historians, writing under the Bourbon régime, flattered their sovereigns at having rescued Spain from the depths of degradation, and treated the century between Philip II and Philip V as one of almost unredeemed mediocrity. The dogma was expressed at its most extreme and concise by the Catalan historian Antonio de Capmany: 'What was the whole of Spain before the august

---

[1] Letter of 29 Nov. 1700, quoted in Manuel Danvila y Collado, *El poder civil en España* (6 vols), Madrid, 1885, vol. 3, pp. 369–70.

House of Bourbon came to the throne? A corpse, without spirit
or strength to feel its own debility'.[2] In this way the decline of
Spain, bewailed by scores of *arbitristas* under the later Habsburgs,
combated by increasingly impotent ministers of state, and eagerly
awaited by the capitals of western Europe, passed into the official
historiography of Spain and became a concept to challenge and
concern historians of a later day.

What is certain is that the loss of self-confidence among upper
circles in the government of the last Habsburg reflected a real
disillusion with the state of the monarchy. The French ambassador
Rébenac, writing in 1689 to Louis XIV, was expressing not his
own prejudices but the actual feeling at Madrid when he reported
that:

if one examines the government of this monarchy at close quarters, one
will find it in an excessive state of disorder; but, things being as they
are, one could hardly introduce changes without being exposed to
more fearful inconveniences than the evil itself, and what is needed is a
complete revolution before establishing good order in this state. Such
a revolution can be found only by changing the form of government,
and enlightened people agree that the government of the House of
Austria is leading them inevitably to total ruin.[3]

The House of Austria had, however, to contend with problems
whose size dwarfed the isolated attempts of occasional ministers
to grapple with them. Spain in 1700 was still at the head of a vast
empire stretching from Milan to the Philippines. It was expected
to produce military and political leadership, and financial aid, for
territories that it was hardly in its interest to maintain. Long
before the mid-seventeenth century the strain had become
obvious. America had brought in the life-blood of bullion to
Spain, but 'the court of Rome, the subsidies to Germany, the
upkeep of Flanders, the wars in Milan and Catalonia, drain the
blood out of this body through all its veins'.[4] America itself, said
the same writer, Luis de Salazar y Castro, was of little profit: 'it

---

    [2] Cited in Charles Weiss, *L'Espagne depuis le règne de Philippe II jusqu'à l'avènement
des Bourbons* (2 vols), Paris, 1844, vol. 2, p. 371, note 1.
    [3] Dispatch of 20 May 1689, quoted in *ibid.*, vol. 2, p. 55.
    [4] Luis de Salazar y Castro, 'Discurso Político sobre la flaqueza de la Monarquía
Española en el reynado de D Carlos Segundo, y valimiento del Conde de Oropesa'
(1687), printed in Antonio Valladares de Sotomayor, *Semanario Erudito*, Madrid,
1788, vol. 2, p. 132.

does not keep its doors closed to foreign merchandise, and we ourselves have not the means to maintain its great mass'.[5] The definitive loss of the Netherlands had been a severe shock to the might of Spain; more severe, because more indicative of a malaise within the peninsula itself, had been the loss of Portugal, the temporary secession of Catalonia, and the reverses by land and sea in the middle of the century at the hands of the French and the Dutch. The severe blow to Spanish morale in the 1640s led to the perpetuation of a mood that accepted with acquiescence the ills of the monarchy and abstained from active efforts to prop up the tottering structure. Under Charles II political and court life centred around the ambitions and activities of Don Juan of Austria, a bastard son of Philip IV whose career illustrated several of the factors contributing to the fragmentation of the realm. His general popularity attested to national disgust at a feeble and corrupt court; his tenure of power in the late 1670s betrayed the impotence and indifference of the grandees who were his chief rivals; and his strong support in Aragon pointed both backwards and forwards to 1640 and 1705, when the Aragonese refused to follow Castile in its descent to inglorious decay. Political life became a thing of public contempt, and the king, sick both in mind and body, a subject of seditious rhymes such as the last verse of one current in May 1691:

> Ay de ti, España oprimida
> En tan tirano govierno,
> Ay de ti, Reyno sin Rey
> Y ay, infeliz Rey sin Reyno.[6]

The end of the seventeenth century still saw Habsburg power undiminished in Europe. Territorially the House of Austria was largely unshaken by the wars of Louis XIV. But in every other way the Habsburgs were in eclipse. The Spanish court had long ceased to work in conjunction with Vienna, and no perceptible bond united the two sections of the dynasty. Louis' campaigns had been waged inevitably against his Spanish neighbour, whose possessions in northern Italy, the Rhineland and Flanders were still a bulwark against French expansionism. Particularly after the

---

[5] *Ibid.*, p. 138.
[6] B Nac., MS 3918 f.124. Alas for you, Spain oppressed/by so tyrannical a government;/ alas for you, kingdom without a king;/ and for you, unhappy king without a kingdom.

Treaty of the Pyrenees, Louis was anxious to secure as much territory as he could claim by virtue of his wife's rights to the Spanish throne. He was not to know that his wars against Spain contributed to the decline of a monarchy his grandson would one day inherit, so that his aggression merely aggravated the problems facing the Bourbons on their arrival in Madrid. The cost of all this to Spain was immense, not only in men but in money. Expenses outside the realm, whether in Milan, Germany or Flanders, had to be met in silver coin, of which there was naturally a shortage in a country whose currency was almost exclusively copper or *vellón*.

If the European empire was a deadweight, so was America. The wealth of the Indies now represented little or nothing in the coffers of the Spanish treasury. What bullion did arrive was invariably pledged in advance to financiers who had pressing claims.[7] Nor was America still an open market for Spanish produce. Interlopers in the Caribbean and Pacific had flooded American markets with Dutch, English and French produce, and even the official monopoly trade from Seville was largely controlled by foreign merchants operating through agents. The crown consequently reaped little benefi⁺ from the New World, yet it was still committed to the expense and trouble of organising and protecting the convoys that plied between Seville and the American ports.

Spain could conceivably continue to exist, even to flourish, without her empire. But there were pessimistic contemporaries who doubted even this. The ruin and depopulation of Spain, claimed the archbishop of Saragossa in 1703, derived primarily from the need to maintain a vast empire which bled the country of manpower. But this was only the extrinsic cause of depopulation. The intrinsic cause, he said, was the excessive number of taxes.[8] Whatever the true cause, there was no doubt about the depopulation. The very vague estimates made by historians suggest that a population decline in the peninsula occurred in the first half of the seventeenth century and checked itself during the

---

[7] For some bullion figures see Henry Kamen, 'The Decline of Castile: the last Crisis', *Economic History Review*, 2nd Series, XVII, 1 (1964), p. 67.

[8] 'Consulta del exᵐᵒ sr Arᵖᵒ de Zaragᵃ que puso en manos del R. Cardenal de Etré en el mes de Henero de 1703 pa q la passase a las del Rey ... y es conforme con la otra que hizo a Carlos 11, siendo presidente de Castilla', BM, MS 21536 ff.185–6.

second half, when population actually began to rise again, without however attaining the level of 1600. In a Castilian town of the middle of the century the adults would remember the shrinking villages of their youth, and their children would probably live to experience the devastation caused by epidemics and famine in the 1680s. For both generations depopulation would remain the principal reality facing a struggling agricultural economy.[9] After the crisis of 1676–86 a period of comparative tranquillity ensued. Whether the war of the Spanish Succession interrupted this process is debatable, and is one of the questions to be discussed in a later chapter. The very great uncertainty of global estimates of population remains to baffle any historian attempting to analyse the demographic state of seventeenth-century Spain.

Within the peninsula the mass of the population and wealth had in the sixteenth century been concentrated in Castile, giving this province a distinctive preeminence in the government of the realm. Covering over 65 per cent of the surface of the peninsula (including Portugal), Castile at the end of the sixteenth century possessed nearly 73 per cent of the population. Secure in this superiority, the Castilians had dominated the Spanish empire in both Europe and America. Castilian nobles had controlled the Netherlands and the Italian states, in Seville only Castilians were officially permitted to take part in the trade to America, and in the provinces of the crown of Aragon (a term used here to cover the three realms of Valencia, Catalonia and Aragon) the principal administrative posts had invariably been allotted to Castilians. Emigrants to the Indies were also for the most part subjects of the crown of Castile, which thereby exercised hegemony over both the New and the Old Worlds.

Agriculture remained the dominant industry over most of the peninsula, but it had by the end of the seventeenth century begun to suffer severe dislocation from taxation as well as natural causes. The overriding privileges of the sheepowners' guild, the Mesta, meant that much common land available for tillage was forcibly reserved for pasture alone. But even pasture-land was diminishing, according to common complaints. The city of Jaén in 1669 pointed out that common land was being enclosed and royal land

<hr>

[9] The best demographic study of the seventeenth century is in A. Domínguez Ortiz, *La Sociedad Española en el siglo XVII*, Madrid, 1963, pp. 53–157. For the population crisis under Charles II see Kamen, 'The Decline of Castile'.

alienated, so that the few cattle that remained had little grazing ground. The most important victim of the land-holding system in Spain was, naturally, the peasant. Often owing rent to a lay or ecclesiastical lord, and expected at the same time to pay his taxes, whether to the lord or to the crown, the average peasant never accumulated enough capital to improve his land, or even to pay his way and support his family. The indefatigable *arbitrista* Francisco Martínez de la Mata had this class in mind when he proposed the reestablishment of credit-banks or *montes de piedad* – a solution tried before, but never with success – to enable the productive sector of the population to draw on capital resources. But the energies of the ruling élite were directed elsewhere. No books on agricultural improvement appear to have been published in Spain under Charles II, and it was notorious that the nobility spent less time on their estates than at court in Madrid. The depopulation which was both a cause and a symptom of agricultural decay resulted in substantial movements of population from the countryside to the larger cities.

The state of industry, if we judge by the little evidence at present available, was even more deplorable than that of agriculture. There is little doubt that native industry, not only in Castile but also on the Mediterranean littoral, had declined markedly during the reign of Charles II and shown no tendency to recovery. In Catalonia and Castile this decline had allowed many foreign, and mostly French, manufacturers to establish themselves. But the old centres never decayed totally. In 1703 an official of the government, Gaspar Naranjo y Romeiro, undertook a tour through Cuenca, Sigüenza, Soria, Burgos, Palencia, Toledo, Córdoba and Jaén, and found the state of manufactures to be desperate but not irreparable. He stayed eight months in Burgos, Palencia and other centres, and reported back that the textile factories 'only needed to be activated'.[10] In 1715 a French commercial agent reported that the old manufactures 'still subsist, at Segovia, Peñaranda and Valencia as well as elsewhere in Spain for linen and wool, and at Seville, Granada, Valencia, Toledo and

---

[10] Quoted in J. Carrera Pujal, *Historia de la Economía Española* (5 vols), Barcelona, 1943–7, vol. 3, pp. 84–9. The report by Naranjo, entitled *Antorcha que alumbra*, is still in manuscript form and is normally in the possession of the Academia de Ciencias Morales, Madrid. I have been unable to consult it, since for the past seven years it has been in the custody of Don Carmelo Viñas y Mey, who has promised to publish it.

Madrid for silk'.[11] The War of Succession played some part in the recovery of the textile industry, which the government was anxious to promote for both military and commercial reasons. Other industries received less preferential treatment, though one outstanding exception was the armament factories. The exigencies of war made it difficult for the government to promote one of the most common remedies suggested by *arbitristas*, namely the foundation of trading companies, particularly for internal trade. Gaspar Naranjo's suggestions for reform, which included one for trading companies, were ignored almost immediately after they had been made.[12]

The decisive guide to Spanish decline is the commercial decay consequent on industrial stagnation. Contemporary writers and officials were, however, concerned less with peninsular and European commerce than with the distant riches of the Indies. The American trade, which brought to Seville and Cadiz tobacco, chocolate, cacao, Brazil-wood, campeche, cochineal and bullion; and the American market, which received the produce of Spain; were looked upon as the mainstay of the economy. Successive *arbitristas* pointed out that this was an illusion, and that true wealth lay in developing the native resources of Spain. Equipped with the necessary figures, they could have pointed out that the average annual tonnage from Spain to America had fallen regularly and disastrously from about 19,800 toneladas in 1600 to 4,650 in 1680. Two principal reasons for this decline stand out. The degeneration of Spanish naval forces before the power of the maritime states, in particular England, reduced the number and effectivity of warships available to protect trans-Atlantic trade and to enforce the Cadiz–Seville monopoly. In addition, the increasing volume of European goods unloaded on to the American market by English and Dutch interlopers, created a glut which severely hit the Spanish export trade. This adverse situation was paralleled in Europe. It was a standard complaint that Spain exported valuable raw materials (particularly wool) and imported rather more manufactured goods, the balance being made up by bullion. Figures available for the early eighteenth century substantiate these complaints. Anglo-Spanish trade in this period saw a greater volume of exports to Spain than imports from it. Similarly, the

---

[11] Memoir by Partyet, 17 May 1715, AE Mèm et Doc. (Esp.), 32 f.69.
[12] 'Memoire sur la Junte du Commerce', AE Corr. Pol. (Esp.), 154 f. 425.

French sent more goods to Spain than they bought from that country.[13]

What Spaniards themselves thought of their country may be gauged by the many suggestions for reform which poured in to the French government. The very appearance and quantity of these memoranda suggest a faith and hope in the new dynasty that had been lacking under the old. Inevitably the complaints, and the solutions proffered, were old ones. The year 1701, for instance, sees the reissue of Francisco Martínez de la Mata's *Epítome de los Discursos*,[14] which had first appeared in Seville in 1659. Martínez de la Mata, who used to describe himself as a 'servant of the poor' (*siervo de los pobres afligidos*), had laid down sixty points for discussion in his original pamphlet, and the publisher of the new edition added a sixty-first, in which he observed that all the old points were still causes for complaint. An attack on the export of raw materials and the import of manufactured goods; on the resort to *juros* and *censos* (that is, government and municipal bonds) to make up for inefficient financial administration; on the excessive number of clergy and of university students in the country; on the decay of the *gremios* or guilds; these were the basic points of the memorandum. They were repeated substantially in an important anonymous memorandum presented to Philip v at the end of 1700. This work[15] listed twenty-five articles for complaint. It was claimed that inefficiency and tyranny in taxation had led to depopulation of the country and impoverishment of its people: when a peasant could not pay taxes, for example, his plough would be taken away from him, which led to his ruin, neglect of the soil, and eventual harm to the state. All outstanding tax debts, it was suggested, should be remitted by the crown, notwithstanding the fact that the debts were really owed not to the crown but to tax-farmers and the like. Only a clean start would solve the confusion in finances. One

---

[13] See the graphs in Jean McLachlan, *Trade and Peace with Old Spain 1667-1750*, Cambridge, 1940, and in J. Vicens Vives, *Historia Económica de España*, Barcelona, 1959, p. 449.

[14] *Epítome de los Discursos que ha dado a su Magestad Francisco Martínez de Mata, siervo de los pobre afligidos, en que prueba como la causa de la pobreza y despoblación de España . . . ha procedido de la omision comun de los vassallos, en no pedir el cumplimiento de las leyes*, AE Corr. Pol. (Esp.), 90 ff.77-82.

[15] 'Memorial que a la Mag^d de nro Rey y Señor D^n Phelipe quinto . . . le ofreze un Basallo en 25 Capitulos mirando en todos al mayor servizio de Dios, aumento de la R^l hazienda, y alibio general de los Basallos', *ibid.*, 93 ff.4-25.

article complained bitterly about the notorious *millones*, a tax imposed principally on food, and claimed that the crown received only half of the revenue extracted from the population, since the balance went on administration. Another complained that a decree of 1670 ordering every individual to plant four trees, had not been observed, with the result that when wood was required houses had to be torn down, resulting in depopulation. It was claimed that there was a great shortage of mules in Spain; and a complaint about the shortage of soldiers and the superfluity of government officials went on to say that 'Your Majesty will find more secretaries than captains, more wielders of the pen than of cannon'. One article described a common method of tax evasion which cheated the government of income while also increasing the wealth of the propertied classes: families would put their property under the nominal ownership of a clergyman or a noble, and thereby qualify for exemption from taxation. There was a plea for all taxes to be reduced in number to one only, and the constant outflow of money from Spain to Rome was condemned. Emphasis was put on the great universal evils caused by the export of raw wool from Spain, and it was claimed that the lack of wool within Spain, together with the entry of foreign manufactures, had led in the province of Toledo alone to the depression and depopulation of the towns of Cuerva, Yebenes, Ajofrin, Casasbuenas, Santo Domingo and Yebes. Finally, we find once again the old complaint of *arbitristas* that facility of emigration to America had contributed to the depopulation of Spain. While some of these grievances, as well as others not listed here, rest on an inadequate understanding of the ills afflicting the country, they do give a fair idea of what in the eyes of contemporary Spaniards appeared to be wrong with Spain.

This unhappy picture of the peninsula at the opening of the eighteenth century cannot be used, as it once was, to set a contrast with the achievements of the new Bourbon dynasty. Many of the factors active in previous decades continued to operate under Philip v. Changes in monarchy and administration had very little effect on the economic position, and the year 1700 therefore has no more than symbolic meaning. But if the origins of recovery from decadence must be sought, they should be located in the reign of Charles ii. The great monetary devaluation of February 1680 occurred in the midst of crisis and itself precipitated another, but the confidence that was thereafter restored to Spanish currency seems to have encouraged financiers and manufacturers. From about 1686, the year of another monetary adjustment, greater stability was restored to prices, and moderate inflation, reflected in non-agricultural prices, characterised the Castilian economy. In Catalonia too the last years of the reign may be taken as a period of readjustment and equilibrium. Philip v entered a Spain substantially removed from the profound monetary chaos that had been its hallmark for nearly a century.

Politically, however, the country was thoroughly degenerate. 'Though this be a great monarchy,' reported Alexander Stanhope from Madrid in 1691, 'yet it has at present much aristocracy in it, where every grandee is a sort of prince.[16] The ascendancy of the nobles and the sordid intrigues at court had almost totally eclipsed the authority of the crown. Charles ii was no more than a shadow king. Government in his minority was controlled by his mother, the queen regent, and in his later years by a succession of ministers and favourites. Orders and decrees were issued in the king's name, yet they were seldom submitted to him for his signature, and official documents of the reign usually bore only facsimiles of the royal hand. The unhappy psychotic Charles, *el Hechizado*, reduced monarchy in Spain to a mockery of its ancient self. Under him the régime of the aristocracy reached its fullest – and final – period of fulfilment.

The empire which Philip v inherited was centred on Castile, but the laws, customs and tax system of Castile did not govern it. On the contrary, disunity of government (its apologists might have termed it decentralisation) characterised the various realms which made up the monarchy.[17] The Spanish crown was essentially the crown of Castile, and its writ was unrestricted only in Castile. Even in this realm the Cantabrian provinces of Vizcaya (Biscay), Guipúzcoa and Alava maintained considerable autonomy of laws and taxation. These autonomous laws, or *fueros*, were also the special pride of the crown of Aragon, which included the realms of Valencia, Aragon, Catalonia, Sardinia and the Balearic Islands. Aragon, associated with Castile ever since the reign of Ferdinand

---

[16] Stanhope to Nottingham, 22 May 1691, in *Spain under Charles the Second; or, Extracts from the Correspondence of the Hon. Alexander Stanhope, 1690–1699*, London, 1844, p. 18.

[17] This section on the monarchy and the councils is based on a 'Descripzion de la Monarchia de España' (1701), in A E Corr. Pol. (Esp.), 91 ff.233–43.

and Isabella, had always remained independent of Castile, and neither Philip II in 1591 nor Philip IV in 1640 had attempted to subject it to royal authority. Each of the constituent realms of the crown of Aragon was governed independently, with its own coinage and administration, and in each the king of Spain had a viceroy. Castilian authority was even more restricted in Italy, where states with their own distinctive institutions were governed through a viceroy: these were the realms of Sicily and Naples, held in fee of the papacy. The duchy of Milan, held in fee of the empire, was ruled through a governor appointed by the king of Spain. In addition to these three great Italian territories, Spanish authority and troops held several fortified towns which together made Spain the principal power in Italy. A few strongholds on the north African coast completed this picture of Spanish possessions in Europe. The governmental affairs of all of them were regulated by the councils sitting in Madrid.

Government at the top was exercised through a system of councils, staffed by nobles and by a few administrative officials. Foremost of the councils in 1700 was the council of state, which deliberated on all important affairs of state, peace and war, and foreign policy. This council had no president, since the king was supposed to be its convener. It had two secretaries, one for the affairs of northern Europe and one for Italian questions. It was correctly regarded as the chief organ of government in the monarchy, and any detailed business arising from its deliberations was discussed in the other councils. Next in general importance came the council of war, whose deliberations concerned only peninsular Spain together with adjacent territories such as the Canaries and the African forts; the military affairs of Italy, Flanders and America being dealt with largely by officials in those territories. All the councillors of state were *ex officio* members of the council of war, which had two secretaries, one for land and one for sea, and no president, for the same reason as the council of state.

There were five superior or supreme councils which functioned independently of each other. In order of precedence (an important issue at official gatherings) these were the council of Castile, the council of Aragon, the council of the Inquisition, the council of Italy and the council of Flanders. By the end of the War of Succession the councils of Aragon, Italy and Flanders had ceased to exist, for reasons we shall outline later. The council of Aragon was the highest governing body, under the crown, of the three realms of the crown of Aragon. Formed in 1494, it provided the model for government of territories which the king of Castile could not govern directly. The council acted as a liaison body between the king in Madrid and the viceroy in Saragossa. Its membership, like that of the other councils, varied according to period and circumstance, but all the councillors, with the exception of the treasurer-general, had to be natives of the crown of Aragon. In 1555 the Italian states, which had till then been represented on the council of Aragon, were allotted a separate council of Italy. The council of Flanders was set up in 1588 to help govern the Netherlands; while that of the Inquisition, dating from 1483, helped to keep the Holy Office under the control of the government. Each of these councils had a president and one or more secretaries, usually allotted on a geographical basis.

The most important of the councils in the early eighteenth century was the council of Castile. In 1700 it had four chambers and a membership of twenty councillors. After 1707 it took over the work of the suppressed council of Aragon. It was usually presided over by a 'governor', sometimes also called a 'president' though the real president was the king. The membership and functions of this council fluctuated widely during the early years of the reign of Philip v, thanks to the administrative changes of the period. In the golden age of empire the council of state had been the most prominent because of Spain's great international commitments; as these commitments receded (particularly after the territorial losses at Utrecht), the internal affairs of the monarchy and hence the activities of the council of Castile gained in importance. The council was entrusted with the administrative and judicial government of the crown of Castile alone, but the growing Castilianisation of the peninsula after the suppression of the Aragonese *fueros* gave it an added authority over Spain as a whole, so that in the course of the eighteenth century it became the principal organ of government in the monarchy. All other councils not already named depended on the council of Castile. One tiny body, consisting usually of three members chosen from that of Castile, was the *Cámara* or chamber of Castile: this dealt with Church affairs and with administrative appointments. A subordinate body of the council of Castile, the *Sala de Alcaldes*, exercised jurisdiction over finance and other matters touching the court. The council of Orders represented the interests of the three military Orders of Santiago, Calatrava and Alcántara in Castile, and that of Montesa in Aragon. The council of the Crusade (*Cruzada*) was concerned exclusively with a tax, the *cruzada*, granted by the pope to finance the fight against the Moors.

The last two councils depending on that of Castile were of the highest importance: the council of the Indies, with a president and two secretaries, was concerned with all American affairs; the council of Finance (*Consejo de Hacienda*, by which name it will be called in these pages), dealt only with taxes levied on Castile, but since in effect Castile alone financed the upkeep of the monarchy, the Hacienda had international responsibilities.

Historians are accustomed to the picture of a highly centralised administration in Madrid, with the king and his secretaries at the centre of a complex conciliar machine which tried to govern the country and did so rather inefficiently. But the efficiency or otherwise of the administration must be set in focus against the stark fact that there was no proper centralisation, even in Castile. Where France by 1700 had embarked seriously on an intendant system, and England had created a reliable body of local government officials, Spain totally lacked any proper liaison between the periphery and the centre. The councils at Madrid all governed indirectly rather than directly. Thus the Hacienda, which had most need for a bureaucracy directly under its control, had to rely for tax-collecting on the activities of tax-farmers with no accountability to the government or to the people. Similarly the regional councils had no full-time administrative officials in the provinces under their control. Perhaps the only council which functioned at all properly in these circumstances was the Inquisition. It is not surprising therefore that the conciliar system was seriously discredited.

Ironically enough in a system which lacked a proper administrative bureaucracy, much of the inefficiency could be traced to a superfluity of bureaucratic personnel. The pursuit of office, which was so serious a blight on the administrations of other countries, became in Spain a fatal disease. As Melchor de Macanaz observed at the time in his memoirs,

all the officials in the councils and the chanceries make their posts not only perpetual but also hereditary in their house and family. The method of it is this. In the three leading universities of Spain there are six *colegios mayores* where the young enter to study. Those who enter are the sons, nephews, brothers and cousins of officials. The student who applies himself manages after several years to get a lectureship. For every one who succeeds, twenty fail and obtain posts outside. As many as enter the university, therefore, leave with an official post in the audiencias or chanceries, and from there they go to the councils. There is no instance of anyone, however ignorant he may be, being refused an official post.[18]

Macanaz knew what he was talking about, since he had been through two universities. His account suggests that there was a closed circle which tended to monopolise both administrative employment and university entrance, the two being interdependent since it was necessary to have a degree to become an official. 'Offices *de capa y espada*, as they are known, are given to brothers, relatives, friends or dependents of officials.' The result was a self-perpetuating bureaucracy with no claim to academic distinction or administrative competence. The evil was a long-established but increasingly grave one, since the great number of office-seekers churned out by decadent universities had brought all honest and efficient administration to a full stop. The crown had not improved the situation by constant recourse to the sale of government offices, a common expedient when money could be raised in no other way. Alienation of offices had flourished under Charles 11, and Philip v continued the practice in order to meet the fiscal demands of war.

The organs of representative government and of judicial administration offered little hope of reform. The chief judicial bodies in Castile, all subordinate to the control of the council of Castile, were the chanceries (*Chancillerías*) of Valladolid and Granada, and the audiencias of Seville and La Coruña. These courts were essentially delegations of royal authority, and acted as courts of justice as well as of appeal. Their corruption and lengthy procedures were well known; more serious, if we can accept Macanaz's strictures, was the fact that their personnel were ill-qualified in legal matters and owed their jobs only to nepotism. Independent justice could hardly function under such conditions, so that it was inevitably the vested interests of money or of

---

[18] BUV MS 24. See also appendix 7 for a note on this source. The theme of education and employment is examined in the illuminating Cambridge thesis (1968) by Dr. Kagan on 'Education and the State in Habsburg Spain'.

influence that prevailed in legal judgments. Nor was there adequate encouragement given to the study of the law: in this we have the testimony of Macanaz that only the study of Roman law was allowed in the universities, and that scholars were forbidden to devote themselves to the laws and customs of Castile.[19] Constitutional government was likewise in decay. The cortes of Castile, which had for over a century been little more than an empty conference of the eighteen or so[20] chief Castilian cities, with no authority over legislation or taxation, had failed to meet at all throughout the entire reign of Charles II. Between 1665 and 1701 the only realms to have any meeting of their cortes were Navarre and the province of Aragon. Both the tradition and practice of representative government were therefore defunct. The crown, no less than the people of Spain, suffered from this situation, for the lack of an efficient centralised administration weakened the monarchy at its roots.

The fault lay to a very great extent with the feudal character of the Spanish countryside. Government officials could not function adequately where the king had no jurisdiction over taxation or the dispensing of justice. The *corregidor* or municipal governor, appointed by the crown since the late fifteenth century, was supposed to act in liaison with the government, but this seldom occurred. More often, the cities rejected any royal interference; and the *corregimientos* themselves became, as in Barcelona, the perquisite of a narrow oligarchy. By far the greatest threat to royal authority, however, was the preponderance of aristocratic control. It is not often realised (and further research will serve only to emphasise the fact) that the greater part of Spain was not ruled by the king. The French foreign minister Torcy was advised in 1710 by his ambassador in Spain that the king had jurisdiction over only about two hundred of the seven hundred towns and villages in Castile.[21] This is a just estimate. The face of the Spanish countryside changed very little between the fifteenth and the eighteenth century, so that any estimates made within that period are generally valid for the whole period. Detailed analysis of the province of Salamanca in the eighteenth century, for example,

---

[19] *Ibid.*
[20] By the 1660s there were about twenty-one cities represented. See Antonio Domínguez Ortiz, *Política y Hacienda de Felipe IV*, Madrid, 1960, p. 234.
[21] Report to Torcy dated 22 Apr. 1710, AE Corr. Pol. (Esp.), 203 f.141.

shows that only 30·5 per cent of the territory and 33·7 per cent of
the population came under direct royal control; while 63 per cent
of territory and 60·4 per cent of population lay in the hands of
secular lords; the balance being in the hands of the Church.[22] A
similar picture can be obtained for the neighbouring province of
Valladolid, where the chief cities were in the king's jurisdiction,
while all the major towns and villages were in the hands of secular
lords. Even outside Castile, in Valencian territory for example,
the king was an overlord rather than a direct ruler. The advisers
of Philip v regarded such a situation as intolerable, and we shall
be examining their reactions in the context of the provinces of
Aragon, where conquest by Bourbon forces enabled them to
implement far-seeing administrative reforms.

The territorial preponderance of the nobility was paralleled by
their control of political and social life in Spain. The greatest
cities of Castile – Toledo, Seville, Avila, Ciudad Real – were controlled absolutely by aristocratic families,[23] so that even if a city
was technically in the king's jurisdiction it was administered by
an oligarchy not necessarily in sympathy with the crown. Philip v
was to witness the results of this when during the War of Succession Toledo wavered in its loyalty to him. The day of aristocratic
influence was nevertheless waning. Many of the leading families
had mortgaged their own futures by conspicuous consumption
resulting in accumulated debts. The apogee of power achieved
under Charles ii had gone to their heads. Holders of the greatest
fortunes, they also had the greatest debts.[24] Under Philip v they
further compromised themselves by their political attitudes, and
found themselves at variance with the new administrative
machinery set up by the Bourbons.

The overriding impression to be had by an observer of Spain
in 1700 was therefore that of the failure of government. The
arbitristas who patiently laid their remedies before the eyes of
their sovereign were only too well aware that a multiplicity of
economic and social factors had brought Spain into decay and
disrepute, but there was little, they felt, that could not be cured
by firm government. In 1701 their hopes were high. There had

[22] María Dolores Mateos, *Salamanca*, in the series *La España del Antiguo Régimen*
(ed. Miguel Artola), Salamanca, 1966.
[23] Domínguez Ortiz, *La Sociedad Española en el siglo XVII*, p. 258.
[24] *Ibid.*, pp. 235 ff.

been a peaceful succession to the throne, and there was every possibility that a dynasty renowned for its administrative efficiency would rejuvenate the monarchy. The king of France, however, was looking beyond the present to the consequences of the succession. Admitting the great need for structural reforms, in a letter to his ambassador extraordinary in Spain, the comte de Marcin, he observed nevertheless that one consideration above all should be given precedence:

It is to be wished that one could carry out a general alteration in all the different states of the monarchy. But as this idea is too vast, he [Marcin] must try as far as possible to remedy the most pressing evils and think principally of enabling the king of Spain to contribute in some way to the war that the king [of France] is preparing to endure.[25]

The question of reform consequently took second place to the one great cause on which the whole dynasty depended: the prosecution of the war.

[25] A. Morel-Fatio and H. Léonardon (eds), *Recueil des Instructions données aux Ambassadeurs . . . de France depuis les traités de Westphalie jusqu'à la Révolution Française* vol. 12, *Espagne*, Paris, 1898, pp. 8–9.

3   Court and Government

When Philip v crossed the frontier into Spain in January 1701 there were many who looked back to a precisely similar event in September 1517. Then, too, a seventeen-year-old boy with no knowledge of Spain or its language, and dependent on non-Spanish advisers for guidance in matters of state, had instituted the rule of a new foreign dynasty. Those who believed in the omens would have greeted in Philip v the beginnings of a new *Siglo de Oro,* a golden age to compensate for the humiliations of the last years of Habsburg rule. But through the general rejoicing there still remained a strong undertone of dissatisfaction from those who, as in 1517, were not easily convinced that the young foreign king would accommodate himself to the ways of the peninsula. The first signs were unconvincing: Philip refused to attend an *auto de fe* held in 1701 to celebrate his accession; his French advisers began to take sides in the quarrels between factions at court; he himself showed excessive deference to the wishes of his grandfather in Versailles. But the fact remained that he was the *king,* and the war was to make both him and his people better acquainted with each other.

For several years the young king was inclined to defer in everything to his grandfather. Louis on his side was kept thoroughly informed of everything that went on in Spain, and the constant correspondence[1] he had with Philip guaranteed a direct control over all decisions. More directly than correspondence, however, control was exercised through the ambassadors who became the instruments of Louis's policy in Spain. The envoy to the last Habsburg, the marquis d'Harcourt, was instructed to abstain from any part in the new government, but his successor, the

[1] Excellently utilised in Alfred Baudrillart, *Philippe V et la Cour de France* (5 vols), Paris, 1890–1900.

comte de Marcin, was permitted to become a member of the cabinet council or *despacho*. It is no exaggeration to say that Spain was governed, in the years before 1709, from Versailles and through the French ambassador.

Philip v was accompanied to Madrid by an entourage chosen carefully by the French king and his advisers. His tutor, the marquis de Louville, was on hand to advise him about immediate affairs; his grandfather was at Versailles to advise him on weightier matters. Decisions affecting the monarchy were often made not in Madrid but in Paris. The new king's bride, Marie Louise of Savoy, was chosen for him without consultation: the proxy marriage took place on 11 September 1701. The new queen, already at thirteen years a woman of character, had her ladies-in-waiting and confessor chosen for her by the king of France. Though governed by others, she herself governed the spirit of her husband, who doted on her. One person above all gained an ascendancy over Marie Louise, and through her over the king. This was the princess des Ursins,[2] a domineering woman of French origin, chosen expressly by Versailles as *camarera mayor* or head of the queen's household. Her control over the impressionable royal couple, together with her considerable political acumen, made her and with her the court a centre of political intrigue for several years to come.

The growth of faction at the Spanish court had become particularly pronounced in the last months of the previous reign, as adherents of the Bourbon or the Habsburg party vied for advantage in the succession dispute. Under the régime of the princess des Ursins, the factions tended to divide into a court clique devoted to the princess and to French ascendancy; and a Spanish party devoted to the eradication of foreign influence. There was also, however, an occasional French splinter group, generally in league with the French ambassador, which heartily opposed the influence of Ursins and complained bitterly of her to Louis xiv. The court consequently became a focus of constant rivalry and intrigue, as each faction sought for supremacy and drew upon itself the hatred of all others. These struggles were no doubt

---

[2] Born the daughter of the duc de Noirmoutier in 1635, her second husband was the duke of Bracciano, of the Orsini family. After his death in 1698, she became known by the French form of the Orsini name. Perhaps the best study of her is by François Combes, *La princesse des Ursins: essai sur sa vie, et son caractère politique* Paris, 1858.

important in the regulation of government policy, but will receive little mention here.

In Spain Madame des Ursins achieved an eminence perhaps greater than that of Madame de Maintenon in France. Louis xiv treated directly with her as though she were arbiter of the destinies of Spain, and ministers appointed in Madrid had invariably to pass under her scrutiny. In her correspondence[3] with ministers such as Torcy and Chamillart, but above all with Madame de Maintenon, she displayed a firm grasp of policy and policy-making at the Spanish court. Inevitably, experienced politicians in both countries resented this matronly interference in matters of state. In 1709 Maintenon informed her, with a strong hint of displeasure, that 'on n'aime pas ici que les dames s'occupent d'affaires'. It is difficult to make an assessment of her character and motives. Ursins should probably be viewed not as a quarrelsome shrew, but rather as Baudrillart sees her, a moderate woman whose undeniable ambitions were not wholly personal, being exercised largely in the service of others.[4] There can be no doubt of her importance. Round her, though not necessarily subordinate nor even sympathetic to her, grouped the most outstanding personalities in the government, among them Orry and Amelot.

The direct instruments of Louis' policy in Spain were, as we have noted, the French ambassadors, nearly all of whom incurred the enmity of Ursins. This may have been due to the fact that their position as exponents of the policy of France threatened the predominance of Ursins, but it is also likely that they were relatively poor public relations men, since many of them were on no better terms with the Spaniards. The first French ambassador appointed during the reign, the comte de Marcin, saw little political activity and remained in Spain only from August 1701 to April 1702. His successor, Cardinal d'Estrées, took up his appointment in October 1702 in Milan, where Philip v was about to complete a tour of his Italian territories, and returned to Spain with the king in January 1703. His haughty bearing instantly provoked the princess des Ursins and all the court. In October he was recalled and left Madrid. He was replaced by his nephew the Abbe d'Estrées, already resident in the Spanish

[3] M. A. Geffroy (ed.), *Lettres inédites de la princesse des Ursins*, Paris, 1859.
[4] *Philippe V et la Cour de France*, vol. 1, p. 131.

capital. Like his uncle, he was fitted for intrigue rather than diplomacy, and devoted his efforts to securing the dismissal of Ursins. Louis XIV was won over, and put pressure on his grandson to dismiss Ursins, who was recalled to France in April 1704. Philip and Marie Louise thereupon turned their hatred on Estrées, who was obliged to retire to France in July 1704. His replacement arrived in Madrid in June. This was the duc de Gramont, a distinguished soldier and administrator on whom Louis relied for complete conciliation with the court of Spain. Whatever his other qualities, Gramont was neither conciliator nor diplomat. As personal representative of Louis he claimed a principal part in the government of Spain: to achieve this he was prepared to cross Marie Louise and even the king.[5] A bitter opponent of the return of Ursins to Spain, he faced defeat when in spring 1705 Louis gave in to the urgent representations of his grandson and sent the princess back. 'Sire,' wrote Gramont to Louis in March, 'recall me promptly from here.' On 23 May he left Madrid, four days after the arrival of his successor, Amelot. On 5 August Ursins came back triumphantly to the capital.

Michel-Jean Amelot, marquis de Gournay since 1693, a prominent diplomat who had already served as ambassador to Venice (1682–5), Portugal (1685–8) and Switzerland (1688–98), had since 1699 been one of the directors of French commercial policy and in 1700 was elected to the presidency of the council of commerce, at which post he remained until his appointment as ambassador to Spain.[6] He stayed in the peninsula in this capacity from 8 May 1705 to 2 September 1709. His term of office was to mark the highest point ever reached by French influence in the peninsula.

At the time of his arrival Bourbon fortunes could hardly have been lower. Militarily the year 1704 had been a bad one in the peninsula. The archduke had landed at Lisbon in May, and in August the Allies had captured Gibraltar. Discontent with these failures and with the predominance at court of French advisers who initiated no reforms but spent their time in complicated intrigues, led to the rise of widespread anti-French sentiment in Spain. It was Amelot's task to begin the recon-

[5] Ibid., vol. 1, pp. 199 ff.
[6] For further biographical details see Dictionnaire de Biographie française, Paris, 1936, vol. 12, pp. 618–22.

struction on which the hopes of the Bourbon monarchy rested.

From the moment of his arrival in Spain the new ambassador won the confidence of all the factions at court, something not achieved by any of his predecessors. He had strict principles of conduct, and political beliefs which won him respect in some quarters but bitter hostility in a few others. Never depressed by opposition, he worked his way methodically towards a rational system of government in Spain.

With a firmness that nothing weakened, and which commanded immediate obedience, he did not fail to win by his manners the hearts of all orders in Spain, through his attitude which remained gentle, cautious, polite and respectful amid this great power, just as his capacity and probity won him unanimous esteem and confidence, and even the friendship of the princess des Ursins.[7]

Such was the tribute of a diplomat and historian who, just over a decade later, served as ambassador to the same court.

Among the many other officials who aided the Spanish crown, one deserves particular attention. This was Jean Orry. Perhaps the first and most important of the tasks facing the government of Philip v was reorganisation of the finances, but this could only be achieved by someone who would approach the task in a radical frame of mind. Louis xiv was asked whether he could lend such a man to Spain. Instead of choosing a distinguished public servant Louis sent an obscure official of no previous distinction. It was an odd choice to make, but by no means a regrettable one, for Jean Orry, sieur of Vignory,[8] was to become the most prominent of all the French servants of Philip v. He arrived in Madrid on 21 June 1702 and immediately began to study the papers of the royal treasury. Over the next few months he analysed and catalogued the tax structure of the monarchy in a vast series of memoirs which are still available in the French archives.[9] 'In all this work,' he wrote to Torcy in August, 'I shall make every effort to set the

---

[7] Louis de Rouvroy, Duc de Saint-Simon, *Mémoires* (45 vols), ed. A. de Boislisle, Paris, 1879–1930, vol. 18, pp. 81–2. Cited hereafter as *Mémoires de Saint-Simon*.

[8] Orry is given this title in French books, but I am not sure whether it is a French title. The fact is that when Orry returned to Madrid for the last time in April 1713 he was given the title of Conde de Vinaroz by Philip v: see A E Corr. Pol. (Esp.), 221 f.221. The similarity of this title to Vignory is too great to be a coincidence. Born in Paris on 4 Sept. 1652, he died 29 Sept. 1719. His son, Philibert Orry, comte de Vignory, was to become controller-general of the finances of France.

[9] A E Corr. Pol. (Esp.), 119.

people of Spain in motion to make them undertake the restoration of some manufactures'.[10] His labours were interrupted by
two visits to France, one from September to December 1702, the
other from June to July 1703. While Orry achieved much that
was useful (and this will be evaluated in a later chapter), it was at
the expense of the hostility of most of his colleagues, who were
provoked by the man and his manners rather than by his proposed
reforms. The enmity of French ambassadors and of Spanish
officials forced him to leave for France in August 1704, but the
influence of the princess des Ursins, his constant but not uncritical
protector, secured his recall the following year and he returned to
Madrid on 25 May 1705. Once again widespread hostility forced
France to recall him, and he arrived back in Versailles in July
1706, not to return to Spain for another seven years.

Orry's difficulties illustrate clearly the significant part played by
intrigue in the formation of court policy. As long as the court
continued to be racked by petty faction there was little hope of
winning the confidence of the Spanish aristocracy. The result was
an inevitable series of desertions to the enemy. Moreover the
French presumption, right or wrong, that they alone were capable
of introducing order and reform into a country that had been
betrayed by its natural rulers, was certainly calculated to alienate
Spaniards. There were several ardent Francophiles at court, but
these were outnumbered by the many patriotic Spaniards who
refused to accept foreign innovation unless it could be shown to
be necessary.

With the five years of Amelot's ambassadorship, latent tensions
reached their peak. During his régime the most significant
reforms of the war, excepting only the introduction of intendants,
were put into effect. Changes in the administration led to the
alienation of several nobles who profited by the Allied occupation
of Madrid in 1706 to desert to the enemy. Further discontent
occurred at the news in 1707 that the government had revoked the
fueros of Aragon. But while these crises served to rid the Bourbons
of unstable and unreliable elements in the administration, they
also served to consolidate the ranks of those, whether French or
Spanish, who believed that only rigorous measures would set the
monarchy on its feet again. This is where Amelot's real importance lies. Under him a group of ministers came into existence,

---

[10] *Ibid.*, 107 f.90.

devoted to the resurrection of their country. It is misleading to call the ambassador 'the Colbert of Spain'.[11] However strong Amelot's 'colbertist' opinions may have been he did not put them into the service of Spain but reserved them for his work on the French council of commerce. But there is no doubt that during his tenure of office he gave his unselfish and indefatigable attention to promoting the interests of the Bourbon monarchy. Perhaps his most useful long-term achievement here was the encouragement he gave to the careers of young Spaniards anxious to serve the crown. He fostered a whole school of administrators who put into practice the measures he helped to formulate, and it was from this group of men that the reforms characteristic of Bourbon rule in Spain took their origin. The years of his ambassadorship were not therefore simply the high point of French influence in this period: they were also the most active years of change and development during the war, and the most favourably remembered.

Notable among those who first came to the attention of Amelot was a future prime minister of Spain, Joseph Patiño.[12] But the most important of the Spanish administrators to emerge during the war was Melchor de Macanaz.[13] Born 1670 in Murcia, Macanaz studied law at Salamanca and then went to Madrid to further his career. He was taken into the royal entourage and eventually became a secretary of the council of Castile. While in this post he prepared several memoirs analysing the constitutional position of Valencia and Aragon: one of these, on the method to be adopted in governing the provinces, brought Macanaz to the attention of Amelot, who decided to make some use of him. As a result Macanaz was sent to Valencia in 1707 to reform the finances and administration. By his labours in the eastern provinces and by his unflagging literary output written to defend his actions, Macanaz has earned himself a primary place in the ranks of those who

---

[11] Baudrillart, *Philippe V et la Cour de France*, vol. 1, p. 229.

[12] As early as 1707, Amelot considered Patiño (or the reference, which is not clear, may be to his brother the marqués de Castelar) the only suitable administrator for Valencia, but Orléans opposed the appointment: AE Corr. Pol. (Esp.), 176 ff.196, 244. Patiño had to wait until 1711 for his first big advancement, as one of the first intendants.

[13] For an estimate of his career see Henry Kamen, 'Melchor de Macanaz and the foundations of Bourbon power in Spain', *English Historical Review*, Oct. 1965, pp. 699-716.

established the new dynasty on foundations that were essentially Spanish.

The revocation of the *fueros* of Aragon in 1707, an act in which Amelot was the chief agent though the real arguments for the measure were in fact put forward both by Louis XIV and by Macanaz, was one of the last important administrative steps taken by the ambassador in Spain. Henceforward he was occupied by two general issues of the greatest gravity: the problem of Philippe d'Orléans,[14] and the French decision to withdraw from the peninsula.

From 1707, as we have already seen, the duc d'Orléans, uncle of Philip V, was supreme commander of the Bourbon forces in Spain. Although he took no part in the victory at Almansa, his later military services to the régime were outstanding. Unfortunately the duke soon began to show impatience at the policy of the Spanish court and government, and his dissatisfaction took the form of a marked hostility towards Ursins, Amelot and even the king. It is possible that he wished to assume sole control over decisions in the field, without having to refer back constantly to Madrid. But suspicions of his attitude took a sinister turn. His conduct in the province of Aragon, where he openly followed a policy of moderation to the conquered, in complete contrast to the harsh policies dictated by Madrid, provoked the belief that he was trying to gain the sympathies of the people. To Philip V and his advisers it appeared that the duke was attempting to gain a party which might aid him in a claim to the throne of Spain. The young king was not impressed when his grandfather minimised the importance of the whole affair and urged him to hush up matters.

It was therefore with some relief that Philip greeted the withdrawal of Orléans from Spain in 1709. However, this was merely part of a wholesale French disengagement, which Philip refused to accept. Indignantly repudiating as cowardly the peace terms which Louis was urging him to agree to, he informed his grandfather that 'I shall never quit Spain save through death; I would rather prefer to perish fighting for it foot by foot, at the head of my troops'.[15] Much as Louis admired and agreed with his grandson, for him the withdrawal was a regrettable necessity, and the

[14] Baudrillart devotes most of his second volume to this subject.
[15] Baudrillart, vol. I, p. 341.

only possible way to make peace with the Allies. The ambassador, of course, was bitterly opposed to the whole operation. Rather than become the mouthpiece for this complete reversal of policy, Amelot wrote to Versailles demanding to be recalled. With his departure in August 1709 the period of French preponderance at the Spanish court came to an end. Only Ursins remained to provide some sort of continuity with the former régime. The new French representative, Blécourt, was an envoy extraordinary rather than an ambassador. This diplomatic downgrading completed Louis xiv's disengagement from Spain.

The critical state of the monarchy in 1710, and the serious Spanish reverses of that year, together with the Allied occupation of Madrid in September, overshadow all purely administrative problems. By 1711, however, the advantageous situation created by the victory at Villaviciosa enabled Philip to turn his attention once more to matters of government. Instead of appealing for help to France he turned to his own dominions and sought the employment of one of the most remarkable administrators of the time. Jean de Brouchoven, comte de Bergeyck,[16] has received no recognition for his work in Spain from any historian, yet his plans to resurrect the country were more ambitious and profound than any others conceived in this period, and if fully carried out may well have remedied over a century of disorder and neglect. A distinguished Flemish administrator who spent all his working life in the financial service of the Brussels government, he became treasurer general of the Spanish Netherlands in 1688. After 1701 he cooperated with the French officials who took over the Netherlands, and in 1702 became *surintendant gènèral* of war and finance. When Brussels fell to the Allies in 1706, Bergeyck went to live in France, at Mons, Versailles and Paris. From here he corresponded regularly with Philip v.[17] In the peace negotiations of 1709 he acted as spokesman in France for Philip.[18] At the end of 1710 Philip wrote to Bergeyck, then at Namur, and asked him to come and help him in Spain: Bergeyck accepted gladly, and left for Spain via Paris the following June. On 20 July 1711 he was

[16] There is an excellent life by Reginald de Schryver, *Jan van Brouchoven, Graaf van Bergeyck 1644–1725*, Brussels, 1965, which however has very little on Bergeyck's work in Spain.

[17] See the forty-four letters from Bergeyck to Philip, dated 1708 to 1711, in AHN, Estado leg. 2460¹ atado 18.

[18] AHN, Estado leg. 2460² atado 8.

received by Philip in the royal camp at Corella (about seventy kilometers from Pamplona), and took part immediately in meetings of the *despacho*. By August it was well known that Bergeyck's purpose was to institute a general reform of the government. In September he told Torcy that he was going to Madrid but intended 'not to take charge of war or finances but only to offer help with my ideas and suggestions to those who have charge of these matters, this being I think the best part I can play at my advanced age'; at the same time, however, he had a plan which, given the prerequisite of peace, would help to make Philip 'master of his states independent of all his councils'.[19]

The several proposals made by Bergeyck dealt with naval matters, finance and administration; and will be discussed later in their appropriate context. It was he who introduced the system of intendants into Spain. It was he also who encouraged the establishment of native industries in the peninsula. His position in this period was unique. All the chief ministers of Philip v from 1701 to 1715 were French, and from 1705 to 1709 the French ambassador was the unquestioned ruler of Spain. Bergeyck alone, in his brief spell of influence from 1711 to 1712, was not ultimately devoted to the interests of France.

At the end of September 1711 Bergeyck was made superintendant of finances, which placed him at the head of all financial matters. 'The disorder I have found here is beyond all imagining,' he wrote to Torcy in October. 'I am not going to bother about correcting the details, for that would take years. I am cutting through the disorganisation and disorder at one blow by a new plan I am proposing.'[20] At precisely the same time, as we shall see later, he was setting about the establishment of intendants in Spain. But his ambitious work in these and other fields was interrupted at the end of the year when Philip decided that he would be the best man to represent Spain at the forthcoming peace conference with England. At the end of October we find Bergeyck complaining that he would be unable to complete any of his reforms before his departure. It is quite possible that Philip v was also concerned at the impending loss of an able administrator, but he knew that Bergeyck was probably the only man experienced enough to defend Spain's interests at the

[19] Bergeyck to Torcy, 5 Sept. 1711, AE Corr. Pol. (Esp.), 209 f.61.
[20] *Ibid.*, 19 Oct. 1711, *ibid.*, 209 f.234.

congress. Louis xiv chose this moment to betray a hypocritical concern for Spain. Writing to the ambassador Bonnac at the end of November, he urged him to delay the departure of the Spanish plenipotentiaries, on the grounds that their presence, and notably that of Bergeyck, was essential to the reforms being effected in Spain.[21] The fact was that the French had a good reason for wanting Bergeyck out of the way, since he had always refused to agree to France handing the Spanish Netherlands over to Bavaria. Eventually, in the first week of January 1712, he left Spain for France.

The French ambassadors in the post-1709 period were faced with a peculiarly difficult situation in which the open hostility of Spaniards to an ally that had deserted them in the hour of greatest need, was aggravated by a growing impatience in the court itself. French military aid did not assuage suspicions that France was preparing to betray Spain at peace conferences with the Allies. The embassy of the marquis de Blécourt (1709–11) was a particularly disastrous one. His successor, the marquis de Bonnac, arrived at Corella on 2 September, eight days before Blécourt's final departure from Madrid. Bonnac remained at his post until November 1713, when he was relieved by the marquis de Brancas, who kept this position until March 1714. None of these men managed to retrieve the sinking fortunes of France in Madrid.

By August 1712 Bergeyck had grown weary of his tasks as a plenipotentiary, and asked to be recalled to Spain. His one desire now was to take up his reforms where he had left off. But the short absence had been disastrous. Already in 1711, before his departure, a perceptive observer had forecast that 'when he returns from the congress monsieur de Bergeyck will hardly find the memory of his plan',[22] referring in this instance to the plan for establishing intendants. The prophecy turned out to be only too true. 'So many dents have been made in this minister's plans during his absence,' it was reported, 'that it will take him some time to smooth them out.'[23] Bergeyck found the opposition invincible. Meanwhile Philip, impatient with the failure of one minister, wrote to Louis requesting the return of Orry as the only

[21] Louis xiv to Bonnac, 23 Nov. 1711, *ibid.*, 210 f.32.
[22] Bourke to Torcy, 23 Nov. 1711, *ibid.*, 210 f.78. For Bourke, see below, p. 86 n. 7.
[23] *Ibid.*, 30 Jan. 1713, *ibid.*, 220 f.61.

other man he knew to be competent to reform the finances.[24] By 29 April Orry was back in Madrid. After this Bergeyck faded into the background, assisted only formally in the *despacho*, and in March 1714, after a quarrel with Orry, ceased to come to any meetings of this body. On 14 April that year he and his family left Madrid.

Withdrawing eventually to his estates at Leefdael in Brabant, Bergeyck died there quietly in May 1725. His work in Spain shows him to have been a brilliant statesman of great promise, whose talents were never effectively utilised by the Spanish government. On his journey homewards he stayed at Versailles for several months as a guest of Louis xiv, who is said to have remarked that 'he regarded it as a tragedy for the king his grandson that Bergeyck no longer managed his affairs'.[25] It is difficult to estimate a man on promise alone, but there is no doubt that Bergeyck could have been one of Spain's greatest ministers. He had every experience in all fields of public service, and required only the necessary time and encouragement, neither of which he got. 'He was the most sincere man in the world, the most devoted to truth; he loved and sought the good for its own sake, and was the most attached to the interests of the king of Spain'.[26] Saint-Simon's tribute seems in every way deserved.

With Bergeyck's disappearance the administration fell into Orry's hands. Ursins and Orry now became close associates in the government. On the Spanish side the most prominent official in power was Macanaz, since 1713 attorney general of the crown. Although these three personalities are frequently described as members of the same coterie, it would be wrong to accept this at face value, since Macanaz is on record as an opponent of some of Orry's measures.[27] At the time, however, the public identified them with each other; hatred directed at one affected them all.

---

[24] Philip v to Louis xiv, 13 Mar. 1713, *ibid.*, 221 f.27.
[25] *Mémoires de Saint-Simon*, vol. 24, pp. 304–5.
[26] *Ibid.*, p. 246.
[27] In his *Regalías de los Señores Reyes de Aragón* (1729) he refers to 'la planta de gobierno o desgobierno de Juan Orri'. See the work of the same name publ. 1879, p. 199. Modesto Lafuente, *Historia General de España* (2nd ed., 30 vols), Madrid 1869, says in vol. 18, p. 370, note 1: 'Don Melchor de Macanaz nunca estuvo conforme con las medidas rentisticas de Orri . . .; no convenían en el modo de ver las cosas, y Macanaz se queja en muchos lugares de sus obras y de sus apuntes de la confusión que dice haber introducido el ministro francés, asi en la hacienda como en la justicia.'

C

Greeted in 1713 as the man who would save the monarchy, by 1714 Orry was the most hated man in Spain. Much of our evidence for this statement comes from ambassador Brancas, a man who loathed Orry so much that he informed his government in 1714 that 'an ambassador of France who wishes to do his duty can never put up with a man who has neither honour nor probity, and who pushes insolence to an unimaginable degree'.[28] But the general tenor of other reports besides those of Brancas confirms a growing popular hatred of Orry and indeed of all things French. Brancas reported cases of public outrages against Frenchmen in Madrid, Málaga and Alicante, including one or two stabbings.[29] Orry was accused both by Brancas and by Spanish politicians of arrogating to himself supreme power over all aspects of the administration, and a reorganisation of the conciliar system on 10 November 1713 aroused hostility throughout the peninsula. 'These last few days,' reported Brancas on 25 January 1714, 'they have found posters set up in all corners of the city ordering all the French nation, in the name of the people, to leave Madrid immediately. The posters threaten M Orry and M de Macanaz with some dire accident if they do not suspend the new taxes.'[30]

It is difficult to explain the anti-French mood on any rational grounds. To some extent it was a continuation of the reaction against France after 1709; to an extent also it was xenophobia and impatience with the pretensions of the court's French advisers, particularly Orry, a man about whom virtually no contemporary or subsequent historian has ventured to say a kind word. There is no evidence that the Spanish aristocracy played any part in sponsoring the movement: the mood was genuinely popular.[31]

[28] See his comments on the letter from Orry to Pontchartrain, 13 Feb. 1714, AN Aff. Etr., B¹ 777.

[29] Letters to Torcy, 30 Jan. 1714, AE Corr. Pol. (Esp.), 228; and 2 Mar. 1714, *ibid.*, 229 f.9.

[30] Brancas to Torcy, 25 Jan. 1714, *ibid.*, 228. Popular hatred of Orry is illustrated by a pamphlet, circulating in Madrid, showing a portrait of the king between Ursins and Orry, and below them the couplet: 'Esta disoluta y este borracho/tienen perdido este muchacho' (This strumpet and this drunkard/have corrupted this boy): BUV MS 456 f.282.

[31] Cf. Bourke to Torcy, 2 Dec. 1714, AE Corr. Pol. (Esp.), 237 f.99: 'Le bruit s'est répandu la semaine passée qu'on avoit assassiné a Cordua dans sa maison un François nommé Turgis, ancien commis ou secretaire de Monsr. Orry, qui est allé depuis peu en ce pays la pour quelque administration des rentes du Roy, et on ajoutte qu'on a répandu dans les principales villes d'Andalousie un imprimé par lequel on menaçoit du meme sort tous les François qui se melleroient de l'administration des rentes'.

The stage was at any rate set for the demise of French influence at the Bourbon court in Madrid.

By 1711, as we shall see later, the Italians had begun to make inroads into the most senior offices controlled by the crown. The inquisitor general as well as the viceroy of Peru nominated in 1711 were both Italians. This new orientation was attributed by a contemporary to the Savoyard queen, Marie Louise. With her death on 14 February 1714 the trend might well have stopped. However, the serious split between Versailles and Madrid over peace terms, and the factionalism between Brancas and the princess des Ursins at court, lowered French stock in Spain. Philip v's advisers proposed that he take an Italian princess, Elizabeth of Farnese, as his new queen. On 16 September the two were married by proxy, and Farnese commenced her journey through France to Spain. On 23 December she was met in Jadraque, just north of Guadalajara, by Ursins, who was anxious to assert her authority over her new mistress. Ursins was to receive a rude shock. Instead of an impressionable young girl she encountered a commanding young woman who refused to brook the *camarera mayor*'s superior attitude. Their meeting resulted in a quarrel that caused Farnese in a violent rage to order her guards to take 'that mad woman' away. Ursins was promptly bundled into a carriage and transported immediately to the French border. She was given no time even to collect her personal effects.

On 24 December Philip v married his queen in Guadalajara, and the bridal carriage entered Madrid three days later. The fall of Ursins had come as a thunderbolt to everyone. So drastic a procedure boded ill for Ursin's colleagues in the government. It was noted that the Abbé Alberoni, seen by many as the new power behind Farnese, had been having meetings with other members of the Italian circle at court. Orry in a state of concern approached the queen, and was given a verbal reassurance. Despite this he was dismissed from office on the morning of 7 February 1715, and a special decree the same day dismissed and banished Macanaz. With the departure of these two men from the government the first formative period of Bourbon rule in Spain came to an end. Drastic changes were decreed in the central administration, and all trace of French influence was eradicated. 'The court of Spain,' wrote the French *chargé d'affaires* after the fall of Ursins, 'is totally different from what it was ten days ago. It is a completely new court and a completely new system.'³² There was some exaggeration in this, but there is no doubt that Philip v had at last grown out of his reliance on Versailles and its servants.

³² Pachau to Torcy, 31 Dec. 1714, in Baudrillart, *Philippe V et la Cour de France*, vol. 1, p. 622.

4 The Conduct of the War

How far was Spain capable of maintaining a ten-year war on her own territory? According to all contemporary accounts, and according to Allied expectation, the country was ready to collapse at the slightest sign of military intervention. The Venetian ambassadors under Charles II were unanimous on Spanish decline. 'The ancient valour of Spaniards has perished',[1] reported one of them in 1678. Another, Giovanni Cornaro, reported in 1682 that the coasts were undefended, that there were no material forces within the country, that the forts were unmanned and munitionless, and that the roads into the kingdom were unguarded: 'tutto esposto, niente custodito. E incomprensible come la monarchia sussista.'[2] As late as 1698 the envoy Pietro Venier could claim that the coastal defences of Spain were undermanned, that artillery was lacking in most of the country's fortresses, and that even the royal guards were entirely ignorant of the use of arms.[3] When a decree for general enlistment was issued by the government on 17 July 1691, it stated that Spain had 'insufficient ships and soldiers for our defence . . . and that in most towns one can hardly find a musket, arquebus or pike'.[4]

If this was true of Castile, it was even more true of the provinces of the crown of Aragon. In 1685 in Saragossa the military stores in the palace of the Aljafería were totally lacking in artillery, since all usable pieces had been sent over the previous few years to help the defence of Pamplona; in 1693 the viceroy of Aragon himself

---

[1] *Relazioni degli Stati Europei lette al Senato dagli Ambasciatori Veneti nel secolo decimosettimo* ed. Nicolò Barozzi and Guglielmo Berchet, Venice, 1860, Serie I, *Spain*, vol. 2, p. 433.

[2] *Ibid.*, p. 489.

[3] *Ibid.*, pp. 647–8.

[4] Cited in Antonio Domínguez Ortiz, *La Sociedad Española en el Siglo XVIII*, Madrid, 1955, p. 368, note 4.

reported 'the poor and needy state to which the garrisons of this realm have been reduced'; and in 1695 it was reported from Barcelona that the prevalent torrent of desertions from the army was to be expected, since 'every dispatch of recruits turned out to be a row of wretches incapable of bearing arms'.[5]

The accounts given at the beginning of the eighteenth century bear out these reports. A distinguished native soldier who served in the War of Succession claimed, though with considerable exaggeration, that:

from Rosas to Cadiz there was not a castle or fort which had a garrison. . . . The same negligence was to be seen in the ports of Biscay and Galicia. The magazines lacked munitions; the arsenals and workshops were empty. The art of constructing ships had been forgotten.[6]

Such complaints were to be of prime importance later during the events in Aragon, when the defencelessness of the realm was to be cited as a reason for surrender to enemy forces. Certainly Castile was better defended with men and arms than the eastern provinces of the peninsula, yet even in Castile it was possible for the fortress of Gibraltar, defended by only a small garrison, to be captured by the Allies. Nor was Cadiz at all adequately defended, according to Marshal de Tessé, who visited the city at the beginning of the war.[7]

The resources of the Spanish crown in 1702 were limited, above all at sea, where the English and Dutch posed the greatest threat. In Mediterranean waters the crown controlled twenty-eight galleys in all: seven of these made up the 'squadron of Spain'; six others, based on Genoa, were by contract under the command of a Doria, the duque de Tursis; seven were stationed at Naples, six in Sicily, and two in Sardinia.[8] As an effective striking force, this motley navy had no existence, and the principal claim of the navy on royal finances was in the wages of the otherwise unemployed admiral, Fernan Núñez. What naval power did exist was devoted exclusively to the protection of the trade with

---

[5] José Camón Aznar, 'La situación militar en Aragón en el siglo XVII', *Jerónimo Zurita. Cuadernos de Historia*, viii-ix (1959), pp. 108, 128, 142.

[6] San Felipe, *Comentarios*, p. 25.

[7] *Mémoires et lettres du Maréchal de Tessé* (2 vols), Paris, 1806, vol. 2, p. 174. But contrast Parnell, who says, perhaps more reliably, that the garrison and defences were very good, *The War of the Succession in Spain during the reign of Queen Anne 1702–1711*, p. 24.

[8] AE Corr. Pol. (Esp.), 91 f.243.

America. In 1701 the total strength of Spanish warships deployed in the Caribbean and the Atlantic was twenty, under the command of Pedro Fernández Navarrete as Admiral General of the Ocean Sea.[9] Four of this number made up the Barlovento fleet, whose principal task in this period was to escort the trading and silver vessels across the Atlantic. Apart from these vessels, the Spanish crown had ceased to exist as a naval power, and the great traditions of the sixteenth century were watered down in the eighteenth to total dependence on the protecting hand of France.

Within its frontiers the country was not completely defenceless. A reasonably reliable memoir drawn up in 1703 estimated the Spanish military establishment at that date as follows:[10]

Infantry

In Galicia, five companies totalling	355 men
In Biscay, four companies totalling	378
In Extremadura (Badajoz), nine companies totalling	528
In Andalucia (Cadiz), 116 companies totalling	4,727
In Gibraltar, 32 companies totalling	431
On the frontiers of Portugal (Zamora)	1,000
In Catalonia (Barcelona)	3,116
In Africa (Ceuta, etc.)	2,733
Total	13,268

Cavalry

In Galicia, maximum total of	640 horse
In Extremadura, maximum total of	1,227
In Andalucia, maximum total of	2,162
In Catalonia, maximum total of	1,068
Total	5,097

So small a military establishment, even before the age of standing armies, was more than surprising in a country which had been intermittently at war with France and other nations for the past

[9] 'Razon de los Navios que ay en Indias', *ibid.*, 87 f.224. I was unable to gain detailed information of these ships in the Archive of the Indies at Seville, since the relevant documents were being bound at the time of my visit.

[10] 'Reconnoissance de l'Etat present des Troupes', *ibid.*, 119 ff.276–9. The memoir was drawn up by Orry.

century and more. The lack of any figures for troops in Valencia will be seen to be significant when we come to deal with the history of that region, and it is natural to find the Allies landing troops without opposition in Valencia as a prelude to their seizure of Barcelona. The concentration of forces in Andalucia, and especially Cadiz, was part of the build-up of defences against frequent Allied naval operations in the south during the first few months of the war. On the whole, we may assume that the figures cover military garrisons as well, which helps us very easily to understand why Cadiz – the key to the Indies trade and a prize long sought by the English navy – should have withstood attacks so well, and why Gibraltar should have fallen with so little effort.

The figures by themselves justify all the pessimistic reports of Spanish strength. This, however, was in 1703, at the very beginning of the war and before the commencement of any land operations. Within the ensuing year, efforts were made to raise troops sufficient to defend the Portuguese border, and French help brought the total armed forces up to a respectable figure. Yet three years later the French ambassador was complaining that the total number of Spanish infantry in Andalucia, Extremadura, Castile and Galicia was only 17,242 men.[11] In the event, this was of no great consequence, for as French intervention increased the Spanish troops were restricted to a predominantly defensive or supporting role. French commanders distrusted the ability of Spaniards in battle,[12] and the direction of campaigns was invariably entrusted to French generals, while defensive commands in Andalucia and Galicia were left for Spanish noblemen.

Perhaps the principal problem facing the Spanish government was not men, but supplies. In 1703 it was claimed that the infantry and cavalry had no arms, and that the troops lacked clothing completely.[13] At the same time the troops on the Portuguese frontier were deserting because they were not being paid, sheltered or fed.[14] These problems were only gradually

---

[11] Amelot to Louis XIV, 28 Jan. 1706, *ibid.*, 157 f.133.

[12] Thus Tessé to Amelot, 17 June 1705: 'I would not trust a Spaniard, however brave, with the defence of a steeple. They fight duels; but as a body, and for their country, is an idea which never enters their heads'. Quoted in Coxe, *Memoirs of the Kings of Spain*, vol. 1, p. 343.

[13] Orry to Torcy, 20 Oct. 1703, AE Corr. Pol. (Esp.), 120 f.187.

[14] Louville to Beauvilliers, 8 Oct. 1703, *Mémoires de Saint-Simon*, vol. 11, p. 531.

solved in the course of the war, and then with French help. The one drawback was that the speed of the war overtook the pace of reforms, so that when the Allies spread over eastern Spain in 1706 there was no material hindrance in their way: this was to have significant results in the realms of Aragon.

The French came to a country which had for over two centuries been in the habit of fighting wars abroad or at the national frontiers, not in the heart of the homeland. Spain's inability to deal with the crisis was characterised by financial bankruptcy in the exchequer, and military ineptitude in the ruling classes. These two reasons were enough to necessitate French control of the war-effort. The several commanders-in-chief of the peninsular war were all French, and French control alone made it possible to coordinate military and naval strategy in a theatre where support from the sea was of immense importance. Spanish armies undoubtedly benefited from foreign advice which rationalised the methods of recruitment, organisation and equipment of Spaniards, and, most vital of all, which supplied the war materials needed to fill the enormous gaps in Spanish equipment.

The reform of the Spanish armed forces is a subject that needs to be studied in its own right, and will be touched on very briefly here.[15] Spanish military recovery under Philip v derived principally from two factors: the adoption of more functional weapons and the rationalisation of military organisation. The first was catered for by a decree of 29 January 1703 which abolished use of the musket, arquebus and pike as standard equipment, and replaced them by the plug-bayonet rifle. The appointment simultaneously of D Francisco Fernández de Córdoba as commissary-general initiated the series of organisational reforms. In the same year, Córdoba formed twelve new *tercios* of six hundred men each. This was followed by other measures throughout the kingdom to improve recruitment and to create more *tercios*. A decree of 3 March 1703 ordered the enlistment of one man out of every hundred of the population. A significant break with the whole Spanish military tradition occurred with a decree of 28 September 1704, which abolished the term *tercio* and substituted for it that of *regimiento* or regiment. A month after this the office

---

[15] The information here is drawn largely from A. Ballesteros y Beretta, *Historia de España*, Barcelona, 1929, vol 6; A. Domínguez Ortiz, *La Sociedad española en el siglo XVIII*, pp. 371–3; Danvila y Collado, *El poder civil*, vol. 3, pp. 454, 532–5.

of commissary-general was replaced by that of director-general of the infantry. Subsequent decrees aimed for the most part at keeping recruitment to a high level and integrating the new regiments into a rationally organised army. The other military measures are also noteworthy. A royal bodyguard in four companies was created on 21 June 1704. Its novelty lay in the fact that half the companies were non-Spanish in origin, a reflection of French distrust of Spanish military capacity, since Orry was primarily responsible for the measure. Reform of the cavalry, along French lines, seems to have been postponed until 1707. The corps of artillery began to be centralised as early as 1702, under a colonel-general; by 1710 the corps had expanded enough to be divided into battalions. The engineers formed part of the artillery and became a separate corps only in 1711, when the Fleming George Prosper Verboom was entrusted with their reorganisation.

Spanish production of war materials was virtually non-existent. According to Orry, 'in 1701 the king of Spain drew almost no gunpowder from any factory in the realm',[16] with the result that Spain was forced to rely heavily on France until her own factories increased production. On 1 October 1702 Cardinal Portocarrero signed a treaty with Aufroy de Servigny, a Frenchman resident in Spain, to supply gunpowder, and in 1703 Orry drew up contracts for the supply of powder from Aragon, Granada, Navarre and other places, to a total of 12,250 hundredweight. With the onset of war, production was stepped up, but at least until 1706 Spain relied largely on France for powder. She also relied on France completely for most grades of artillery, and almost completely for flints; and so long as the factories in Biscay and Navarre remained undeveloped, she had to import bullets and explosives from France.[17]

Marshal Tessé in 1705 summed up his own difficulties in a letter to the French minister of war. Spain, he wrote, could supply only a limited number of mortars, and a foundry should therefore be set up in Pamplona. Little powder was available and some should be sent from France through Bayonne. Bullets and explosives were being promised in Spain, but more explosives and fuses, together with saltpetre and sulphur, should be sent.[18]

16 Guerre, A¹ 1884 f.126, Memoir of 20 Mar. 1705, p. 21. 17 Ibid., pp. 24–5.
18 Tessé to Chamillart, 9 Dec. 1705, Guerre, A¹ 1888 f.220.

The same shortages appeared when it came to uniforms, because of the low state of cloth production in Spain. The first care of Orry and other French administrators, aided by reforming Spaniards such as Gaspar Naranjo, was to develop the textile industry so as to make Spain self-sufficient in war materials. Despite some important advances,[19] urgent needs could nevertheless be met only by imports from France, and for this reason French weapons played a key role in the earlier years of the war.

The amount of French war materials supplied to Spain is of importance for two principal reasons. In the first place it provides evidence of precisely what goods Spanish suppliers were incapable of producing; and, secondly, it allows us to calculate the cash value of purchases from France. It should be noted that the convenience of standardising equipment in a Franco-Spanish army would to some extent explain the need to fit out Spanish troops with French weapons.

Orry seems to have initiated the series of orders placed by the Spanish government with French suppliers. Early in 1703 an order was placed with Maximilien Titon, director general of military factories and stores at Paris, for the supply, *inter alia,* of 1,440 sabres, 2,200 pistols of various kinds, 780 flintlocks of different calibres, and other weapons to arm at least five regiments of cavalry and one of dragoons: the cost of this order came to 110,744 livres (or, in Spanish money, 553,720 reales).[20] At the same time Philip v bought a large quantity of field tents, enough for six thousand officers and horse, and ten thousand cavalry. The purchase of such elementary weapons, added to the buying of tents, emphasises the shortcomings of Spanish production. This is reaffirmed in a letter from Orry to Chamillart, the French minister of war, in March 1703, reporting that he had placed an order with a Toulouse cloth manufacturer for three thousand complete uniforms, costing 405,000 reales, and had also ordered

---

[19] Orry in 1705 claimed that he had helped 'a establir trois manufactures de gros draps, charges d'en fournir 100,000 aunes par an pour l'habillement de toutes ces troupes; a aporter une reforme et un arangement dans la fabrique des armes de Biscaye, de laquelle on en devoit tirer 12,000 par an sur les meilleurs models de ce qui se fait presentement en France, et a l'epreuve, on estoit de meme parvenu a faire reussir cinq differentes fabriques de poudre qui en donnoient 65 milliers par mois, et une de plomb', Guerre, A¹ 1884 f.126.

[20] *Ibid.*, 1696 ff.6–7.

six thousand hundredweight of gunpowder.[21] Later the same year another order placed with Titon called for ten thousand flintlocks with bayonets, 1,280 sabres, and 5,280 swords, the whole totalling 273,064 livres (1,365,320 vellon reales).[22] Orry considered the flintlocks essential for the equipment of the infantry, and said that the order was meant to supplement a presumed future production of two thousand flintlocks a month by the Spanish factories.[23] All these orders were for the troops of Spain alone, and the urgency with which they were demanded confirms the impression that the Spanish forces had till then been virtually defenceless for lack of arms and munitions.

No continuous record of purchases appears to have been kept in Spain for the duration of the war. Available details do suggest, however, that very large orders continued to be placed with French manufacturers throughout the war, due no doubt in part to the failures of Spanish industry. On 30 June 1704 a contract was signed with the Paris manufacturer Jean Lelarge, to clothe all the soldiers in Philip v's infantry guard with uniforms in the French style: the total cost of this was 176,394 livres[24] (881,970 reales). In December 1704 Philip ordered 7,000 uniforms, of which 4,400 were for the infantry and 2,600 for the cavalry.[25] On 4 July 1705 the treasurer of Spain, the conde de Moriana, forwarded to Paris six bills of exchange worth 3,501,532 reales, to the account of Jean Lelarge, who was to supply clothing for that amount. On 27 August Moriana sent seven bills of exchange worth 500,000 reales to the account of Titon. On 4 May 1706 Moriana again paid 3,151,505 reales to Lelarge's account, for the supply of 1,541 cavalry uniforms, 5,360 infantry uniforms, 2,000 pairs of boots, 10,000 pairs of shoes, and 680 uniforms for the officers of the infantry guard. These and other sums credited to Paris between 1705 and 1707 came to a total of 7,970,537 reales.[26]

On 17 December 1706 another contract was signed with Le-

[21] *Ibid.*, 1695 f.50. In February he stressed the importance of sending at once four thousand hundredweight of powder to La Coruña, and two thousand to Cadiz: *ibid.*, f.30.

[22] Orry to Torcy, 11 Sept. 1703, AE Corr. Pol. (Esp.), 120 f.72.

[23] *Ibid.*, 20 Oct. 1703, *ibid.*, 120 f.187.

[24] Guerre, A¹ 1791 f.84.

[25] Ribas to Chamillart, 7 Dec. 1704, *ibid.*, 1786 f.358.

[26] All these payments are given in AGS Dirección General del Tesoro, Inventario 16, guión 19, leg.1².

large, for the supply of ten thousand more uniforms.[27] The accounts of the central military stores at Madrid, under the care of Juan Manuel de Villagarcía, show that from June 1705 to June 1707 the sum of 1,254,334 reales was paid directly or indirectly to French suppliers in the following way:[28]

166,365 vellon reales to Jean-Jacques Yon and Company,[29] for cavalry and infantry uniforms, being an advance for 998,195 reales, the total sum due.

382,958 reales to the same, for another order of uniforms costing 1,221,800 reales.

87,925 reales to Guillaume Coulon, master-weaver at Bayonne, towards the 30,500 livres owed him for 1,000 infantry tents and 500 cavalry ones.[30]

66,593 reales as an advance to N. Morasin and N. Berton of Bayonne, for the supply of sacks and 1,500 infantry tents and 500 cavalry tents.

315,020 reales to Jean Baptiste Duplessis, for 2,497 tents supplied in 1707; this payment was towards a sum of 369,000 reales owed for 3,000 tents.

234,973 reales to the same, for 2,115 pairs of boots and 1,062 pairs of stockings supplied in 1706 and 1707.

Substantial purchases continued to be made right through to 1709. The accounts of the Spanish treasury from 1707 to 1709 show that in that period Jean Lelarge supplied shoes, tents and uniforms worth 975,821 reales; Duplessis supplied the same to the total of 1,094,840 reales; and Yon supplied from France uniforms worth 2,621,845 reales.[31] In 1708 the enormous sum of fifteen million reales was assigned by Philip to pay debts to French suppliers;[32] among these debts were the following:

To Yon, for cavalry uniforms and equipment, 600,000 livres.

To the brothers Gallois, drapers of Paris and bankers of Madrid, 94,954 livres.

To the same, for clothing 5,000 infantry, 298,125 livres.

To Yon, for clothing 6,100 cavalry, 521,345 livres.

[27] Amelot to Chamillart, 10 Jan. 1707, Guerre, A¹ 2048 f.33.
[28] AGS Dirección General del Tesoro, Inventario 16, guión 21, leg.3.
[29] Yon was a Franco-Spanish financier. See below, p. 77.
[30] This sum was paid in the first instance to the financiers Bernardo Cambi and Gianbattista Spinelli, for a bill of exchange on the Paris banker Masson to be made payable to Coulon.
[31] AGS, Tribunal Mayor de Cuentas leg.1878.
[32] AE Corr. Pol. (Esp.), 186 f.79.

In 1709 a contract with Titon provided for the supply of twelve thousand infantry flintlocks with bayonets, costing 193,700 livres (968,500 reales).[33] By this time Louis XIV, under pressure from the Allies, had decided to disengage himself from Spain in order to simplify the peace negotiations being carried on by his diplomats. The French forces were almost all withdrawn from the peninsula, and Spain was thrown back on her own resources. For over a year after the French withdrawal, there appear to have been no purchases of armaments from France. It is possible that Spanish production had now improved and was helping to fill the gap, but of this no certain information is available.

Purchases were continued when France resumed aid to Spain. In March 1711 the Spanish war minister, the marqués de Canales, negotiated with Noë Dufau, a Lyons financier, the purchase of six thousand flintlocks with bayonets, two thousand carbines, and two thousand pairs of pistols, at a total cost of 158,000 livres; the price was subsequently raised to 171,000 livres (855,000 reales).[34] On the same date, 3 March 1711, another contract was agreed upon with Titon for the supply within a year of eighteen thousand flintlocks, eight thousand muskets, a thousand carbines and seven thousand pairs of pistols, at a total cost of 585,000 livres (2,925,000 reales).[35] 'Our magazines are completely exhausted and we have nearly half our infantry and part of our cavalry weaponless', the French commander, the duc de Vendôme, was complaining at this time.[36]

The next major purchase after this occurred in 1714, during the siege of Barcelona by royal troops. Large shipments of arms from France were made, such as the delivery from Toulon, in a convoy of five ships, of guns, bombs and bullets for the besieging forces.[37] It has not been possible to estimate the value of the shipments. At the same period, early in 1714, Orry also sent

[33] Bergeyck to Philip V, 10 Dec. 1709. AHN, Estado leg. 4004.

[34] Letter from Voysin to Alba, 18 Apr. 1711, AGS, Secretaría de Estado leg. 4308; AE Corr. Pol. (Esp.), 206 f.79; AGS, Secretaria de Estado leg.4309, where the revised estimate is given. The arms were to be supplied by Duplessis, director of the armaments factory at Saint Etienne.

[35] AGS, Secretaría de Estado leg.4309.

[36] Vendôme to Torcy, from Saragossa, 21 Mar. 1711, AE Corr. Pol. (Esp.), 206 f.78.

[37] AGS, Guerra Moderna leg.1590. The inventory of arms delivered is headed 'Toulon: second envoy d'artillerie', signed 'De Veuvré' and dated 1 May 1714.

400,000 livres to France, to the merchants Le Leu and Morasin, for military uniforms and equipment.[38]

These are all the contracts relevant to the war of the Spanish Succession which seem to be traceable in the archives. The total value of purchases made from 1703 to 1709, that is, the period of extensive French commitment in Spain, may be put roughly at not less than 37,000,000 reales. This is 32·5 per cent of the total government revenue in 1703. Put another way, the annual average spent on purchases of equipment from France came to about 5 per cent of the government's yearly income. It is important to note that these contracts answer for only a part of the total volume of French arms entering Spain: the other part consisted of armaments, both light and heavy, bought by the French command in Spain to supply their own troops.

There are some indications that the war effort gave an impetus to armament production within Spain, and that the country was becoming less dependent on foreign supplies. But the recovery was very slow. The majority of contracts made by the government with Spanish suppliers from 1704 to 1709, concern the provision of food rations, clothing, and gunpowder; and contracts for munitions are noticeably infrequent. French arms must therefore have played a cardinal role in the maintenance of Spanish forces. Contracts such as the one made in 1705 with a Navarrese supplier,[39] for bombs, grenades and other explosives, show a native capability in gunpowder production, but less of one in the production of guns. The military stores at Madrid from 1705 to 1707 received all their gunpowder from places within Spain – Murcia, Orihuela and Granada. But even gunpowder supply was in foreign hands, the official company for its provision being controlled after 1707 by two Frenchmen, Jean Baptiste Duplessis and Jean Baptiste Milhau. It is difficult to say what held arms production back. Certainly by the end of the war many obstacles had been cleared, for the greater part of the artillery bought by the government between 1713 and 1716 came from the manufactories of Cantabria.[40] But financial difficulties hindered the expansion of the war industry, and one company formed to

---

[38] Brancas to Torcy, 5 Mar. 1714, AE Corr. Pol. (Esp.), 229 f.19.

[39] Asiento with Adan de Maculaiz (or Maculair), 'administrador de las fabricas de muniziones de Guerra en el territorio de la harmeria de Egui, en el reyno de Navarra' AGS, Contadurías Generales leg.189.

[40] AGS, Dirección General del Tesoro, Inventario 16, guión 21, leg.6.

provide arms complained in 1711 that the factories in Plasencia, Tolosa and elsewhere in Cantabria were in a depressed state because of government debts to them; this led to lower production, and the need to buy arms from France.[41] Some progress seems to have been made with textile production. If we may believe Orry, by 1705 three new factories to produce heavy cloth had been set up, with a planned output of 100,000 yards a year for clothing the troops.[42] The efforts of Gaspar Naranjo to promote industry also had some success, for by a decree of 3 December 1703 the government placed an order with manufacturers for 70,000 yards of woollen cloth and 300,000 of serge.[43] Presumably this sort of order was repeated.

On another level, however, import of arms continued because of the adoption of French weapons as standard Spanish equipment. This is most clearly seen in the case of the royal household of Philip v, on whose behalf Orry in 1714 sent the sum of 400,000 livres noted on a previous page, for uniforms and arms for four new companies of guards.

The problem of supplies for the armies was no less difficult than that of arms. It is unfortunate that this question is not well documented, for it involves that small body of men who did more than anyone else to promote the war effort – the financiers. The provision of supplies was carried out in the same way as administration of the taxes: it was farmed or contracted out. The contracts went to financiers who could command the necessary capital outlay, so that the army relied for grain and munitions on a network of private companies not subject to the central control of the government. The disadvantages of this system were obvious, but insuperable.

All possible provisions were contracted out, usually on a geographical basis. The south-east of Spain, for instance, was catered for by a contract of 16 June 1702 between the government and Luis González del Olmo, for the supply for ten years of six thousand hundredweight of gunpowder a year, to be delivered at Cartagena and Málaga. In 1707 Jean Baptiste Duplessis and

---

[41] 'Si acian cien armas, se les pagaba la mitad o menos, de que nace que se deve a las fabricas de atrasados 30,000 doblones ... Por esta razon no podia su Mag⁴ tener las armas que se necesitavan, y le ha sido precisso proveerse del Reyno de Francia cassi del todo.' AGS, Guerra Moderna leg.1576.

[42] Guerre, A¹ 1884 f.126.

[43] Jaime Carrera Pujal, *Historia de la Economía Española*, vol. 3, p. 84.

Jean Baptiste Milhau were, as we have seen, contractors for powder in Castile. In 1712 Juan Francisco Goyeneche and Company were described as contractors for arms from Cantabria. The contractors and regions varied according to circumstance.

The most important group of contracts was that for grain and food supplies to the army. The history of this group can be traced in more detail. Orry's reforms in 1703, which we shall touch on later, resulted in the drawing up of various contracts for the provision of food and grain: typical is that agreed upon on 31 October 1703 and confirmed on 23 December 1703, with Manuel López de Castro. This contract was to run for six years from 1 November 1703, and supplies were to be made to forces in the provinces of Andalucia, Extremadura, Old Castile, and Galicia. Payment for this contract, as for others, took the form of taxes being assigned totally to the contractor.[44] The system of assignations vitiated the whole supply line, and contractors often refused to extend their agreements because they were assigned revenues that had already been spent or pledged years in advance.[45] López de Castro turned out to be an inefficient supplier, and his contract was terminated prematurely. By 1704 Francisco Esteban Rodríguez de los Rios, later marqués de Santiago, was contractor for Extremadura and Castile, while the other regions of Spain were covered by Cristobal de Aguerri (administrator of the banking house of the marqués de Valdeolmos) for Andalucia, the marqués de Campoflorido for Galicia, Jose de Soraburu for Navarre, and Esteban de Moriones for Aragon. By 1707 Santiago was considered the most efficient of these contractors, and was given the contract for supplies to Aragon and Catalonia, in which the majority of campaigns were being conducted. Because of government inability to meet expenses, however, Santiago refused to carry on further than the first half of 1708, and Amelot set about organising fourteen financiers of Madrid into a company for supplies.[46] This company appears to have continued

[44] AGS, Contadurías Generales leg.188.

[45] The marqués de Santiago in 1707 refused to contract for supplies to French troops in Spain for this reason. See the letter from Amelot to Chamillart, 31 Jan. 1708, AE Corr. Pol. (Esp.), 187 f.26.

[46] Amelot to Orléans, 1 June 1708, AE Corr. Pol. (Esp.), 187 f.188. The head of the company was a certain Duchaufour, and the man proposed as director was D Thomas de Capdevilla: *ibid.*, f.265. Each member of the company advanced 4,500,000 reales for the immediate purchase of supplies: Amelot to Orléans, 13 May 1708, AE Corr. Pol. (Esp.), Supplément 11 f.32.

successfully until 1710, in which year a company of Frenchmen under Antoine Sartine undertook supplies for Aragon, Valencia and Catalonia.[47] On 1 November 1711 this contract was extended for another year.

Government failure to grant reliable assignations on taxes led to another change on 1 November 1712, when the prominent financiers Juan Francisco Goyeneche, and Pedro López de Ortega (who had succeeded Aguerri as head of the firm of Valdeolmos), took over the provision of grains to Aragon, Valencia and Catalonia for one year, the full value of this contract being 45,948,930 vellon reales. Astonishingly, Goyeneche and Ortega were at the same time contractors for Extremadura and Castile. [48] The enormous debt of the government to these two financiers will become clearer when we examine the general relation between bankers and the tax structure of Spain. With respect to the war, it is certain that the Bourbon monarchy would have fallen but for the frequent and opportune loans made by financiers at critical moments in the struggle. Some space must be devoted to this question.

The financiers relevant to our study can be divided into two distinct groups, the French and the Spanish. The French operated principally in Cadiz and Madrid; their energies in this period were directed towards the French war effort in Spain, and the trade to the Indies. The most important single group was the Guinea Company, which had in 1701 been granted the Asiento for the slave trade, and which both Louis xiv and Philip v exploited to the extent that it never became a paying concern.[49] The financial history of the Asiento, however, is a subject by itself. Spain at this time had no public bank, nor was paper money in circulation. Financial transactions were carried out through banking houses and individual financiers, whose bills of exchange became the principal machinery of credit and were valid throughout the Spanish dominions and, particularly during

---

[47] Bourke to Torcy, 8 Feb. 1712, A E Corr. Pol. (Esp.), 212 f.123, implies that Sartine began operations in 1710, but I have found contracts only for 1711. On Sartine, see my article 'El establecimiento de los intendentes en la administracion española', *Hispania*, xxiv (1964), p. 382.

[48] A G S, Dirección General del Tesoro, Inventario 24, leg.556.

[49] On the Guinea Company, see particularly G. Scelle, *Histoire politique de la Traite Négrière aux Indes de Castille* (2 vols), Paris, 1906, vol. 2; and Léon Vignols, 'El Asiento francés e inglés y el comercio franco-español desde 1700 hasta 1730', *Anuario de Historia del Derecho Español*, V (1928).

the War of Succession, at international fairs such as those of Lyon. Outside Barcelona, with which we are not here concerned, the principal centres of finance were Madrid, as the capital, and Cadiz (with Seville), as the focal point of the Indies trade. Other parts of the realm seem to have been relatively backward: Saragossa, for example, had little or no banking facilities, and hardly half a dozen financiers.[50]

The study of relations between financiers and the state, carried out so brilliantly for the sixteenth century by Carande, Lapeyre and others, becomes increasingly difficult to formulate for the seventeenth century, and by the eighteenth the subject loses both its significance and its interest. The principal reasons for this are the decline of the great banking houses, and the greater autonomy of the state in financial matters. The financiers of the reigns of Charles II and Philip V are remnants of a once powerful breed. Perhaps the most outstanding of them was Francisco Bàez Eminente, whose firm had served the Habsburgs 'for a period of over forty years, with credit, industry and zeal that were well known'.[51] Failure of the crown to repay its debts, and, no doubt, the effects of the prosecution undertaken against Eminente by the Inquisition in about 1691, meant that the firm under his son, Juan Francisco Eminente, had to ask in June 1702 for a moratorium which was extended up to 1711 and probably beyond that,[52] because it was unable to provide credit for the bills of exchange it issued. This collapse of credit meant that by the time of Juan Francisco's death on 23 February 1711, and the succession of Joseph Franco as its head, the firm had declined to a minor position in the ranks of the financiers.

This fatal failure of the crown to meet its obligations was an old phenomenon, and was repeated again in the case of one of Philip V's most prominent financiers, Bartolomé de Flon y Morales. Flon distinguished himself from the beginning of the reign by placing his credit at the service of the crown. His principal achievement was the salvation of the treasure when the Allies sank the plate fleet off Vigo in 1702. 'I have kept Monsieur Flon

---

[50] Guerre, A¹ 1985 f.6, Méliand to Chamillart 2 Jan. 1706: 'Le Royaume d'Aragon est sans resource et sans facultés ... La Banque y est presque inconnue, il n'y a que deux ou trois marchands au plus qui entretiennent quelque petit commerce de lettres de Saragosse a Madrid; les autres ne connoissent que celuy de marchandises.'
[51] *Cédula* of 19 Aug. 1712, AGS, Contadurías Generales leg.190.
[52] Relevant details are in *ibid.*, leg. 188.

here almost by force,' reported the distraught French admiral of the fleet at the time; 'he wanted to go off to his own business, but now he is here, and needed on all sides'.[53] At his own expense Flon raised troops to repel the Allies, saved a large part of the silver, and sent to France the French survivors from the fleet, for which he was rewarded by Louis XIV with a chain (in Spanish, *cadena*) of gold. In 1710, a particularly critical year for Philip, he lent the crown fifty million reales and also made a gift of 600,000 reales to the king. In 1711 he advanced a further six million reales to the crown.[54]

The numerous transactions of Flon with the government do not seem to be dealt with in available documentation, but there is no doubt that his efforts for the new dynasty were magnificent. In July 1702 we find him attempting to raise money for the Bourbons through Samuel Bernard in France and Gaetano Ametrano in Naples.[55] In 1707 he was one of the two principal financiers on whom the French ambassador relied for immediate monetary help,[56] and again in 1709 the government turned to him for help in the emergency after Louis XIV's withdrawal from Spain.[57] Between these dates Flon had certainly been giving money to the crown, for the accounts of the treasury show that he had forwarded 1,577,468 reales to Philip V 'for a secret purpose'.[58] I have found no trace of Flon administering taxes except in 1711 when he was given the farm of tobacco on condition of an advance of six million reales.[59] Flon's reward came on 22 December 1711, when Philip V issued a decree by which:

in consideration of the outstanding services rendered by Don Bartolomé de Flon since the beginning of my reign, in negotiations (among other things, with his capital and credit in all sorts of business both in these realms and in the Indies, from which have resulted silver escudos that have been of such great help in the urgent needs of war) . . . I have decided to grant him a title of Castile in perpetuity to him and his heirs, under any title he chooses as a count or a marquis.[60]

[53] Chateaurenaud to Larrea, 5 Nov. 1702, AGI, Indiferente leg. 2714.
[54] The preceding details are from a memoir of 1732 in AGS, Secretaría de Hacienda leg.85.
[55] AE Corr. Pol. (Esp.), 106, ff.3, 126.
[56] Guerre, A¹ 2048 f.16.
[57] AE Corr. Pol. (Esp.), 194 f.199.
[58] AGS, Tribunal Mayor de Cuentas leg.1875.
[59] Bonnac to Louis XIV, 21 Dec. 1711, AE Corr. Pol. (Esp.), 210 f.170.
[60] AN Aff. Etr., B^{III} 326 f.97.

The title he chose was that of conde de la Cadena. The honour did nothing to wipe out the fact that the crown had heavy debts to him: these remained unpaid. On Flon's death, his son Bartolomé de Flon y Zurbarán, conde de la Cadena, was faced with severe financial difficulties, and on 16 March 1728 Philip v had to grant him a moratorium of two years. In 1732 Flon applied for another moratorium, this time for four years. On this note of decline his firm fades from our documentation.

Of other Spanish financiers only a few, scattered details are available. Juan Francisco Goyeneche belonged to a family firm which gained greater prominence later on in the eighteenth century. The Goyeneches and Eminentes played an important part in the War of Succession, but few of their compatriots were equally outstanding. Instead, foreigners domiciled in Spain came to the fore. Among them was Hubert Hubrechtz, a leading banker of Madrid, whose activities during the war were ubiquitous and untiring, but of whom no account can be given here because of the absence of any continuous evidence of his transactions. Also at Madrid were the Italian bankers Rubini and Spinelli, and the Englishman Francis Arther.

Arther is of special interest because he seems to have done business with both sides during the war. His name occurs regularly in transactions with the Bourbon government of Spain. At the same time he helped the English invasion forces. A letter from him to General Stanhope in the Spanish archives, dated 29 August 1711, runs:

I must acquaint you of my impossibility to continue supplying Col. Nevill with more money. I have already engaged all my own and ye little credit I had w. my friends in England and Holland, but they begin to faile me, seeing that no manner of care is taken to satisfye your and ye Collonels bills. They and I were promised that all should be paid as soon as the Parlam. had setled the fonds, but as yet my correspondents have not recovered any but the first £6,000 upon account of about £60,000.[61]

Obviously the letter fell into Spanish hands, yet no action was taken against Arther, who continued to operate well after this. For the period of the war, Arther conducted business in association with a partner called Edward Crean. In 1715 the two terminated the partnership.[62]

[61] AHN, Estado leg.3469.
[62] Letters to this effect in AGS, Secretaría de Estado leg.7838.

The principal ways in which these financiers helped Philip were by direct gifts and loans, or by advancing credit to help pay for food supplies and weapons. Often they worked together with French officials and financiers to promote the joint war effort of the two nations. A typical loan was that demanded of the Spanish financiers in the 1709 emergency: on that occasion Juan de Goyeneche, the conde de Moriana, the marqués de Campoflorido and others advanced 120,000 reales each, and Juan Francisco Eminente, Arther and others advanced 60,000 reales each.[63] It has unfortunately been impossible to examine what loans and credits were issued by these financiers. To take one instance, the treasury accounts from 1703 to 1706 show that the sum of 205,723,470 maravedis (6,506,570 reales) had been paid to Goyeneche for bills of exchange advanced by him,[64] but it is likely that the sum was much higher for the period, and in any case this figure is of little use if we cannot compare sums advanced by other financiers. The last big loans called for during the war were in order to pay for the campaigns in Catalonia. The treasury accounts show that various bills of exchange were issued by the government on Madrid bankers, to be payable in Barcelona, in order to help the pacification of Catalonia in 1714 and 1715. Cambi and Spinelli in January 1715 gave bills for 1,500,000 reales; Arther and Crean, with others, in December 1714 gave bills for 750,000 reales; Jacobo Flon y Zurbarán in January 1715 gave bills for 600,000 reales; and others helped likewise.

Despite pressing economic difficulties, the financiers in Spain seem to have been vitalised by the war. Certainly the money market in the peninsula became a thriving one as the result of the efforts of several foreign governments, particularly the French and English, to find adequate supplies for their troops in the peninsula. The impetus this gave to the activities of financiers may safely be presumed. At the same time the corresponding growth of multilateralism[65] and the international negotiations of Spanish financiers, prepared the way for a greater participation of Spain in European commerce. It was an awareness of this development that led Campomanes at the end of the century to

[63] AGS, Secretaría de Estado leg.7835.
[64] AGS, Tribunal Mayor de Cuentas leg.1870.
[65] A discussion of multilateralism in exactly this period, is given in J. Sperling, 'The International Payments Mechanism in the Seventeenth and Eighteenth Centuries', *Economic History Review*, XIV, iii (1962), esp. pp. 455–65.

emphasise the beneficial aspects of a war which had stimulated Spanish finance.[66]

A few lines should suffice to outline the Spanish war expenses to which the financiers contributed. In 1702 it was calculated that the ensuing six-month campaign could cost the royal treasury 17,981,060 reales.[67] This, of course, was before the war had got under way. By 1704 it was estimated that for the food, clothing and pay of the Spanish troops a minimum of 70,615,870 reales per annum was needed, this figure not including the cost of armaments and transport which should raise expenses to 100,000,000 reales.[68] In 1706 the same figure was given.[69] In 1707 the Jacobite ambassador in Madrid, Toby Bourke, estimated that to pay the 48 infantry battalions and 110 cavalry squadrons of Philip v, about 4,500,000 reales a month were needed, this sum excluding all armaments, clothing and garrisons.[70] By 1708, according to the French ambassador, the figures given by Bourke had swollen to 73 infantry battalions and 131 squadrons of horse; and besides this, Philip had had to finance sieges in Portugal, Castile, Aragon, Valencia and Catalonia.[71] When these expenses and figures are compared with what was competently estimated to be the ordinary income in 1703 of the Spanish crown – 96,730,447 reales,[72] the enormous financial weight of the war becomes plain.

In addition to the upkeep of her own troops, Spain had to contribute towards the support of French troops helping to defend Philip v. Here difficulties arose. Chamillart, the French minister of war, wanted Philip in 1704 to undertake to supply most of the food and artillery and other special needs of the French troops,[73] but in the following year he was informed that this was impossible.[74] Nevertheless, Spain made an effort to aid the French, and helped to bear the brunt of war expenses up to

[66] 'Entonces se formaron casas españolas de hombres de negocios, y aprendieron nuestros españoles el manejo de los asientos, que quedaron privativamente dentro de la nación': *Discurso sobre la Educación Popular de los Artesanos, y su Fomento*, Madrid, 1775, p. 420.
[67] A E Corr. Pol. (Esp.), 105 ff.191–3.
[68] Ozon to Torcy, 17 Sept. 1704, *ibid.*, 139 ff.50–4.
[69] Amelot to Louis xiv, 28 Jan. 1706, *ibid.* 157 f.133.
[70] Bourke to Torcy, 3 Jan. 1707, *ibid.*, 166 f.15.
[71] Amelot to Louis xiv, 6 Feb. 1708, *ibid.*, 178 f.122.
[72] See Table 7 in chapter 9, page 215.
[73] Chamillart to Orry, 26 Jan. 1704, Guerre, A¹, 1886 f.72.
[74] Amelot to Chamillart, 16 July 1705, *ibid.*, 1886 f.75.

and beyond 1705.[75] French officials were quite aware of the burden being imposed on Spain, and in February 1708 the French ambassador, Amelot, pointed this out in a remarkably impatient letter to Louis XIV.[76] But in general the opinion was that Spain was only playing her proper part in aiding soldiers who had come unselfishly to her defence.

When in 1709 France withdrew most of her troops from the peninsula in order to facilitate a peace settlement, the remaining battalions were left to operate prinicipally at the expense of Philip V.[77] Formal agreement on their upkeep was not reached until the convention of 14 April 1711 at Saragossa, between the duc de Noailles and the marqués de Castelar, by which Philip undertook to pay for the twenty battalions and fifteen squadrons of French serving in Spain.[78] Differences soon arose even over this, for the French understood that Philip was to pay the complete expenses of the French, whereas the Spanish ministers denied this.[79] The dispute over payments seems never to have been settled. All these expenses taken together clearly amounted to a formidable sum, and we shall later examine the resources and methods used by the government to liquidate the burden of war.

The burden was shared by French no less than by Spanish financiers. Several French actually operated principally in Spain, but others were satisfied to do their main business in France and keep subsidiaries in Spain. The two main centres of their activity were Cadiz and Madrid, but there were a few who operated in other provincial cities. The financiers at Cadiz were the most cosmopolitan, their main interest being naturally the trade to America. Many of them had been established in Andalucia for over half a century, passing the business down from father to son. By the end of the seventeenth century the French colony,

---

[75] *Ibid.*, 1891, f.61, Méliand to Chamillart, 22 Nov. 1705, 'Le Roy d'Espagne a payé jusques a present la plus grosse partie de la depense des equipages des vivres et de l'artillerie'. Tessé on 11 Dec. 1704 informed Chamillart that France owed Spain 750,000 reales a month for the victualling of French forces in Spain that year: *ibid.*, 1789 f.237.

[76] AE Corr. Pol. (Esp.), 178 f.122.

[77] On 26 June 1709 Louis wrote to Amelot that he planned to leave in Spain 'jusqu'a 25 bataillons, independamment des garnisons que je laisserois pareillement dans les Rozes, Pampelune, Fontarabie, Saint Sebastien et les forts du Passage': M. le baron de Girardot, *Correspondance de Louis XIV avec M. Amelot, son ambassadeur en Espagne*, Nantes, 1864.

[78] Guerre, A¹, 2329 f.210.

[79] Bonnac to Voysin, 2 Nov. 1711, *ibid.*, 2329 f.208.

consisting not only of financiers and merchants but also of small traders and artisans, outnumbered all other foreign groups in number and importance. In 1701 the French merchant financiers in Cadiz totalled over twenty-nine.[80] In 1710 they numbered over forty-five.[81] In 1714, as we shall see later, there were over eighty.

Among those particularly active in Cadiz in 1710 were Masson, Stalpaert and Romet, Sarsfield and Fenel, Gilly and Company, and Villebague-Eon. Masson was the merchant Jean-Baptiste Masson, who had been in Cadiz in 1701. Stalpaert, Romet et Compagnie was a firm based on Cadiz, but operated by the Flemish financiers Stalpaert frères, of Nantes, and by the banker Louis Romet, of Paris. The company was established at Cadiz in 1705, and was of inestimable service to the French forces during the war; it went into liquidation in 1715.[82] Jean-Jacques Fenel, a trader and financier of Seville, appears less often in documentation of the war than his colleague Jacques Sarsfield, a merchant who was already in Cadiz in 1701, but whose other connections I have been unable to trace. Gilly and Company, known also as Gilly frères, were natives of Calvisson (Gard), and had important trade connections in Languedoc; as proprietors of substantial sugar plantations in the Antilles,[83] they had a natural interest in the trade to America. Guillaume Eon, sieur de la Villebague, whose financial negotiations proved invaluable to the French armies in Spain, had been in Cadiz for nearly a generation.

The most prominent of the French bankers in Madrid was Jean-Jacques Yon.[84] His kinsman Louis Yon was a Paris banker, specialising in payments to Spain, and together they gained a considerable amount of control over financial transactions between the two countries during the War of Succession. Bayonne, on the Franco-Spanish frontier, was another centre for commerce, and here the banker Morasin,[85] and the brothers Barthélemy and

[80] Albert Girard, *Le commerce français à Séville et Cadiz au temps des Habsbourg*, Paris, 1932, p. 551.

[81] A list of the chief French merchants at Cadiz in 1710, in AN Aff. Etr., B¹ 218, f.55, lists 'Monsʳ Masson; Mʳˢ Luis Hays y Compᵃ; Mʳˢ Stalpaert Romet & Compᵉ; Mʳˢ Sarsfield & Fenel; Mʳ Macé; Mʳ Musq & Compᵉ; Mʳ Gilli & Compᵉ', and thirty-seven others. It is obvious that some of these names represent firms rather than individuals, so that the total number of merchants is uncertain.

[82] Herbert Lüthy, *La Banque Protestante en France de la Révocation de l'Edit de Nantes à la Révolution vol. I, Dispersion et Regroupement (1685–1730)*, Paris, 1959, pp. 77, 189, note 5, 261.

[83] *Ibid.*, p. 368, note 27.   [84] Cf. *ibid.*, p. 159, note 13.   [85] Cf. *ibid.*, p. 401.

Laurent de Ville, who described themselves as bankers of Madrid, Bayonne and Paris, were active.

The French bankers were a necessary part of Louis xiv's plans for his troops. The French king was reluctant to send specie into Spain, and therefore financed the forces in the peninsula through Cadiz. The war-treasurer at Paris would send bills of exchange to Cadiz to be converted there by the French traders who controlled the city's economic life,[86] and from Cadiz the money would be transported to the troops in the interior of the country. The bankers would be repaid in France, at their French branches. Time and again it was the financiers in Madrid or Cadiz who saved the French forces in Spain. In 1706, for example, at a desperate point in the campaign, the French bankers in Madrid and Cadiz offered to advance up to 900,000 reales a month to pay the troops; and the seven or eight French traders in Málaga offered to send silver for the same purpose, to an estimated total of 600,000 reales.[87] By January 1707 the financiers had raised their offer to about 1,800,000 reales a month, to be given in bills of exchange payable at Lyon.[88] The excessive reliance of the French on credit from Lyon had bad results when in the summer of 1707 a failure in payments occurred: bills issued in Spain were protested when presented at Lyon,[89] and the result was to threaten a total collapse of French credit in Madrid and Cadiz, since Spaniards refused to accept French bills. The intendant of the French troops in Spain, Méliand, wrote to Chamillart to report that 'since the disturbance caused among bankers here by the default in payment of bills on Lyon, I have been unable to persuade anyone to accept further bills'.[90] French credit in Spain continued at a low level, reflecting the development of the crisis of payments at Lyon, and in January 1708 Amelot was bewailing the evil effects this would have on the war in the peninsula.[91]

[86] Guerre, A¹ 2049 f.299, Fiennes to Chamillart, 23 Aug. 1707: '... les François estant les seuls qui y fassent a l'heure qu'il est le peu de commerce qu'il y a'.

[87] Amelot to Chamillart, 20 Dec. 1706, Guerre, A¹ 1978 f.289.

[88] *Ibid.*, 31 Jan. 1707, *ibid.*, 2048 f.86.

[89] Marqués de Santiago to Chamillart, 11 July 1707, *ibid.*, 2049 f.187. The Lyon banker refusing the bills was Ollivier, but the default was general: see for example Lüthy, p. 185.

[90] 22 Aug. 1707, Guerre, A¹ 2049 f.296.

[91] Amelot to Chamillart, 16 Jan. 1708, *ibid.*, 2104 f.21: 'Cela ruine absolument notre credit et fait un tort presque irreparable à la place de Madrid, qui d'ailleurs n'est pas bien abondante en argent'.

Hard on the heels of these difficulties came the tragic autumn of 1708, the failure of the harvests, the grim starvation in France and Spain during the winter of 1708–9, and then the financial crash at Lyon and Geneva in 1709 when Samuel Bernard lost a fortune and the French were forced to withdraw from Spain. By the end of 1709 the desperate French paymaster-general reported that of all the Paris bankers only Samuel Bernard had offered to advance money for the troops in Spain, and then only a single sum of six thousand livres.[92] This marked the end of full-scale French military intervention in the peninsula.

Because of the extent to which Philip v helped to pay for the expenses of the French troops, it is difficult to estimate with any accuracy how much the Spanish campaigns cost France. In 1704 a memoir[93] stated that the upkeep of the French forces cost 400,000 livres (two million reales) a month, but that this sum was obtainable only with great difficulty, because since the money was paid through bills of exchange on Cadiz and Seville, the distance from these cities delayed payments in Madrid. The memoir further noted that at this date all the cannon and munitions in the field were French; and this must obviously have laid a greater burden on France in the first stages of the war, before Spain could commence her own industrial production. Even later, however, the French preferred to use their own standardised equipment rather than Spanish goods, and the military correspondence of the war indicates that the French bought as little as possible in Spain, preferring to import material through Bayonne. By 1708 the cost of the war had gone up: Chamillart observed that France was contributing ten million livres for general expenses, six millions of this to be sent through Samuel Bernard in bills of exchange at the rate of 500,000 livres a month, the balance to be sent in the form of grain for the troops.[94] In 1709 costs were regulated at the same level of ten millions,[95] and negotiations to supply this were entered upon with the bankers Yon and de Ville.

[92] Montargis to Voysin, 5 Dec. 1709, *ibid.*, 2178 f.300. For an introductory sketch of Bernard's activities, see Jacques Saint-Germain, *Samuel Bernard, le banquier des rois*, Paris, 1960. His part in the 1709 crash is described in Lüthy, pp. 188–225.

[93] Guerre, A¹ 1791 f.196.

[94] Chamillart to Amelot, 16 Jan. 1708, AE Corr. Pol. (Esp.), 184 f.10. Amelot's reply, 31 Jan. 1708, *ibid.*, 187 f.26, claimed that the six million would produce only an effective 4,800,000 in Madrid; this seems to refer to the current rate of exchange.

[95] Desmaretz to Amelot, 20 Feb. 1709, *ibid.*, 195 f.121.

This outline of the means used to promote the war effort illustrates the extent to which Louis XIV was committed to helping his grandson in the peninsula. The conflict saw a remarkably unselfish effort by the French to aid a weaker neighbour. But for such help, Spain would have fallen to the English, Portuguese and Dutch. Even after the French withdrawal in 1709, Spain benefited enormously from the introduction of French reforms, reorganisation and equipment. Yet when we examine the aims and methods used in the conduct of the war, a certain reserve must be expressed, for it is obvious that Louis was not helping Spain without hope of requital. Only a fuller examination of the issues involved can elucidate this point.

PART TWO

The Objectives of
French Policy

5 Grandee Power and Administrative Change

On 18 January 1703 the elderly Cardinal Portocarrero, archbishop of Toledo, primate of Spain and regent of the realm at various periods during the absence of Philip v, informed the French foreign secretary Torcy of his intention to retire from active political life. With his letter to Torcy the cardinal enclosed a remarkable memoir analysing the evils of the realm as he saw them. The two principal objects of the cardinal's wrath were the decadent nobility and the inefficient administration. Probably never before had the aristocracy been so denounced by an eminent member of their own class:[1]

In the last few years of the reign of the king our lord Charles the Second, the nobility were brought up and educated without any application, in pure idleness, accustomed to the fact that with the aid of the Palace and with bargaining tricks they could obtain the principal employment in military and political government, as well as royal grants and graces, without knowledge or experience or any merit of their own, exercising these appointments thereafter with ambition, pride and self-interest, so that the natural results of this unhappy procedure were repeated ill successes, squandering of the treasury, and the ruin of the state . . . And through these gates opened up by the upper nobility came in also individuals of all classes, solely through flattery, favouritism and the basest self-interest.

From this total failure of the governing classes most of the other evils outlined by Portocarrero sprang. Administration was neglected by the nobles, and left to others whose only interest was the profitability of office. This resulted, the cardinal said, in:

salaries which were doubled and multiplied, not for any great merit or need, but only brought in through bad example and continued through

[1] AE Corr. Pol. (Esp.), 114 f.25.

inevitable error; succession rights pledged in governorships and commands; offices and superfluous posts which were never created for good merit.

Venality of office and multiplicity of officials meant that men were paid for posts which they did not fill, while those who did the actual work of administration were not paid enough and so tended to neglect their duty. According to Portocarrero, this had worst results in the army, where the number of posts and officials was incompatible with efficiency. The cardinal's reproaches were not entirely original, but their tenor and timing was important, for at this very time the new Bourbon government in Madrid, closely advised from Paris, was concerned about the need to create a more efficient administration by superseding the personnel and structure of the old one. The need for reform was universally recognised, and at the beginning of the reign various plans for change were submitted to the French authorities,[2] the most influential being that drawn up by Jean Orry in 1703 as part of his general scheme for reforming the realm of Spain. Many prominent Spaniards, to cite only Portocarrero and the marqués de Villena, were in favour of reforms, but the French alone had the will and power to carry out changes according to a deliberate programme, and after them native administrators in the French tradition carried on the work.

The most pressing problem therefore, at least in the eyes of Louis XIV, was reform of the administration. The French king, as Torcy later observed:

saw himself forced to enter into the details of governing Spain and its dependent states. And since the whole weight of the war which occurred immediately after fell solely on France, the king felt it

---

[2] In 1701 the president of the council of Castile submitted a plan for reforming the Spanish government, AE Mém. et Doc. (Esp.), 102 f.68. In Feb. 1703 the French marshal Boufflers submitted a plan for establishing the Spanish government along French lines, suppressing the power of the grandees, unifying the realms of the peninsula, and uniting the taxes into one general farm: AE Corr. Pol. (Esp.), 122 f.38. See also the interesting letter from Fénelon to Louville, 10 Oct. 1701, in Marquis de Louville, *Mémoires secrets sur l'établissement de la Maison de Bourbon en Espagne* (2 vols), Paris, 1818, vol. 1, p. 55. Fénelon stated that 'un royaume est bien gouverné quand on travaille 1. à le peupler 2. à faire que tous les hommes travaillent selon leurs forces pour bien cultiver les terres 3. à faire que tous les hommes soient bien nourris 4. à ne souffrir ni fainéans ni vagabonds 5. à récompenser le mérite 6. à punir tous les désordres 7. a tenir tous les corps ... dans la subordination 8. à modérer l'autorité royale en sa propre personne 9. à ne se livrer a aucun ministre ni favori.'

necessary to allow his ambassador to assist at the councils of the king his grandson and to become as it were his prime minister.[3]

This had not been the practice at first. In order to persuade Europe as well as the Spaniards that France had no intention of taking over Spain, Louis had in 1700 forbidden the marquis d'Harcourt, last ambassador to Charles II and for a while envoy to Philip, to assist at meetings of the king's council. But from Marcin onwards, that is from 1701, the French ambassadors were instructed by Louis to enter the council in order to influence and direct policy. The body in whose meetings they now took part was a cabinet council known as the *despacho*. The name itself was no novelty. The king's secretary, who acted as the principal link between the council of state and the king, and who executed the royal orders, had in the seventeenth century been known as the secretary of the *despacho universal*. But the secretary's function had been limited largely to 'despatching' orders issued by the king or by his prime minister. Louis' advisers felt that this nucleus of a king and a secretary could be expanded. The French argument was put at its clearest in the instructions issued to the ambassador Gramont in 1704.

Just after the arrival of the Catholic king in Madrid [went the instructions], his council consisted of Cardinal Portocarrero, archbishop of Toledo, of Don Manuel de Arias, then president of Castile and now archbishop of Seville, and of Don Antonio de Ubilla, secretary of the *despacho universal*, now known as the marqués de Ribas. This was a new departure. Previous kings of Spain had had no other council but the council of state. They would usually leave the administration of all the business of the monarchy to their prime minister, and it was from him that the secretary of the *despacho universal* would receive and then transmit orders. After the disgrace of the conde de Oropesa, the late King Charles the Second had no prime minister. He himself gave his orders to Don Antonio de Ubilla. It was not judged appropriate to let Ubilla be the only one to bring affairs of state before a young king, inexperienced in matters on which the accomplished secretary of the *despacho* might speak to him. It was this reason that led to the institution of this new council.[4]

If we accept this explanation, the *despacho* was formed in order to give Philip V the benefit of the advice of his most experienced

---

[3] Instructions to the ambassador Bonnac in 1711, Baudrillart, *Philippe V et la Cour de France*, vol. 1, p. 683.

[4] *Recueil des Instructions données aux Ambassadeurs*, vol. 12, p. 94.

D

councillors. The period when such advice came only from Spanish officials was of very short duration. No sooner had the French ambassadors begun to attend meetings of the *despacho* than their authority came to supersede that of the grandees, who protested vigorously against the invasion of their rights. In November 1705 the duque de Medinaceli and the conde de Aguilar brought their grievances to Amelot, demanding that whatever the form of government the king might choose to adopt, 'whether cabinet or junta, the French ambassador must not be included'.[5] Their wishes remained unfulfilled, for under Amelot French authority reached its zenith.

The preeminent role played by Amelot in Spain is too obvious to be documented at length. Through the *despacho* he exercised direct control over all administrative matters. As chief adviser to Philip, his influence prevailed over that of anyone else in the government. Financial policy was in the hands of Orry, but Orry was directly responsible to Amelot. The ambassador informed Louis in June 1705 that the king:

sends me every day the memoirs and reports regarding war and finance, and after I have examined them with Orry I take him the replies or the orders which I have drawn up. He usually approves them and then sends them on to be put into effect.[6]

By 1706 it was clearly recognised that Amelot was in effect prime minister. In November that year Toby Bourke[7] wrote to Torcy to say that Amelot 'works day and night. Everyone here believes that he deserves all the credit and authority he has, and that nothing essential is done without him.'[8] Simultaneously the

[5] Amelot to Louis XIV, 11 Nov. 1705, AE Corr. Pol. (Esp.), 149 f.149.

[6] Amelot to Louis XIV, 22 June 1705, *ibid.*, 147 f.190.

[7] Bourke, whom we have already encountered, is of considerable importance in this narrative. An Irish colonel, he was technically the representative of the Old Pretender at Madrid, but his salary was in fact paid by the French government. He seems to have arrived in Spain in about 1705, and stayed till 1715 when, having entered the service of the Spanish crown, he was appointed envoy of Spain to Sweden. François Combes, in an article entitled 'Gazette inédite et hebdomadaire de la Guerre de la Succession d'Espagne, par le colonel chevalier du Bourk, agent de Chamillard', in *Lectures Historiques à la Sorbonne et à l'Institut* (2 vols), Paris, 1883-5, vol. 2, pp. 111-42, describes Bourke as a paid correspondent of the minister of war. In fact, most of his correspondence is directed to the foreign minister, Torcy, and supplies by far the best-informed and most balanced reporting of events in this period.

[8] Bourke to Torcy, 16 Nov. 1706, AE Corr. Pol. (Esp.), 162 f.58.

princess des Ursins was writing to Madame de Maintenon: 'The ambassador is killing himself with work ... since he fulfils the functions of a prime minister rather than those of an ambassador.'[9]

Despite this great activity, a reader of Amelot's correspondence with Louis would be liable to get the misleading impression that the actions of the ambassador were a consequence of orders from Versailles. Certainly Amelot took care to have all that he did approved by Louis. But the fact is that Louis' correspondence often amounts to little more than commentary on actions which had already been resolved upon in Spain. 'I approve', 'I very much approve', are stock phrases in the letters from the Grand Monarch. In June 1705 Torcy wrote to Amelot, 'The king has recognised with pleasure in your first dispatch the true style of a minister who is an accomplished ambassador'.[10] The compliment could as validly have been phrased the other way round: Amelot was an ambassador who, for the four years of his stay in Spain, became one of the greatest ministers of the Spanish crown.

The two most striking alterations achieved under Amelot were in the position of the grandees, and the functions of the central administration. The two questions are interconnected, for the grandees, as the ruling class, dominated conciliar government. The grandees, as we have already seen, were entitled by tradition to the first place in social and political life, but by the end of the seventeenth century it was already notorious that they were a degenerate and effete caste, and the Bourbons rightly saw in them the principal barrier to an efficient monarchy. From the very outset, therefore, the new dynasty clashed with a class that had grown to wealth and prominence under two centuries of Habsburg rule. French officials found the pretensions of the nobles intolerable. 'The more I see them, the less I view them as worthy of the esteem that I used to believe one could not refuse them,' reported Ursins in 1702. 'All these people have but one principal object – to bring down the authority of the king', wrote Marshal Tessé in 1705.[11] The marquis de Louville remarked to Torcy of the duque de Medina Sidonia that 'he was seven times grandee of

---

[9] Ursins to Maintenon, Nov. 1706, *Lettres inédites de la princesse des Ursins*, ed. M. A. Geffroy, Paris, 1859, p. 252.

[10] Baudrillart, *Philippe V et la Cour de France*, vol. 1, p. 231, note 3.

[11] Ursins to Torcy, 9 July 1702; Tessé to Chamillart, 11 Apr. 1705. Both quoted in L. Mandon, *De l'influence française en Espagne sous Philippe V, 1700–1713*, Montpellier & Cette, 1873.

Spain, and consequently seven times more corrupt than the others'.[12]

This attitude was almost equalled by arrogance on the Spanish side from nobles conscious of their own transcendent origins. In an attempt to promote a closer understanding between France and Spain, Louis had suggested that the nobility of the two countries introduce some degree of equivalence in their ranks and honours. The refusal of the Spanish grandees to accept equivalence with even the highest French peers, was led by the duque de Alba and his family of the house of Toledo, including the marqués de Villafranca and the marqués de Mancera.[13] This opposition reached its peak in the formal protest published by the duque de Arcos on 22 July 1701, in which he enumerated the ineffable dignities of the grandees.[14]

Such differences of outlook only increased the pressure placed on the nobles, who in their turn schemed against the new régime. A large number of the leading grandees were holding secret meetings at each other's houses in 1703,[15] apparently in order to concert opposition to the government. At the same time the princess des Ursins was trying to forge a working alliance with a number of nobles including the duque de Medinaceli, the duque

---

[12] Louville to Torcy, 19 July 1702, *Mémoires du Duc de Noailles*, Paris, 1828, vol. 2, p. 157.

[13] Ozon to Torcy, 3 July 1701, AE Corr. Pol. (Esp.), 91 f.177. Villafranca gave evidence of his hostility to France in 1702, when it became known that Philip v, then in Italy, had freely pardoned the people of Messina for their past revolts against the crown. '"Ce sont là les conseils de France", s'écria d'un ton emporté Villafranca': Noailles, *Mémoires*, vol. 2, p. 158.

[14] The Arcos memorial, addressed to Louis xiv, contains these phrases: 'Hallara V.M. en los Grandes todas las calidades que en las otras tres clases ... En los Grandes Españoles, o en los mas de ellos, concurra con la dignidad de Grande, la de principe de la Sangre que, aunque en grado remoto, les da derecho para poder suceder en todas las coronas de España': BN, fonds Espagne 378. There are several copies of this document, which also includes the reply to Arcos by the peers af France. It is noteworthy that Arcos was brother-in-law to Alba. Both Arcos and his brother the duque de Baños were exiled to Flanders to serve in the army, but were later allowed to return.

[15] 'Por medio de persona fidedigna se a savido estan mui unidos los duques de Medina Zeli, Montalto, Infantado, Condestable, el marqués de Leganes, Carpio, conde de Frigiliana, y otros señores, juntandose mui frequentemente en Cassa de Medina Zeli, y Carpio, donde tienen largas y secretas conversaciones, sospechandose ser poco faborabiles y mui perjudiciales al Rey nro señor', AE Corr. Pol. (Esp.), 114 f.281. Later, in 1709, according to Coxe, *Memoirs of the Kings of Spain*, vol. 1, p. 457, this practice of secret meetings was continued when 'the house of Montellano became the resort of all who were discontented with the government'.

de Veraguas, and the conde de Aguilar.[16] Such efforts at compromise were eloquently denounced by Louville in 1703. In a letter to Chamillart he wrote that the main reason for the little progress made was that no single or efficient policy had been followed till then:

There is still another matter which has no less prejudiced affairs, namely, that the grandees have been confused with the Spaniards, as if these grandees composed the whole nation, whereas nothing in the world could be more mistaken. It is a gross error to think that the grandees have all the authority; on the contrary, there is only one authority in Spain, that of the king, and the grandees will fall into dust as soon as they have a king with the strength to desire their fall. It is quite certain moreover that the grandees are both hated and despised in Spain and that their authority, separated from that of the king, is nothing.[17]

With the appointment of Amelot as ambassador in 1705 all possibility of cooperation and compromise vanished. As he himself wrote to Louis XIV in July 1705:

I came to Spain persuaded that we could do nothing without them, that we must convince them with good reasons . . . but I had been here hardly a fortnight before I knew it useless to imagine we could succeed this way . . . so I realised that it was only firm action which could bring some hope of a change in affairs.[18]

The ambassador was supported by the precise instructions of Louis XIV in August 1705:

The principle you are to lay down with regard to the grandees is a valid one. It is convenient to preserve all the external prerogatives of their rank, and at the same time to exclude them from all matters cognisance of which might increase their credit or give them a part in the government.[19]

The direct attack now launched on the privileges of the grandees was facilitated by the conservatism, inefficiency and quarrels of the nobles themselves. From the beginning of the reign they had fallen into factions which cut across pro-Habsburg or pro-Bourbon party lines. When in November 1705 Amelot and

---

[16] Louville to Torcy, 14 Feb. 1703, AE Corr. Pol. (Esp.), 114 f.166.
[17] Louville to Chamillart, 23 Aug. 1703, *Mémoirs de Saint-Simon*, vol. 11, p. 531.
[18] Amelot to Louis XIV, 26 July 1705, AE Corr. Pol. (Esp.), 147 f.288.
[19] Louis XIV to Amelot, 20 Aug. 1705, in Girardot, *Correspondance de Louis XIV*.

Ursins conferred with Medinaceli and Aguilar about some government posts:

these two gentlemen appeared always to think that only the duque de Veraguas and the two of them were suitable to become ministers. . . . We went through all the other councillors of state and it was agreed that Mancera was decrepit, the marqués del Fresno silly and immoderate, Fuensalida about the same, San Esteban small-minded and full of evil tricks, Medina Sidonia unpleasant and ignorant of affairs, Palma spineless and kin to the marqués de Leganés, Canales less than nothing, Castelrodrigo quite lively-minded but Italian and too young . . .

It is depressing to have to choose between such people.[20]

Faced by such petty squabbling among the grandees, Amelot chose to ignore them all. This was done in the first place by excluding them from the *despacho*. From the comte de Marcin onwards, the French ambassadors had already begun to assist in the *despacho* and influence policy, to the disgust of the grandee councillors. By 1705 Louis considered that all the Spaniards in the *despacho* could safely be dispensed with, save for just one 'whose name would suffice to persuade the public that the king of Spain does not wish to exclude all Spaniards from his counsels'.[21] The one chosen for this unenviable role, the duque de Mancera, already in 1705 an old man of ninety-eight, had the good sense to comprehend the significance of his position, and cleverly proposed that the *despacho* be suppressed as unnecessary.[22] Louis opposed this strongly, for official French policy now was, as we shall see, to supersede the apparatus of conciliar government, which was anyway in the control of the grandees, by concentrating power in the *despacho*. All the French advisers were agreed that conciliar government was a prime obstacle to efficiency and that an alternative must be found. The marquis de Louville in 1701 stressed the benefits of abolishing the councils,[23] and two years later he wrote to Chamillart: 'The people want an absolute king, the grandees want a figurehead.'[24]

[20] Amelot to Louis xiv, 11 Nov. 1705, AE Corr. Pol. (Esp.), 149 f.149.
[21] Louis xiv to Amelot, 14 June 1705, *ibid.*, 147 f.111.
[22] *Mémoires du Duc de Noailles*, vol. 2, p. 321.
[23] He wrote to Torcy: 'Si vous cassez le conseil de Flandre, vous ferez crier ceux qui le composent, mais les choses en iront mieux en Flandre, et vous aurez une grande économie. Si vous cassez le conseil des Indes, vous donnerez à notre maître de bonnes armées et de bonnes flottes, mais vous ferez crier le marquis del Carpio et une foule de gens qui enrichissent Madrid', *Mémoires secrets*, vol. 1, p. 154.
[24] Louville to Chamillart, 23 Aug. 1703, *Mémoires de Saint-Simon*, vol. 11, p. 531.

The inevitable crisis came when the fall of Barcelona to the Allies on 9 October 1705, a disaster for which the Francophile government was blamed, released a flood of fury among the nobility in Madrid. The *consulta* or memorandum issued by the fourteen councillors present[25] at a meeting of the council of state on 9 November, is a document of some historical importance, for in this protest the grandees summarised their principal complaints against the policy of the French, and denounced the mismanagement of the war. The meeting was opened by Cardinal Portocarrero, who regretted that the council had not been consulted on the defence of Barcelona; after him, each speaker in turn delivered a bitter and hostile speech, the conde de Fuensalida going so far as to say that the Catalans had rebelled only because of mistreatment. Among the demands contained in the *consulta,* it was declared that there must be:

A good intelligence between the king of Spain and his tribunals, by which alone he can defend his realms. . . . That as for the troops, it would be necessary above all for a report on those of the realm to be sent to the council of war and that the tribunals should be in touch with what concerned them. . . . That the tribunals are the depositaries of wise counsel, of the oath taken by the king of Spain, and of that which he has received from his subjects. . . . That they should have cognisance of everything, to give their opinion, the decision belonging to the king of Spain. . . . That one may form particular juntas in certain situations, and give commissions to those most fit to have them, but that they must act in public and be guided by superior minds such as those in the *despacho.* . . . That the king of Spain must try to make himself loved, and that there has been more good intention than prudence in breaking up the household of the late king, who had recommended its members in his testament. . . . That Charles the Fifth indeed made changes, but one reads that he was obliged to send back to Germany the Archduke Ferdinand whom the peoples loved better because he adapted himself more to their customs. . . . That this is the way to defend the realms, since it is this that wins over the affection of the people. . . . That for the expenses of the war, it is necessary to consult the councils of Castile, of Finance, of the Indies, of Orders, and of the Cruzada.[26]

[25] The fourteen councillors were Cardinal Portocarrero, marqués de Mancera, conde de Frigiliana, duque de Montalto, conde de Monterey, duque de Medinaceli, marqués del Fresno, conde de San Esteban, conde de Fuensalida, duque de Veraguas, duque de Medina Sidonia, conde de Palma, marqués de Canales, marqués de Castelrodrigo.
[26] A E Corr. Pol. (Esp.), 149 f.134.

These demands read like an open challenge to the government, and the ultimatum appears unmistakable, yet in fact the practical importance of the *consulta* is negligible. As Amelot wrote to Louis XIV in 1706, 'the grandees are not to be feared, because they have no power, or unity among themselves'.[27] Because of this, the historical significance of the *consulta* lies in it being no more than a last threat from a vanishing aristocracy.

The nobles were excluded from effective government, and the councils reduced to a minimal role. At the same time, the grandees were denied their historic privileges in the army when in 1705 Philip V decided to grant military commands only to nobles trained in war.[28] This trend was accentuated by plans to give the king a large personal bodyguard, plans to which the nobles objected because they considered it an insult to their ability to protect Philip themselves, and even more because half the guards were foreign troops or under foreign command.[29] When in August 1705 the duty captain of the bodyguard, the prince of Tserclaës Tilly,[30] was given the task of standing immediately after the king at mass in the royal chapel, so giving him apparent precedence over the grandees of Spain, the nobles of the household refused in a body to attend mass. The incident caused a major scandal in the government, and hardened attitudes on both sides. Tserclaës Tilly was created a grandee of the first class

---

[27] Amelot to Louis XIV, 28 Jan. 1706, *ibid.*, 157 f.133. Cf. also Bourke to Chamillart, 28 Aug. 1705, Guerre, A¹ 1886 f.295: the grandees, he says, 'ne sont pas aussi formidables que l'on ne les imagine dans les pays etrangers; ils n'ont ni credit, ni argent, ni pouvoir sur les peuples . . . toute leur habilité consiste a mener par des canaux soutterains de petites intrigues de Cour'.

[28] Amelot to Louis XIV, 5 Aug. 1705, AE Corr. Pol. (Esp.), 148 f.11.

[29] Amelot to Torcy, 5 June 1705, 'Les Grands ne dissimulent pas qu'ils n'ont rien plus a coeur que de detruire les Gardes du corps, regardant cela, disent ils, comme une injure faite a la nation', *ibid.*, 147 f.124. The guards, to some extent an innovation in Spain, were formed in spring 1703 by Orry, at the direct request of Louis XIV. 'Four companies of cavalry were formed, two of Spaniards, one of Italians, and one of Walloons, consisting of 200 gentlemen each. The captains, who bore the rank of colonel, were the count of Lemos, the dukes of Sessa and Popoli, and the prince of Tserclaës Tilly. To these companies of parade were added an efficient force of footguards, consisting of two regiments of 3,000 men each, one Walloons and one Spaniards': Coxe, *Memoirs of the Kings of Spain*, vol. 1, p. 361. Of the captains, Popoli was an Italian and Tilly a Walloon.

[30] Albert-Octave de Tserclaës Tilly (1646–1715) was invited to Spain from Flanders in 1703. Created captain general of Extremadura that year, then captain of the guards, he became a grandee on 14 August 1705, viceroy of Navarre in September 1706, second in command in Aragon and Catalonia in 1709. He died at Barcelona on 3 September 1715.

in order to circumvent opposition; the two Spanish grandee captains, Lemos and Sessa, were dismissed from the royal guard;[31] Montellano was dismissed from the presidency of the council of Castile and replaced by a noble detested by the grandees;[32] Montalto, then president of the council of Aragon, was dismissed from the government and replaced by the conde de Aguilar. Medinaceli took the opportunity to publish a pamphlet claiming that the grandees were entitled to the first place after the king.[33] The object and occasion for protest may have been petty, but, to be fair to the nobles, they were correct in seeing any alteration of custom as the thin end of a wedge. Their defeat in this affair, with both the French king and his advisers firmly against any concession on the part of Philip v, was a significant reversal. There appears to have been some renewal of grandee influence just after 1709, when the French had withdrawn most of their troops and advisers from Spain, but the old days were irretrievably gone, and the war took its toll in disgraces and desertions.

The military ineptitude of most of the Castilian nobility was widely recognised at the time. There are strong indications of it in the lack of military leadership shown by Castile after the 1640s, and in the prominent role played by Italian commanders. In 1700 when the marqués de Villena wrote to Louis xiv,[34] he pressed for the reformation of the armed forces and the need to attract the nobility to a service which was tending to be reserved for mercenaries and criminals. Bourbon policy responded ably to the challenge. Military appointments, as we have seen, were reserved for serving soldiers. A decree of February 1704, resumed in a *cédula* of 8 November 1704, abolished the name *tercio* and substituted for it that of *regimiento*: the hundred regiments planned by this decree were part of a positive move to create an officer corps. In the words of the decree:

These regiments are to serve as a school to the nobility of my realms. . . . I order them to receive in each company up to ten cadets, nobles

---

[31] Amelot to Louis xiv, 2 Sept. 1705, A E Corr. Pol. (Esp.), 148 f.109.

[32] This was Francisco de Ronquillo, formerly *corregidor* of Madrid: Amelot to Louis XIV, 5 Sept. 1705, *ibid.*, 148 f.125.

[33] Amelot to Louis xiv, 25 Sept. 1705, *ibid.*, 148 f.182. To add to the general comedy, the papal nuncio also claimed to be seated immediately after the king.

[34] Danvila y Collado, *El poder civil en España*, vol. 3, p. 370.

and gentlemen, who are to be distinguished from the others in both dress and salary.[35]

The fruits of this policy were slow to ripen. During the War of Succession, the crown had to continue to rely on generals from Flanders and Italy, men such as Tserclaës Tilly, Popoli, the Príncipe Pio and Francisco Caetano y Aragón, not to mention the generals of France.

The decline and fall of the grandees of Castile is a subject to occupy a volume in itself, and will be discussed rather summarily here. Aristocratic disillusion with Bourbon government was profound, even among those who had initially supported the new dynasty, and the number of desertions to the enemy side during the war contains elements of personal tragedy. Thwarted ambitions, personal resentment, attachments of honour to the House of Habsburg, the pull of family loyalties, were among the many factors which drove men to sacrifice their families and fortune in order to serve under an alien flag. Defections came at the very start of the reign. In July 1701 the duque de Nájera, commander of the galleys of Spain, resigned his post;[36] later, in 1706, he left Madrid with the Portuguese troops that had occupied the capital. The conde de Oropesa, former prime minister of Charles II, found that he was not in favour with the new régime,[37] and deserted to the archduke in 1706, becoming the puppet premier of his régime and dying unsung at Barcelona on 23 December 1707, at the age of sixty-five years.

The most startling defection of all those that occurred in the early years was that of Don Juan Tomás Enríquez de Cabrera, duque de Rioseco and conde de Melgar, admiral of Castile, grandee of the first class.[38] As the most eminent in lineage of all the nobles, his adherence to the Bourbon cause was particularly welcome. He seems, however, to have become quickly disillusioned with the new court and with the administration of Portocarrero, who had been acting as regent during the king's

---

[35] Guerre, A¹ 1787 f.73. Discussion of this measure is given in Antonio Domínguez Ortiz, *La Sociedad Española en el siglo XVIII*, p. 372. 'Nobles and gentlemen', is, in the original, 'hidalgos y cavalleros'.

[36] Blécourt to Louis XIV, 3 July 1701, AE Corr. Pol. (Esp.), 91 f.174. Nájera was of the Manrique de Lara family.

[37] See his letter of 6 July 1701 in *ibid.*, 91 f.215.

[38] Cesareo Fernández Duro, *El último Almirante de Castilla, Don Juan Tomás Enríquez de Cabrera*, Madrid, 1902.

absence in Italy. The Almirante then suggested that he be appointed ambassador to France. Portocarrero agreed, but lowered his salary as an economy measure, a step which automatically lowered the status of the embassy. Not betraying any displeasure, the Almirante asked permission to convey his goods with him to Paris, and left Madrid on 13 September 1702 with a retinue of three hundred persons in a hundred and fifty carriages and luggage including a great amount of jewels and paintings. He set out towards France then suddenly made a detour and fled to Portugal, where he issued a denunciation of the Bourbon government. He remained in the service of the archduke until his death on 29 June 1705 at the age of fifty-nine. Much later, on 12 January 1726, a royal decree suppressed the title of *Almirante de Castilla*.

Another defector of importance was the conde de la Corzana, a former viceroy of Catalonia and friend of the Almirante, who found, like Oropesa, that the ministers of the new régime 'are not favourable to me, since they have not recommended me for any employment'.[39] A dwindling income and growing resentment drove him in 1702 to defect to the archduke, who took care to reward him in 1707 by appointing him viceroy of Valencia, a post he held for only a few months. Forced into exile with his family after the end of the war, he died at Vienna on 14 July 1720, and it was not until 1738 that the rest of his family was allowed to return to Spain.

In November 1704 the conde de Cifuentes was arrested for treason and taken to prison in Fuenterrabia. A peer of Aragon, he fled to Saragossa where 'the people rioted in his favour, and, being persuaded that their liberties were threatened, accepted all the accusations made by this gentleman against the government, and thence broadcast them throughout the realm'.[40] At the same time as Cifuentes was arrested, the conde de Eril was confined in the Alhambra at Granada.

The year 1705 witnessed the first major conspiracy against the Bourbon monarchy. On 10 June the marqués de Leganés, a

[39] Antonio Rodríguez Villa, *Don Diego Hurtado de Mendoza y Sandoval, Conde de la Corzana (1650–1720)*, Madrid, 1907, pp. 197–8.

[40] Agustín López de Mendoza y Pons, conde de Robres, *Historia de las guerras civiles de España* (written in 1709 but published in Saragossa 1882), p. 252. Throughout 1705 Cifuentes was hiding in Aragon: see BNac., MS 5805 for correspondence relative to this. In 1706 he joined the Allies in Barcelona.

senior grandee, was arrested by Tserclaës Tilly in his capacity as captain of the royal guard, and escorted to the fortress at Pamplona. From there he was later transferred to France, where he died in the fortress of Vincennes, outside Paris, on 28 February 1711. Several other grandees were believed to have been involved in this plot, which had ringleaders in Cadiz, Málaga and Badajoz,[41] but little evidence was found to substantiate suspicions. The centre of the conspiracy was Granada, where several suspects, including a friar, were executed.[42] Startled by this affair, the government drew up an oath of loyalty which it demanded that the grandees take. When Leganés was tendered the oath, he predictably refused to take it. The other nobles were considerably disturbed by the demand. Amelot informed Louis that the oath 'has mortified and appalled the grandees: they had convinced themselves that someone of their rank could shirk his duty with impunity'.[43]

By 1706 the loyalties of several nobles were near breaking point, and it only needed the successful capture of Madrid by Allied forces that year, for them to desert Philip v. At the very start of the year three of the four gentlemen of the royal chamber were deprived of their keys for refusing to follow the king to the army at Burgos: these three were the duque de Béjar, the conde de Peñarada, and the conde de Colmenar.[44] When the Allies occupied Madrid in June, several grandees, including those who had already deserted, came forward to take a solemn oath of loyalty to King Charles III, as the archduke titled himself. Among these were the conde de Oropesa, the conde de Haro (son of the constable of Castile), the duque de Nájera, the conde de Elda, the marqués de Mondéjar, the conde de la Corzana, the conde de Cifuentes, the conde de Cardona, the conde de

---

[41] *Mémoires de Saint-Simon*, vol. 13, p. 56: 'On fit mourir a Grenade plusieurs convaincus de la conspiration. Elle s'étendoit en plusieurs autres villes; on en arrêta à Cadix, à Malaga, à Badajoz, même le major de la place, et on leur trouva des lettres de l'Amirante, mort fort peu après, du prince de Darmstadt, et de l'Archiduc même.' Prince George of Hesse-Darmstadt had been the last Habsburg viceroy of Catalonia, 1698–1700.

[42] Conde de Robres, *Historia de las guerras civiles*, pp. 228–9, says that the rising in Granada was set for the day of Corpus. The arrested friar was taken to Pamplona and hung in an iron cage, 'donde acabó sus dias, o en los principios de 1707 o en los fines de 1706, casi comido de piojos.'

[43] Amelot to Louis xiv, AE Corr. Pol. (Esp.), 147 f.288.

[44] Amelot to Louis xiv, 4 Jan. 1706, *ibid.*, 157 f.36.

Miraflores, the conde de Galbe, the conde de Eril, and the conde de Santa Cruz.[45] The conde de Lemos, former captain of the royal guard, together with his wife, sister of the duque del Infantado, attempted to join the defectors but was arrested by loyalists, and both of them were sent prisoner to Pamplona.[46] Several others compromised themselves gravely during these happenings. Among them was the marqués de Ribas, a former secretary of the *despacho*. Perhaps the most important of these sideline casualties was Don Juan de Dios de Silva y Mendoza, tenth duque del Infantado.[47] A fundamentally loyal grandee who had, however, never fully committed himself to Philip v, Infantado was brother of the conde de Galbe and brother-in-law of the conde de Lemos, whose defections could not fail to implicate him. Arrested by the government in February 1707 on suspicion of commerce with the enemy, he was confined in the Alhambra at Granada and released in August the same year when no proof could be found. But even after his release suspicion continued to weigh on him, and he retired to his estates, away from political life. Apart from Infantado, the two other principal casualties of the recapture of Madrid by Philip v in 1706 were the marqués del Carpio, and the conde de Palma, a nephew of Cardinal Portocarrero. Both these grandees were banished from Madrid, the latter to San Sebastián, the former to Oviedo.[48]

The year 1710, which witnessed the second fall of Madrid to the archduke, was also responsible for the defection of several nobles whose patience with the Bourbon monarchy had long since run out. The most startling case was that of Don Luis Francisco de la Cerda, ninth duque de Medinaceli, the most prominent and active of all the grandees, and the one whose opposition to the régime had been the most honest and

[45] For this list, see Domínguez Ortiz, *La Sociedad Española en el siglo XVIII*, p. 79; and the 'Memoria de las personas que acompañaron el Estandarte de la proclamacion del señor Archiduque en Madrid', in Valladares, *Semanario Erudito*, vol. 7, p. 96. Santa Cruz, who commanded the galleys of Spain, was responsible for handing over Cartagena, Spain's naval base, to the enemy. Nájera commanded the galleys at Cadiz.

[46] 'Memoria de los presos de Estado que el día 25 de Agosto entraron en el castillo de Pamplona', Valladares, *Semanario Erudito*, vol. 7. p. 98. Others sent to Pamplona were the conde de las Amayuelas, the conde de Sacro Imperio, and the conde de Valdecabra.

[47] Cristina de Arteaga, *La Casa del Infantado* (2 vols), Madrid, 1944, vol. 2, pp. 147–75.

[48] Amelot to Louis xiv, 13 Sept. 1706, AE Corr. Pol. (Esp.), 161 f.26.

vociferous. A man of great wealth and influence both in Castile and in Valencia,[49] he was one of those most feared by the French advisers to the crown. Arrested secretly on 15 April 1710, he was tried in secret on charges that were never made public,[50] and was condemned to prison. He was confined under close guard in the fortress of Segovia from May to August, but the advance of Allied troops in the latter month made it imperative to move him to a place of greater security near the French frontier. In September he was moved for a couple of weeks to Fuenterrabia, but, as his custodian informed the government, in that province 'he is regarded as the protector of the country',[51] whereupon for greater security he was moved to the fortress in Pamplona. There he became violent and temperamental in confinement, and suffered extreme depression and insomnia. Finally, after refusing to eat any food for eleven days he died at 7.30 a.m. on 26 January 1711 'of a sudden accident in the head',[52] probably a stroke.

The Allied advance also compelled Philip v and his court on 9 September 1710 to withdraw from Madrid towards Valladolid, but a number of grandees refused to follow him and stayed in the capital to greet the archduke, who entered on 28 September. The three principal defectors on this occasion were the conde de Palma, who had already been in disgrace; the conde de Paredes, marqués de la Laguna; and the duque de Hijar.[53] At about this time the Bourbon government ordered the arrest and imprisonment of the príncipe Luc Spinola, eldest son of the duque de San Pedro.[54]

The duque de Uceda, a distinguished grandee who had been viceroy of Sicily, president of the council of Orders and then of the Indies, and for the duration of the War of Succession had served as ambassador to Rome, also defected to the archduke in

---

[49] According to the French ambassador at the time, Blécourt, Medinaceli 'étoit le principal protecteur des titules et barons de Castille, qui ont dans ce païs plus de villes et villages que le Roy, qui de 700 villes ou villages qu'il y a dans ce Royaume n'en a qu'environ 200': A E Corr. Pol. (Esp.), 203 f.141. For Medinaceli's possessions in Valencia, see appendix 4.

[50] San Felipe, a contemporary of these events, suggests that Medinaceli's correspondence with the pro-imperialist minister of Tuscany in the United Provinces, may have led to his arrest: *Comentarios de la guerra de España*, pp. 190–1.

[51] Patricio Laules to Grimaldo, 21 Sept. 1710, AHN, Estado leg. 2975.

[52] *Ibid.*, 26 Jan. 1711, *ibid.*, leg.2975: 'Il vient d'expirer en ce moment d'un accident subite qu'il a eu a la tete'.

[53] San Felipe, *Comentarios de la guerra de España*, p. 207.

[54] *Mémoires de Saint-Simon*, vol. 20, p. 129.

1710. His complaints were of long standing. In 1707 he had felt insulted by the decision of the court, made without his consultation, to lodge the duc d'Orléans in his palace in Madrid because there was nowhere else suitable. In 1710 he kept up a secret correspondence with the duque de Medinaceli even while the latter was in prison in Segovia. In August 1710 we find Uceda complaining that 'at the same time that I have been exerting myself in an unparalleled way that has ruined my income and health, I receive no satisfaction, even verbally, while all others who are my enemies and who strive even more to be enemies of the king, receive inflated honours'.[55]

The number of these defections illustrates clearly that a large section of the nobility had been alienated from the Bourbon monarchy. Of the twelve grandees of the first class alive in 1701,[56] four were disgraced for having commerce with the enemy. Though less than a third of the other grandees and títulos deserted or were disgraced, the moral reflection on the honour of the nobility was profound. As a consequence the monarchy was enabled to adopt a firmer attitude towards the Spanish aristocracy, and the humiliation of the grandees during the war prepared the way for their removal from the administration of the country. This does not mean that the government was adopting an intrinsically anti-aristocratic attitude, but only that it welcomed in the fall of the nobles the removal of an effective barrier to efficient administration.

Besides this, there was something to be gained in cash terms from the defection of wealthy individuals. The following tables give some details of the confiscation of property carried out against delinquents in 1706 and 1710. Table 1 details the annual value to the treasury of money and crops confiscated from nineteen nobles, mostly Castilians, in 1706.[57]

[55] Letter dated 5 Aug. 1710, from Genoa, to Felix de la Cruz, secretary of the council of the Indies: AHN, Estado leg.2989. Cruz had formerly been secretary to Uceda in Rome. In Mar. 1711 he was arrested and confined in the castle at Segovia: see Bourke to Voysin, 10 Mar. 1711, Guerre, A¹ 2328 f.59.

[56] The admiral of Castile, constable of Castile (duque de Frias), duque del Infantado, duque de Albuquerque, duque de Arcos, duque de Nájera, duque de Béjar, duque de Medina Sidonia, marqués de Villena (Escalona), marqués de Astorga, conde de Lemos, conde de Benavente. This list is drawn from AE Corr. Pol. (Esp.), 114 f.219. Compare the list for 1707 given in Domínguez Ortiz, La Sociedad Española en el siglo XVII, Madrid, 1963, pp. 360-1.

[57] Taken from AHN, Estado leg.2973. Confiscations in Aragon and Valencia are dealt with in later chapters.

This short list obviously includes only those whose bodily defection to the archduke was penalised; it does not include those guilty of treason and imprisoned (such as Leganés), those dismissed from power and banished (such as Béjar), or all those who withdrew to their own estates and refused to give further support

TABLE 1. ANNUAL VALUE OF APPROPRIATIONS AND CONFISCATIONS IN CASTILE IN 1706 (GRAIN VALUES IN *fanegas*, OIL IN *arrobas*)

	Reales	Wheat	Barley	Rye	Olive oil
Almirante de Castilla	63,203	5,240	2,826	674	
Conde de Oropesa	332,250	10,464	4,372	205	893
Conde de Cifuentes	90,422	1,645	570	14	
Duque de Nájera	16,873	318		243	
Conde de Elda	10,562	230	126		
Conde de Galbe	19,901	76	76		
Conde de Sástago	4,067				
Conde de la Corzana	6,149	282	181		
Marqués del Villar	1,845	187	187		
Marqués de Miraflores	3,259	9	4		
Marqués de Mondéjar	21,142				
Conde de Santa Cruz	11,881	400	200		
Marqués de San Marcelino	5,067	443			
Marqués de la Fuente	37,445				
Duque de Monteleón	8,441				
Marqués de Campotejar	38,065	826	148		
Conde de Requena	11,786	331	154		
Condesa de Foncalada	61,905	695	747		
Vizconde de Santo Domingo	7,598				

to the régime (such as Infantado). An unsatisfactory aspect of the table is that it fails to specify any details about the figures given, and the data can be fully interpreted only with some knowledge of the economic position of the nobles in question. Moreover, the list gives no indication of whether the confiscations were levied on individuals alone or on their families as well. Despite these drawbacks, some comment on the table is appropriate.

The estimates for grain would seem to represent the payment of rent or of *juros* in kind, though they could also refer to the yield from confiscated lands. Their cash value would have to be added to the monetary income for a rounded total. In many of the cases in table 1, even this total would appear derisory as the annual value of a nobleman's estate. Several considerations must therefore be borne in mind when surveying the table. In the first place, many confiscations had not been completed at the time this list was drawn up in 1706: the final figure for confiscations from the admiral of Castile, for instance, was to be nearly five times the amount cited in table 1. In the second place, few if any nobles suffered the confiscation of their whole estate, since the crown was bound to make allowance and provision for the maintenance of the other, usually innocent, members of the nobleman's family. In the third place, the economic assets of the Castilian aristocracy must not be overestimated. Several nobles were at least as poor as the confiscation lists indicate. As Domínguez Ortiz has indicated, large numbers of the Castilian nobility were, or pretended to be, in a precarious economic position.[58] The marqués de Mondéjar had already in 1667 claimed that all his property had been used up in the service of the monarchy; and even the admiral of Castile had had to ask Charles II for a moratorium on the payment of his debts.[59] As a result, the government at Madrid found to its sorrow that several of the noble houses whose property was confiscated during the War of Succession, were so burdened by debts that their administration became more of a liability than an asset: the duque de Monteleón is an example of this.

It may help to place the confiscations in focus by comparing them with some aristocratic incomes. The brother of the duque de Arcos in the mid-seventeenth century had an annual income of 118,000 reales, clearly a very comfortable sum but not in the region of great wealth. The conde de Cantillana, on the other hand, claimed in 1682 that his effective income was only 4,500 ducats (49,500 reales), a sum which he considered very close to poverty, since it did not suffice to pay off his creditors.[60] At the same period, noble houses with incomes far greater than this were crying poverty, and for exactly the same reason. In these circumstances we cannot judge the wealth of a house by its income alone, since conspicuous consumption and accumulated debt were

[58] *La Sociedad Española en el siglo XVII*, pp. 223–52.
[59] *Ibid.*, pp. 231, note 21, 237–8.
[60] Both examples from *ibid.*, pp. 367–8.

striking at the fortunes of all nobles, both great and small. There is, no doubt, evidence available that some of the defections in the War of Succession were caused by the crown's failure to come to the help of ailing aristocratic lineages. The sole documented case I have found is that of the conde de la Corzana, who seems to have had an effective income in 1700 of only 12,671 reales; his financial situation, and royal indifference, drove him into defection.[61]

The confiscation details that now follow,[62] give a later and more complete picture of the situation among the Castilian nobility. Reasons for the variation from table 1 in some figures can only be guessed at. According to data from inventories drawn up after the war,[63] the total annual revenue from the confiscated property of the almirante de Castilla was 305,785 reales, and the net revenue after deduction of expenses was 212,169 reales. The larger figure was made up of the income from the estates at Medina de Rioseco, an annual 297,930 reales, and the income from the *almirantazgo* tax in Seville, an annual 7,855 reales. The admiral's three mansions in Madrid were also confiscated: one was given to the duque de Popoli, another was used as a royal factory, and the third was given to Baron Ripperda for the space of two generations.

The conde de Oropesa also seems to have lost all his possessions. The total of his confiscations was put at an annual 440,129 reales, a net 173,815 after expenses. The income comprised that from his estate of Oropesa and other lands, valued at 379,301 reales; that from *juros* and *censos,* 42,536 reales; and the balance from estates in Jaén and Córdoba after some property had been granted to the duque de Popoli, 18,292 reales. Several of the conde's mansions, which were gifted away, do not enter the calculations.

---

[61] Antonio Rodríguez Villa, p. 192.

[62] A minor footnote to this account of confiscations is the 'Relacion de las casas confiscadas en esta Corte cuia administracion esta a cargo de D. Asensio Mocha', in BNac, MS 18718, no. 24. *Inter alia,* the relation refers to 'Unas casas principales que pertenecieron a el Almirante . . . en la cercania del Convento de Nra. Sra. de los Aflijidos, que sirven de avitacion a los Sres Duque de Populi, y D. Juan Bap^ta Orry' and to 'otras cerca de el beaterio de San Joseph q pertenecieron a D. Fran^co Ber^do de Quiros que ocupa el S^r Dn. Melchor Macanaz'. The confiscated houses belonged to the admiral, Monteleón, Nájera, and others.

[63] AGS, Secretaría de Hacienda, vol. 972: 'Reynado de D. Phelipe Quinto: Bienes confiscados por la Guerra de Succesion'. The account for Castilian confiscations is dated 1721. All details in the next few paragraphs are from this source.

The conde de Cifuentes' confiscations were put at an annual total of 157,729 reales, a net 103,025 reales. The total was made up of possessions in Andalucia, 85,269 reales; the estate of Velilla in Toledo, 25,285 reales; property in Talavera, 34,040 reales; in the town of Cifuentes (Guadalajara), 4,387 reales; and in Cuenca province, 7,648 reales. In addition, 1,140 reales came in annually from *juros*.

Less detail is available for other grandees. The duque de Nájera's total confiscations, an annual 19,727 reales which left a net 7,205, were drawn from property in Soria and *juros* in Madrid. The marqués de Mondéjar's confiscations, an annual total of 21,154 reales, came from *juros* in Madrid, 11,044 reales; estates in Guadalajara, 509 reales; pasture in Extremadura, 8,922 reales; and a house in Segovia, 679 reales. The duque de Monteleón's confiscations are of interest. Most of his possessions were not in Spain but in America, so that the confiscations in the peninsula came to only 4,228 reales, all of which went on expenses. In America, his principal property was the Marquesado del Valle de Oaxaca in New Spain: this was taken into administration by the government in 1707, but with little profit, for despite the moderate running costs of the estate (in 1706–7 less than a tenth of its income of 101,501 pesos went on administration), its income was almost totally pledged to the payment of debts run up by the duque. Last in this survey comes the condesa de Foncalada, whose total annual confiscation of 79,822 reales (a net 58,177 reales) was drawn from the estate of Foncalada in Talavera, 47,250 reales; the estate of Huerta in Ocaña (Toledo), 29,327 reales; and various *juros*, 3,245 reales.[64]

Further evidence can be drawn from a list of confiscations made in about 1710 in Castile:[65]

---

[64] There are some important differences between the 1706 list and the 1721 account in the following cases: the conde de Galbe's total confiscations in the latter account are put at 79,728 reales net; the conde de Elda's at 18,257 total and 11,305 net; the conde de la Corzana's at 11,390 total and 10,400 net; the marqués del Villar's at 6,336 net: the marqués de Miraflores at 1,884 net; the conde de Santa Cruz's at 22,272 total and 10,258 net; the marqués de San Marcelino's at 3,837 total and 2,281 net; and the conde de Requena's at 28,002 total and 24,492 net. Galbe's property was mostly in *juros*, Elda's came from land in Córdoba, Corzana's from property in Alava, Miraflores' from property in Córdoba, San Marcelino's from possessions in Alcalá, and Requena's from various rights in Toro, León and Avila.

[65] Taken from A HN, Estado leg.2973.

TABLE 2. ANNUAL VALUE OF PROPERTIES CONFISCATED IN
CASTILE IN 1710 (GRAIN IN *fanegas*, OIL IN *arrobas*)

	Reales	Wheat	Barley	Rye	Olive oil
Conde de Palma	93,523	2,559	666	16	
Conde de la Puebla de					
Montalbán	107,082	456	350	18	
Marqués de Valdetorres	26,068		100		
Vizconde de Ambite	20,465				
Conde de Paredes	39,672	635	286		
Conde de Siruela	113,071	1,293	701	109	34
Marqués de San Vicente	41,026	915	849		
Marqués de Valparaiso	66,946				
Marqués de Tejares	11,670	161	153		
Marqués de la Conquista	53,476				
Marqués de Monrreal	5,872				
Conde de Belmonte	28,185	47	47		
Marqués de Cusano	3,000				
Conde de Sacro Imperio	21,997				
Marqués de Campi	2,233	27		20	

The same criticisms hold for this table as for the preceding one.
Once again, however, we dispose of details of the confiscations.[66]
The total income confiscated from the conde de Palma came to an
annual 159,830 reales, a net 84,103. The figure appears to exceed
that given in the 1710 list, but it is possible that not all confisca-
ations were included in that list. Of the total, 122,538 reales
derived from property in Córdoba, and 37,292 from the estate of
Montes Claros in Guadalajara. The conde de la Puebla de Montal-
bán, better known as the duque de Uceda, had all his property
confiscated and granted to the duque de San Pedro. The conde de
Paredes, whose confiscations are estimated at 71,250 reales by
the 1721 account (a net 48,940 reales), lost this sum from his
rights in the town of Paredes (Palencia), 21,908 reales; from similar
rights in the town of Alcaraz (Toledo), 12,000 reales; from rights
in León, 642 reales; and from *juros*, 36,700 reales.

The conde de Siruela suffered confiscations totalling an annual
176,857 reales (a net 78,617): these came from rights in Siruela

[66] Also from AGS, Secretaría de Hacienda vol. 972.

(Extremadura), 85,598 reales; in Roa (Burgos), 65,665 reales; in Cerbera (Palencia), 23,594 reales; and from lands in Cuenca, 2,000 reales. The marqués de San Vicente lost an annual total of 48,834 reales, a net 19,971. The money came from *censos* in Madrid, 3,235 reales; rents in Madrid, 3,433 reales; pastures in Palencia, 17,211 reales; agricultural land in Leganés, 20,749 reales; the estate of San Vicente in Zamora, 3,070 reales; and *censos* in Granada, 1,136 reales. The marqués de Tejares suffered confiscations worth an annual 14,740 reales, a net 12,665, from pastures and *censos* in Toledo.[67] Finally, the marqués de Campi, whose property was in Salamanca, suffered confiscations amounting to 2,719 reales annually, a net 2,653.

Meticulous as these details may appear, they are none the less valuable evidence of the extent and manner of confiscations suffered by the nobility. At the same time they reveal the differing ways in which aristocrats held their wealth, whether in *juros*, land-rents or simply seigneurial rights. There is little doubt that these defectors helped the treasury appreciably, while at the same time relieving the government of their presence. The Bourbon war effort could well be grateful to the grandees for the money realised through confiscations. The defection of Oropesa alone brought to the treasury an annual income totalling about half the value of all the confiscations made in Castile in 1706.[68]

Nor was this the end of the story. Among the many other Castilian nobles who deserted to the Allies were those who, though not in possession of confiscable property at the time of their defection, were heirs to the vast fortunes of great houses. The most prominent example of this is the conde de Haro, a grandee of Spain and son and heir to the constable of Castile, the duque de Frias. Haro had defected in 1706. On 19 January 1713 his father died, and he automatically inherited the family property. At once the government stepped in and confiscated all his

[67] Variations between the 1710 and 1721 accounts are notable in the cases of the following: the marqués de Valdetorres, estimated at 10,911 reales, none of it net, by the later account; the vizconde de Ambite (marqués de Legarda), estimated similarly at 4,250 reales net; the marqués de Valparaiso, estimated at 29,118 reales (17,864 net), most of it in pasture in Toledo; the marquesa de la Conquista (it is not clear here whether the husband or wife suffered), 39,990 reales (33,478 net), whose estate was in Trujillo (Extremadura); the conde de Sacro Imperio, whose property, all in Toledo, was put at 5,350 reales, none of it net.

[68] The annual total for 1706 was 853,066 reales, 23,151 *fanegas* of wheat and 10,267 of barley: AHN, Estado leg.2973.

possessions. The income from this source registered with the treasury was an annual total of 559,520 reales (net 377,225), a greater fortune even than Oropesa's. The sources of this income were: nine estates in the province of Burgos, worth 287,840 reales annually; property in Segovia, 48,710 reales; in Valladolid, 66,230 reales; in Palencia, 52,622 reales; in Soria, 38,540 reales; and the estate of Jodar in Jaén, 65,578 reales. To this total must be added the sum of 37,828 reales, mostly in *juros*, which reverted to Haro in 1717 on the death of the condesa de Medellin.[69]

This was, for all practical purposes, the end of the grandees of Castile. Their numbers were diminished, their honour compromised, their incompetence exposed. By 1711 they were complaining, and with some justice, that they had been excluded from public affairs and that Italians and Flemings were running the country.[70] In September 1711 an Italian, the principe de Santo Buono, was appointed viceroy of Peru, and it was reported that the king had become so disgusted with Castilian grandees losing his territories (the marqués de Villena had lost Naples in 1707; the marqués de la Jamaica, later duque de Veraguas on the death of his father in 1710, had lost Sardinia in 1708; and Don Francisco de Velasco had lost Catalonia in 1705) that it seemed appropriate to honour a non-Castilian for a change.[71] In fact Italians were advancing rapidly to favour. The duque de Popoli had now become one of the most distinguished generals of the monarchy. Created a grandee of the first class in 1706, and captain general in 1710, he subsequently commanded the Spanish forces in Catalonia, and became a knight of the Golden Fleece and governor of the heir to the throne. In February 1714, despite Spanish complaints, a Milanese, the príncipe Pio, was appointed governor of Madrid and captain general of the province.[72] Another of the Italians prominent at court, according to a memoir of 1713 drawn up by the French ambassador, was the marqués de Crèvecoeur, son of the príncipe de Masserano. According to

[69] All details from AGS, Secretaría de Hacienda vol. 972.

[70] The Spaniards complained, according to the French ambassador, 'sur ce qu'ils n'ont nulle part aux affaires; sur ce que les Italiens et les Valons sont preferés en tout au naturels': Noailles to Torcy, 9 June 1711, AE Corr. Pol. (Esp.), 211 f.233.

[71] Bonnac to Louis XIV, 9 Sept. 1711, AE Corr. Pol. (Esp.), 209 f.74.

[72] Brancas to Torcy, 17 Feb. 1714, *ibid.*, 228 f.153. The principe was Francisco Pio de Saboya, marqués de Castelrodrigo; he was known either by his title of prince or that of marquis. He was later to command Spanish forces in Catalonia.

the same memoir, 'in general the Italians seem to be more agreeable than any others; they are entrusted with the principal posts both in war and in the government of the provinces, and one can expect that the queen, who put them there, will keep them there'.[73] Last, but of greatest importance, in this list of Italians comes the powerful Giudice family: Domenico del Giudice, duque de Giovenazzo, was a councillor of state; Francesco del Giudice was cardinal inquisitor general; and the duke's son, the príncipe de Cellamare, was later to become ambassador to France. Clearly the Italians were well entrenched in Madrid long before Alberoni or Elizabeth Farnese had begun to orientate Spanish policy towards the Mediterranean.

For all this, royal policy towards the grandees was directed against individuals only, and not against their social class. Philip's advisers were concerned to break the power of the grandees, but not to undermine the aristocracy. 'The opinion that His Catholic Majesty holds in general of the grandees of Spain,' reported ambassador Bonnac to Louis xiv in 1711, 'is that so long as they are not in office they will be incapable of harm, hated as they are by their subjects and odious to the lower nobility. But he is careful to display his regard for those who are in his entourage.'[74] While he cast aside the wreckage of grandee casualties with one hand, therefore, with the other Philip encouraged and created a new noble tradition of advancement based on service and loyalty. The response was such that during his reign he felt himself called upon to create no less than two hundred new titles of nobility, a record equalled before him only by Philip iv. The War of Succession consequently sees the death of one concept of nobility and the birth of another, more beneficial to the monarchy and to the nation.

The collapse of grandee power consisted principally in their removal from the central administration. They may well have retained considerable authority in their country seats, a subject of which we know virtually nothing, but it is safe to say that their influence in Madrid declined with the reformation of the conciliar system.

The elaborate network of councils, together with their

[73] 'Memoire concernant l'Estat présent de la Cour d'Espagne', AE Corr. Pol., (Esp.), 223 ff.15–26. Also printed in Recueils des Instructions données aux Ambassadeurs, vol. 12, pp. 214–28. The date of the memoir is August 1713.
[74] Bonnac to Louis xiv, 20 Sept. 1711, AE Corr. Pol. (Esp.), 209 f.126.

subsidiary juntas, had long been considered inefficient, for a variety of reasons. Progress was slow, jurisdictions clashed, conservative nobles at the top and self-interested office-holders at the bottom blocked reforms; if positive decrees ever did emerge from the maze of councils there were no civil servants under central control to enforce them. The one hope of success under the old system lay in the executive. A strong minister or efficient royal secretary could override and bypass the councils in order to carry out necessary measures. Additional support might come from the *despacho* which, consisting as it did of the king and a handful of picked ministers, could ignore the normal processes of conciliar machinery. When, however, there was no strong king or minister or secretary, initiative returned unfailingly to the grandees who sat on and controlled the councils.

Under the Bourbon monarchy the council of Castile began to establish its superiority over the council of state, which specialised in foreign affairs, in proportion as Spanish questions became more important than those of a rapidly disintegrating European empire.[75] It is possible that the decline of the council of state occurred soon after Philip v's arrival,[76] but there are no definite indications of this. The first change made by Philip v was a decree on 28 February 1701 limiting the size and cost of the council of Castile and subsidiary bodies in the provinces: the council was limited to twenty members, and the size and number of salaries were specified.[77] By its supremacy over the judicial machinery of provincial audiencias (in Seville and La Coruña) and chanceries (in Granada and Valladolid), and its control over civil governors or *corregidores*, the council already held important influence,[78] and Marshal Tessé claimed that it abused this power in order to block orders of which it disapproved.[79] The French

[75] G. Desdevises du Dézert, *L'Espagne de l'Ancien Régime* (3 vols), Paris, 1897–1904, vol. 2, *Les Institutions*, pp. 59–86.

[76] *Mémoires de Saint-Simon*, vol. 8, pp. 153–4: 'Je ne m'étends point sur le conseil d'Etat parce qu'il tomba fort peu après l'arrivée du roi, et qu'il est demeuré depuis en desuétude. Il a fait rarement des conseillers d'Etat, mais toujours sans fonction'.

[77] AHN, Consejos suprimidos leg.13222 f.10.

[78] *Mémoires et lettres du Maréchal de Tessé*, vol. 2, p. 160: 'C'est le president de Castille qui nomme quasi tous les corregidors ... c'est donc l'esprit du conseil de Castille qui règne en Espagne'.

[79] Tessé to Chamillart, 11 Apr. 1705, in *Ibid.*, vol. 2, p. 160: 'J'ai vu des ordres et des lettres de lui [the president of Castile] particulières et des corregidors et des juges totalement contraires à ce qui avait été réglé dans le despacho; de sorte que par là il combat quasi toujours ce que le despacho, dont il est, a réglé.'

were impatient with the delays which the conciliar system imposed on administration, and from the start it became Bourbon policy to eliminate any barriers to efficiency set up by the grandees and councils. The method adopted was that of centralisation. This was carried out in two ways: firstly, effective power was moved from the council chamber to the *despacho*; and, secondly, the number and personnel of councils were reduced until only one principal body remained – that of Castile.

The second of these developments was a swift and simple one. On the outbreak of the War of Succession, Spain handed over military control of the Netherlands to France. The French drew up a new form of government for the country,[80] which brought an energetic but futile protest from the privy council of Flanders in 1702.[81] Because Versailles now controlled Brussels, the relevant conciliar machinery became superfluous, and the council of Flanders in Spain was suppressed, its president, the conde de Monterey, being allowed to assist in the *despacho*. The papers of the defunct council were passed to the council of state's secretary for northern affairs.[82] The next council to disappear was that of Aragon, which was suppressed on 15 July 1707 after the revocation of the liberties of the realms of Aragon. The functions of the suppressed council were merged into those of the council of Castile. In June 1715, after the expulsion of Philip's French advisers, changes made during the war were recapitulated and the merging of the functions of the councils of Aragon, Flanders and Italy into that of Castile were confirmed. By this date, therefore, the complexity of the old system had been eliminated, and Spain had a single supreme advisory body.

The first development, involving executive control, was more complex. Instructions given by Louis XIV to his ambassadors show that he was at pains to supersede conciliar government by royal cabinet control: the result was to antagonise conservative Spaniards.[83] When in 1704 Mancera and Portocarrero resigned

---

[80] This is given in AE Corr. Pol. (Esp.), 102 ff.58–74.

[81] Memoir of the Privy Council dated 27 Mar. 1702, *ibid.*, 104 f.67.

[82] Gaceta de Madrid for 11 Apr. 1702, BN, fonds Lorraine 970.

[83] San Felipe, *Comentarios de la guerra de España*, p. 51: 'El cardenal de Etré ... resolvía lo más principal, y dispuso que nada despachase en su casa Portocarrero, y que llevase todo al Consejo del Gabinete. Esto le empezó a conmover, y más cuando vió que no era su voto atendido; hablaba mal de los franceses, y que no debían usurpar el mando a los españoles'.

from the *despacho* in protest against neglect of the councils, Louis assured Philip v that the *despacho* was essential and must not be suppressed: 'far from suppressing it, you must have all the most important business of your monarchy carried on there'.[84] The young king appears to have learned his lesson well, for at the first *despacho* meeting attended by Amelot in May 1705 the king agreed that a certain matter be referred to a council, 'and turning to me', reported Amelot, 'he added that there were some matters on which two hundred councils should be consulted before a decision, but there were others on which none must be consulted'.[85]

The first step, then, was to remove all important business to a selected cabinet at which the French ambassador was usually present. The size of this cabinet depended on current needs and policies, but the general trend was to exclude the majority of grandees, even those favourable to France. In March 1703, for example, the *despacho* consisted only of two grandees (Mancera and Manuel Arias, the latter of whom was president of the council of Castile and later cardinal archbishop of Seville), two secretaries, and the French ambassador.[86] At Amelot's arrival there appear to have been four grandees in the *despacho*, but he soon reduced this number to two.[87] By January 1709, however, the *despacho* had swollen to a membership of six,[88] because of the degree of cooperation achieved with the grandees. In July 1709 a change reduced the number to five;[89] by 1710 the number was four,[90] at which level it stood in 1713.[91] But by August 1713 it had become clear that even this select *despacho* was no more than a sham. A memoir of that date prepared for Torcy stated that the

---

[84] Baudrillart, *Philippe V et la Cour de France*, vol. 1, p. 183.

[85] Amelot to Louis xiv, 27 May 1705, AE Corr. Pol. (Esp.), 147 f.64.

[86] *Mémoires de Saint-Simon*, vol. 11, p. 320.

[87] Amelot to Louis xiv, 26 July 1705: 'Depuis que le despacho n'est plus composé que du marquis de Mansera et du duc de Montellano, les affaires passent presque sans aucune opposition. Je crois qu'il n'est pas possible que le despacho soit composé d'une maniere plus convenable', AE Corr. Pol. (Esp.), 147 f.288. The eliminated grandees were Montalto and Monterey.

[88] *Ibid.*, 21 Jan. 1709, AE Corr. Pol. (Esp.) 189 f.60. The six were Francisco Ronquillo, the conde de Frigiliana, the duque de Medina Sidonia, Montellano, Veraguas and the duque de San Juan.

[89] *Ibid.*, 1 July 1709, *ibid.*, 192 f.7. Montellano and San Juan went out, the marqués de Bedmar came in.

[90] San Felipe, *Comentarios de la guerra de España*, p. 197.

[91] *Recueil des Instructions données aux Ambassadeurs*, vol. 12 ,*Espagne*, p. 221.

despacho was reduced to mere approval of decisions already taken, and those not the most important; moreover, it frequently referred to the councils for opinions.[92] Obviously, therefore, the form of the *despacho* had been superseded by other executive machinery. This important development deserves some examination.

Between 1701 and 1713 the only considerable change in the councils occurred in 1706, when the number of personnel in the councils of Castile, Aragon, Italy, Finance, the Indies, and Orders, was reduced from 108 persons to 56, and a cut made in conciliar officials from 382 persons to 240.[93] On 10 November 1713 an entirely new form was given to the councils of Castile, the Indies, Finance, and Orders, with the issue of a *nuevaplanta*, or new régime, inspired by Jean Orry and Melchor Macanaz.[94] By this reorganisation the chamber of Castile was suppressed and the existing president of the council replaced by five presidents, one for each of five chambers. Similarly, the council of the Indies was given three presidents, that of Finance four presidents with a special official known as the *veedor general* or supervisor (a post meant for Orry himself), and that of Orders two presidents. At the same time the total personnel of the councils was more than doubled, and meetings made more regular. The purpose of this surprising resort to conciliar government seems to have been to create a broader and more comprehensive administration divided into clearly defined departments. Executive decisions were, however, reserved to government ministers sitting in a series of *despachos*

---

[92] *Ibid.*, p. 221: 'On ne rapport dans ce conseil que des affaires de peu d'importance, et quand on y traite des autres, ce n'est qu'après qu'elles ont été décidées en particulier, et seulement pour les faire approuver . . . Il ne décide pas même sur-le-champ la plupart des affaires qui y sont rapportées'.

[93] Amelot to Louis XIV, 5 Oct. 1706, AE Corr. Pol. (Esp.), 161 f.132.

[94] Details of the *planta* are listed in AN Aff. Etr., B¹ 776. It was known at the time as the *planta Macanaz*, but Orry seems to have had even more responsibility than Macanaz for it. The scheme was very unpopular, as were the ministers behind it: pasquins on them may be found in Isidro Planes, *Sucessos fatales de esta Ciudad y Reyno de Valencia*, BUV MS 456, f.279. One verse given here says of the scheme: 'Estas Plantas en Castilla, producirán Catalanes'. For a discussion of the council of Castile in 1713 see Janine Fayard, 'La tentative de réforme du Conseil de Castile sous le règne de Philippe V (1713–1715)', *Mélanges de la Casa de Velázquez* vol. 2, 1966, pp. 259–81. The reform of the council was to some extent a political move, because of its opposition to the 1712 Law of Succession excluding female heirs from the throne. A consulta by the council to Philip V was burnt by order of the king, who secured the opinion of the councillors individually and thus broke the pretensions of the council to be a constitutional authority.

devised by Orry along lines he had planned as early as 1703.[95] According to Orry's plan, decreed on 31 January 1714,[96] the *despacho* was to sit six days a week, but different business was to be transacted each day and the personnel of the *despacho* was to differ each time. On Monday ecclesiastical affairs were to be discussed, with three others present besides the comte de Bergeyck, Orry and the secretary; on Tuesday, affairs of state, with three grandees and Bergeyck, Orry and the secretary present; on Wednesday, judicial affairs, with two grandees and the last three named; on Thursday, financial affairs, with the same number of personnel; and similarly for Friday with military affairs and Saturday with business concerning the Indies.

Essentially this scheme altered nothing at all, as Toby Bourke shrewdly pointed out to Torcy, beyond increasing the size of the *despacho* with people who neither decided business nor carried it out. One of the grandees remarked sardonically to his colleagues at a meeting of one of these swollen *despachos*: 'Gentlemen, this is only to have more witnesses to the fact that nothing is done here!'[97] Even this alleged reform, then, could not mask the fact that the cabinet was not the deciding body in the government, and that it had been developed under French influence largely as a means of undermining the power of the grandees as expressed in the councils. Where then did the true centre of government lie?

There can be no doubt that in the period with which we are specifically concerned, that of French preponderance from 1700 to 1715, the guiding influence was that of foreign advisers. The French ambassadors from Marcin onwards were encouraged by Louis XIV to advise, control and manipulate the Spanish administration. In every case where the ambassador assisted in the *despacho*, it was he and not the grandees who most guided policy,

---

[95] AE Corr. Pol. (Esp.), 119 f.195 gives Orry's suggestions in 1703.

[96] *Ibid.*, 228 f.108.

[97] Bourke to Torcy, 5 Feb. 1714, 'Ce qu'on a fait ne change rien dans la nature du gouvernement ni meme dans la forme. On a seulement divisé les matieres dont on devra parler dans le dispacho les six jours de la semaine, et on a augmenté le nombre de ceux qui composoient le dispacho ... mais comme tous ces messⁱˢ n'ont d'autre connoissance des affaires que celle qu'on leur donne dans le meme dispacho, et que pas un d'eux n'est chargé de l'execution de rien, l'autorité demeure dans le meme canal ou elle etoit auparavant ... ce qui a fait dire malicieusement a Mʳ le comte de Frigiliana dans la chambre de dispacho en parlant a ces messieurs auxquels on venoit de donner entree, Señores, esto es solo tener algunos testigos mas de que no se haze nada aqui'. AE Corr. Pol. (Esp.), 228 f.130.

this situation reaching its climax under the ambassadorship of Amelot. Before 1706 and after 1712 the counsels of Orry were also of great importance, and from 1711 to 1712 it was the comte de Bergeyck who controlled the policies of Spain. In all these cases, the chief minister (whether ambassador or not) worked through the *despacho* with the active help of the secretaries of this body. It is with these secretaries that we approach at last the answer to our question.

Under Charles 11 and for the first three years of the reign of Philip v, the *despacho* had only one secretary, Antonio de Ubilla y Medina, created marqués de Ribas in 1701.[98] In September 1703 this post was split in two, and the marqués de Canales was given charge of foreign affairs, finance and war. In 1705 Ribas and Canales were replaced, and a decree of 11 July 1705 put in their place Joseph Grimaldo[99] for war and finance, and the marqués de Mejorada for other business. For the whole length of Amelot's stay in Spain, he seems to have worked exclusively with the two secretaries, to the virtual exclusion of the grandees in the *despacho*. When, after 1709, the French ambassadors ceased to play any part in the administration as a result of Louis xiv's policy of disengagement, the secretaries were left in full control of the administrative machine. By 1713 the initiative that they were taking was so obvious as to worry conservatives.[100] The importance of their posts was now established beyond all question. Orry's cabinet system in 1714 was transparently framed to fit a nucleus of secretary and *veedor general*: the secretaries were still Mejorada (for church, foreign and administrative affairs), and Grimaldo (for finance, war and the Indies). On 30 November 1714 a new decree created four secretaries in the *despacho*: Joseph Grimaldo for foreign affairs, Bernardo Tinajero for marine and the Indies, Miguel Durán for war, and Manuel de Vadillo y Velasco for justice and the clergy.[101] Each of these secretaries had the official title of 'secretary of state'. This measure seems to have meant

[98] Ribas, as we have already noted, fell into disgrace in 1706.

[99] Born 1660, a Basque, he was secretary to Orry, then appointed to war and finance in 1705. Gentleman of the chamber Aug. 1707, received a commandership of the Order of Santiago in Apr. 1714, and created marqués in October that year.

[100] *Recueil des Instructions données aux Ambassadeurs*, vol. 12, p. 223: 'Quoique l'usage soit que les secrétaires d'Etat ne fassent que rapporter les affaires sans dire leur sentiment, le marquis de Mejorada s'est mis sur un autre pied. Il joint toujours son avis au rapport qu'il fait et souvent détermine'.

[101] Pachau to Pontchartrain, 12 Nov. 1714, AN Aff. Etr., B¹ 777.

that the secretaries were very near to exercising ministerial powers, and it would no doubt have led to greater efficiency in the *despacho*.

The situation was altered when the expulsion of Orry and Macanaz from Spain in the first week of February 1715 led to a suspension of all the former's administrative changes. On 18 February 1715 a provisional number of ministers[102] was named to exercise the government, pending fundamental changes. Despite these ministers, however, observers reported that all effective authority remained in the hands of the secretaries of state,[103] and subsequent legislation repealing all changes in the councils made in the preceding fifteen years, did nothing to alter fundamentally the status and function of the secretaries. On 2 April 1717 their number was raised to three, but this was later raised to four, at which level it stayed for the rest of Philip's reign.

After the first decade of Philip's reign, then, the centre of government lay in an efficient minister (such as Amelot, or, later, Alberoni) working through secretaries of state who grew rapidly in importance as their duties expanded. This development was made possible only by Bourbon policy, which succeeded in excluding the grandees of Castile from any important or active part in the government. The significance of this is greater than might at first sight appear. The fall of the grandees, with which this chapter began, has led logically to a discussion of the administrative changes of the period. Exclusion of the grandees, contraction of the councils, resort to the *despacho*, centralisation of business in the hands of secretaries: this meant in practice the restoration of responsibility to the centre of the state by the elimination of an irresponsible governing caste. It was the centre of the state, and the movement to centralisation, that absorbed Philip's Bourbon advisers.

Our conclusions may be summarised as follows. If the French in this period laid emphasis on the *despacho*, it was not in order to govern through this body, but simply to take away initiative from the grandees and the councils. The true source of government decisions was rather the nucleus that consisted of a chief

---

[102] Cardinal del Giudice to control judicial and church affairs, Veraguas trade and marine, Bedmar war, Frigiliana the Indies, and the marqués de Campoflorido finance: Saint-Aignan to Pontchartrain, 19 Feb. 1715, AN Af. Etr., B¹ 778.

[103] Bourke to Torcy, 25 Feb. 1715, AE Corr. Pol. (Esp.), 239 f.84.

minister aided by a number of secretaries, sitting in or out of the *despacho* according to circumstances. This nucleus expanded until the secretaries themselves became the chief ministers of the crown.

It should be emphasised that the fall of the grandees, though of fundamental political and administrative importance, is of lesser significance in the social history of Spain. As in previous reigns, the nobility remained entrenched in their privileges and estates. Their authority remained unquestioned in the day to day ordering of life in the court and in the country, and cultural as well as economic organisation continued to be dominated by the values of the ruling class. The question of loyalty to the new régime ceased to be an issue after 1725, when, as one of the terms of the Treaty of Vienna between Vienna and Madrid, it was stipulated that exiles could return home to their fortunes and estates.

The Bourbons had rejected the upper aristocracy, but they took the lower nobility to their hearts. The reign sees the rise to eminence of administrators who boasted no title higher than that of 'Don', and who earned loftier titles than this simply by faithful service to the crown. The most prominent field of service of these new administrators was in the intendancies. The introduction of intendants into Spain is one of the most interesting developments in the Bourbon policy of centralisation.

Intendants were part and parcel of the financial and administrative reforms introduced during the war.[104] As early as 1703 Orry had been convinced of their necessity if any permanent reforms were to be introduced into Spain. He saw in the existing Spanish office of *corregidor* or municipal governor a perfect basis for the introduction of the new system. For various reasons, however, no steps towards implementation of these suggestions were taken until 1711, when Philip v took on Bergeyck as his prime minister. Bergeyck very swiftly and efficiently created regulations for the introduction of intendants, who were nominated to serve as from 1 December 1711. Approval of the *despacho* for these

[104] For further details and documentation on the subject of intendants see Henry Kamen, 'El establecimiento de los Intendentes en la administración española', *Hispania*, XXIV (1964), pp. 368–95; and the interesting article by J. Mercader on the establishment of intendants in Catalonia, 'Un organismo-piloto en la Monarquía de Felipe v: La Superintendencia de Cataluña', *Hispania*, CIII (1967).

measures was obtained, and the experiment went ahead. Among those who shared the distinction of being the first intendants in Spanish history, were Don Joseph Patiño for Extremadura, and Don Rodrigo Cavallero for Valencia.[105]

The Spanish intendants were, as Bergeyck admitted, modelled entirely on the French pattern, and were empowered to perform all duties of finance, police (i.e. administration), justice and war, with sole responsibility to the Madrid government. The project achieved only limited success. Bergeyck was called away to the peace conferences in France very soon after the establishment of the intendants, and in his absence, as we have already seen, the whole scheme began to flounder. The intendancies were certainly continued in places such as Saragossa, Barcelona and Valencia, where their services in the task of pacification and reorganisation were invaluable; but elsewhere in the peninsula they were quietly dropped, so that by 1715 no real progress had been made in Castile towards the creation of an administrative class dependent on and responsible only to the crown. The relative failure of the *institution*, however, is balanced by the remarkable success of the *personnel* involved. Many of the earliest intendants, of whom Patiño is justly the most famous, blossomed into the most distinguished ministers of the Spanish monarchy. Others, whose names are not so well known, spent their most formative years of service in the intendancies during the War of Succession, and were the vanguard of a new administrative class devoted to reform and impatient of the accumulated weight of generations of misgovernment.

The conciliar reforms of the war period were all undone in 1715 with the advent of Elizabeth Farnese. Reasons for the reaction are not difficult to find. Most of the 'reforms' (if they can be called such, for they had had little chance to prove their value) were closely associated with the policies of a faction, and when it fell from power the reforms also collapsed. Individuals who had implemented the reforms, such as Bernardo Tinajero de la Escalera, secretary of the council of the Indies, or Miguel Guerra, president of the council of Castile, were dismissed from office. Others who had cooperated unenthusiastically with Orry and Macanaz were retained, and promoted. It may be, as Torcy

---

[105] Among intendants nominated at this date were Thomás Moreno Pacheco for León, Antonio de Ozas y Córdoba for Burgos, the conde de Torrepalma for Zamora, and Antonio Orellana for Salamanca.

tended to think,[106] that the changes in 1715 were inspired by hatred of France; but other pressures certainly operated as well: opposition to radical and sudden alterations in administrative procedure, concern by office-holders for the security of their posts,[107] and quite simply hatred of Orry. The faction that now assumed office was the Italian one: a Spinola became governor of Valencia, a Grimaldi governor of Cadiz, while Italians took over the chief ministerial posts and, cruellest cut of all, an Italian became Spanish ambassador to France.[108] On 9 June 1715 the council of Castile reverted to the form specified in a decree of 17 July 1691. On 4 August the council of finance reverted to its form in 1701. On 23 August all decrees relating to the council of war made since 1700, were repealed. The whole apparatus of government stood as it was on the accession of Philip v to the throne. With these moves all the reforms of the French period were disowned.

The reaction of 1715 was only a temporary one. The administrations of Alberoni and still more of Patiño saw the further development of reforms initiated under the French. Under them the system of secretaries of state and provincial intendants was brought to perfection, and Bourbon government found its ablest exponents in men like these who had served the French during the War of Succession.

[106] Torcy to the marquis de Saint-Aignan, ambassador in Spain, 13 May 1715: 'Tinajero . . . passoit pour françois; ainsy le motif de la disgrace.' AE Corr. Pol. (Esp.), 240 f.97.

[107] E.g. the case of the minister of war, the marqués de Bedmar, who profited by the change in 1715, so that 'ce nouvel etablissement etendra les fonctions de sa charge, qui se reduisoient tres peu de chose sous le regne de M. Orry': Pachau to Pontchartrain, 19 Feb. 1715, AN Aff. Etr., B¹ 778.

[108] The ambassador was Cellamare, of the Giudice family.

6 The Techniques of Control

The unprecedented nature of war and invasion in this period was paralleled by the degree of control exercised over the Spanish executive by foreign ministers and advisers. Within the part of Spain controlled by the Bourbons, this control was definitive up to the year 1709. The evidence of the preceding chapter has shown clearly that French direction of the administration was of profound importance during the war. The role of the French ambassador was, of course, the key factor, since it was through him that Louis xiv intervened in the government of Spain. Baudrillart has described in some detail the extent to which official nominations were made in Versailles: 'the king of France,' he says, 'knew all the administrative personnel; no change or appointment was made without him.'[1] Examples can be multiplied to show how effective this control was. In 1706, for instance, Louis xiv tried to have the marqués de Jamaica nominated as next viceroy of Mexico; in 1707, he proposed the marqués de los Balbazes as next viceroy of Sicily.[2] Through Louis and his ambassador Amelot, governors of provinces were dismissed and appointed, and foreigners were nominated to govern Spanish kingdoms.[3]

As we have seen, the principal aim of this control over appointments was to exclude the grandees from the government and to force through reforms which the Spaniards themselves were apparently unwilling to institute. Most of the French, including Amelot, considered this use of force necessary. 'You never get anywhere in this country without forcing nature. . . . All the

[1] Baudrillart, *Philippe V et la Cour de France*, vol. 1, p. 121.
[2] Amelot to Louis xiv, 15 Jan. 1706, AE Corr. Pol. (Esp.), 157 f.91; Louis xiv to Amelot, 14 Mar. 1707, in Girardot, *Correspondance de Louis XIV*.
[3] Amelot to Louis xiv, 27 Sept. 1706, AE Corr. Pol. (Esp.), 161 f.79; 11 Nov. 1706, *ibid.*, 162 f.35; 5 Sept. 1706, *ibid.*, 161 f.3.

Spaniards, great and small, are opposed to everything called novelty, without considering whether it is better.'⁴ Whether the use of force was wise is another matter. There is no doubt that French hostility to conciliar government meant that a very large number of junior officials resented the attempt to destroy institutions that were their sole livelihood.

The effectiveness of French control can be proved simply by the resentment it provoked among Spaniards. Such resentment was linked to military events. When Gibraltar fell to the English on 2 August 1704, there was anger and dismay in Spanish ruling circles; when Barcelona fell on 9 October 1705, this anger was turned against the French. The mood was general in all classes, and particularly among the aristocracy, who saw their country being ruined by the depredations of a foreign monarchy and its adherents. Amelot in 1706 tried to placate and exhort a special meeting of the grandees. He was sharply answered.

The duque de Medinaceli spoke up and said that if there was anything which could give offence to the nation and cause it to be not as faithful to its prince as it had been to all its other kings since the establishment of the monarchy, that could arise only from the contempt shown to it, seeing how the armies were commanded by foreigners, secret councils were held without the participation of the principal leaders, a number of people had come into the realm only to plunder it, and the principal governorships of Spain and the Indies were placed in the hands of a woman⁵ who sold them publicly; and that these four reasons were only too powerful in causing division and making people lend an ear to numerous manifestos which the enemies of the two crowns had distributed.⁶

All these charges were undeniably true. Most of the principal military commanders in the field were French, and the commander-in-chief of forces in the peninsula was always French: Spanish generals either held subordinate posts or were given defensive commands. The Castilian nobles also resented the number of appointments granted to prominent generals from Flanders or Italy: among these were Tserclaës Tilly and the duque de Popoli, both captains of the royal guard and both brilliant soldiers.

---

⁴ Amelot to Louis xiv, 10 Nov. 1708, in Girardot, *Correspondance de Louis XIV*.
⁵ The princess des Ursins.
⁶ AE Corr. Pol. (Esp.), 159 f.207. The speech is dated 6 June 1706 by Coxe, *Memoirs of the Kings of Spain*, vol. 1, pp. 379–80.

Councils had undeniably been held without the participation of grandees, and Ursins had certainly exercised her influence in the distribution of offices. Finally, a factor of some importance, numbers of Frenchmen had come into Spain looking for an easy fortune. It is difficult not to sympathise with the viewpoint of Castilians who, long accustomed to exploiting other countries, were now for the first time to experience the techniques of exploitation by another.

The French community in Spain had long been important because of its contribution to the economic life of the country, particularly in the commercial centres of Barcelona, Valencia and Seville. Other foreign communities also existed, but the advent of the Bourbons meant that the French would tend to be preferred above them. Already before 1700 they had been an important minority, estimated in 1680 at about sixty-five thousand by the French ambassador.[7] Most of these were workers and artisans, and only about a tenth were traders. Many Frenchmen after 1700 began to look south for opportunities, and one even located a legendary castle of Moorish treasure in Spain.[8] The quality of immigrants worried the French government for a number of reasons, and Louis XIV informed Amelot in 1705 that 'several vagabonds or people with a bad past . . . have crossed into Spain since 1700, and have thought themselves entitled to obtain employment by the sole virtue of being French'.[9] Immigrants made a recognisable impact on the Spanish economy, and a memoir of the same year, 1705, claimed that 'all the cities of Spain are full of a great multitude of artisans and workers from France'.[10]

Anti-French feeling would naturally tend to exaggerate the number of immigrants, making it very difficult to arrive at a just estimate of numbers. The French ambassador would have no special reason to minimise his figures, so that we can probably accept, with some caution, the statement given by the ambassador

[7] Dispatch of Villars, 25 Jan. 1680, quoted in Charles Weiss, *L'Espagne depuis le règne de Philippe II*, vol. 2, pp. 147–9.

[8] This was the correspondent who wrote to Torcy of a friend who 'm'a dit qu'il sçavoit un vieil chasteau en Espagne, desert et abandonné depuis plusieurs siècles, dans les caves duquel il y avoit un grand tresor qu'on croit estre du tems des maures et sarazins'. AE Corr. Pol. (Esp.) 87 f.474.

[9] *Recueil des Instructions données aux Ambassadeurs*, vol. 12, p. 146.

[10] AE Corr. Pol. (Esp.), 154 f.385.

Bonnac in November 1711: 'according to the report made to me, I believe there are from twenty to thirty thousand French scattered throughout Spain, and I am certain that not more than a hundred of them return in the year to France'.[11] Though this figure is less than half that given by Villars in 1680, it is no less acceptable, if Bonnac is referring to the semi-permanent French population. But his estimate for the annual movement back to France is more doubtful, since there is little doubt that the flow of seasonal labour was fairly large, particularly in the Franco-Spanish border regions. The great fear of the French authorities, as we shall shortly see, was that the number of French skilled workers and entrepreneurs entering Spain would be enough to resurrect the industrial potential of the peninsula.

Available reports on the position of the French in Spain date from the later years of the war. There was little doubt in the minds of contemporaries that the immigrants were of even more benefit to France than to Spain. As Amelot, then occupied with the business of the council of commerce in Paris, wrote in 1712:

How many French business houses of Nantes, Saint-Malo, La Rochelle and Marseille, have grown powerful at Cadiz, Málaga, Cartagena, Valencia and in the other principal ports of Spain? A host of people living in Auvergne and other neighbouring provinces cross the Pyrenees every year, and return to France after a certain time, each with a sum proportionate to the price of his labour. If some French marry and settle down in Spain, they are usually only simple workers such as cobblers or tailors, or if they are people with some capital in commerce, very rarely do they cut all links with the part of their family in France.[12]

The core of Amelot's argument, namely that France did not lose by temporary emigration, but in fact gained by it, can be reinforced by the testimony of the abbé de Vayrac, who was also acquainted with the internal affairs of Spain:

It is true that every year one sees arriving in Spain a large number o artisans and workers from the provinces of Auvergne, Limousin, upper and lower Guienne, Languedoc, Bearn and the Basque country; but usually they return after having stayed a short while, and bring with them a considerable amount of money.[13]

---

[11] Bonnac to Pontchartrain, 23 Nov. 1711, *ibid.*, 211 f.423.
[12] Amelot to Pontchartrain, 21 Jan. 1712, *ibid.*, 218 f.42.
[13] Abbé de Vayrac, *L'Etat présent de l'Espagne*, Amsterdam, 1719, p. 48.

While these two quotations emphasise the role of seasonal immigrants, they should not divert attention from the fact that the vast majority of French in Spain were reasonably settled in profitable commercial enterprises, and only returned home if the political situation demanded it. In Seville and Cadiz, as Girard has shown, the French performed a financial role which was duplicated in the other cities of Spain. A memoir of 1715 reports that:

one sees in Madrid very many French employed in crafts and trades, there being several surgeons, a few hatmakers, many wigmakers, and numerous comb-makers, tailors, shoemakers and four or five tapestry-workers who are nearly all members of the *gremios*, or craft-guilds. There are also in Madrid several French bankers, a few wholesalers, and a great number of small traders who draw their merchandise from France.[14]

While there is no evidence that the French dominated or controlled finance and the retail trades, it seems indubitable that their *preponderant* role in these enterprises attracted popular hostility in all the major cities of the peninsula. In Barcelona, Saragossa and Valencia anti-French feeling played a major part in the civil disturbances that accompanied the war; and this question will be discussed later in the context of the rebellion of the eastern provinces.

Valencia appears to have been a very important centre of French trade, and the merchants there probably came second only to those of Cadiz. One indication of their wealth is the offer made in 1705 by four of them to the governor of the city of Valencia, of one and a half million reales for the defence of the realm.[15] The Allied occupation of Valencia was a disaster for many of the merchants: some fled to France, some joined the royal forces, others were taken prisoner, confined and murdered. In 1708 only sixty or seventy of them were left in all Valencia.[16] By 1713, a sign of better times, the authorities estimated that there were fifty French traders in the city of Valencia alone.[17] In

[14] Memoir by Partyet, AE Mém. et Doc. (Esp.), 32 f.69.

[15] AHN, Estado leg.265, f.14. The four merchants were André Gombau, Charles Brun, Pierre Tornier and Thomas Destrem.

[16] 'Lista de los negoziantes franzeses que fueron saqueados de los rebeldes del Reyno de Valencia y que an buelto, y estan actualmte en dho reyno', AHN, Estado leg.345.

[17] AGS, Guerra Moderna leg.2356 f.6.

Cartagena, the principal port of Murcia, the number of Frenchmen (considered either as individuals or as heads of firms or households) registered as resident in 1714 came to forty-four.[18] The principal French colony, however, was based on Andalucia. As we have already seen,[19] the number of merchants in Cadiz in 1710 was put at forty-five. At approximately the same date the French colony in the adjacent town of San Lucar was estimated at about thirty families, most of them being petty traders in oil, coal and the like, while of the eight larger traders in the town only two, Savalette and Fournier, were important enough to be classified as merchants.[20] A survey made three years later, in December 1713, when the war had for all practical purposes ended, is far more comprehensive than these previous estimates.[21] According to this account, Seville at the time had seven wholesale merchants and four retailers; Santa María had twenty-six merchants and eleven retailers; Cadiz had eighty merchants and thirty-one retailers; and San Lucar, as in 1710, had only two merchants of note. Since these figures represent firms and not individuals, they need to be multiplied by an appropriate number to reflect the total of business associates and household dependents.

Fragmentary as these data on the French are, they help towards outlining the number and position of the French community in Spain.[22] The importance of this small group of foreign traders in the peninsula will become clearer as we study the development of Franco-Spanish relations in this period. Essentially, the merchants were the vanguard of French economic penetration. French officials of Philip v did their utmost to secure for their compatriots economic and commercial privileges denied to other nations, while at the same time they discouraged any attempts by French entrepreneurs to bring industry into the country.

[18] 'Lista del Repartimiento hecho por la Ciudad de Cartaxena a los de la Nazion franzessa', AE Corr. Pol. (Esp.), 231 f.144. The names of forty-four are given.

[19] P. 77 above.

[20] AN Aff. Etr., B^1 218 f.211.

[21] The survey is in AN Aff. Etr.,B^1 221 ff.16–99 and gives a complete list of names, not reproduced here for reasons of space. The list names the place of origin of each trader.

[22] The French vice-consul in Galicia, Bru, made a note in 1714 of the number of French settled in this province. In general, he emphasised 'la pauvreté des François establis en Galice', and named only seven Frenchmen in La Coruña (two being wig-makers, 'métier méprisé en Espagne'), seven in Santiago, five in Pontevedra, and two in Vigo: Bru to Pontchartrain, 21 Jan. 1714, AN Aff. Etr., B^1 456.

The state of Spanish industry was, of course, notoriously bad, but the accession of Philip v raised hopes that a new, more vigorous policy in encouraging manufactures would be adopted. Among the many pamphlets issued to greet the new king was, as we have seen, a reprint of the *Discourses* of Martínez de la Mata, first issued at Seville in 1659: if things were so bad in 1659, said the new edition of the pamphlet, how much worse must they be now in 1701! On 18 May 1701 the junta of commerce, a body set up in 1679 to promote trade and manufactures, ordered all cities, through their *corregidors* and *alcaldes,* to send in reports of existing industries.²³ The lack of response to this appeal led to the tour made in 1703 by Gaspar Naranjo, whom we have already encountered. Naranjo's report resulted in no action, and as late as 1705 he was still waiting for something to be done.²⁴ His seems to have been the only considerable effort made by a native in the war period, to reform Spanish industry: all other important measures were originated by foreigners.

It was to the interest of both France and Spain to revive industry in the peninsula in so far as this might help the war effort. But there were very clear limits to what the French were willing to do to help Spaniards. The French position was made clear from the very beginning. In July 1701 the president of the council of Castile had asked the French government:

to allow into Spain, 1. workers to establish manufactures, 2. of cloth of all kinds, 3. of hats, 4. of mirrors, 5. of cloth of gold, 6. of silks, 7. of glass, 8. and of paper. He asked also for 9. jam-makers, saying that they are brought from Genoa, much jam being eaten in Spain and a great deal of money going out because of that.²⁵

Foreign Minister Torcy's reply to this request is of considerable interest since it lays down the basic pattern of French policy:

1. For the last few years many workers have left France. For permission to be given now to other workers to go, would do great harm to our

²³ André Mounier, *Les faits et la doctrine économiques en Espagne sous Philippe V: Gerónimo de Uztáriz (1670–1732)*, Bordeaux, 1919, p. 99.

²⁴ AE Corr. Pol. (Esp.), 154 f.425, Mémoire sur la Junta du Commerce, 'D. Gaspar Naranjo a travaillé depuis trois ans a l'establissement des Manufactures de Laines et de soye en Espagne; il a fait un livre sur ce sujet: il a presenté son travail au Roy, S.M.C. l'a renvoyé a la jonte'. The junta was still discussing the question. The little evidence available tends to show that the junta of commerce failed to become an effective instrument in promoting Spanish industry.

²⁵ A Foreign Ministry report in AE Corr. Pol. (Esp.), 91 f.464. This also includes Torcy's replies.

manufactures, and since both sides must bear in mind the advantages of each nation, it is necessary to lay down once and for all that France does not ask for what will harm Spain, and vice versa.

2. There are many French Catholic workers in Holland. They have made a move to return to France. Depending on the offers made them, they could go to Spain. The king of Spain may order as he sees fit.

The materials included in articles 3, 4, 5, 6 and 7 have always been carried easily from France to Spain. This will be even easier after the union and will greatly hurt the trade of the English and Dutch.

8. The workers asked for by this article can be sent.

9. The king agrees that his subjects should go for this purpose into Spain and so keep much money within the realm of Spain.

Torcy's reply amounts to a rejection of all the requests except the last two, and shows no concern for the promotion of Spanish industry. On the contrary, it seems to accept that with the exclusion of Anglo-Dutch trade the Spaniards must now reconcile themselves to becoming an open market for French goods alone. In short, French policy was diametrically opposed to Spanish aspirations as enunciated by Naranjo or propagated by Martínez de la Mata and other *arbitristas,* who aimed at making Spain self-sufficient in manufactured goods and rescuing it from the position of a dumping-ground for the manufactures of foreign countries. Throughout the war, therefore, there was a basic conflict between the commercial and industrial aims of France and Spain. Both sides had the same theoretical presuppositions: an adverse balance of trade meant a corresponding loss of specie or bullion, therefore trade must be extended at another's expense; one must export or die. Louis xiv was of course concerned not only with peninsular trade, but also with the traditional outlet for peninsular goods – the Indies. As the senior partner in the alliance of the two crowns, the French king had all the advantages, and he used them.

The instructions on trade given to each French ambassador in this period were virtually identical. Those issued to the ambassador Blécourt in 1709 said:[26]

The Spanish trade is considerable because of the quantity of silver to be drawn from it, and the more one takes goods to the Spanish, the more does one bring back specie in gold and silver, so he [the ambassador] must pay particular attention to maintaining and increasing the

[26] 'Mémoire du Roy concernant le Commerce et les Colonies, pour servir d'Instruction au M de Blécourt', 24 July 1709, AN Aff. Etr., B¹ 771.

trade which the French do there, by all the means he considers most suitable. . . . The negligence which the Spanish have hitherto shown in founding manufactures obliges them always to take from foreign countries the goods they need for the lands they possess in the Indies. . . . The other nations, above all the French, have long profited from this trade, and H.M. has always paid particular attention to preventing his subjects giving to Spaniards the means to establish their own manufactures. Since the present union between the two crowns gives, more than ever, opportunities to Frenchmen to settle in Spain and take their manufactures there, he [Blécourt] must prevent them as far as possible, being careful nevertheless to take all necessary precautions so that the Spanish do not see into H.M.'s intentions in this matter, or into the motives which influence him.

Forthright in its lack of altruism, this quotation is an invaluable and concise summary of French policy during the War of Succession. Louis XIV had several initial advantages. On 13 June 1702 a Spanish decree declared illegal and prohibited 'any trade with the subjects of the emperor, England and Holland, and all trade in their produce and manufactures'.[27] On 1 December, the entry of enemy goods through Portugal was prohibited, and decrees of 3 December and 12 December reinforced this ban in detail.[28] On 22 September 1703 another decree prohibited all trade with the Dutch.[29] Simultaneously, France received most-favoured-nation treatment, on the basis of favourable provisions in previous peace treaties. On 28 February 1703 a decree banned duties on various goods, which were allowed free entry through Cadiz and other ports, while on 30 April a decree basing itself on article 15 of the Treaty of Rijswijk prohibited Spanish officials boarding and searching French ships.[30] The way thus lay wide open for French traders, with virtually the rest of Europe officially excluded from Spanish markets. Restriction of duties on their goods, and the freedom granted from inspection for contraband, gave French importers opportunities denied to any other nation.

The authorities in Paris were not slow to respond to the opportunity. In Paris the secretary of state for marine, Pontchartrain, presented a memoir to Louis in which he asked that a council of

27 AN Aff. Etr., BIII 323 f.61.
28 Ibid., 323 ff.73, 74, 76.
29 Ibid., 323 f.119.
30 Ibid., 323 f.84.

commerce be set up to help, *inter alia,* to regulate trade with Spain.[31] This council was created on 29 June 1700, one of its founder members being Amelot. From the very first one of the council's chief preoccupations was trade to the peninsula: proceedings in May and June 1701, for instance, were concerned with this question.[32] In subsequent months the council discussed and decided on various proposals concerning manufactures in, and exports to, Spain. A typical suggestion was that from the deputy of Nantes, in March 1701.

> One could draw great benefits to French trade from the relations we have with the Spanish [he wrote]. The principal means would be to make the peoples of this monarchy, both in America and Europe, cast off their black clothing in order to adopt our fashions and dress in the French way. That would bring a great demand for our silks and woollens . . . and attract much specie into the kingdom.[33]

To promote Franco-Spanish trade, tariffs must be kept low and commerce with the enemy prohibited. The French, to their annoyance, found that it was no easy matter to get their way on these two points, which threatened to diminish the value of the trade privileges they officially enjoyed. Customs duties were regulated by Madrid, but were never administered by the central government. Instead, they were farmed out to four companies which administered each of Castile's four frontiers, and there was little guarantee that the official rate would be observed. The two principal routes of Franco-Spanish trade were through Cadiz and over the Pyrenees;[34] war disturbed the former, so that the land route became the principal one. It was an unpleasant surprise for the French when the tax-farmer for the border route succeeded in February 1705 in raising the rate of the customs levy. Despite French pressure, nothing could be done because of the war, until September 1709 when one of Amelot's subordinates

[31] A. M. de Boislisle, ed., *Correspondance des Contrôleurs Généraux des finances avec les Intendants des provinces* (3 vols), Paris, 1883, vol. 2, p. 467.

[32] Procès-verbaux of 27 May, 3 June, 10 June and 23 June 1701, in Pierre Bonnassieux, ed., *Conseil de Commerce et Bureau du Commerce 1700–1791*, Paris, 1900, p. 3.

[33] Boislisle, *Correspondance*, vol. 2, p. 499.

[34] 'La principale entrée de ce commerce se fait par Cadiz pendant la paix . . .; ce meme commerce a une autre entrée de terre par la Navarre d'ou nous introduisons nos marchandises en Aragon et en Castille; par cette meme entrée nous retirons les laines de Castille et d'Aragon qui tombent a Bayonne pour estre voiturées en France . . .', 'Mémoire touchant le commerce de France en Espagne, pour . . . Bonnac. Envoyé par M. Desmarets'. AE Mém. et Doc. (Esp.), 32 ff.61 *et seq.*

in the treasury at Madrid, Quenneville, succeeded in drawing up
a new table of rates which was given official sanction.[35] The new
schedule did not fully satisfy French demands. 'Reductions have
been made on some of our manufactures in respect of the previous
tariff, but some articles have been left with excessively heavy
taxes which do harm to our workers', wrote the French finance
minister Desmaretz to ambassador Bonnac in 1711, at the same
time instructing him to work for further concessions.[36] This
was clearly a question on which no satisfactory agreement would
ever be reached, and the French do not seem to have progressed
any further than the 1709 tariff.

Commerce with the enemy, which was the other principal
ground for discontent, went on intermittently despite French
disapproval. There seems to be no doubt, however, that it was
the Spanish more than the French who had reason to complain.
It was obvious to everyone that the French were operating a
double code of conduct. Louis wished to close all Spanish ports
to the maritime powers, on the grounds that one should not trade
with the enemy; but France itself continued to trade openly with
the Dutch for the greater part of the war down to 1710. The
Spanish decision to cease trading with the Allies was a voluntary
one, but it is doubtful if the ban on trade with nations that brought
in a large proportion of the commodities habitually consumed in
the peninsula was meant to be observed literally. The junta of
commerce, for example, had thought the ban inadvisable, but the
council of state in June 1705, and the *despacho* after it, both reaffirmed the correctness of the decision. Not surprisingly, the
French ambassador also supported the prohibition. The final
decree, issued on 16 October 1705, stipulated that only Spanish
or neutral vessels could trade directly to and from the peninsula;
foodstuffs were allowed to be imported from, and exported to,
enemy countries, but only in Spanish or neutral ships; inferior
quality wool could be exported to enemy countries, but only
after paying a special additional tax; and on no account were
enemy manufactures to be permitted into Spain.[37]

Some French officials realised that it would not do to be too
strict about prohibiting Spaniards from trading with the enemy,

[35] The new customs schedule is given in AE Corr. Pol. (Esp.), 197 f.68.
[36] AE Mém. et Doc. (Esp.), 32 f.61 ff.
[37] AN Aff. Etr., B^{III} 324 ff.7, 23.

partly because this might be impractical, and partly because France itself was not setting a good example. Such at least was the view of the minister of war, Chamillart, who told Amelot in December 1705 that if the Spaniards really pressed for an 'open ports' policy, it would not be too unreasonable to grant it to them; but in such a case 'you must try to limit this permission only to Dutch ships, excluding the English, *whom we have never received* in France during the present war'.[38] When, however, a concrete proposal was made in 1706 to allow trade with the enemy because of the glut of produce in Spain, Amelot would have none of it:

> The most destructive and sensible way of making war on the Dutch and English is to interrupt their trade. . . . In order to establish the reciprocal trade [with the enemy] that has been suggested, it is necessary for the advantages to balance the need. Spain has metals and fruits of her own; silk, woollen and linen textiles can be obtained in France; and what else may be lacking is not absolutely necessary. Spain therefore has no need of help from the English and Dutch.[39]

Great as the ambassador's authority was, he seems not to have opposed a decree issued on 19 February 1707 in favour of trade with the enemy. On the same day that the decree was issued, the duke of Gramont wrote an alarmed letter from Madrid to Chamillart:

> I enclose the copy of a decree that the king of Spain has just issued, from which you will see that not only does it allow English and Dutch ships into the ports of Biscay with certain kinds of merchandise, but it even enables them to transport all sorts of contraband goods on paying a duty of 7 per cent of the value. I can hardly believe that the decree has been issued with the consent of M Amelot, who would have doubtless seen that this new introduction of foreign goods is going to halt completely the trade that the French do in Spain. . . . Spaniards, accustomed to prefer foreign goods to ours, will resume their old tastes without any difficulty.[40]

This letter is typical of the excessive alarm shown by the French authorities whenever even minor threats to their trade arose. The fact was that the decree was a particular one, applicable only to one case, and was not intended as a general relaxation of the

---

[38] Chamillart to Amelot, 13 Dec. 1705, AE Corr. Pol. (Esp.), 154 f.280.
[39] *Ibid.*, 155 ff.234–5.
[40] *Ibid.*, 172 f.98.

ban on trade with the enemy. The reference to Amelot is signifi-cant. No decree of this sort could have been issued without his connivance, particularly since naval licences issued by Philip were valid only if countersigned by the French ambassador. Amelot appears to have consented to allow entry to enemy traders only in cases of emergency. In December 1708, for ex-ample, four Dutch ships were commissioned to bring grain from northern Europe to a starving Andalucia;[41] and on 24 October 1709 a royal decree opened the ports of Spain to all ships, whether neutral or enemy, that could bring grain into the country. The latter decree tried to encourage merchants to bring grain by allowing the provisional entry of all prohibited goods save English and Dutch silks and woollens.

The Franco-Spanish effort to limit, control or prohibit trade with the enemy could hardly have been other than a failure. With half the peninsula under Allied control, and with enemy fleets off the coast, no adequate measures could be taken to stop the trade. Pontchartrain at least had no illusions about this. He observed in 1711 that:

despite the war, the prohibitions against the enemy doing any trade with Spain, and the decrees issued by His Catholic Majesty during the present war, enemy ships daily introduce all kinds of manufactures, spices and other forbidden merchandise traded or produced by the enemy, who possess in the principal towns of Spain, and above all in Cadiz and Bilbao, a great number of houses and shops occupied by traders of their nation acting as their agents.[42]

It is true that the official trade figures, of England for instance, reflect an almost total cessation of commercial exchange;[43] and that Pontchartrain was unquestionably exaggerating; but the activities of unofficial traders and of pirates, who fall outside the scope of the present study, leave little doubt that trade with the English and Dutch was at no time completely suspended.[44]

Unsuccessful in the attempt to control Spanish commerce, the French authorities tried their hand at the regulation of industry

[41] Amelot to Pontchartrain, 2 Dec. 1708, AN Aff. Etr., B¹ 771.
[42] Memoir of 12 Aug. 1711. AE Corr. Pol. (Esp.), 208 f.175.
[43] See the graph in Jean McLachlan, *Trade and Peace with Old Spain*.
[44] Cf. for example the French consul at Cadiz, Mirasol, writing to Pontchartrain, 10 Apr. 1712, AN Aff. Etr., B¹ 219 f.130: 'Il est entré en cette Baye la semaine passée deux v^aux anglois avec passeports du Roy d'Espagne, l'un venant d'Ostende entierement chargé des marchandisses de Flandres, et l'autre de Douvres chargé des marchandises d'Angleterre. On admettra l'un et l'autre en payant le droit ordinaire.'

within the country. Their policy falls into two categories: firstly, attempts at monopoly and exclusion; secondly, attempts at suppression.

The first category concerns French attempts to corner the peninsular market. This would have been a natural wish of French merchants anxious to expand their exports to Spain. Spanish officials, however, showed a strong reluctance to depart from established practice, and as a result only limited success was achieved in this category. The citation of one or two commodities as examples will illustrate the position. France used to reexport to Spain a considerable amount of cocoa brought from the French Indies, in contravention of the rule that traffic with the Indies could be carried on directly only from Spain. In 1702 these imports were prohibited, to the consternation of the council of commerce in France.[45] In 1705 a new crisis arose over this question, and it became clear that a great deal of cocoa was being introduced into Spain through Nantes, Bordeaux, La Rochelle and Bayonne, with the active cooperation of the authorities in Biscay;[46] not to mention the amount being carried directly from the Indies to Cadiz in French ships. The Spanish authorities promptly took action. On 26 August 1705 the council of war issued a *consulta* saying that the American trade was a government monopoly, and that no foreign nation had any right to participate in the carrying trade.[47] It was in the light of this principle, said the council, that they had forbidden the Basque officials in February 1705 to import cocoa from France; and it was by the same principle that they now forbade the unloading of three French ships in Cadiz which had arrived with cocoa and sugar from Santo Domingo.

The French were also interested in promoting the sales of other produce. In December 1706, for example, Pontchartrain complained to Amelot that there were reports of Brazilian sugar and tobacco circulating in Andalucia. To trade in Portuguese sugar, he pointed out, was to finance the enemy to the extent of four or five million livres a year.[48] French policy, he emphasised to the ambassador, should be 'to increase the demand for sugar from the French colonies, and accustom the Spanish to it, so that at the

[45] Procès-verbal of 7 Sept. 1702, in Bonnassieux, *Conseil de Commerce*, p. 10.
[46] Mémoire des Députés du Commerce, AE Corr. Pol. (Esp.), 154 f.444.
[47] AN Aff. Etr., B^{III} 324 f.5.
[48] AE Corr. Pol. (Esp.), 156 f.327.

peace a part of this commerce should remain to us'.[49] For 'sugar' one can read any other commodity. The highly privileged position enjoyed by France opened great possibilities to French manu-facturers, and this was nowhere more true than in the example of textiles. The peninsula had always been a market for French cloth; whether the war caused any appreciable improvement in French exports to Spain is something that awaits quantitative assessment. All the indications are that the war indeed saw the creation of a large new market for French textiles. This would have been true not merely in the case of military uniforms, which we have touched on already, but also in the case of court fashions. The Spanish ruff, or *golilla,* went out of fashion with the new dynasty, which looked on it as a reactionary, expensive and un-comfortable form of dress. By 1706 Amelot was reporting that the leading councillors and household officials of the king had ceased to wear the *golilla*[50]; after the battle of Almansa in 1707, according to the same source, nearly everyone had stopped wearing it, 'which will produce here a very considerable demand for French cloth and fabrics'.[51] The subsequent adoption of French forms of dress by the Spanish nobility had important results for French manufacturers, since native cloth production did not approach the required quality for some considerable time. By 1709 it was estimated that the abolition of the *golilla* benefited the factories of Lyon to the extent of four million livres a year.[52]

The pattern of trade between France and Spain was not altered by the war. France continued, as before, to extract basic materials and to send in manufactures. The balance of trade in manufactures being unfavourable to Spain, the difference was usually made up with bullion. Of the basic materials extracted from the peninsula the most important was wool, which had figured as the principal item in English, French, Flemish, Hanseatic and Dutch trade.[53] The outbreak of war gave the French an opportunity to dominate the wool trade. A memoir drawn up in Madrid in June 1702, apparently under French influence, proposed the foundation of a

---

[49] Pontchartrain to Amelot, 19 Jan. 1707, *ibid.,* 172 f.15.
[50] Amelot to Louis XIV, 29 Nov. 1706, *ibid.,* 162 f.91.
[51] *Ibid.,* 30 May 1707, *ibid.,* 168 f.142.
[52] 'Projet général pour l'année', Jan. 1709, AE Corr. Pol. supplément (Esp.), 11 f.215.
[53] Jean McLachlan, *Trade and Peace with Old Spain,* pp. 8–9.

Franco-Spanish company to direct and control the wool trade.[54] The proposal was discussed at a meeting of the council of commerce in France on 11 August 1702.[55] There was in fact little alternative to French control, since trade with England and Holland had virtually ceased, and the Mesta, the official wool corporation, was in severe financial difficulties. But the Spaniards were foreseeably hostile to the plan, and at least one French adviser, Jean Orry, thought that the scheme was ill-considered and 'benefits neither Spain nor France'.[56] The plan was followed by another one in 1703, this time to form a purely French company. Negotiations on the Spanish side were led by Orry, who proposed that the company should pay sixty reales of vellon for every twenty-five pounds of finest wool, but the French merchants refused to pay more than forty-eight reales, and the scheme fell through.[57] The export of wool continued to be an important subject for negotiation even after these failures, since Spain urgently needed to market its produce. The councils of state and of Castile continued to discuss the subject throughout 1705. In January 1705 the duc de Gramont made it clear to the Spanish government that France opposed the export of wool in enemy ships, and obediently Philip v on 20 January issued a decree banning the entry of enemy ships into Spanish ports, and allowing wool exports only in neutral ships or by an overland route. Since France controlled the only land route, it was in an excellent position to direct the wool trade between Spain and the United Provinces and northern Europe, where the principal markets lay.

On his arrival in Spain, Amelot seems to have wavered at first in his attitude to official French policy. In June 1705 we find him writing to Pontchartrain in concern at the fact that unsold wool was piling up: 'it is absolutely necessary for the king of Spain to issue passports to the English and Dutch to come and fetch wool, otherwise the flocks cannot be maintained'.[58] But only a few weeks after this his attitude had completely changed. Urgent

[54] AN Aff. Etr., B¹ 769.

[55] 'Mémoire sur la proposition de l'établissement d'une compagnie pour l'achat et le commerce de toutes les laines d'Espagne', in Bonnassieux, *Conseil de Commerce*, p. 10.

[56] Orry to Pontchartrain, 24 Aug. 1702, AN Aff. Etr., B¹ 769.

[57] 'Sur le fond du commerce entre la France et l'Espagne', 31 Dec. 1720, AE Mém. et Doc. (Esp.), 153 ff.136–41.

[58] 19 June 1705, AN Aff. Etr., B¹ 770.

discussions had been going on in the junta of commerce between a large number of Spanish representatives and two French representatives, Nicolas Mesnager and Ambrose Daubenton. A lengthy *consulta* issued by the junta on 14 July 1705[59] opposed the idea of direct trade with the enemy, a conclusion agreeable to the French. Taking his cue from this, Amelot came out firmly against the issue of licences to enemy ships, and stressed the great value of the overland route, in particular the generous concessions offered by France, which was willing to waive all exit duties on the wool when it left France on the way north, but required half the duty levied on the wool at Antwerp.[60] The complex and lengthy negotiations that ensued took up a great deal of administrative time, but ultimately resulted in failure for French expectations. The junta of commerce came to a final agreement in the third week of September 1705, overruling the two French participants,[61] and on 12 October a composite regulation was issued, defining the conditions of export for all goods.[62] The details of the regulation are worth summarising as a guide to Spanish trade policy during the war. All Spanish produce could be freely exported, but only on Spanish or neutral ships. The same ships could also import any goods, even enemy goods, save for 'drugs, spices, manufactures and other items of enemy produce, make or trade'. Both fine and low-quality wool could be exported even to the enemy, but only in Spanish or neutral ships, and only from the ports of Bilbao, Alicante and Seville. 'Every sack of washed fine or lamb's wool taken for England or Holland will pay a duty of 30 reales of vellon; 15 reales on thick washed wool, and $7\frac{1}{2}$ reales on unwashed wool'. The income from this was to go towards making up the loss on six thousand sacks of wool which were to be allowed into France every year at a reduced rate of duty; any wool exported by land over and above this figure was to pay the full duty of sixty reales on every sack of washed fine wool, and thirty reales on unwashed wool. The small amount of wool conceded to France represented nothing less than failure for the French negotiators.

59 In AN Aff. Etr., B[III] 324 f.50.

60 Amelot's memoir, dated 8 Aug. 1705, is in AN Aff. Etr., B[1] 770. An earlier memoir of his, dated 2 Aug. 1705, is in AE Corr. Pol. (Esp.), 154 f.419.

61 Amelot to Pontchartrain, 28 Sept. 1705, 'Les Srs. Mesnager et Daubenton n'ont pu s'opposer au torrent de la Jonte', AN Aff. Etr., B[1] 770.

62 AN Aff. Etr., B[1] 770.

The failure must, however, be set in perspective. Though France had failed to dominate the Spanish market, it had nevertheless begun to consolidate its position to such an extent that the reign of Philip v, and indeed the rest of the eighteenth century, saw an enormous expansion in trade between the two countries. From 1716 to 1750 the total volume of Franco-Spanish trade expanded from an index of under 50 in 1716 to one of over 140 in 1750.[63] This development is ironic. For all his attention to peninsular trade, Louis xiv's interests really lay elsewhere. As he informed Amelot explicitly in 1709, 'the main object of the present war is the Indies trade and the wealth it produces'.[64] Spain was to be of use, but only as a stepping-stone to the Indies. Yet, as we shall see, France reaped little profit from the Indies during this war, and all the most significant gains were made in the peninsula. In view of the many reversals suffered by their trade representatives, this is a tribute to the effectiveness of French control in the period.

The second category discussed above deals with French attempts to suppress industry in Spain. The issue does not arise in the case of industries that supplemented the war effort. French officials in Spain were very anxious that native sources of iron, gunpowder and other war materials should be developed and their production extended. Where the competitive factor, and hence the issue of suppression, arises is in the case of articles of commerce. This brings us back to the substance of Torcy's reply to the president of Castile. The premise underlying the French foreign minister's statement was that workers must not be allowed to contribute to the resurrection in Spain of industries which might disturb the balance of commerce between the two countries. The most important preventive step, then, was to control the volume of immigration into the peninsula. This problem, which troubled so many others, did not trouble Amelot excessively. He believed, as we have already seen, that the majority of emigrants from France soon returned to their own country, and that those who settled rarely contributed much to Spanish industries; writing in 1712, he saw no danger of an industrial revival in the peninsula.

---

[63] See the graph in J. Vicens Vives, *Historia Económica de España*, p. 499.
[64] Louis xiv to Amelot, 18 Feb. 1709, in Girardot, *Correspondance de Louis XIV*.

There was still, however, great reason for alarm, since substantial measures to promote industrial efficiency had been
undertaken by foreign advisers, chief among whom was Bergeyck.
This Belgian statesman's principal opponent at the Spanish court
was the French ambassador, Bonnac, who complained to Louis
XIV in 1711 that Bergeyck thought too much of himself. Louis
agreed fully, and replied that 'the comte de Bergeyck certainly
has the zeal and capacity necessary to a good minister, but he is a
bit too obsessed with his projects'.[65] The reason for this petulance
was, as we have already seen,[66] Louis' annoyance at Bergeyck's
opposition to the proposal that the Spanish Netherlands be given
to Bavaria at a peace settlement. But Louis' ministers were also
visibly concerned at the measures taken by Bergeyck to encourage
Flemish clothworkers to settle in Spain. As Bonnac reported in
September 1711:

The comte de Bergeyck has, among the plans he has formed to restore
the affairs of Spain, not forgotten that of augmenting manufactures. He
has had several clothworkers sent from Flanders. I hear that they have
arrived near Madrid and that he wishes to set them up a few leagues
from the city. He is sending some of them into other parts of the kingdom, where some manufactures still remain. I shall be on the look-
out for further information, since these establishments can have a
prejudicial effect on the trade of France.[67]

According to another informant in Spain, the clothworkers were
fifty in number, 'all Flemish and nearly all from Brussels'.[68]
There is some doubt about the date at which they were brought
into Spain, and even about the number of workers involved.[69]
The workers were put under the direction of Don Joseph Aguado
Correa, who chose his own native town of Valdemoro as the
place to start a factory. A plan drawn up by Aguado and presented
to the junta of commerce on 31 December 1711, envisaged the
setting up of twelve looms in the first four years. The junta gave
its permission for the enterprise in a decree of 2 October 1712,

[65] Louis XIV to Bonnac, 18 Nov. 1711, AE Corr. Pol. (Esp.), 200 f.17.
[66] Above, p. 52.
[67] Bonnac to Louis XIV, 23 Sept. 1711, ibid., 209 f.134.
[68] Gibaudière to Voysin, 17 Nov. 1711, Guerre, A¹ 2332 f.217.
[69] Eugenio Larruga y Boneta, Memorias políticas y económicas sobre los frutos, comercio,
fábrica y minas de España (45 vols), Madrid, 1787–1850, vol. 9, p. 139, says that
'El Conde de Berguich, que conocía la importancia de establecer en Castilla manu-
facturas de paños finos, traxo a Madrid de Flandes en el año de 1710 veinte y siete
personas'.

from which date we can probably trace the commencement of the factory. The French were very hostile to the undertaking. A French report of 1715 painted Bergeyck and his factory in the blackest possible colours.[70] The Belgian, it was reported:

had views very favourable to Spain, and wished to establish the cloth factory at Valdemoro, which still exists, though feebly. Bergeyck wished all those employed there to enjoy all the possible advantages, saying that one must sow in order to reap, that the Catholic King must devote an unalienable and reliable fund to be applied without any distraction to the upkeep of this manufacture; that one must purchase the most skilful workers with their weight in gold, in order to found this establishment; that they must be employed with good treatment, and encouraged to look on Spain as their native land and educate their children there; that the Spaniards, stimulated to enjoy the status of these foreigners and to partake of their privileges, would apply themselves to what was necessary in order to obtain it. In brief, that it was time to awake out of the stupor in which they were, so that Spaniards would think of their own interests and the glory of the Catholic King.

As for Valdemoro, says the report, it was unprotected after Bergeyck's departure from Spain, so that of the workers 'most have deserted, eight or ten have joined the Walloon royal guard, no doubt in despair rather than from choice, and as a result the factory today lacks dyers, carders, spinners and founders, so that there is little chance that it will last much longer'. This account was written in hope rather than truthfully. In fact the Valdemoro factory never looked back: in 1726 the number of looms had risen to twenty-five, and in 1730 it had thirty-four working looms.[71]

Valdemoro was the first real step taken in the eighteenth century towards the revival of industry in Spain. French alarm was understandable, for textiles had always been the principal item exported to the peninsula.[72] Louis xiv naturally had no control over the immigration of Flemish workers, since these were not his subjects. But the attitude to French immigrants was uncompromising. The author of the above report on Valdemoro, Partyet, a deputy of the French council of commerce, insisted that there should be strict limitation on the entry of Frenchmen into

[70] Memoir by Partyet, 17 May 1715, A E Mém. et Doc. (Esp.), 32 f.69 ff.

[71] Larruga, *Memorias*, vol. 9, p. 164. For the later history of Valdemoro, see *ibid.*, vol 8.

[72] Albert Girard, *Le commerce français a Séville et Cadix*, pp. 338–71.

Spain. All must have passports, and should make a declaration of the reasons why they were going to Spain. Any textile workers who slipped through the net should be sent back to France by the local consul. The French ambassador must be given instructions to protect all French traders, but to refuse his protection to French working men.

When in March 1707 the French minister of war, Chamillart, discovered that a Frenchman in Córdoba was asking for Spanish permission to set up twelve looms to manufacture English-style cloth,[73] he wrote immediately to Amelot, ordering him to 'do everything possible to prevent this establishment taking place', and emphasising that his aim was 'to avoid the bad effect it could have on our manufactures'. Whatever the fate of the merchant from Córdoba, he was no doubt more fortunate than the sieur de la Pomeraie. The Pomeraie affair began when Spanish merchants interested in promoting glass manufactures in Spain persuaded Louis XIV to allow Jean Baptiste Pomeraie to come to Spain to help them. He went to Spain in the summer of 1713 and established a factory near Gerona. This aroused the authorities in Paris, who feared Spanish competition, despite the assurance of the French ambassador in Madrid, who saw no threat to a virtually non-existent commerce in glass.[74] Finally in 1714, after accusations that Pomeraie had conspired to make glassworkers emigrate to Spain, the French authorities put several people on trial in Paris and sentenced them: Pomeraie's wife and son were, in his absence, imprisoned in the Bastille.[75] The Spanish merchants in retaliation threatened to stop the dispatch of basic materials for glass manufacture if Madame Pomeraie were not freed.[76] There is no indication of the later history of the affair, though it is certain that Pomeraie's work was after all of no avail, for the

[73] 'Douze mestiers pour fabriquer des Bayettes, Sempiternes, et Escarlatilles façon d'Angleterre, en luy accordant l'exemption de la moitié des droits ordinaires sur ces sortes d'etoffes pendant dix années', Chamillart to Amelot, 9 Mar. 1707, A E Corr. Pol. (Esp.), 172 f.114.

[74] Bonnac to Pontchartrain, 31 July 1713, A N Aff. Etr., B¹ 776: 'Je pourrois vous asseurer que l'Espagne n'a pas tiré de France pour mil pistolles de glaces, soit que les Espagnols qui sont acoutumés a celles de Venise ne se soucient pas de celles de France; soit que le transport en soit plus difficile, n'ayant que le seul port d'Alicante ou on les puisse faire venir a Madrid par charrois.'

[75] D'Argenson to Controller-General, July-Oct. 1714, in Boislisle, *Correspondance des Contrôleurs Generaux*, vol. 3, p. 546, no. 1683.

[76] A E Corr. Pol. (Esp.), 239 f.107.

glass factory he established very soon ceased to function.[77] The incident illustrates the extreme precautions taken by France to protect its export markets.

The dark side of this preventionist policy is exposed when we realise that advisers who had the principal voice in the government of Spain (that is, the ambassadors and representatives of the French crown) devoted their efforts to isolating and crushing any efforts from outside to revive industry; so that if Spain benefited at all from the immigration of Frenchmen in this period it was *despite* the methods of those in power. There were, of course, limits to the suppressive policy of France. Only up to 1709 did Louis xiv have a direct voice, through his ambassador, in the formation of policy. After that date, the disengagement practised by France meant that the ambassadors played no part in the government of Spain, and though French influence continued to preponderate advisers in Madrid were able to shape policies more beneficial to the country's interests. Bergeyck stands out as the first non-French minister of the new dynasty to be actively concerned in promoting the recovery of Spain, as distinct from serving the ends of French commercial policy. The ministers of France in Spain must not on the other hand be judged too harshly. While some of them were undeniably concerned only with the interests of Versailles, others – notably Amelot and Orry – were genuinely preoccupied with the well-being of the country which fortune had engaged them to serve, and on whose behalf they laboured so briefly and yet so brilliantly.

[77] A decree of 13 Jan. 1720 states: 'No habiendo tenido efecto la fábrica de cristales de que se encargó Don Tomás del Burgo y compañía, desde al año de 1712 que le concedí el privilegio; ni establecidose tampoco la que emprendió Don Juan Bautista Pomeraye, en virtud del privilegio que le di cerca de dos años ha . . .', in Larruga, *Memorias*, vol. 10, p. 54. Subsequently, however, success was achieved by Juan de Goyeneche. We learn from Bernardo de Ulloa, *Restablecimiento de las Fábricas y Comercio español* (2 vols), Madrid, 1740, vol. 1, p.221, of 'la Fábrica de Cristales que emprendió Don Juan de Goyeneche, y la consiguió con toda perfección; sin embargo de los exemplares de no averla podido conseguir Don Thomás del Burgo y Compañía, ni Don Juan Bautista Pomeraye; y la grande utilidad de que se conserve'.

7 The Pursuit of Commercial Privileges

It has been convincingly argued that the War of the Spanish Succession can be best explained in naval terms.[1] The planning of campaigns, the movement of commerce, depended directly on the outlay of naval power; the transport route through the western Mediterranean and the trade route across the Atlantic were both at the mercy of naval resources on either side. Spain, however, lacked these resources completely. As we have noted in a previous chapter, the Spanish naval forces were inadequate either to protect the peninsula or to safeguard the *carrera de Indias*. The art of shipbuilding had certainly not been forgotten, in spite of statements to the contrary by many contemporaries. But sheer inefficiency and incompetence had meant that contracts for ships were seldom fulfilled, if at all.[2] Not until after 1710 were any serious steps taken towards rebuilding the naval power and merchant marine of Spain, and this meant that for the greater part of the war the country had to depend on French protection. Nominal recognition of this came on 18 May 1702, when the comte de Toulouse, head of France's navy, was appointed by Philip to be head of the virtually non-existent Spanish navy. Thereafter it was French power that patrolled the coasts of Spain, guarded the routes of the galleons from America, and helped to reduce the rebel city of Barcelona.

Spain could hardly fail to be grateful for this immense naval

---

[1] The point is illustrated in G. N. Clark, 'War Trade and Trade War, 1701–13', *Economic History Review*, I, ii (1928). See also J. S. Corbett, *England in the Mediterranean, 1603–1713* (2 vols), London, 1904.

[2] One case is documented in AGS, Contadurías Generales leg.189. A contract was made with a Basque firm in 1697 for eight ships, of an average 750 *toneladas* each. The original contractors then defaulted and passed the contract to another firm, which eventually floated one ship (984 *toneladas*) in 1701 and another (1233 *toneladas*) in 1703. As late as 1709 no further ships had been manufactured, officialdom misplaced the plans, and the cut wood was rotting.

aid, but the price of such dependence was heavy. The brief outline that follows in the next few pages cannot do justice to the
complexities and fascination of a subject which is thoroughly
documented in the French naval archives, and which forms a
unique chapter in Spanish history. Never before, nor indeed
again, was a foreign nation to enjoy so many privileges, legally
guaranteed, in peninsular and American waters.

The question of privateering rights is illustrative. Spain possessed several privateering craft along the coastline, particularly
in Biscay, where the natives were the most enterprising. France,
however, probably possessed more privateers than any nation in
Europe, and the government had a particular interest in seeing
that they worked unhindered, since they were even more effective
than the official naval forces in destroying and capturing enemy
ships. In view of the old rivalry between the two countries,
measures would have to be taken to control Franco-Spanish
rivalry over possible prizes, and even to prohibit naval clashes
between their nationals. The question of prizes was a particularly
delicate one, since although Spain had officially prohibited all
direct trade with the Allies, France still continued (notably after
1704, when the Dutch refused to renew the recently expired
Anglo-Dutch agreement banning trade to France) to trade with
the United Provinces. Spanish privateers found that they would
consequently have to discriminate between enemy ships trading
to France and those *not* trading to France. They had their instructions in this matter from a decree of 18 March 1705, by which
Philip v forbade them to capture enemy ships licensed to carry
goods for France; this decree was reaffirmed on 8 April.[3] But, as
Pontchartrain observed at a later date, this decree 'was only on
condition that French ships of war should similarly respect
enemy ships bearing passports from the king of Spain', a condition
which tended 'to destroy French privateering entirely'.[4] Louis
xiv wrote to Amelot demanding the repeal of the decree. Obediently, Philip on 16 August 1705 issued a decree, addressed in
particular to the Basque privateers, allowing the Spaniards to
capture licensed enemy ships provided this was done in the open
sea and not in ports or rivers. Chamillart and Louis for their

[3] AN Aff. Etr., B^{III} 324 f.55.
[4] Pontchartrain to Champigny, intendant of Havre, 16 Sept. 1709, AN Aff. Etr.,
B^{III} 361.

part were satisfied that this would secure adequate safety for the Dutch ships which traded regularly to Bordeaux.

The Dutch trade[5] was of particular importance to France, since only Dutch carriers could relieve the country of produce destined for the north European market. It was quickly realised, however, that even the reaches of the Gironde did not guarantee the safety of Dutch ships from Spanish privateers; and as a result new orders went out to the ambassador in Spain. A letter of Amelot's dated 4 October outlines developments up to that date:

M Chamillart having informed me in several letters that the king wished me to secure a decree from the king of Spain on the subject of privateers, I obtained this decree on 16 August last. But since it was observed that the execution of this would be prejudicial to the traders of Bordeaux, and that the Dutch who had been given French passports would not come to take our wines and our brandies, I received an order from H.M. through the same channel, instructing me to ask for the suspension of the 16 August decree for three months. I have carried out this order, and have sent the new decree to M Chamillart.[6]

The Spanish decree suspending that of 16 August was issued on 3 October. On the fourteenth of that month Louis reciprocated by banning French privateers from attacking enemy ships licensed by Spain.[7] The Spanish suspension was renewed on 20 December, and was extended for six months up to 15 May 1706. Thereafter it was renewed every six months for the duration of the war. No clearer example could be given of the subordination of Spanish legislation to French wishes. There is no reason to believe that the French were reciprocating the Spanish measure. On the contrary, in France the ban was interpreted to apply implicitly to Dutch ships only, and in 1708 and 1709 we find Amelot complaining that English ships licensed to carry grain to the ports of Spain were being attacked. The blame cannot be placed solely on the French government, which was making painstaking efforts to control the illegal activities of its privateers. The fact remains that, inhibited by the French-influenced legislation of their own government, and overwhelmed by the superior power

[5] This is discussed in J. S. Bromley, 'Le commerce de la France de l'Ouest et la guerre maritime (1702–1712)', *Annales du Midi,* lxv (1953). French passports issued to Dutch ships are detailed on p. 66 of the article.

[6] Amelot to Torcy, 4 Oct. 1705, AE Corr. Pol. (Esp.), 148 f.226.

[7] *Ibid.,* supplément 10 f.282.

of their ally's corsairs, Spanish privateers were labouring under a considerable disadvantage. In the winter of 1708–9 Amelot was obliged to protest vigorously to his own government against the uncontrolled marauding of French privateers in the Canaries and on the Basque coast.[8] On one occasion the privateers seized a ship and took it to Brest despite the fact that it was licensed by Philip v. Aware of its own crumbling authority over the privateers, the French government tried to stem the tide by issuing several prohibitory orders: in February 1709, for instance, Louis ordered all French vessels to respect Basque ships carrying passports countersigned by Philip and Amelot.[9] But it is doubtful if these measures were ever effective. The whole question served only to reveal the inferiority of Spanish naval power, and the readiness of Madrid to tailor its legislation to suit France.

French naval initiative was even more marked in the Atlantic trades. Louis xiv's principal objective was to gain entry into, or control of, the commerce of America, and France's superior position in the alliance of the two crowns brought the attainment of this objective at last within reach. French interloping in America was by now a phenomenon of long standing. Could more than illegal profits be obtained from the new king of Spain? The French offered their military protection, and it was because of this that the Spaniards were initially inclined to be generous to their allies. America was after all too rich a prize to be allowed to fall into English or Dutch hands.[10]

From the very beginning, in 1701, Spain allowed French expeditions into America in order to combat Allied marauders. A royal decree of 11 January 1701 addressed to the governor of Cartagena in the Indies, informed him of 'the friendship and unity of this crown with that of France, and that in consequence of this alliance and these close ties I have resolved to allow entry into the ports of the Indies to French vessels'.[11] The ships were only allowed to buy stores and other necessary material, and trading was firmly prohibited. Subsequent decrees renewed this privilege: in 1705 Philip v reported that

[8] Amelot to Pontchartrain, 10 Dec. 1708 and 11 Feb. 1709, AN Aff. Etr., B¹ 771.
[9] *Ibid.*, 4 Mar. 1709, AN Aff. Etr., B¹ 771.
[10] Thus the French carried arms to America: see the 'Mémoire des armes et munitions portées à la Vera Cruz par un batiment de l'escadre de M. de Coetlogon', AE Corr. Pol. (Esp.), 105 f.318.
[11] AN Aff. Etr., Bᴵᴵᴵ 323 f.51.

by decrees of 31 May 1702, 20 January 1703 and 10 February 1703, I ordered that the commanders of warships of the Most Christian King which go to America to frustrate the designs of the English and the Dutch, should be received in the ports of my domains, and should be allowed to take on board goods to the value of only 1500 to 2000 livres in French money, to be employed as refreshment, and that if any of my subjects traded goods of higher value they would be punished.[12]

These concessions appear to be mild and reasonable only, but in fact they were of unprecedented generosity. Never before had the warships of a foreign nation been allowed unrestricted entry into American ports, and Spaniards could well feel that they were playing their part in the alliance of the two crowns.

The French were duly grateful. The official permission they now received served as an excellent cover for the extension of an interloping trade that had been flourishing for several years. Complaints began to pour in from officials in America that French vessels were trading under the protection of the decrees mentioned above. Blame cannot be attached exclusively to the French. The breakdown of the annual fleet system resulted in a severe shortage of many commodities in America, and local traders, often aided openly by officials, were only too glad to buy the necessary produce from French (or English or Dutch) ships if there were no Spanish ships to supply them.[13] The alarming increase in French interloping, however, justified the protests sent to Philip v from both sides of the Atlantic. In 1702 and 1703 the council of the Indies presented *consultas* of protest to the king.[14] The authorities in Vera Cruz reported in January 1703 that French ships were trading illicitly to New Spain, and the viceroy in November 1704 added his own confirmation.[15] The result of

---

[12] 'Decret du Roy d'Espagne touchant la visite des vaisseaux de Guerre et des navires françois qui entreront dans les ports de l'Amérique Espagnole, 3 juin 1705', AN Aff. Etr., B[III] 361.

[13] French interloping in the Indies has been excellently, though not exhaustively, studied by E. W. Dahlgren, *Les relations commerciales et maritimes entre la France et les côtes de l'Océan Pacifique. Vol. I Le commerce de la Mer du Sud jusqu'à la paix d'Utrecht,* Paris, 1909. A second volume by Dahlgren, covering the rest of the reign of Philip v, exists in manuscript form at the University of Rennes. My account of French interloping here is meant to supplement Dahlgren's account, to which reference should also be made.

[14] *Consulta* of 27 Sept. 1702, AN Aff. Etr., B[III] 323 f.69. Memoir of 26 Jan. 1703, in Dahlgren, p. 249.

[15] 'Decret du Roy d'Espagne, 3 juin 1705', AN Aff. Etr., B[III] 361.

these protests was Philip's decree of 3 June 1705 reinforcing the rules which stipulated confiscation of the goods of all those engaged in illicit trading. As with other legislation on this subject, the decree remained a dead letter. Spain had no adequate naval power in the Indies capable of stopping interlopers, and the French therefore had a free hand.[16] The coast adjoining the Pacific was particularly favoured by foreign traders, since it was completely defenceless, and extremely short of many commodities. 'The Armada of the South (Sea)', wrote viceroy Castelldosrius in August 1707 to Philip v, 'consists at present of only three vessels, the *capitana,* the *almiranta* and its cutter, and the galleon *Ave Maria.*'[17] The marquis had just taken over the viceroyalty of Peru on the death of its previous holder, the conde de la Monclova. He was shocked to discover the condition of trade in his province:

> They say that for the last ten years this realm has lacked any trade in clothes and goods brought by the galleons,[18] for it is as many years since the last fair was held in Portobelo. The frequency of French ships in these seas has been and is extremely well received by those who have had and still have their capital lying idle with nothing to do; and from this results the ease in defrauding, the non-observance of laws, orders and prohibitions, the contempt of danger and the ruin of all.[19]

To set the background to the debate over interloping, it is as well to examine in detail some data on French ships in the Indies. In May 1707 the Spanish merchants at Seville estimated that since the beginning of the war thirty French ships had traded to the ports of Campeche and Vera Cruz, and over eighty-six to the ports of Tierra Firme, while fifteen French vessels could be detected in Pacific waters at the end of 1706.[20] These figures, as we shall see, are not exaggerated. In 1701 only one French ship, the *Marin,* is recorded as having called in at Vera Cruz in Mexico. But in Cartagena a squadron under Belleisle called in during

[16] There are useful discussions of interloping in the articles by Henri Sée, 'Esquisse de l'Histoire du commerce français à Cadix et dans l'Amérique espagnole au XVIIIᵉ siècle', *Revue d'Histoire Moderne*, 13 (1928); and by Henri Sée and Léon Vignols, 'La fin du commerce interlope dans l'Amérique espagnole', and Léon Vignols, 'L'ancien concept monopole et la contrebande universelle', both in *Revue d'Histoire Economique et Sociale* (1925).

[17] The terms *capitana* and *almiranta* are explained in the next chapter.

[18] The last fleet for Tierra Firme to sail from Spain was in 1695.

[19] Castelldosrius to Philip v, Lima 31 Aug. 1707, AGI, Indiferente leg.2720.

[20] Dahlgren, p. 484; Consulado of Seville to Grimaldo, 10 May 1707, AHN, Estado leg.319.

August and unloaded the following goods:[21] 147 bales of Brittany,
Rouen and other linens; 9 large lined cases; 2 barrels of hats;
29 cases of ham; 13 heavy crates; 12 large barrels of tools and
other objects; 12 barrels of wine; 6 cases of worked wax; 81
barrels of liquor; 2 barrels of towels and other goods; one of
guns and pistols; 2 of pepper; 8 pipes of wine; and 471 barrels of
flour. Enumeration of these items will serve to illustrate the sort
of goods easily sold and readily bought on the coasts of the Caribbean and the Pacific. The profits from such trade were immense.
The Seville merchants in 1707 claimed that one French ship
trading to Mexico in May 1706 had returned to France with
three million pesos on board. In 1702, the first year of the war,
anger over interloping was so great as to move the council of the
Indies to issue a number of *consultas* on the subject, one of which,
dated 23 August, complained of:

the great disorder and liberty with which the French continue their
trade of introducing considerable amounts of clothing throughout
America, and especially in the ports of Vera Cruz, Santa Martha,
Cartagena and Portobelo. . . . In May this year there arrived at Saint
Malo a ship that had sailed from the same port for America, laden with
merchandise which it sold in Portobelo, and brought back 108,000
pesos in silver, not to mention an unassessed amount of gold. At the
beginning of July another ship arrived at the same port, from which it
had likewise sailed with a cargo of merchandise, and after trading in
Caracas, Santa Martha and Portobelo it touched on the north coast of
Santo Domingo and from there continued to France, bringing more
than 100,000 pesos in silver, and other produce. . . . Trustworthy
people in Havana have written this May to say that the French there
were buying and dealing in almost all the sugar in the city and island,
in order to carry away in their ships.'[22]

In the years after this, French activities grew even greater. The
trade carried on by individuals from the French possessions in the
Caribbean was supplemented by the expeditions made by various
French companies such as the China Company, the South Sea
Company, and the East India Company.[23] The China Company's
ships seem to have given most trouble to the viceroy of Peru, who
in October and November 1704 reported to Philip v the presence

[21] 'Relacion de las ordenes dadas a los Minros y Govres de los Puertos de Indias',
AGI, Indiferente leg.2716.
[22] AGI, Indiferente leg.2716.
[23] All these are discussed in Dahlgren.

in the ports of Callao and Concepción of eight French vessels.[24] In the course of the following year, 1705, a total of ten French ships called in at Vera Cruz, according to the viceroy of New Spain.[25] In 1706 there was a still larger French presence in both the Caribbean and the South Sea. Nine ships are recorded as having called at Vera Cruz. In addition there were two ships which came in from Havana during the month of June: the larger of these 'came under the pretext of bringing Negroes, since it held the asiento, but it brought no more than fifty or sixty, and a great deal of clothing'. Later in July the same year two more vessels called in from Campeche.[26] In Peru, meanwhile, the majority of ships calling in seem to have come from Saint-Malo.[27]

One of the peak years for French interloping in South America was 1707. The authorities at Vera Cruz recorded twenty-one French vessels as having called at the port,[28] without including in this number those French ships accompanying the naval

[24] Five of these eight were the *Saint-Esprit, Saint-Joseph, Baron de Breteuil, Saint-Charles* and *Murinet*, all discussed in Dahlgren, pp. 293, 306. See also letters of Conde de la Monclova to Philip V, 8 Oct. and 7 Nov. 1704, AGI, Indiferente leg.2720. The *Saint-Charles, Murinet* and another ship were estimated to have brought back nearly 1,900,000 pesos in gold and silver to France: Dahlgren, p. 314 fn. 4. In his *Voyages français à destination de la Mer du Sud avant Bougainville (1695–1749)*, Paris, 1907, Dahlgren attempted to list French vessels trading to the Pacific. His necessarily incomplete figures for departures from France are less valuable than the details given of each ship's movements.

[25] Viceroy of New Spain to Philip V, 28 Feb. 1706. AGI, Indiferente leg.2751. The ten ships were the *Intrépide*, of Martinique; the *Faucon*, owned by the Guinea Company; the frigate *Sirène* and the brigantine *Société*, both of Martinique; the *Subtil*, of Brest; the corvette *Saint-Jean* and the frigate *Patriarche*, which had sailed from Rochefort; the frigate *Mercure*, of Marseilles; the *Paix*, of Brest; and the *Précieuse*.

[26] 'Razon de los navios franceses que an entrado en el Puerto de la Veracruz desde el año de 1701', dated 10 May 1707, AGI, Indiferente leg.2751. The nine ships calling at Vera Cruz were the *Americain, Sirène, Mercure, Duc-de-la-Force, Fort, La Motina* (this may be a Spanish version of the name), *Saint-Jean, Rose Marie* and *Anne*.

[27] In May the *Beauvais, Capricieuse, Savant* and *Saint-François* called in at the port of Arica; the *Galère d'Or* arrived at the same port in August, and the *Brilhac, Confiance* and *Danycan* in November: see Dahlgren, pp. 317, 359, 363, 365, 371.

[28] The twenty-one were the *Triomphant*, of La Rochelle; *Franche-Comté-de-Lorraine*, of Saint-Malo; *Licence*, of Nantes; *Vengamin* (thus in Spanish), of Nantes; *Marquis-du-Roy*, of Brest; *Chico San Pablo* (perhaps *Petit Saint Paul*), of Nantes; *Saint-Malo*, of Saint-Malo; *Saint-Jean-Baptiste*, of Saint-Malo; the frigate *Marie-Angélique*, of Brest; the frigate *Vengeur*, of La Rochelle; *Duc-de-la-Force*; *Gaspar*, of Saint-Malo; *Saint-Jean-Baptiste*, of Marseilles; *La Motina; Comte-de-la-Bedoyère*, of Rochefort; *Isabelle*, from Martinique; *Venture*, from Mobile; *Sirène; Volante*, from Santo Domingo; the frigate *Comte-de-Toulouse*, from Nantes; and the *Marie Galère*, of Marseilles. All these names come from AGI, Indiferente leg.2751.

squadron under Ducasse, whom we shall encounter in the next chapter. This number may very well be incomplete, since it includes only ships officially boarded by American customs officials in the ports of Mexico. In Peru the viceroy was also having trouble with French contraband ships which claimed that they had been licensed to sail to China and to make discoveries. At least eighteen French vessels were in the South Sea in the course of the year.[29]

The details for these few years have been given merely to illustrate the extent of French participation in the commerce of South America. It is clear that the allies of Spain were profiting quite openly from the decay of Hispano-American trade and the absence of adequate naval power in the Indies. The result was that when in 1706, for the first time in over ten years, a Spanish fleet brought merchandise from the mother country to be traded in the fair at Portobelo in America, it was found that there was no demand for the goods, so thoroughly had the French done their job of glutting the market with contraband. A committee of the Consulado of Lima reported to this effect in September 1706, saying that:

in the ports along the coast markets are being held for which the French supply the goods, and the kingdom is thereby provisioned, so that the holding of the fair at Portobelo will be more of a hindrance than a service, seeing that in Chile they do not need the clothing that was transported from here when the armada came, because they already have more than enough and at very moderate prices.[30]

The introduction of contraband was clearly ruinous to the monopoly theoretically exercised by the traders of Seville. This should not lead us to view it as essentially disadvantageous to the economic life of Spanish America. On the contrary, we may consider it a healthy corrective to the evils both of the monopoly system and of its collapse. Contraband supplied America with essential goods, kept prices down, introduced new items of non-Spanish manufacture, and stimulated commerce which would otherwise have decayed. These and other advantages to the Americans are not, however, our primary concern. More relevant to our purpose is the fact that, regardless of the laws and regu-

[29] See the ships listed in Dahlgren, *Voyages français*.

[30] Sergio Villalobos, 'Contrabando francés en el Pacífico 1700–1724', *Revista de Historia de América*, 51 (1962), p. 65. I owe this reference to Dr John Lynch.

lations of Spain, French officials were actively conniving in the commerce of the interlopers. Amelot summed up the situation in 1707:

On the accession of Philip v to the crown, the French saw the lack of action in the Spanish court, and wished to have their share in the profits from this rich trade. They made military preparations, and carried their goods to Peru by the South Sea, with immense gain. The use of this route, which had till then been regarded as sacred, and forbidden even to the Spanish, caused a great outcry in this country even before I had come to Spain. On our side we replied to complaints by saying that since the Spaniards were not themselves trading, it was more just that we should profit from it, rather than our common enemies who were employing the riches of the Indies to make war on us.[31]

It is true that the English and Dutch were at this time particularly active in the Caribbean, but there is no doubt that the French were the principal participants in the interloping trade in South America.[32] The authorities in France made few serious efforts to stop the activities of their nationals who made privateering voyages to the Pacific;[33] indeed, they stood to gain by an extension of interloping, because of the very considerable profit extracted by way of a duty on imports of bullion. Pontchartrain expressed his opposition to the illicit trade fairly firmly, and others in France and Spain, including Amelot, were of the same mind, but the position of the French government became clear when in August 1705 Louis xiv granted eight passports to merchants of Saint-Malo to trade in the South Sea.[34] This was nothing less than a green light to all interlopers. Appearances were of course preserved. Chamillart informed the minister of marine that 'since the king does not wish to give any public title or personal authorisation to their enterprise, it is necessary for the passports to state some other purpose, such as going to our American islands, or going on exploration, or some other pretext'.[35] At the same time

---

[31] Amelot to Torcy, 21 Nov. 1707, AE Corr. Pol. (Esp.), 171 f.69.

[32] In addition to Dahlgren, see N. M. Crouse, *The French Struggle for the West Indies 1665–1713*, London, 1943 (repr. 1966).

[33] Thus the 'Memoire sur ce qui regarde trois vaisseaux de Saint-Malo qui ont été faire commerce dans la Mer du Sud et qui sont partis au mois d'aoust 1703', AE Corr. Pol. (Esp.), 147 f.261, justifies the expedition by saying, 'Il n'y avoit encor en ce temps aucune deffense publique ni particuliere d'envoyer des vaisseaux dans la Mer du Sud'. For the expedition, see Dahlgren, pp. 293-306.

[34] Torcy to Amelot, 14 Dec. 1705, AE Corr. Pol. (Esp.), 155 f.177.

[35] Chamillart to Pontchartrain, 25 Aug. 1705, cited in Dahlgren, p. 338.

F

he stoutly denied to Amelot that any permissions whatsoever had been given to go to America. 'You may assure the Spaniards,' he wrote in October to the ambassador, 'that the king has not given and will not give any permission to his subjects to go and trade in the American territories ruled by the king of Spain. All that have been issued are some permits given in the normal way for the French islands in America and for going on explorations'.[36] Such deception was so transparent that it is difficult to see whom the French government was trying to delude, and the only result was to increase the distrust felt in Madrid of all plans which the French might propose regarding the Indies. This distrust was shared also by French interests in Spain: the Company of the Asiento necessarily suffered from the competition offered by individual French traders and interlopers, and never became a profitable concern; while the French merchants in Cadiz objected strongly to interloping because it hurt their own trade from Cadiz.[37]

Even when the French offered naval assistance to the trading ships of Spain, the offer was looked upon, quite rightly, with unconcealed suspicion. In 1705, for instance, a Spanish pamphlet complained that the Indies trade had been:

taken away by the French, so that merchants have declared their unwillingness to send any goods to the Indies, because the French vessels which act as an escort themselves trade to the Indies.[38]

In 1705 Louis XIV offered to send a French escort to accompany the galleons sailing from Cadiz to the Indies: the offer was rejected outright by the consulado of Seville (the corporate body of merchants trading to America), the junta of commerce, and the council of the Indies.[39] A similar refusal was given in the same year when France offered to help expel English marauders from the coasts of Florida and Carolina.[40] The Spaniards quite stubbornly maintained that their own resources were sufficient. Pontchartrain, however, urged Amelot to press on the Spaniards the need to accept a French armed escort for their trading vessels,

[36] Chamillart to Amelot, 11 Oct. 1705, AE Corr. Pol. (Esp.), 154 f.2.
[37] G. Scelle, La Traite Négrière aux Indes de Castille (2 vols), Paris, 1906, vol. 2, p. 168.
[38] 'Memoire sur la perte de Barcelone', AE Corr. Pol. (Esp.), 154 f.385. The memoir also claimed that Saint-Malo had become a better mart than any in Spain.
[39] Amelot to Louis XIV, 8 Dec. 1705, AE Corr. Pol. (Esp.), 149 f.231.
[40] 3 Nov. 1705 consulta of the council of the Indies, AN Aff. Etr., B[III] 324 f.34.

adding in cipher that such an escort might secure the Indies if any trouble were to arise there.[41] This military preoccupation was a valid and sensible one, but not calculated to please the Spaniards. A year later Amelot was planning to arrange for the new governor of Havana to hand the city over to the French if war broke out in the Indies.[42] It is doubtful if such a negotiation actually succeeded, for the very idea of a French military presence would have been anathema to Spaniards.

Opposition to French help crumbled after the Allied occupation of Madrid in 1706. With the future of the monarchy threatened, Philip feared not only for his crown but for the Indies. A French frigate, the *Aurore,* was sent from Bayonne to warn the viceroy of Peru to prepare defences. This set sail in December 1706, under the command of Captain de la Rigaudière Froger, and reached Concepción in March 1707. Further French help was now employed on a large scale, primarily to escort the treasure fleet from Mexico to Spain. A squadron under Michel Chabert was to sail to Lima and bring back the treasure from Peru, while another under Admiral Ducasse was to go to Vera Cruz and sail back with the plate fleet.[43] For the first time, therefore, Spain confessed its complete reliance on France for protection of the treasure fleets, and the union between the two countries led to some degree of cooperation in regulation of the Atlantic crossings. As a result of this cooperation, the fleet arrivals in 1708, 1709 and 1712 were all accomplished under French escort. The mutual understanding achieved as a result of these successful efforts led to a proposal in 1706 to arm and send six French frigates to the Indies, with Spanish merchandise on board: the scheme was not a selfish one, and was accepted by the Spaniards. But though it was ultimately put into practice, the financial difficulties which emerged at the end turned the whole plan into a disastrous failure, and this first and last attempt at joint trading to the Indies embittered relations between the two countries long after the peace of Utrecht.[44]

[41] Pontchartrain to Amelot, 26 Nov. 1705, AE Corr. Pol. (Esp.), 154 f.219.

[42] *Ibid.,* 7 Nov. 1706, *ibid.,* 156 f.245.

[43] *Ibid.,* 25 July 1706, *ibid.,* 156 f.48. A full account of the voyages of the *Aurore* and of Chabert's two ships, is given in Dahlgren, pp. 401–72. Dahlgren gives no account of Ducasse's expedition containing seven warships and two frigates.

[44] A brief account of the plan, which is fully documented in the archives, is given in Dahlgren, pp. 353–7. The two French warships associated particularly with the plan were the *Apollon* and the *Triton.*

The decline of good relations was inevitable. Chabert's expedition, for example, brought back a small fortune from Peru, but almost none of it, as we shall see in the next chapter, reached the Spanish treasury. This incident would have taught the Spanish authorities not to trust any further offers of French help. Meanwhile, interloping had in no way stopped. France made no move to stop illicit trading until all possible advantages had been gained from its continuation. The official (but not openly professed) attitude is shown by a memoir on the American trade presented to Louis xiv in 1707, in which it was noted that recent traders from Saint-Malo had had to sell their goods at well under half price because of the glut of European goods illegally taken to America:

It is therefore certain that the South Sea trade will stop of itself, and that five or six years will pass before one can return there. On this principle there is no risk in banning commerce and sailings to the South Sea by a severe public ordinance of the king.[45]

In other words, prohibition was feasible only when there was nothing to prohibit. Amelot, like a few other French officials in Spain, was seriously concerned not only with the propriety of this attitude but also with its morality. His position was a peculiarly delicate one. He was chief minister of Spain, but he was also the ambassador of the king of France. How could he reconcile these duties if a conflict of interest arose? The truth was that he was first and foremost a servant of Louis xiv, so that he never allowed a conflict of loyalties to arise, and he always gave his allegiance to French policy. But his honesty and probity compelled him to speak out, even to the king of France, if he felt that the line of conduct being pursued was indefensible. His letter of 31 March 1708 to Louis xiv is a tribute to his unfailing integrity:[46]

The continuous reports which have come from Peru and New Spain, of the almost total ruin of commerce and of the rights of the Catholic King, through the abundance of European goods which French traders have taken to the Indies via the South Sea, and also the North, have more than ever aroused the Spanish. All who return from there, even the French, speak openly of the frightful disorder into which everything is fallen. Among the crippling duties I am charged with, I

45 AE Corr. Pol. (Esp.), 174 f.241. Cf. Dahlgren, p. 489.
46 Amelot to Louis xiv, 31 Mar. 1708, AE Corr. Pol. (Esp.), 179 f.187.

can assure Your Majesty that this is one of those which most pains me, knowing the justice of the complaints against us, and seeing that what should assure the greatness of the king of Spain and bring about a close union between the two nations, becomes absolutely useless to His Catholic Majesty.

In fine, Amelot says, the fault lies with:

the licence of our French merchants, who by their uncontrollable greed have found a means of bringing to ruin the richest commerce in the world.

Amelot consequently pressed continuously for a French ban on interloping, and in November 1708 he was assured by Pontchartrain that Louis was going to decree this soon, and that no more passports for trade in the Pacific were to be issued.[47] This did not happen: in January 1709 the ambassador was again complaining of interloping.[48] Obviously matters were being deliberately delayed, and Amelot was curious to know why. He had in fact already been informed of the reason in May 1708. Negotiations had been going on in Madrid between France and Spain over a scheme for a joint promotion of trade with the Indies. The deputy of the French council of commerce, Mesnager, took the lead in talks on the French side, and Versailles was waiting to see what would result. While these talks were going on, Amelot was sent a copy of the projected ordinance to ban interloping. The covering letter said:[49]

Basically, the main motive for sending M Amelot this project of the ordinance, is to allow him, under the pretext of negotiating changes or additions, to press for the conclusion of the tariff agreement on which Mesnager has been working under his orders. It is with this in view that we have not put into the project all that can be put.

The ambassador saw in this letter a complete betrayal of the good faith that France should observe in high policy. Of what use were all the promises to ban interloping if they were no more than a pretext to further the commercial aims of France? He thought back to the many occasions that he had himself concurred in

---

[47] Amelot to Pontchartrain, 12 Nov. 1708, AN Aff. Etr., B¹ 771.
[48] Ibid., 28 Jan. 1709, AN Aff. Etr., B¹ 771.
[49] Dahlgren, p. 504, cites this letter as Pontchartrain to Amelot, 13 May 1708. The copy I have seen is from Desmaretz to Amelot, 24 July 1709, AN Aff. Etr., B¹ 771.

interloping and had suppressed information that might have been embarrassing to his government; the occasion in April 1707, for instance, when he had prevailed on the secretary of the council of the Indies to suppress letters from Peru which had complained of French interlopers.[50] Was French policy always to be one of dishonesty? In October 1708 he made his position clear to Desmaretz, the minister of finance:[51]

With regard to the French being hurt to see that after all the immense efforts that they make daily in order to preserve the Spanish monarchy, the Spaniards now wish to take from them the small profit that they are able to make in the Indies from the sale of their goods: permit me to say, Monsieur, that nobody has worked more than I have to protect the trade of the French in the Indies, taking great care to soothe and even to stifle the protests that have been raised perpetually against this trade. What matters is not the advantage of the Spaniards, since my intention is not to gratify them.

What mattered, he emphasised, was to preserve the good faith of France. 'These frauds, which are unforgivable in the merchants, bring nothing directly to the king, and take a great deal from the king of Spain.' The strong position taken up by Amelot found its clearest expression in his memorable letter to Pontchartrain, written in 1711 after his return to France, when he outlined the duty of all rulers, great and small, to observe the dictates of honour:[52]

It remains to be seen whether it is suitable for His Majesty to grant, now and until the peace, unofficial permits to go to the South Sea, even though he has promised not to give any more. I am, Monsieur, fully persuaded that it could never be to the service of the king nor to the welfare of the state, to oblige His Majesty to break his given word. The first and most noble of all interests is to establish good faith and to observe religiously what one has promised. If, as I think, that is true for individuals, it is incomparably more so for great princes, whose position relies infinitely on opinion and repute. It is a principle from which I think one should never depart, and which, I have always observed, has served well in all matters both great and small in which I have had a part.

Substantial blame for French prevarication must fall on Pont-

---

[50] Amelot to Louis xiv, 11 Apr. 1707, AE Corr. Pol. (Esp.), 167 f.187.
[51] Amelot to Desmaretz, 29 Oct. 1708, *Mémoires de Saint-Simon*, vol. 16, p. 340.
[52] Amelot to Pontchartrain, 26 Dec. 1711, AE Corr. Pol. (Esp.), 211 f.475. Printed in full in Dahlgren, pp. 671–3.

chartrain, who as secretary of state for naval affairs was in a position to enforce the prohibition he desired, but did nothing about it.[53] The main influence behind the interlopers, however, seems to have been Chamillart, the secretary for war. As a correspondent wrote to Amelot in March 1707:

About the voyages to the South Sea, I must tell you that it is not Pontchartrain who needs to be shaken up. He has always opposed them as much as he could. But M Chamillart has looked to the succour coming from them as necessary in the current shortage of silver.[54]

Chamillart remained quite unrepentant. 'If you were in my place,' he wrote to the ambassador that same month, 'you would ignore all the great rules of policy, even of propriety, in order to make silver come into France, no matter by what means.'[55] If we had listened to the counsels of Madrid, we would have been outdone by the Allies in the Indies; he should not therefore be reproached simply for doing his duty. So long as Chamillart remained a minister, active help continued to be given to interlopers. In June 1709 he was dismissed and replaced by Voysin. This brought the expected decree no closer, and it was only on 18 January 1712, in circumstances outlined elsewhere,[56] that the French government officially banned all illicit trade to the South Sea. The prohibition did not of course stop interloping, and had to be repeated in 1716; but it marked a new departure in government policy, and was the beginning of the end for French interlopers. Under the regency, Amelot once again added his voice to the pressure for a ban, which duly followed in 1724. After this date the French concentrated on trading through the Cadiz merchants, and left the profits of interloping to the English.

Despite French naval superiority, despite the Asiento, despite the volume of illicit trade carried on through Saint-Malo, for France the whole question ended in failure. Louis xiv never managed to break into the monopoly exercised by Cadiz over the Indies, and the various plans and negotiations of the period, culminating in the acceptance of Mesnager's plan for the Indies trade in July 1708,[57] came to nothing at the final settlement of

[53] The comments of Dahlgren, p. 280, are appropriate.
[54] Daguesseau to Amelot, 8 Mar. 1707, AE Corr. Pol. (Esp.), 172 f.112.
[55] Chamillart to Amelot, 13 Mar. 1707, ibid., 172 f.130.
[56] Dahlgren, pp. 661–703.
[57] For this and other plans, see Dahlgren, passim.

Utrecht. This failure was of course due not only to the resistance of the Spanish, but also to the competition of the English, backed as it was by superior maritime strength.

From French efforts abroad we now turn to the French in the peninsula. Here the traders attempted to establish their privileges on the basis of consular organisation.[58] In addition to their own consular officials Frenchmen had to rely on a judge-protector or *juez conservador* appointed by Madrid, with authority over all civil and criminal cases of first instance that involved that nation. In theory, therefore, the French were under the jurisdiction of their judge-protectors and their local consuls, but the extent of their privileges under this jurisdiction was seldom clearly defined. In practice, the consuls always had to fall back on privileges granted in previous treaties to friendly powers, and the basis of all French claims during the War of Succession was that Frenchmen were entitled to all the rights accorded to foreigners by the treaties of 1648 (Münster), 1659 (Pyrenees), and 1667 (with England).[59]

From 1701 to 1709 the French in Spain enjoyed privileges which probably allowed them a more favourable position than they had ever had before or were to have again. These were the years of close liaison between Versailles and Madrid, when French forces were more committed to defence of the peninsula. Traders benefited implicitly and explicitly from the terms of the treaties cited above, as confirmed by several royal decrees: one in February 1706, for instance, in the case of Jacques Albert, a merchant of Málaga, confirming that the French nation as a whole enjoyed all the privileges formerly confirmed to the Hanseatic towns; or one in April 1706, confirming that Frenchmen had the right to be tried before their judge-protector, even in a criminal suit, in accordance with the terms of the Treaty of Münster.[60] Few or no complaints were made by the French in the years before 1709 in respect of their privileges under treaty. The concessions they enjoyed were no doubt enough to convince them that they had never had it so good. To take one example of an extension of privilege: on 10 February 1703 the French merchants in Cadiz

[58] An account of this organisation in the seventeenth century is given in Albert Girard, *Le commerce français à Séville et Cadiz*, pp. 89–130.

[59] 'Extrait de la lettre de M de Blécourt du 23 mars 1710', AN Aff. Etr., BIII 360.

[60] *Ibid.*, 324 ff.90, 104.

were granted by decree the right to trade freely to Africa, paying
no taxes save the normal customs duty. This concession was
enjoyed by the French up to 1718, when Alberoni stepped in to
suppress it.[61] The privileges of foreign traders included exemption from extraordinary taxation levied on residents and natives:
this was confirmed, for instance, to the French merchants of
Orihuela (Valencia) in September 1707.[62] In 1708 when plans
were afoot to reform the customs duties payable at the Spanish
border, Philip v issued a decree, dated 9 November, confirming
that the French traders in Aragon, Valencia and Catalonia were to
pay no more than the old duties on goods from France, and were
not to be liable to new or extraordinary taxation.[63] These cited
instances are typical of a great number of concessions made to
French traders by a government strongly under the influence of
French advisers and, above all, the French ambassador.

Naval privileges were likewise confirmed according to the
terms of previous peace treaties. A regulation issued by the
Spanish government on 5 August 1702 ruled that naval prizes
made by privateers of both nations could be sold in the ports of
either France or Spain, and that prizes were to be free from all
taxes.[64] This regulation was reinforced by subsequent decrees:
on 20 March 1703 it was decreed that goods from prizes could
be sold free of tax; on 23 August that year the tax-commissioners
of La Coruña were forbidden to levy duties on English prizes
brought in by French ships, on the grounds that this contravened
the 1702 regulation;[65] and on 13 April and 20 July 1704 a general
ban on taxing French prizes was again decreed.[66] The number of
such legislative prohibitions shows clearly that Spanish officials
found the privilege distasteful and were attempting to enforce
duties on prizes in defiance of their government. A test case in
Galicia led to a royal decree of 10 October 1705, whereby French
privateers had to pay some taxes on sales from prizes, but Amelot
protested so vigorously that the decree was revoked by another
on 4 December.[67] Elsewhere in the peninsula, as in Valencia,[68]

[61] 'Memoire de Mssrs les Commissaires du Conseil', Jan. 1724, *ibid.*, 361.
[62] Grimaldo to Padilla, 12 Sept. 1707, *ibid.*, 325 f.32.
[63] *Ibid.*, 325 f.81.   [64] *Ibid.*, 323 f.63.
[65] *Ibid.*, 323 f.112.   [66] *Ibid.*, 323 f.147.
[67] *Ibid.*, 324 ff.18, 70.
[68] Decree of 11 Aug. 1705, *ibid.*, 324 f.52.

French prizes continued to be duty-free. Not content with these privileges, Louis XIV worked to gain complete immunity for French shipping in Spanish waters. Opposition to this would have been based on the secure knowledge that a considerable amount of smuggling was carried on from French vessels, but as usual the strong foreign influence at Madrid prevailed. A decree of 30 April 1703 prohibited all Spanish officials from boarding French ships, a privilege based on article fifteen of the Treaty of Rijswijk.[69] A year later French ships were given the extraordinary privilege of being allowed to board and inspect any foreign ships in Spanish 'harbours and seas, and if they find any trading and trafficking in goods and supplies to enemy ports, they may detain and arrest them'.[70] These two decrees are of fundamental importance, for they virtually granted the freedom of the western Mediterranean to all French ships, whether for smuggling or for piracy. At the same time, the only recognised authority over French mariners in Spain was held to be the French consul of the region: thus when in November 1707 the authorities at Málaga tried to assert their jurisdiction in a matter of prizes taken by French ships, the Madrid government decreed that the question be reserved to the consul alone.[71]

Up to 1709, then, the relations between French traders and the Spanish authorities continued to be satisfactory because the former were granted unrestricted exercise of their treaty privileges, and any native protests were stifled by the French advisers who dominated the central government. In that year, however, a radical change in policy occurred. Louis XIV decided to withdraw all but nominal support of Philip's régime, most of his troops left Spain, and nearly all the French advisers were recalled. Among the last named was Amelot, who finally left Spain on 2 September 1709.

Although it was Amelot who brought French power to its peak in Spain, he seems never to have suffered for it in the estimation of Castilians. He was hated in Valencia and Aragon, where his name was indissolubly linked with the revocation of the *fueros,* but, as we have already seen, in Castile he was revered as few native ministers of the crown had ever been. Whenever a

[69] *Ibid.,* 323 f.84 ff.
[70] Decree of 13 Apr. 1704, *ibid.,* 323 f.148.
[71] 'Decre tdu Roy d'Espagne', 29 Nov. 1707 ,*ibid.,* 361.

French privilege was successfully upheld, it was the ambassador who invariably bore the credit; whenever the wishes of Louis XIV were acted upon, it was at the instance of Amelot. Yet despite this, when a Castilian pamphleteer of 1714 chose to vent his wrath on the mismanagement caused in Spain by French, Flemish and Italian advisers, he made an exception of 'Monsieur Amelot, who was more intimately attached to the advice and policy of Spaniards, and made the effects of his ministry shine more brightly'.[72] A French colleague of the ambassador reported that 'the nobility and the people of Andalucia and Castile, provinces which will always decide the fate of Spain, put their hope in him'.[73] And over a decade later, when the duc de Saint-Simon arrived in Madrid as French ambassador, he spoke of Amelot and of

this great reputation which after so many years is still revered in Spain and where, twelve years after his recall, everyone I saw pressed me for news of him, praised him at great length, and showed astonishment at the fact that he was not at the head of affairs in France.[74]

Disengagement from the peninsula was a mistaken policy bitterly opposed by Amelot, who saw it as yet another example of French bad faith. In February 1709 he urged Torcy to reconsider the implications of such a step:

Considering that the ambassador of the king has laboured for nearly four years in this country to repair the fortunes of the king of Spain, has made it a cardinal principle to ensure that France should never abandon Spain, and has endeavoured by all practicable means to engage thousands of people to attach themselves to the fortune of their rightful king; he would be far less suitable than someone else to execute a plan of retreat for which one would have to employ totally contradictory language.[75]

This letter shows that Amelot preferred to be recalled rather than be associated with the new policy of France. This alone may have contributed to his standing with the people of Spain. The new envoy, the marquis de Blécourt, who arrived in Madrid on 23

---

[72] Anonymous letter of 16 Apr. 1714, AE Corr. Pol. (Esp.), 229 f.113.
[73] Marquis de Louville, *Mémoires secrets sur l'établissement de la Maison de Bourbon en Espagne* (2 vols), Paris, 1818, vol. 2, pp. 164–5.
[74] *Mémoires de Saint-Simon*, vol. 18, pp. 81–2.
[75] Amelot to Torcy, 15 Feb. 1709, in Baudrillart, vol. 1 p. 346, note 1.

August 1709, was given specific instructions by Versailles not to take any part in the direction of affairs.[76] His stay proved to be the most frustrating of any experienced by an ambassador during the War of Succession.

As Amelot may have foreseen, the departure of the French forces led to an immediate Spanish reaction. Officials great and small, traders and merchants, anyone who had had any reason to resent French influence, control and privileges; all now saw their opportunity to right the balance. In April 1710 Pontchartrain caught the mood when he complained to Torcy of 'the extraordinary outrages that have been carried on these last few months against the French in Spain'.[77] It was Blécourt who now had the unhappy task of trying to remedy the multiple complaints that kept pouring in from consuls and traders in Spain. The first and undoubtedly most drastic sign of the new mood came with a decree of 1 December 1709, which complained of French frauds and contraventions of the 5 August 1702 regulation on prizes. As a result, the decree reinforced the disciplinary clauses of the 1702 regulation, but deprived consuls of any jurisdiction over prizes, which were to be subject to the competence of the local governor or judicial officer, and ordered that 'French privateers may come to Spanish ports with their prizes, but on the express condition that they pay the duties appertaining to my treasury in the same way as any other trader, and that they be subject to boarding and inspection by the captains general, governors and justices of the ports'.[78] To maintain parity, Spanish privateers were also now required to pay the duties on prizes; but it was clear, since the vast majority of prizes were in fact made by Frenchmen, that the decree was aimed at France. With this one measure all the principal privileges enjoyed by French ships were destroyed. The French in Spain and in Paris were stunned by the decree, and Blécourt was hastily directed to see if he could settle the question. But this time pressure did not succeed, and the ambassador

[76] *Recueil des Instructions données aux Ambassadeurs*, vol. 12, pp. 156–64. He was not an ambassador, for Louis had downgraded the post as part of his disengagement policy.

[77] Pontchartrain to Torcy, 16 Apr. 1710, AE Corr. Pol. (Esp.), 203 f.127. Note also Amelot to Pontchartrain, 1 July 1713, AN Aff. Etr., B³¹¹ 360: 'Depuis mon retour de Madrid, sachant les dispositions peu favourables des Ministres d'Espagne sur tout ce qui regardoit le commerce et les privileges des François . . . .'

[78] AN Aff. Etr., B³¹¹ 325 f.157.

was forced into negotiations which dragged themselves out and which were continuously embittered by new complaints. Neither Blécourt nor his successors managed to reach full agreement on the issues involved, and discussions were still being carried on in 1715 when the last of the French advisers were ordered to leave Spain. The December 1709 decree was not repealed, and was confirmed again by a schedule of 31 July 1711.[79] French pretensions were finally shattered when on 3 April 1712 a Spanish decree made all ships, both friendly and neutral, liable to inspection by the authorities, irrespective of privileges granted by peace treaties.

This resolution [Pontchartrain observed] is absolutely contrary to article 6 of the Treaty of the Pyrenees, confirmed by an ordinance of the queen regent in 1670, and to the Treaties of Aix-la-Chapelle, Nijmegen and Rijswijk. It is in consequence of these treaties that the French have always enjoyed the privileges of the Hanseatic towns. Article 22 of the treaty between Spain and these towns states expressly that their ships will not be boarded on any pretext whatsoever.[80]

The curtailment of other privileges was swiftly put into effect.[81] Blécourt could with justification complain to Philip v that 'the peace treaties between Spain and France have in the last four months been violated so publicly in Your Majesty's dominions that I am forced to bring it to Your Majesty's notice'. An unusual royal decree of 30 October 1709 forbade any commerce in bills of exchange by foreigners: this was widely interpreted as a blow directed against the French bankers in Spain. In a civil case concerning four Frenchmen in Jaén, two of whom had been in prison without redress for five months, the appellants claimed that since October 1709 they had been clamouring in vain to have their case transferred from the *corregidor*'s court to that of the judge-protector, in accordance with their recognised privileges. 'In Madrid itself three other French traders cannot likewise obtain a summons before the judge-protector of their nation.' In La Coruña in October 1709 a French merchant, Dubilla, had his house forcibly searched by the local authorities; in January 1710 a municipal official in Madrid broke into the house of the

79 *Ibid.*, 326 f.87.
80 Pontchartrain to Torcy, 18 May 1712, AE Corr. Pol. (Esp.), 214 f.39.
81 The cases in this paragraph are taken from Blécourt's letter to Pontchartrain, 7 Dec. 1709, AN Aff. Etr., B¹ 771; and from his Jan. 1710 memoir to Philip v, AN Aff. Etr., B¹¹¹ 361.

merchant Marsiac and took away his account book; while in Málaga the consul, Fleury de Vareilles, had his house forcibly searched by the municipal authorities. In La Coruña a trader named Henri Augey had been under arrest for the past six months because of a dispute over a prize. At the end of November 1709 the governor of San Lucar boarded and searched a French vessel moored in the reaches of Seville. In December in Alicante the governor ordered special taxes to be levied on French traders, and in Valencia the military commander forced the resident French to contribute to the winter-quartering of troops. Such were some of the official and unofficial steps taken against the French at the turn of 1709. It is most probable that there was good reason for each action, but the timing and intensity of them all together made a distinct impression on the French authorities.

The new year, 1710, witnessed legislative support for many of the unofficial steps taken against French privileges. On 11 January 1710 the customs duty on goods entering Aragon from France was raised by 5 per cent, while the exit duty on Aragonese wool was raised from two to four reales an *arroba*.[82] A royal order of 24 January raised a fruitful point for discussion when it allowed the military commander in Aragon to tax only those French who were 'established' in the province; and a decree of 5 April 1710 repealed that of 23 November 1708 which had exempted the French from all extraordinary taxation.[83] The special status of Frenchmen in Spain was now almost completely overthrown, and they were reduced to the level of any other foreign colony. A long explanation sent to Blécourt in May 1710 by the secretary of the *despacho* contains an interesting attempt to justify the new Spanish attitude. According to this letter,

all Frenchmen married to Spaniards holding landed property, or resident for ten years continuously in Spain, or holding offices reserved by law to naturals of the realm, should contribute to the extent that they enjoy the prerogatives of Spaniards; moreover, French craftsmen who have married Spaniards or lived ten years continuously in these realms, should be considered as naturals, even though they have no landed property.[84]

[82] Blécourt to Pontchartrain, 8 Feb. 1710, AN Aff. Etr., B¹ 772.
[83] AN Aff. Etr., B¹¹¹ 360; also 326 f.18.
[84] Manuel de Vadillo y Velasco to Blécourt, 12 May 1710, AN Aff. Etr., B¹¹¹ 360. This ten-year period for domicile was later enshrined in a controversial decree of 8 Mar. 1716.

This view was a great blow to French pretensions to special treatment, and led to acrimonious disputes in the following months.

Meanwhile the number of incidents involving Frenchmen increased. Taxes were imposed on traders in Santa María; disputes occurred with the guilds in Madrid; in Granada an army colonel

has kidnapped and robbed over one hundred Frenchmen, holding them prisoner and conducting them by force to Aragon. At Alicante they have violently seized all the horses of the French traders without paying them, and have imposed exorbitant taxes on them. At Tortosa they have gone into the house of a merchant named Lasalle and seized a quantity of merchandise on which duty had been paid: all the other French merchants are being forced to pay an extraordinary tax, in addition to supplies, winter-quarters and lodging for troops, and they have been compelled to help with fortification. The violence is even worse in Galicia. The governor of Vigo has imprisoned the captain of a French ship, *La Colombe*, from Martinique, and seized part of the cargo. He has forcibly boarded another French ship, belonging to M Dominique Grangent, from the Canaries; and has caused to be boarded and seized another ship, belonging to captain Estienne Grangent, which sank in the port of Guardia. Finally this same governor has had a third ship seized by armed boats in the port of Aldau.[85]

All these incidents occurred before June 1710. Various others occurred after this date, but their recitation would add little more to the point which these examples illustrate: that if there had been any friendly attitude between the two nations before 1709, this had now evaporated. It is not difficult to speculate on the reasons for this development. While some hostility may have been caused by the French decision to abandon Spain, the most likely explanation is that the Spanish had always objected to the special favours enjoyed by the French, and that only the French withdrawal had given them an opportunity to express their resentment.

Still intent on saving something from the wreckage of Franco-Spanish relations, Blécourt began discussions with the Spanish authorities with a view to defining French privileges more clearly. On 22 March 1710 the duque de Giovenazzo, representing Philip v, met Blécourt in the house of the agent of the French council of commerce in Madrid, and proceeded to deliver his interpretation

[85] Details from Blécourt's memoir of 25 June 1710 in AN Aff. Etr., B^I 772. Another 1710 memoir is in AN Aff. Etr., B^{III} 364.

of the peace treaties of preceding years.[86] The sterile nature of the discussions began to disillusion those in Versailles who had hoped that the peace treaties were a suitable basis for defining consular and other privileges. When in addition the Spanish government claimed jurisdiction over all allegedly domiciled Frenchmen, it became clear that a new factor had entered to complicate the situation. By 1711 the new chief minister of Spain, Bergeyck, had evolved his own formula to cover the case of domiciled Frenchmen: *establecido, avezindado;* if settled, then naturalised: residence of a year and a day in Spain made a French man into a Spaniard.[87] Subsequent legislation accepted this view, which provided the fiscal authorities with a convenient yardstick to differentiate between categories of foreigners. A decree in 1712, for instance, exempted from extraordinary taxation only those Frenchmen who 'estubieren de passo', that is, were 'passing through' Spain.[88] The French envoy who succeeded Blécourt, the marquis de Bonnac, was fair-minded enough to see that domiciled foreigners had no real claim to exemption from special taxation.[89] He also adopted the view that France should cease relying on the peace treaties for definition of privileges, and in this he received powerful support from Amelot. The latter, writing to Pontchartrain in 1713, affirmed that:

I agree entirely with the proposal of M de Bonnac. Like him, I think that it would no longer be beneficial to base our rights and franchises on treaties made by Spain with other foreign powers. I consequently consider it suitable to make a particular one between the two crowns, including in it all that has been or will be granted to any other nation. This will not exclude further concessions that the situation of the two realms, the necessary and continuous trade on our frontiers, and the skill of a negotiator, can obtain in favour of our nation, in view of the close blood relationship that unites the two kings, and the great services rendered by France at the cost of the lives of thousands of officers and soldiers, the exhaustion of our finances and the almost total destruction of whole provinces.[90]

[86] Blécourt's letter of 23 Mar. 1710, AN Aff. Etr., B^{III} 326 f.63. A paper presented to Giovenazzo on 'Jurisdicion de los Consules' is given in AN Aff. Etr., B^{I} 772, dated 28 Mar. 1710 for the French version and 4 Apr. for the Spanish.
[87] Blécourt to Pontchartrain, 9 Sept. 1711, AN Aff. Etr., B^{I} 773.
[88] Decree of 7 Mar. 1712, AN Aff. Etr., B^{III} 326 f.104.
[89] Bonnac to Pontchartrain, 18 Jan. 1712, AN Aff. Etr., B^{I} 774.
[90] Amelot to Pontchartrain, 1 July 1713, AN Aff. Etr., B^{III} 360.

The proposed treaty was never obtained, despite a sheaf of suggestions and advice from Amelot.[91] Instead, in March 1714 the Spanish government set up a special junta to examine the status of French traders and consuls: there were ten members, including Melchor Macanaz. The establishment of the junta enraged the marquis de Brancas who, ever since his arrival in October 1713 as the new French ambassador, had been pressing for the appointment of a special government representative to discuss consular questions. His rage was directed especially against Jean Orry, whom he particularly detested. 'This is a trick of Orry's', he wrote to Pontchartrain in March 1714. 'It is Orry's work, and that is saying everything; he is getting out of control and pushing his insolence too far.'[92] Brancas had descended to the sort of petty factiousness that distinguished the French ambassadors who had preceded Amelot. At the end of that month he left Madrid, having obtained nothing in the way of consular concessions.

The last word rests with Orry, then at the summit of his career as chief minister of Spain. Just over a month before his expulsion from Spain, he wrote to Pontchartrain explaining in detail the Spanish government's attitude to the French in the peninsula.[93] There were two principles he had followed since taking control of the government. According to the first, 'I hold that one should not attach oneself either to the terms of the treaties between France and Spain, or to those made between Spain and other nations.' Treaties did not cater for all eventualities, and problems would be better solved without them. Secondly, 'I distinguish between the interest of the state and that of individuals, and consider it an error very prejudicial to the state that individuals should want attention given to their interests when these are contrary to what suits the state.' It was on this principle that he, as a minister of Philip V, had placed Spanish interests above those of individual Frenchmen. He had distinguished between domiciled and non-domiciled traders, for the former were part of the fabric of the nation and should be taxed accordingly. As for consuls, these had jurisdiction over trade and similar matters, but their competence was limited in criminal cases. There had been protests

[91] E.g. his letters of 17 and 18 Aug. 1714 to Pontchartrain, in AN Aff. Etr., B[III] 360.

[92] Brancas to Pontchartrain, 12 Mar. 1714, AN Aff. Etr., B[1] 777.

[93] Orry to Pontchartrain, 12 Dec. 1714, *ibid.*

over the taxation of French artisans in Spain, but he saw no
reason why they should be privileged, nor should France protest,
since they contributed nothing to the extension of French commerce in Spain. French traders were also being taxed, particularly
in Valencia, but this was because all foreigners were required to
contribute to the new tax system introduced into this territory.

Orry's letter was completely contrary to the view of their
privileges that Frenchmen had taken at the beginning of the War
of Succession. At that time they had claimed full benefit of the
treaties, the complete jurisdiction of consuls, and total exemption
from extraordinary taxation: now all these principles had been
perforce abandoned. This reversal of the situation may be dated
from the crucial year 1709. The significant years, however, are
not those after 1709, when the French had to be satisfied with the
status of all other foreigners, but those before that date, for it was
then that the French came nearest to enjoying total and unprecedented freedom of commerce in the peninsula.

8   The Wealth of the Indies

For the maritime powers and for France, what lay at stake in the Spanish Succession was mastery over the commerce and specie of the Indies. In one sense, this motive and purpose was illusory, for it was already widely recognised that the European powers had, by interloping and piracy, long arrogated to themselves a major part of the Caribbean and Pacific trades. French and other European goods, as we have seen, were alleged to have flooded the Indies and robbed a market theoretically open only to the traders of Seville. Even when the fleets from America did bring goods and bullion back to Seville, the major part of the cargo belonged to the French, Dutch, English and Italians. It might have been thought that the enormous profits from interloping would gratify the desires of western European governments. Instead, they only whetted the appetite. Bourbon control of Spain brought before French eyes the glittering picture of a New World open to exploitation, while before the Allies loomed the nightmare of Bourbon power made impregnable because constantly replenished with the wealth of the Indies. As it happened, French control of Spain did not lead to French domination in America, thanks to the obstinacy of Spanish administrators. Louis xiv was consequently obliged to rely on indirect means for his supply of American bullion. The present chapter is concerned principally with this question of monetary relations between France and Spain, and with the movement of bullion from Spain to France. It will end with an analysis of the fleets which brought silver from America between 1700 and 1715.

The most eloquent testimony to the success of the monetary stabilisation of 1686, noted in an earlier chapter, is the way in which Spanish money maintained its value during the War of Succession. Hamilton tends to identify monetary stability with

the advent of the Bourbons, but in fact there was stability continuously through the last years of Charles II, so that the change
of dynasty is of no importance. What is possible, of course, is that
the political security of Spain under Philip v underwrote the
value of Spanish coinage. Certainly the war years did not threaten
any currency inflation, and the generally moderate movement of
prices reflected an economy that weathered the troubles extremely
well. By a royal provision of 24 April 1704[1] the price of silver
was controlled, but this was probably an unnecessary safety
measure. Shortage of specie remained undeniable; thus in December 1705 Amelot was studying the possibility of exploiting the
gold and silver mines of Navarre, and a memoir to this effect was
drawn up for him,[2] though it seems not to have been acted upon.
It seems likely that the greater velocity of circulation provoked
by the financial activity of war compensated to some extent for
shortage of specie, and that in some districts the import of
French coinage made good a deficiency of Spanish currency. A
discussion of inflation, however, can only be entered upon when
we have dealt with other related problems, particularly that of
the role of French money in the Spanish war.

The exchange rate between France and Spain was of considerable importance to both countries, since France was paying its
troops in Spain and the latter was purchasing armaments in
France. Parity between their currencies would have simplified
all aspects of war finance, and have made the Pyrenees non-existent for purposes of convertibility. Unfortunately for France,
Spanish money from the very beginning of the war was quoted
against the livre at disproportionately high rates. Where the peso
was nominally valued at 3 livres, in Spain in 1702 it was 3 livres
16 sols.[3] In 1704 it was at roughly the same level, at 3 livres 14
sols in Cadiz, and not under 3 livres 10 sols in Madrid;[4] on
occasion it reached 4 livres. It fluctuated at just about this level
for the rest of the war. In 1713, however, while it seems to have
kept its face value in Madrid, the price asked in Marseilles was

---

[1] Manuel Danvila y Collado, *El poder civil en España*, vol. 3, p. 474.

[2] AE Corr. Pol. (Esp.), 154 f.344.

[3] The peso, known in French as an écu or piastre, was worth 15 reales 2 maravedis
of vellon. The 1702 value is from Orry to Torcy, 22 July 1702, AE Corr. Pol.
(Esp.), 106 f.311; see also his 23 Jan 1704 'Memoire sur la monoye', Guerre, A¹ 1787
f.93. It was normally taken to be equivalent to the French silver écu worth 3 livres.

[4] Orry to Chamillart, 26 Mar. 1704, Guerre, A¹ 1787 f.192.

between 4 livres 15 sols and 5 livres.[5] The year after this it was valued at 4 livres 10 sols in Spain. The rate of the Spanish doblón[6] was even more inflated. Nominally equivalent to the French louis d'or at a rate of about 12 livres, it soon became an object of concern to those interested in Franco-Spanish commerce. In March 1704 it was reckoned that a louis d'or which cost 13 livres in France would fetch only 11 livres 15 sols in Madrid,[7] and that same year the governor of Bayonne claimed that doblones ('pistoles') were falling out of circulation there because they were selling at 13 livres where the louis cost only 12 livres 10 sols.[8] Pressure by leading French merchants trading to Spain, such as Villebague-Eon of Saint-Malo, in favour of raising the nominal price of the louis and the écu so as to attract Spanish coin,[9] resulted in a decree of May 1704 by which Desmaretz raised the price of the louis to 15 livres, and fixed the écu, formerly worth 3 livres, at 4 livres.[10] In theory, this decree should have established parity between French and Spanish money, but the market price remained unaffected, no doubt because nobody took the decree seriously, and Spanish coin continued to be preferred to French at the old rate. At the beginning of 1706 it cost 15 livres to buy a doblón in Paris, 15 livres 5 sols to buy one in Madrid, and 14 livres 10 sols to buy in Bayonne.[11]

The French authorities could hardly fail to be worried at this unfavourable rate of exchange, because all their troops in Spain had to be paid in Spanish coin bought with French livres, since foreign coinage did not run in the country. Payment of the French armies consequently became a serious financial problem, only soluble through the discreet exercise of pressure on Madrid. It was pointed out to the Spanish authorities that the louis d'or and écu had virtually the same silver content as the Spanish doblón and eight-reales (or peso) piece. Philip v was therefore prevailed on to issue a decree of 5 July 1706 which allowed the two French

[5] Orry to Pontchartrain, 5 Sept. 1713, AN Aff. Etr., B¹ 776.

[6] The doblón, known in French as a pistole, was usually worth 60 reales 8 maravedis of vellon.

[7] Orry to Chamillart, 2 Mar. 1704, Guerre, A¹ 1787 f.131.

[8] Boislisle, *Correspondance des Contrôleurs Généraux*, vol. 2, no. 642, letter of Desmaretz to Gramont, 19 July 1704.

[9] *Ibid.*, no. 39.

[10] *Ibid.*, no. 642, as cited above.

[11] De Gibaudière to Chamillart, 30 Jan. and 6 Feb. 1706, Guerre, A¹ 1981 ff.81, 103.

coins to be accepted as valid currency in Navarre and Castile. 'This will be a great help to us, and a great saving to the king,' the intendant of the French armies reported back to the war minister.[12] Despite the equivalence, however, Spanish money continued to be more expensive. Since there was apparently no intrinsic difference in metallic content, the explanation for this would seem to lie in greater pressure on French money as a result of war commitments. The fact is that, despite all the efforts of the French treasury, French coin was on the defensive. In 1709 the doblón was costing 18 livres in Paris instead of its face value of 12 livres, while in December 1713 the incredible price of 19 livres 10 sols was being quoted, and even in 1714, after the peace, a value of 17 livres was still obtainable.[13]

After all this it is not surprising to find that Frenchmen in Spain suffered acutely from the unfavourable rate of exchange. In 1703 the ambassador complained that 'everything here is extraordinarily expensive'; in 1704 the cost of living in the capital was estimated at being 'double that of Paris'; while Blécourt in 1709 complained of 'the extreme dearness of everything in Madrid, and bankers here tell me that very soon one will have to pay at least 18 francs in Paris for a pistole which is worth only 12, because of the great difference between the new coinage in Paris and that of Spain'.[14] Brancas in 1711 complained to Torcy that his ambassadorial salary had shrunk by a quarter because of the rate of exchange: 'since my nomination to Spain I have received 6,000 livres which, because of the difference in specie, have brought me 380 pistoles. You judge correctly that this has not taken me very far'.[15] On the other hand, there were those fortunate French soldiers who were not paid directly by the French government, as the ambassadors and other senior officials were, but received their money in Spain in Spanish coin, went back across the border, and profited from the difference in monetary values. A French military official explained this situation to the new secretary for war in 1709, Voysin:

[12] Dudoyer to Chamillart, 8 July 1706, *ibid.*, 1977 f.241.

[13] Blécourt to Torcy, 30 Sept. 1709, AE Corr. Pol. (Esp.), 193 f.69; BN, fonds français 21769 f.19; Pachau to Torcy, 7 Nov. 1714, AE Corr. Pol. (Esp.), 233 f.74.

[14] Abbé d'Estrées to Torcy, 29 Aug. 1703, AE Corr. Pol. (Esp.), 117 f.183; Gramont to Chamillart, 4 Dec. 1704, Guerre, A¹ 1786 f.345; Blécourt to Torcy, 30 Sept. 1709, AE Corr. Pol. (Esp.), 193 f.69.

[15] Brancas to Torcy, 14 Dec. 1711, AE Corr. Pol. (Esp.), 210 f.150.

When an officer in Spain is due 1,200 livres, if the treasurer's clerk has cash in hand he pays him 100 pistoles, since the pistole in Spain is worth only 12 livres; if this officer then crosses into France, the pistole with which he has been paid at 12 livres increases its value to his profit. Similarly, should this officer be in need of money and bring some from France, he loses on the pistole he takes into Spain what he gains on the pistole he takes out of the country.[16]

Contemporaries attributed the high costs in Spain to a real or imagined lack of money. There were incessant complaints of the scarcity of ready money, and on a government level the problem became one of how to finance the war when cash was not forthcoming. A crisis hung over the conduct of operations. In the light of this, the decree to allow French coin into circulation must have appeared as a timely method of supplementing the flow of metal within the realm. Even this was not enough. In November 1706 Amelot was considering the need to resort to inflationary measures, by increasing the value of the peso from 15 reales to 20 reales, and that of the doblón from 60 reales to 80 reales; at the same time, he proposed that new coins should be minted.[17] No steps seem to have been taken to revalue the coinage, but new coins were in fact issued at the end of 1706 in an attempt to raise funds for the treasury.[18]

The French, meanwhile, were not slow to exploit the possibilities of the decree of 1706, which had satisfied all their hopes. If payments had to be made to Spain, they could be made in French coin at the nominal exchange rate without losing any money by conversion at the market rate.[19] The benefit this might bring, however, had to be set against the disadvantages of sending coin out of the country. Prior to 1706, for example, France had surmounted many exchange difficulties by making most payments in Spain through bills of exchange on bankers in Cadiz or Madrid. This practice continued even after 1706, because bullionistic doctrine frowned on the export of coin in any appreciable quantity. There was therefore a limit to the possibilities of exploiting the 1706 decree. If, however, one were to mint base coin having

[16] Méliand to Voysin, 7 Aug. 1709, Guerre, A¹ 2178 f.127.

[17] Chamillart to Amelot, 18 Nov. 1706, AE Corr. Pol. (Esp.), 156 f.286.

[18] Earl J. Hamilton, *War and Prices in Spain 1651–1800*, Cambridge, Mass., 1947, p. 39.

[19] One such payment is noted in Pontchartrain to Amelot, 13 May 1709, AE Corr. Pol. (Esp.), 196 f.6.

the same face value as French pieces, and send this into Spain, there was the chance of receiving good Spanish coin in return. French profiteers in Bayonne took this line of action soon after the 1706 decree.[20] By the beginning of May 1709, it was estimated that 800,000 écus of this coin was circulating in Madrid alone.[21] Quick action by the government, in lowering the tariff of the French money, saved the stability of Spanish currency, and the only people to suffer from the incident were those French bankers in Madrid and Pamplona who had connived at the import of the base coin.[22] From time to time other incidents involving base money occurred, as in 1712 when false silver escudos minted at Bayonne were found circulating in Castile;[23] but Spanish coinage was not seriously disrupted. The introduction of Allied coin into Aragon and Valencia likewise caused little alarm at Madrid, after a royal order of 9 January 1711 which banned the use of enemy currency and offered good rates of exchange for any coins that were brought in.[24]

The incidents involving debased money prove that the French were extremely interested in securing good Spanish coin. Bayonne, close to the Basque border, was the centre of this interest in bullion, and through its gates the wealth of the Indies passed from Spain to France. All the available evidence tends to show that the movement of metal was one-way only – northwards across the frontier. This phenomenon was obviously not new, but it gains added importance in this period because of the unprecedented degree of French control over Madrid. Parallel to their interest in Spanish money, the French authorities were concerned to prevent the excessive export of their own coin to the peninsula. In 1704, to take one instance, Chamillart suggested to the French commander in Spain, Puységur, that the money owed by Spain to France for military supplies should be paid directly to the French forces in Spain, so avoiding the need to send French money which would lose by the exchange rate.[25] When it was a question of bullion, Chamillart did not hesitate to

[20] Hamilton, *War and Prices in Spain*, pp. 38–9.
[21] Amelot to Louis XIV, 13 May 1709, AE Corr. Pol. (Esp.), 191 f.31.
[22] *Ibid.*, 7 July 1709, AE Corr. Pol. (Esp.), 192 f.7; Du Pont to Chamillart, 7 June 1709, Guerre, A¹ 2177 f.232.
[23] Vadillo y Velasco to Bonnac, 18 May 1712, AE Corr. Pol. (Esp.), 218 f.239.
[24] Hacienda, Consejo de Castilla impresos, vol. 6549, p. 27.
[25] Chamillart to Puységur, 2 Jan. 1704, Guerre, A¹ 1787 f.1.

emphasise how ready France was to help with supplies. 'The king of Spain,' he wrote to the secretary of the *despacho* in 1704, 'needs powder, arms, bullets, bombs and other munitions; His Majesty will gladly help, and receive payment of what they would have cost in France'.[26] As we have already seen, acceptance of this invitation meant that Philip v placed contracts worth several millions in the pockets of French manufacturers. But while factors of this kind can be measured, it is totally impossible to measure a perhaps far more substantial flow of metal, namely that of smuggled bullion.

Data for smuggling are by definition unattainable. The techniques used under Philip v appear to be the same as had always been used, and there is no definite evidence of a rise or fall in the incidence of smuggling under the new dynasty. One account given in 1704 by the French commandant in Pamplona, a man who no doubt knew what he was talking about, is quite revealing:

What causes the scarcity of specie throughout Spain, despite the silver that comes annually from the Indies, is the exit of this same specie or money in the form of bullion. There is a spot on this sea-coast, namely Bilbao, from which every week there leave at least three pinnaces with twenty oars, going by night to Bayonne. In each of them there are at least fifty thousand piastres. Of this money, which ought apparently to bring abundance to France, only the greater part goes to France: the rest is consumed on lace and fabric at Paris and Lyon, and what goes on takes the Marseilles route to the Levant.

In addition to this sea-route from Bilbao, said the commandant, there was also the trade route, 'bales of wool which pass from Spain to France, to the number of at least twenty thousand a year, and each bale, which is worth twenty-five to thirty pistoles, often contains in its centre a quantity of piastres in bullion'.[27]

These were the old, classic methods of smuggling, with which the authorities on both sides of the border were well acquainted. Less well known, and equally reprehensible, was the smuggling carried on by leading French officials in Madrid, aided and abetted by prominent Spanish financiers. A secret French memoir dated May 1703 illustrates one example of this.[28] Of the money saved from the Vigo disaster in 1702 (described below) a

[26] Chamillart to Ribas, 26 Aug. 1704, Guerre, A¹ 1786 f.125.
[27] Du Pont to Chamillart, 5 Dec. 1704, *ibid.*, 1793 f. 572.
[28] 'Memoire secret sur le transport de l'argent d'Espagne en France', AE Corr. Pol. (Esp.), 123 f.134.

substantial amount was earmarked for Italian financiers who were creditors of the crown. The French authorities were eager to obtain possession of this bullion, and obtained the cooperation of the financiers Bartolomé Flon and Hubert Hubrechtz in carrying out their plan, which was as follows. When Philip v allowed the export of 30,000 pesos to pay for uniforms bought from France, Flon and Hubrechtz secretly made the sum up to 100,000 pesos, and this amount passed freely over the border, without being subject to inspection, because of the royal passport. Subsequently, when further permissions were granted by Philip to export 98,000 pesos to pay for munitions, the two bankers promised to smuggle out over 400,000 pesos under cover of the passport. In each case, the safety of the shipment was assured by Van Duffel, the correspondent of Flon and Hubrechtz in Bayonne. Once the money was safely in France the French government refused to forward it to the Italian financiers concerned, who were told that they could negotiate bills of exchange on it but could not extract the bullion.[29] In this way the debt was repaid in form but not in substance, and the direct beneficiary was France.

The two principal routes for smuggled bullion were the Basque border, which we have noted, and Cadiz. A standard feature of bullion shipments from America to Cadiz was that the metal was often secretly reexported even before it touched Spanish soil. The process continued regularly during the War of Succession, and a few examples can be cited in evidence. In 1704, for example, a plate fleet arrived at Cadiz on 23 January from Buenos Aires. On 10 February a French vessel, the *Saint Pierre*, left the harbour for Marseilles, with 150,000 pesos in silver on board.[30] Again, on 27 April a detachment of ships arrived from New Spain: on 12 May, at one o'clock in the morning, three French vessels slipped out of Cadiz harbour and headed towards Marseilles with 200,000 pesos on board.[31] Similarly, on 1 July 1711 a vessel named the *Phénix* left Cadiz for Marseilles with silver to the amount of 40,000 pesos, and cochineal and indigo worth 100,000 pesos.[32] Two other ships left with the *Phénix*. On 15 August three French galleys left Cadiz before dawn, with 60,000 pounds weight of

[29] *Ibid.*, 124 f.33.
[30] Mirasol to Pontchartrain, 10 and 17 Feb. 1704, AN Aff. Etr., B¹ 215 ff.36, 44.
[31] *Ibid.*, 12 May 1704, *loc. cit.*, f. 119.
[32] *Ibid.*, 4 July 1711, AN Aff. Etr., B¹ 218 f.177.

cochineal and 140,000 pesos in silver.[33] An additional example of semi-official smuggling is given in the case of Samuel Bernard, who on 30 June 1704 applied to the French authorities for a passport to transport 600,000 pesos from Cadiz to Genoa on a neutral ship. This bullion may well have come from the American ships that had arrived two months previously.[34]

It would be impossible to measure the volume of bullion thus smuggled, even if an inventory were taken of all the French ships that left Cadiz harbour shortly after the arrival of a plate fleet. It is similarly impossible to track down all bullion passing over the land route through Bayonne. Nevertheless, at least with Bayonne, a fragment of evidence may lead us to hazard a guess. In March 1706 the commandant of that town informed Chamillart that for the month of February the bullion passing through Bayonne to Lyon and Paris had been valued at 345,954 livres 10 sols.[35] Taking this figure arbitrarily as a basis, the total for twelve months would amount to well over four million livres. It is possible that this estimate is not far from correct, for a French memoir of 1709 (quoted below at length) claimed that France obtained over six million livres a year in specie by the trade at Bayonne and Toulouse. Of the other French sources of bullion, particularly the direct interloping trade organised by the ports of Brittany, nothing need be said here since they do not concern the Franco-Spanish traffic.

The picture that emerges may be summed up at length in the words of a memoir drawn up in January 1709, presumably by a French official, to fortify and encourage the French at a particularly difficult time:

Spain united with France brings us so great an advantage that we must make every effort to support the king of Spain: I shall not speak of the justice of his cause, which alone should animate us, but of the real, effective good of the kingdom.

In the last eight years more than 180,000,000 livres have entered France from the Indies; not that I would deprive the rest of Europe of their share in the profit, but I would let them benefit from it as was done in 1670, and as was so wisely practised last year when the fleet arrived at the port of Pasajes.

---

[33] Ibid., 16 Aug. 1711, loc. cit., f.255.
[34] Jacques Saint-Germain, Samuel Bernard, p. 136.
[35] De Gibaudière to Chamillart, 10 Mar. 1706, Guerre, A¹ 1981 f.212.

Moreover I claim to show that by the trade carried on at Bayonne and at Toulouse you draw annually more than 6,000,000 livres in specie, without counting the wool and silk, the saltpetre to be drawn from Aragon, the timber to be taken from the Pyrenees, and several other things which would take us into too great detail.

I shall say only that the chevalier Bernard[36] has supplied 400,000 livres a month in the past year for the French troops, all in bills of exchange on Madrid, and over 300,000 livres were carried in gold to the army of H.R.H. the duke of Orléans; and this money before the end of the month passed to Bayonne and Toulouse for the payment of what had been taken in clothing and necessities.

The abolition of the *golilla* at Madrid in itself is worth more than 4,000,000 a year to the city of Lyon.

All these are the advantages for the kingdom which make me think of working to maintain a war which is so just and so advantageous.[37]

France's gain was therefore Spain's loss. Spain drew metal from the Indies, but as in times past it flowed out to foreign parts. The French profited not only from smuggling but also from the direct trade with America, as we shall see in the following study of the plate fleets during the War of Succession.

No one since Earl J. Hamilton has attempted to study the volume of silver arriving in Spain during a specific period. Such a study is particularly necessary during the War of Succession, for it would enable us to gauge the importance of American silver in the financing of the war, and it would also help us to decide whether France made any profit out of its intervention in the peninsula. The next few pages will examine each fleet arrival year by year, with a minimum of statistical detail.

Our knowledge of the workings of the Spanish-American trade derives from a number of early Spanish studies of what was known as the *carrera de Indias,* and more especially from a classic modern study by Clarence Haring.[38] More recently, the voluminous work[39] by Pierre and Huguette Chaunu on the trade of Seville has dealt at great length with all aspects of the Atlantic economy and the fleet system. While a detailed background to our study may be sought in these works, it remains essential to outline

---

[36] I.e., Samuel Bernard, the financier.

[37] 'Projet General pour l'année', AE Corr. Pol. (Esp.), supplément 11 f.215.

[38] C. H. Haring, *Trade and Navigation between Spain and the Indies,* repr. Gloucester, Mass., 1964 (first edn 1918).

[39] *Séville et l'Atlantique (1504–1650)* (8 vols), Paris, 1955–60.

briefly the organisation of the Atlantic trade. The departure point for the Spanish fleets was Seville or Cadiz. By 1700 Seville was in decline and traders had shifted much of their business to Cadiz. The monopoly system and its officials continued to operate principally from Seville, where the ships and cargoes were registered with the *Casa de la Contratación* or House of Trade. Ideally the fleets were to sail annually from Seville, and the times of sailing were carefully regulated to coincide with the most suitable weather, wind and tide conditions. One *flota*, destined for New Spain, would leave Seville in the spring (March to May); and the other, for Tierra Firme (the mainland of South America), in August. For the journey back the fleets would reassemble in about January, and then make for Havana; the ships would sail from this port as one fleet in about March. This was the sixteenth-century standard, but later it was seldom adhered to, and the fleets sailed at widely varying times of the year. The cargo carried by the New Spain fleet consisted largely of supplies for Mexico; while the Tierra Firme fleet carried supplies for Peru, which were unloaded at Nombre de Dios and carried overland to the south. In return the ships took back bullion for the king and private merchants, together with some produce of the Indies.

By the end of the seventeenth century Spanish trade with America was highly disorganised. Regular annual sailings were almost unheard of. The fleet to Tierra Firme, as we have seen, sailed in 1695 and then not again until 1706. For the duration of the War of Succession sailings were also disrupted, largely because of superior enemy forces; but a firm effort was made to resume regular traffic. The number of ships registered as sailing between Spain and America during the war, with their approximate tonnage, is shown in Table 3, page 178.[40]

Ships crossing the Atlantic were not necessarily all merchant ships. The essence of the fleet system was that the whole body of trading vessels should be protected by armed escort-ships. During the war the escort consisted of the *armada de Barlovento* or 'windward squadron', so called because of the position it

[40] For a discussion of this table see appendix 2. Tonnage is in *toneladas*. As I explain in appendix 2, the measurement of commercial activity by tonnage in this period is completely meaningless. Moreover, the registers do not list all the ships arriving in the peninsula.

TABLE 3. MOVEMENT OF SPANISH-AMERICAN SHIPPING 1701–15

Year	From Spain		To Spain	
	Ships	Tonnage	Ships	Tonnage
1701	9	1,355	15	2,758
1702	8	1,535	20	4,379
1703	9	1,889	1	81
1704	4	323	9	2,207
1705	6	506	4	616
1706	32	8,390	2	380
1707	7	863	5	1,149
1708	25	3,303	10	2,710
1709	2	165	1	97
1710	10	2,893	11	2,109
1711	14	2,829	6	837
1712	9	1,794	5	764
1713	7	1,070	9	1,731
1714	4	698	1	116
1715	18	3,911	2	819

maintained relative to the fleet.[41] The flagship or *capitana* of the squadron usually preceded the assembled vessels, while the other main command ship, the *almiranta,* brought up the rear together with the escort. Where no armada was available to accompany trading ships, the latter were obliged to make their own hazardous way across the Atlantic. During the War of Succession there were only five fleet sailings from Spain; in 1706, 1708, 1710, 1712, and 1715. Fleet arrivals in Spain will be considered below as part of an analysis of bullion entering the royal treasury.

On 27 January 1701, one day before Philip V crossed the frontier into Spain, the last ships of a *flota* from New Spain entered Cadiz harbour. The eight vessels carried a cargo that consisted principally of cochineal, indigo, leathers, sugar, cocoa and tobacco. In addition, according to the French consul in Cadiz, there were 'one and a half million crowns for the king, almost one million two hundred thousand crowns for the consulado of Seville, and not much for private individuals'.[42] The French ambassador, on

---

[41] The *armada de Barlovento* was originally a defence squadron based in the Caribbean: see e.g. C. H. Haring, pp. 251–5.

[42] Catalan to Pontchartrain, 31 Jan. 1701, AN Aff. Etr., B¹ 214 f.19.

the other hand, estimated that not more than 430,000 pesos had come for Philip v.[43] The discrepancy cannot be solved by examining the actual cargo of bullion, for the king never received more than a proportion of it. It is likely that a considerable treasure was brought, for the *capitana* and *almiranta* alone were carrying 3,200 marks of silver, 43,000 *castellanos* of gold and 2,501,396 peso.[44] The most probable estimate in such cases is always the lowest one, so that we may accept the ambassador's figure as approximately correct, which would mean a sum of 6,450,000 reales (1 peso = 15 reales) accruing to the crown. All this money was apparently assigned immediately to the cost of armaments in Andalucia, so that none reached the royal treasury. This was an inauspicious beginning to the reign.

There was every expectation that the fleet in 1702 would bring in rather more to the treasury. This hope was fulfilled in a peculiarly spectacular way.[45] On 23 September 1702 the plate fleet from New Spain entered the bay of Vigo, a port in Galicia. This destination had been chosen because a powerful English naval force was at the time investing Cadiz. The ships in Vigo included fifteen French warships and two frigates, which provided an escort to the three galleons and thirteen trading vessels owned by Spain. As we have seen in an earlier chapter, on 23 October an Anglo-Dutch fleet sailed in and annihilated the ships in Vigo. It has commonly, and erroneously, been supposed that Spain suffered a disaster on this occasion. Certainly the private merchants of Seville, and no less certainly the merchants of England and Holland with a share in the cargo, suffered heavy losses. But the Spanish crown profited immensely. Representatives of the king superintended the unloading of the bullion from the ships before the arrival of the English fleet. When previous silver consignments had entered Seville, smuggling and export of specie had allowed bullion to melt away before it reached the authorities; this time, however, Seville and its smugglers were far away, and the royal officials were on hand to secure the bullion before any interested parties could arrive on the scene. In addition, Philip v used the Allied attack as an excuse to confiscate the silver that had come on the fleet as part of the merchandise

[43] Harcourt to Louis xiv, 2 Mar. 1701, AE Corr Pol. (Esp), 88 f.6.

[44] AGI, Contratación libro 1968 no. 1.

[45] For a more detailed account of events see the article cited above, p. 11, note 3.

belonging to English and Dutch merchants.[46] The result was that Philip received the largest sum in history ever obtained in any one year from America by any Spanish king. The total amount of bullion was as follows:[47]

	silver pesos
Sent from New Spain for the government	509,353
Reprisals against the English and Dutch	4,000,000
Borrowed from the merchants of Seville	2,000,000
Additional loan from the same	484,940
Deposited in Segovia	2,253,600
Costs of carrying silver to Segovia	121,244
Despatched to merchants of Seville	4,270,093
Total	13,639,230

Of this total, as much as 6,994,293 pesos (104,914,395 reales) entered directly into the royal treasury. The French ambassador, the Cardinal d'Estrées, seems to have been principally responsible for pressure on the Spanish government to contribute to Louis XIV's war effort in Italy and the Netherlands: it was therefore agreed to send a large sum, about one third of the total, to France. The money was meant partly as repayment of debts contracted by Louis on behalf of Spain in defending the Netherlands, and was to be sent in pure specie, in bars of silver.[48] In April 1703 two transports, each containing 800,000 silver pesos, were sent out secretly from Madrid to Bayonne.[49] A third transport was scheduled for the autumn. The total of all these transports came to 2,266,000 pesos (33,990,000 reales). Of the remainder, a sum of 2,800,000 pesos was put at the disposal of Cardinal Portocarrero for government expenses,[50] and 1,184,000 pesos was stored in the castle at Segovia. The total outlay, therefore, was as follows:

[46] Following accepted practice, Philip first consulted 'nearly fifty theologians' (Noailles, Mémoires, vol. 2. p. 234) on whether he had a right to confiscate the property of the Allies.

[47] Letter of Larrea to Aperregui, 16 Aug. 1703, AGI, Indiferente leg.2634.

[48] Card. d'Estrées to Louis XIV, 3 Mar. and 28 Mar. 1703, AE Corr. Pol. (Esp.), 115 ff.34, 181. Of the money sent, one third was to be forwarded to Milan and another third to Bavaria.

[49] AE Corr. Pol. (Esp.), 115 ff.293, 325.

[50] Portocarrero's expenses are detailed in ibid., 139 ff.68–89, particularly f.68.

silver pesos

Sent to Louis xiv	2,266,000
Sent to treasury at Madrid	2,800,000
Other royal expenses	744,293
Kept at Segovia	1,184,000

Total 6,994,293

Examination in detail of the second and third items on this list, shows that they include additional sums which were transmitted to France in payment for armaments and other supplies. Of the money sent to Madrid, for example, at least 80,800 pesos went to France to pay for armaments; and of the royal expenses another 50,000 was paid to France for arms supplied to America. This was not the end of the export of bullion, for Portocarrero's accounts show that an additional sum of 112,750 pesos was sent to the governor of Milan, and another 150,000 to the duke of Bavaria. In short, a considerable amount of silver was sent out of Spain by the government, and a sum in excess of 2,396,800 pesos was dispatched directly to France.

The year 1703 saw no fleet arrival from the Indies. The one vessel which is recorded as having arrived in Cadiz on 17 August had to pay a duty or indult of 6,000 pesos to the crown.[51]

There was some improvement the year after. On 23 January 1704 a richly-loaded ship from Buenos Aires arrived at Cadiz,[52] but there is no indication that anything from it went to the crown. Later, on 26 April, five vessels arrived from New Spain: this was the quicksilver fleet[53] which had set sail from Havana on 25 February. On 8 May two other ships arrived to complete the fleet. Besides an enormous cargo of cochineal, cocoa, sugar, tobacco, leather and campeche, the official list shows that only 208 bars of silver and 492,278 pesos were registered.[54] Well

[51] AGI, Contratación libro 2901 f.131.

[52] Mirasol to Pontchartrain, 27 Jan. and 19 Feb. 1704, AN Aff. Etr. Etr., B¹ 215 ff.19, 49.

[53] The fleet had originally taken mercury to America, and was returning with other goods.

[54] The full cargo list is in 'Memoria de la carga que han traido los siete navios que llegaron ultimamente de Indias a Cadix', AN Aff. Etr. B¹ 215 f.137. A note against the silver, by the French consul, says: 'Il y en a quantité davantage qui ne paroist point'. The amount of silver on the *capitana* of the fleet is estimated in AGI, Contaduría leg.175 no. 4 as 138,592 pesos. An estimate of what each ship carried is given by the French consul in AN Aff. Etr., B¹ 215 f.110.

G

aware that probably ten times this amount was being smuggled, the government promptly laid an indult of half a million pesos on the fleet, and to make sure of this sum sent an armed guard to escort the money back to Madrid. This was certainly all that the government received, for the treasury registered a receipt of only 7,529,412 reales from the fleet.[55] The other ships arriving in this year appear not to have benefited the treasury greatly. One small vessel from Tierra Firme, which arrived in June, had an indult of 600 doblones (36,000 reales) laid on it;[56] but there was no further money forthcoming.

On 5 February 1705 the *capitana* of the Barlovento fleet, which had left Vera Cruz on 11 November, put into Cadiz; and three days later two other vessels of the same fleet put in at San Lucar, in the reaches of Seville. The French consul confirmed that the *capitana* had brought 1,040,000 pesos for Philip v, and that the indult would amount to about 150,000 pesos more.[57] Unfortunately, details of this money are not available in the treasury returns. The French archives do, however, supply a definitive memoir of silver sent on the *capitana* by the viceroy of New Spain: this memoir gives the amount received as one million pesos or fifteen million reales. All this silver was spent immediately on the war effort.[58]

[55] AGS, Tribunal Mayor de Cuentas leg.1870.
[56] AGI Contratación libro 2901 f.132.
[57] Mirasol to Pontchartrain, 8 Feb., 15 Feb., and 4 Apr. 1705, AN Aff. Etr., B¹ 215 ff.263, 266, 298.
[58] 9 Apr. 1705 'Memoria de la distribuzion de los un millon de pesos excudos de plata que vinieron de Nueva España con la Capitana de la Armada de Barlobento', AE Corr. Pol. (Esp.), 152 f.238. To illustrate how silver was swallowed up by the war, the details of the memoir may be summarised thus:

To satisfy bills of exchange advanced by financiers	170,000
Assistance to the citadel at Cadiz	50,000
Payments to the garrison in Ceuta	32,000
Wages and other costs for the siege of Gibraltar	111,284
For the defence of Oran	51,741
To D Juan Eminente, for provisions	62,000
To D Christobal de Aguerri, for provisions	16,000
To the admiral Navarrete, to finance the next fleet	80,000
To the viceroy of Catalonia, for campaign expenses	199,804
For the defence of Mahon	32,000
For transport of artillery in Castile	20,000
To D Gregorio de Mella, for various supplies	88,064
To the royal guard	6,912
To the arms factory at Plasencia	48,000
To pay the army in Castile, January to March	32,195

Total   pesos 1,000,000

In 1706 there were no fleet arrivals from America. The only bullion recorded in the treasury this year was from a private Basque ship, the *Rosario,* captained by Joseph de Ybarra, which arrived at the port of Los Pasajes on 17 March 1706 from America, and from which the crown managed to obtain an indult of 532,500 reales.[59]

There were two years in the period before the Treaty of Utrecht when Spain received virtually nothing from generously laden plate fleets. These years were 1707 and 1709, when the ships from America found it safer to make for a French port than for a Spanish one. The train of events provides an interesting commentary on Franco-Spanish relations during the war. On 27 February 1707 the *capitana* of the Barlovento fleet sailed into the harbour of Brest, in France, in the company of another Spanish ship and two French ships. Its total cargo was estimated to be eight million pesos in silver, of which six belonged to private traders, and cochineal and indigo to the value of three millions;[60] but there is no documentary confirmation of these figures. Philip V on 4 April wrote to Louis XIV offering him one million livres out of the silver meant for himself, and Louis gratefully accepted the offer.[61] The balance of the bullion should subsequently have been transmitted to the Spanish government, but there is no sign in the treasury accounts of any entries relative to the silver. It may be concluded with some probability that most, if not all, of the silver brought from America was seized and utilised by the French government, and that Spain received no benefit whatsoever.

The plate fleet which entered the port of Los Pasajes in Biscay on 27 August 1708 is notable as the first arrival during the war (if we except the 1702 fleet) to have been made under French escort. The whole fleet consisted of nearly two dozen vessels

[59] AGS, Tribunal Mayor de Cuentas leg.1871. This arrival does not, of course, figure in the registers at Seville.

[60] These estimates are made by Boislisle in *Mémoires de Saint-Simon,* vol. 14, p. 284; he also says that most of the bullion belonging to Spain was sent there, and that at the end of February a ship arrived at San Lucar with one million pesos from Mexico. The latter statement is certainly incorrect. The Spanish ambassador in Paris, the duke of Alba, writing to the royal secretary Grimaldo on 6 Mar. 1707, stated that the vessels at Brest 'traen para S. Mgd. un millon de escudos y mas de cien mil para los ministros del Cons° y otros caudales de particulares': AGS, Secretaria de Estado leg.4304.

[61] Louis XIV to Amelot, 18 Apr. 1707, in Girardot, *Correspondance de Louis XIV.*

eight of these were Spanish, including the Barlovento ships. The remainder were French merchant ships and the French naval escort commanded by Ducasse.[62] According to the official statement drawn up in Spain, the total amount of silver brought by the fleet was 1,143,185 pesos, of which 796,403 was intended for the crown, leaving the balance for the council of the Indies and other private individuals.[63] According to Amelot, this round figure of 800,000 was all that came for Philip, but in addition to this the government was going to levy an indult of one million pesos on the fleet.[64] This total figure of 1,800,000 is confirmed by the accounts of the treasury, which show that a sum of 27,635,383 reales was entered from the effects of the 1708 fleet.[65]

While the Spaniards had reason to be grateful to Ducasse and his captains for the protection they had offered the fleet – and Ducasse was eventually to receive the Golden Fleece from Philip as reward for his services – there was also reason for complaint.

I have been assured [Amelot wrote to Desmaretz, the French minister of finance] that the ships of the king's squadron secretly took on board in the Indies silver and other effects which, it is claimed, amount to 800,000 crowns, perhaps more. This would give good grounds for complaint here, if the fact were known. It seems to me that it would be quite just for the king to oblige the owners of this silver and these effects, to contribute as much as the Spaniards to the urgent needs of His Catholic Majesty. It would only be a small help to the king of Spain; but, and this is the important thing, it would serve to establish mutual trust.

[62] For Ducasse, see above, p. 151. A memoir in AE Corr. Pol. (Esp.), 181 f.284 says that 'il y avoit onze gros navires ou fregattes' of France.

[63] 'Relacion de los caudales q en la presente flota del cargo de el Genl Dn Diego Frz de Santillan se han remitido de los Reinos y Provas de la Nueba España', AGI, Contaduría leg.3. The small sum registered is in sharp contrast with the amounts actually sent by officials in Mexico and Peru. Thus the Mexican treasury sent 1,695,771 pesos, but most of this was eaten up by the expense of fitting the fleet, with the result that only 699,154 pesos was actually registered for the government: see AGI, Contaduría leg.892ᵃ no. 49 for detailed figures. Similarly the Peruvian treasury sent 1,357,876 pesos for the government: AGI, Contaduría leg.1762; but it is obvious that only a proportion of this reached Spain, so that to try and reach any general conclusions on the basis of the original sum, an attempt made by M. E. Rodríguez Vicente in her article on 'Los caudales remitidos desde el Peru a España por cuenta de la Real Hacienda. Series estadísticas (1651–1739)', *Anuario de Estudios Americanos*, XXI (1964), is quite misleading.

[64] Amelot to Desmaretz, 3 Sept. 1708, *Mémoires de Saint-Simon*, vol. 16, p. 340. Other correspondence relative to this fleet arrival is also printed in this volume. Amelot sent a duplicate of this letter to Pontchartrain: AN Aff. Etr., B¹ 771.

[65] AGS, Tribunal Mayor de Cuentas leg.1875.

Later he wrote that 'these frauds, for which it is difficult to for-
give the merchants, produce nothing directly for the king, and
take away much from the king of Spain'.[66] Once again, therefore,
Amelot took pains to bring French practice into line with official
condemnations of interloping. Philip v had ample reason to be
dissatisfied with the whole situation, particularly since he was
also committed to meeting all the costs of the French escort –
a sum of 413,528 pesos[67] – out of the silver brought in the fleet.

We cannot leave the year 1708 without mentioning a sizeable
disaster that overtook the *flota* which left Spain in 1706 under the
conde de Casa Alegre. These vessels had been freighted with
bullion in America in June 1708, preparatory to their return home.
They took on silver at Portobelo and were on their way to Cartagena for some more when they were attacked by an English
squadron under Admiral Wager. The *capitana* was blown up,
another ship was sunk, and a third captured by the English: the
almiranta and other ships escaped and took refuge in Cartagena.[68]
The incident represented a serious loss of bullion to the Spanish
government. The only comfort offered by France was a proposal
that nine warships should be sent from Brest to ensure the safety
of the remaining vessels in Cartagena.[69] But by now the Spaniards
had had enough of French generosity.

Spanish discontent reached its peak in 1709. On 27 March that
year, to cite a French report, 'M Chabert, commander of the ship
Aimable, arrived … with seven vessels, six from Saint-Malo
and one from Nantes, all richly laden, coming from the South
Sea. They anchored today in Port-Louis'.[70] Chabert, it will be
recalled,[71] had been sent with a commission from Philip v to
collect bullion from Peru. The bullion loaded on to the *Aimable*
in Callao for Philip v totalled 300,130 pesos.[72] The king of Spain
was therefore entitled to this sum as well as to an indult on

[66] Amelot to Desmaretz, 24 Sept. and 29 Oct. 1708, *Mémoires de Saint-Simon*,
vol. 16, pp. 340 ff.

[67] See the 'Memoire pour servir d'Instruction au sieur D'Aubenton', 18 Apr.
1708, in AN Aff. Etr., B¹ 771.

[68] One account of the disaster is given in Amelot to Louis xiv, 19 Nov. 1708, AE
Corr. Pol. (Esp.), 183 f.70. The remaining ships formed the plate fleet of 1712:
see AGI, Contaduría leg.582 no. 1.

[69] Pontchartrain to Amelot, 12 Sept. 1708, AE Corr. Pol. (Esp.), 185 f.334.

[70] Dahlgren, p. 439. Dahlgren treats fully of the Chabert arrival on pp. 431–80.

[71] See above, p. 151.

[72] AGI, Contaduría leg.1762: Lima treasury accounts for 1708.

anything which the French ships might have brought back on their own account. Not surprisingly, the French ships had managed to accumulate an enormous amount of bullion which, if we adopt the highest official estimate, came to 3,396,174 pesos.[73] The French authorities seized this silver and sent it off immediately to the mints at Paris, Rennes and Nantes, where coin to the value of 10,255,032 livres was produced.[74] Meanwhile a ship that had been separated from Chabert's fleet and had put in at La Coruña, now on 20 May entered La Rochelle. This vessel, the *Vierge de Grace*, brought silver which the government coined to a value of 3,522,065 livres. In addition France now claimed the bullion that had been brought for Philip, as part payment for the expenses of Chabert's expedition. This and other money brought the final total obtained by Louis xiv from this enterprise to 16,255,779 livres.[75]

Spain was predictably furious at this development. Amelot was now faced with the task of disputing the issue with his own government, in an effort to get something substantial for the king of Spain. He pointed out to Pontchartrain that figures available to him estimated the bullion brought back from Peru at 4,390,387 pesos, and that Philip was entitled to an indult of 6 per cent, which should, after payment of all Chabert's expenses, bring in a balance of 319,202 livres to Spain.[76] France agreed on the figure of 6 per cent, but when this was levied it came to only 910,419 livres, which did not even cover the costs of Chabert's expedition.[77] Attempts were made by the French to release the money that had come specifically for Philip v, and this was paid out in small amounts as the money for the indult came in, so that Spain did receive something; but it is unlikely that the sums paid in this way exceeded 250,000 pesos.[78] In any case, there is no record of such a sum, or indeed of any money from the Chabert expedition, entering the royal treasury. Payments were probably made to financiers, from whom at least 2,803,017 reales were

---

[73] Dahlgren, p. 439, citing AE Corr. Pol. (Esp.), 197 f.225. Other estimates differ. One of 15 May in AE Corr. Pol. (Esp.), 196 f.26 gives a total of 3,212,285; and one of 26 March cited by Dahlgren gives 3,369,678.

[74] AE Corr. Pol. (Esp.), 197 f.218.

[75] Dahlgren, p. 475.

[76] Amelot to Pontchartrain, 1 July 1709, AN Aff. Etr., B¹ 771.

[77] Dahlgren, p. 476.

[78] *Ibid.*, pp. 476–7.

borrowed with a promise to repay in silver from the fleet.[79] The whole enterprise therefore brought little help to Spain, and created much contention between the two Bourbon powers. The only American bullion entered in the royal accounts for 1709 was an indult of 300,000 reales from a Basque ship, the *San Antonio de Padua,* which came into port at Brest.[80]

In 1708 the *flota* to America had left Cadiz under the escort of two French frigates, the *Apollon* and the *Triton,* and four French merchantmen. On 2 March 1710 these vessels came into Cadiz harbour in the company of four ships of the Barlovento fleet. Five days later one of their belated Spanish companions put into the bay. The principal cargo of the fleet, apart from silver, was tobacco and leather. The chief items loaded on each ship, excluding anything that may have come for the government, are listed overleaf on page 188.[81]

There seems to have been some doubt, inevitable when smuggling was so frequent, of the precise amount of silver on the fleet.[82] There is also no exact indication of the volume of bullion brought for Philip v and the Hacienda.[83] The French consul in Cadiz informed his government that, according to the official in charge of the bullion, a sum of 1,100,000 pesos had come for Philip; but that with the indult and other grants the royal share should eventually amount to about two millions. A week later he reported that 200,000 of this money was being diverted to military costs in Cadiz and Badajoz, and that a simiilar sum was also being forwarded to the financier Goyeneche; the balance was to be sent to Madrid.[84] We should therefore expect a sum approaching at least 700,000 pesos (the difference between 1,100,000 and the assignations we have noted) to figure in the accounts of the treasury in the Spanish capital. Examination of the entries

[79] AGS, Tribunal Mayor de Cuentas leg.1875.

[80] *Ibid.*

[81] AGI, Contaduría leg.3, 'Mappa de la Plata, Oro y Frutos que se an cargado en la nueva Vera Cruz y puerto de la Havana en los navios de la flota de el cargo de el Almirante General Dn Andres de Pez.' Items for the Hacienda are specifically excluded. The remaining lesser goods on the fleet included chocolate, vanilla and balsam.

[82] A statement in AE Corr. Pol. (Esp.), 198 f.176 estimates the total silver at 5,143,985 pesos, and the amount on the *Apollon* alone at 1,285,920.

[83] At least 706,682 pesos were registered in the fleet for the king: see the statements of 20 Mar. and 16 Nov. 1709 in AGI, Contaduría leg.892ª no. 50.

[84] Mirasol to Pontchartrain, 16 Mar. and 23 Mar. 1710, AN Aff. Etr., B¹ 217 ff.191, 196.

Ships	silver pesos	gold castellanos	silver marks	cochineal in bales	cacao fanegas	leather hides	tobacco (crushed) arrobas	tobacco (in leaf) arrobas	aniline dye cases	sugar cases
Capitana de Barlovento	1,709,665	3,024	880	684	4	450	1,150	—	612	4
Apollon	1,256,769	—	75	419	154	450	1,648	—	260	41
Triton	997,893	—	1,149	214	—	450	275	—	264	—
Saint-François	224,903	—	—	304	70	2,000	4,704	550	92	158
Glorieux	55,510	—	180	63	4	1,106	2,245	585	25	293
Saint-Joseph le Fleurissant	169,749	—	—	189	412	722	1,552	—	139	235
Notre-Dame de la Règle	36,301	—	189	94	4	960	4,938	533	104	240
Nuestra Señora de los Reyes	115,300	—	299	133	392	740	270	110	154	31
Nuestra Señora de Regla	—	—	—	36	311	2,396	3,252	433	54	622
Santo Christo de Maracaibo	—	—	—	—	77	—	4,757	625	10	73
Nuestra Señora de los Remedios	—	—	—	—	—	—	2,093	350	—	—
Totals	4,566,090	3,024	2,772	2,136	1,428	9,274	26,884	3,186	1,714	1,697

reveals that only 11,629,966 reales were paid in this year from the plate fleet.[85] The sum is certainly equivalent to more than 700,000 pesos, but this raises a query about the fate of all the other silver which was presumably owing to the crown. It seems most likely that the balance was paid out to immediate debts and military needs, so that a large proportion of the American silver never saw the inside of the royal coffers. The only other income apart from this to have been received from the Indies in 1710 was a tax of 172,254 reales received from a ship that arrived at the port of Redondela in Galicia.[86]

The following year, 1711, was a lean one for sailings from America, but it saw the arrival of a plate fleet from New Spain. On 31 March the *capitana de Barlovento,* commanded by Andrés de Arriola, entered Cadiz after a crossing of thirty-nine days from Havana. By 4 April a total of five ships, which made up the fleet, had entered the bay. The sum sent specifically for the crown in the *capitana* was a total of 1,155,003 pesos.[87] In addition to this there were sums forthcoming from the indult and other sources. At the end of the month Philip v sent orders to Seville for the distribution of 500,000 pesos to military uses in Saragossa, and 100,000 for the use of troops in Andalucia. The balance of money was sent to Madrid. Royal accounts show that a total of 16,906,108 reales was entered in the treasury from the *flota.*[88] This was the last considerable shipment of bullion to enter the treasury before the end of the War of Succession.

Towards the end of 1711, on 1 November, a French vessel named the *Griffon* came into the port of Pontevedra in Galicia. It was the first of three escort ships under the French admiral Ducasse, who had been sent to conduct vessels from New Spain. The French squadron consisted of the *Griffon,* commanded by the chevalier Touroule; the *Hercule,* under a certain de Broilt; and the *Saint-Michel,* under Ducasse himself. They had left Cartagena on 5 August in the company of nine other vessels, but on the 7th an English fleet scattered some of the vessels and later a

[85] AGS, Tribunal Mayor de Cuentas leg.1880.

[86] Cf. Méritan to Pontchartrain, 31 Sept. 1710, AN Aff. Etr., B¹ 455, describing the ship as 'un Galion d'Espagne venant des Indes et du port de la Vera Cruz'. Méritan was French consul at La Coruña.

[87] 'Carta cuenta de los caudales remitidos por los oficiales R⁸ de Mexico en la Capitana de Barlovento a cargo del Gen⁻¹ Dn Andres de Arriola', AGI, Contaduría leg.784ª no. 46.

[88] AGS, Tribunal Mayor de Cuentas leg. 1881.

storm dispersed the others, with the result that the *Griffon* made Pontevedra unusually early, while one Spanish vessel, the *Nuestra Señora de Regla,* put into San Lucar as late as 20 February 1712, and Ducasse's two remaining ships reached La Coruña only on 25 February. Ducasse's ships were meant to be carrying the remains of bullion from the ill-fated 1708 fleet as well as bullion collected since then. The expedition should therefore have brought in a considerable sum to the Spanish exchequer. For various reasons, however, this did not happen. The accounts show that as much as 489,606 pesos[89] was spent by Ducasse on fitting out the fleet. The *Griffon* brought 258,360 pesos for Philip, but the main fleet brought only twice as much, and the total silver entered in the royal treasury was only 10,006,539 reales.[90] Probably as a mark of gratitude, the Spanish government granted to the *Griffon* soon after its arrival a special concession to trade to Vera Cruz from any port in France with a fixed freight of three hundred tons (*toneladas*), on condition of a payment of 50,000 pesos in silver.[91] The council of the Indies protested in vain against this unusual concession, which, not for the first time, created a formal breach in the long-established Spanish monopoly of trade to the Indies.

One other shipment of bullion in 1712 remains to be noted. This was the sum brought by the French ship *Baron de la Force,* which entered Port-Louis on 5 June. It was supposed to be carrying bullion rescued from the *almiranta de Barlovento,* which had sunk off the coast of Havana. In addition to the silver brought for individuals, there were 500,000 pesos intended for Philip v.[92] A proportion of this money was assigned to France as a final payment towards the costs of Ducasse's expedition,[93] but there is

---

[89] AGI, Contaduría leg.582 no. 1, statement dated 12 Apr. 1712; also AGI, Indiferente leg.2721, the whole of this *legajo* being devoted to Ducasse's fleet.

[90] AGS, Tribunal Mayor de Cuentas leg.1891; AGS, Dirección General del Tesoro, Inventario 24, leg.555 and 557.

[91] Decree of 21 Jan. 1712, AGI, Indiferente leg. 2755. The *Griffon* was luckier than the *Aigle de Nantes,* another French vessel discussed in this *legajo*. Trading illegally to Vera Cruz in the summer of 1712, the captain of the *Aigle* on 1 September had his ship and cargo confiscated by the governor of the city. The vessel was not released till an indult of 50,000 pesos was paid to the king. This meant at least informal collusion in interloping. The *Aigle*'s cargo was worth 186,135 pesos, resulting in an obvious profit to the interlopers.

[92] Manuel López Pintado to Grimaldo, Paris 14 June 1712, AHN, Estado leg. 3028¹.

[93] Bonnac to Pontchartrain, 31 Aug. 1712, AN Aff. Etr., B¹ 775.

no sign that the rest of the bullion reached Spain or the treasury at Madrid, with the result that Philip appears not to have seen a penny of the entire shipment of silver.

The plate fleet of 1713 will be the last to be discussed here, for it was the last one to have any effect on royal finances during the War of the Spanish Succession. On 30 March the *capitana de Barlovento,* commanded by Pedro de Ribera, entered the harbour of Cadiz with four other vessels. The fleet had left Vera Cruz on 19 January, but half the ships were scattered by a storm on 28 February, leading to the loss of one vessel and the late arrival of one in Cadiz and two others in La Coruña. The French consul was informed that the king had been sent 1,200,000 pesos from New Spain, and that the indult of 8½ per cent on other goods in the fleet would add another half million pesos to this sum.[94] This is probably an overestimate, for the sum entered in the royal treasury, 11,973,380 reales,[95] approximates more nearly to a figure of about 800,000 pesos. However, there is every likelihood that a proportion of the silver forthcoming to the crown was assigned away before entering the treasury.

This brief outline of fleet arrivals and the bullion they brought for the crown, throws into perspective only one aspect of the *carrera de Indias.* We have not discussed the general circumstances and significance of the *flotas* that left Spain for America in this period, nor has there been space to discuss in detail the fleets that arrived from America. Inquiry into the amount of silver brought for the crown still leaves undecided the total value of each of the fleets, and the overall volume of bullion brought into the peninsula during the war. Such questions would occupy a volume to themselves. The few results that have been obtained are summarised briefly in table 4 on page 192, which shows the distribution of American silver between 1701 and 1713.

Perhaps the most important question to arise out of this tabulated survey of bullion is the extent to which the silver fleets helped the war effort. Is there any truth in the suggestion that the victory of the Bourbon over the Habsburg dynasty was won by American silver? There can be no doubt that the archduke was

---

[94] Mirasol to Pontchartrain, 4 June 1713, AN Aff. Etr., B¹ 220 f.221. However, the accounts of the Mexican treasury show only 982,790 pesos registered on the *flota:* AGI, Contaduría leg.892ª no. 53, statement of 11 Jan. 1713.

[95] AGS, Tribunal Mayor de Cuentas legs.1891, 1892; AGS, Dirección General del Tesoro, Inventario 24, leg.557.

TABLE 4. DISTRIBUTION OF BULLION FROM AMERICA 1701–13
(IN REALES OF VELLON)

Year	Destination	Estimated total[96]	Philip V	Louis XIV
1701	Cadiz	?	6,450,000	—
1702[97]	Vigo	?	68,962,395	35,952,000
1703	Cadiz	?	90,000	—
1704	Cadiz	45,000,000[98]	7,565,412	—
1705	Cadiz	?	15,000,000	—
1706	Pasajes	?	532,500	—
1707	Brest	125,000,000[99]	—	?
1708	Pasajes	150,000,000[100]	27,635,383	?
1709	Port-Louis	83,000,000[101]	?	81,278,895
1710	Cadiz[102]	78,000,000	17,802,220	—
1711	Cadiz[103]	120,000,000	25,906,198	—
1712	Coruña	?	10,006,539	?
1713	Cadiz	80,000,000[104]	11,973,380	—

at a disadvantage here, but it must be remembered that he was powerfully helped by the financial resources of the Allies, and that Barcelona also witnessed the import of silver – Anglo-Dutch silver.[105] The relative importance of bullion in royal finances is a matter to be discussed in the next chapter. For the moment it may be said that none of the shipments, apart from the windfall at Vigo, made any substantial impact on royal finances. In 1704, for

[96] In all cases the balance of the total is assumed to have gone to individual merchants.

[97] The distribution figures are arrived at by subtracting 2,396,800 pesos (for Louis) from the 6,994,293 that entered the treasury: see text above.

[98] Abbé d'Estrées to Torcy, 14 May 1704, 'L'argent qu'ils aportent ne va pas tout a fait a trois millions d'ecus', AE Corr. Pol. (Esp.), 138 f.49.

[99] Mémoires de Saint-Simon, vol. 14, p. 284.

[100] Amelot's estimate in ibid., vol 16, p. 340.

[101] This minimal estimate is based on the figures given in AE Corr. Pol. (Esp.), 197 f.225.

[102] The total figure is based on an arrival of about 5,200,000 pesos; and the king's share is obtained by adding 400,000 pesos and 172,254 reales to 11,629,966 reales.

[103] The total is estimated by Mirasol to Pontchartrain, 4 Apr. 1711, AN Aff. Etr., B¹ 218 f.85; the royal share adds 600,000 pesos to 16,906,108 reales, as given in the text.

[104] Mirasol to Pontchartrain, 4 June 1713, AN Aff. Etr., B¹ 220 f.221.

[105] For a detailed discussion of silver imports and minting of coinage in Catalonia see Pierre Vilar, La Catalogne dans l'Espagne moderne (3 vols), Paris, 1962, vol. 1, pp. 685–90.

instance, the cost of the war in Spain was put at over a hundred million reales,[106] but the bullion coming to the government that year did not exceed eight millions and for the whole period of the war averaged only fifteen millions a year. The importance of American silver cannot, however, be minimised. It supplemented the flow of specie in Bourbon Spain, and helped to support government credit. The authorities very wisely never used the plate fleets to pay creditors, but assigned the income immediately to current obligations, so that Philip did not waste his silver trying to wipe out old debts.

A secondary question of immense interest is the degree to which France benefited from the plate fleets. We have already seen that enormous profits were made by France out of official and unofficial interloping in the Indies. In years when virtually no bullion reached the peninsula, French vessels from Saint-Malo and other ports were unloading several millions of silver and goods in France. Profits were also made from bullion destined for the king of Spain. Table 4 shows that the totals established for bullion acquired by Louis xiv come to nearly two-thirds of the total received by Philip for the entire period of the war. If in addition it could be demonstrated that Louis received as much from the 1707 arrival in Brest as he did from the 1709 arrival in Port-Louis, then unquestionably the French government received more during the war than the Spanish government did. This possibility, and it is a strong and likely one, introduces a new dimension into the study of Franco-Spanish relations during the war, for it establishes definitely that Spain was benefiting rather less from its colonies than France was.

This evidence does not of course lead to any novel conclusion, but merely reinforces the old *arbitrista* dogma that silver from America never tarried long in the peninsula. Other evidence accumulated from the war period lends force to the dogma. We have already seen that a large but indefinable quantity of bullion was smuggled regularly out of the peninsula, especially from Cadiz and Bilbao. This method may well have accounted for a substantial part of the American silver that went not to the crown but to private merchants who were often agents for French and other foreign interests. To this we may add the money that the king of Spain was obliged to spend in France on war materials,

[106] Ozon to Torcy, 17 Sept. 1704, AE Corr. Pol. (Esp.), 139 f.50.

uniforms and armaments, expenditure which, as we have seen in a previous chapter, amounted to several millions. One quotation, from the French commander in Spain in 1704, illustrates this aspect. 'I am convinced', he wrote to the French minister for war, 'that in order to clothe and arm his troops this winter the king of Spain will have to purchase about 1,500,000 livres of goods from France, and I shall not be surprised if Samuel Bernard accepts the contract for three millions that Monsieur Orry wished to make in France to clothe the troops of Spain.'[107] The Spanish treasury, however, did not limit itself to expenditure on its own troops. Substantial aid was granted to France both within and without the country. 'Last year, in 1707,' Amelot reminded Louis xiv in February 1708, 'the king your grandson aided Your Majesty to the extent of 3,500,000 livres, both by the silver left in France out of what arrived at Brest (1,405,000), and by all that has been supplied in this country to the troops of Your Majesty.'[108] French expenditure in Spain, on the other hand, was very limited. Even French war debts in the peninsula tended to be paid through bills of exchange on French bankers in Cadiz or Madrid, so that little bullion entered the country.

The inescapable conclusion is that the movement of bullion was overwhelmingly one-way only, encouraged and promoted by the instruments of French policy in both countries. This is not to deny that French money did enter the peninsula, particularly after the decree which in 1706 allowed French coin to circulate in Spain. That experiment, however, was of short duration and small financial significance. At least once during the war, in 1706, Louis actually sent bullion into Spain[109] as proof of his devotion to his grandson; but more usually, as in 1705,[110] he made a nominal advance of sums which were used to pay off Philip's debts within France, so that no bullion left the country for Spain. In general it seems certain that only a tiny proportion of French bullion was circulating in the peninsula, and that the French

---

[107] Puységur to Chamillart, 8 Aug. 1704, Guerre, A¹ 1788 f.226.

[108] Amelot to Louis xiv, 6 Feb. 1708, AE Corr. Pol. (Esp.), 178 f.122.

[109] The sum was 783,000 livres, but of this 300,000 was a payment by the Asiento Company, and 103,000 was in bills of exchange, so the cash sent by Louis was actually only 380,000 livres: Amelot to Louis xiv, 2 Nov. 1706, AE Corr. Pol. (Esp.), 162 f.1.

[110] Philip v to Louis xiv, 4 June 1705, AE Corr. Pol. (Esp.), 152 f.432. Louis xiv promised to advance two million livres. The same thing happened in 1709: Amelot to Grimaldo, 22 Aug. 1709, AHN, Estado leg.2313.

authorities were more afraid of exporting coin than of suffering the unfavourable rate of exchange in Spain.

In the light of these observations, there is no basis for claiming that 'the injection of bullion by foreign armies revived the Spanish economy'.[111] Whatever the situation may have been in Catalonia, in Bourbon Spain at least there is no evidence for economic advance fostered by foreign gold. The whole question derives from the writings of the eighteenth-century statesmen Jovellanos[112] and Campomanes. According to the latter, the War of Succession was beneficial because:

in order to finance their undertakings, our enemies introduced immense sums with which to pay their troops. All these quantities built up an effective fund of that which Spain lacked entirely, with the result that the peninsula acquired a monetary circulation greater than any it had had since the discovery of the Indies. Few people would have believed in 1703 that those unjust invasions would turn to the real benefit of Spain. It is from then that the recovery of the country must be dated. This was the first benefit obtained by Spain in the glorious reign of Philip v.[113]

Writing elsewhere on the same subject, Campomanes observed that:

the war was less destructive than is believed. Valencia improved its cloth-production with the War of Succession, since a large number of foreign soldiers, experts in silk-weaving, settled down there. Catalonia recovered in the same way. . . . The great mass of money that foreign troops spent in Spain remedied the shortage of specie that there had been in the time of Charles ii. Military discipline recovered, and with it all the arts connected with the army.[114]

While there was certainly reform and revival in this period, and the war undeniably gave an impetus to new developments, it is impossible to accept the explanations given by Campomanes and

[111] Roland Mousnier, *Histoire Générale des Civilisations*, vol. 4, *Les XVIᵉ et XVIIᵉ siècles*, Paris, 1961, p. 318.

[112] Gaspar Melchor de Jovellanos, *Informe de la Sociedad Económica de Madrid . . . en el expediente de Ley Agraria*, Palma, 1814, pp. 6–7: 'La guerra de sucesión, aunque por otra parte funesta, no solo retuvo en casa los fondos y los brazos que antes parecían fuera de ella, sino que atraxo algunos de las provincias extrañas, y los puso en actividad dentro de las nuestras.'

[113] Pedro Rodríguez, Conde de Campomanes, *Discurso sobre la Educación Popular de los Artesanos, y su Fomento*, Madrid, 1775, pp. 420–1.

[114] *Discurso sobre el Fomento de la Industria Popular*, Madrid, 1774, pp. 170–1.

Jovellanos. Their schema is too purely bullionist to be valid. In Bourbon Spain, more money left the country than came into it. Whatever benefits the war may have had, therefore, they cannot be attributed to bullion.

This situation gives rise to an important theoretical problem. The evidence accumulated above has demonstrated that the balance of payments was unfavourable to Spain and yet that Spain had a more favourable rate of exchange than France. International exchange rates are normally unfavourable to a country with an adverse balance of payments. In addition, according to the bullion-istic concepts of eighteenth-century mercantilism (a doctrine followed by Campomanes), the relative quantity of bullion held by any two given countries was supposed to determine the exchange rate of their currencies,[115] so that it is contradictory to hold that Spain lost bullion to France and yet had a stronger currency than France. The contradiction is, however, a superficial one, and relies for its validity on an excessively bullionistic view of inter-national exchange. As Adam Smith pointed out long ago in an attack on mercantilist doctrine, there is no necessary connection between the balance of payments and the rate of exchange.[116] Although Spain may have lost considerable bullion to France and other countries, this was balanced by the residue of bullion from America, by government policy of drawing on bankers' reserves, and by drawing on coin in circulation through increased taxation, so that the purchasing power of currency remained constant. This stability of coinage insured Spain against the worst effects of war inflation.[117] France, on the other hand, suffered prolonged inflation, financial credit collapsed sensationally in 1709, and the government had heavy bullion commitments, particularly in the Netherlands. No imports of silver were sufficient to meet the demands of expenditure. Under these circumstances the rate of exchange was bound to favour Spain, despite the movement of bullion out of the peninsula.

[115] See Eli F. Heckscher, *Mercantilism* (2 vols), London, 1934, vol. 2, p. 250.

[116] Adam Smith, *An inquiry into the nature and causes of the Wealth of Nations* (2 vols) ed. E. Cannan, London, 1950, vol. 1, pp. 440–1: 'The ordinary course of exchange can afford no sufficient indication that the ordinary state of debt and credit is in favour of that country which seems to have, or which is supposed to have, the ordinary course of exchange in its favour'.

[117] For a graph of prices, see below, p. 374.

PART THREE

The Finances in a Disunited Spain

9 The Finances of the State[1]

The Habsburg monarchy in Spain was submerged by and ultimately vanished in a morass of accumulated debts. Something approaching a miracle would have been needed to put the finances of the state in order, and though nothing comparable materialised during the first two decades of the century, serious attempts were certainly made to reform the system by which taxes were administered. There were two distinct problems to be considered. In the first place there were the taxes themselves, an enormous mass of impositions affecting most commodities and nearly all sections of the population. In the second place there was the administrative system, only occasionally under the direct control of the central government. *Arbitristas* of the seventeenth century had on the whole been convinced that the excessive number of taxes was to blame for the ills of the country's economy. Government reformers, on the other hand, assumed that despite its imperfections the tax-system could be properly and beneficially operated, but that the *unum necessarium* was a radical change in the method of collecting and administering taxes.

There was at the end of the seventeenth century no one body responsible for the finances of the monarchy as a whole. Each

[1] Far from being an adequate contribution to the history of the Hacienda in the eighteenth century, this chapter merely concentrates on factors more or less relevant to the war of the Spanish Succession. A fuller survey of the tax-system and the Hacienda up to 1700 is given in the two modern works by Ramon Carande, *Carlos V y sus banqueros* (2 vols), Madrid, 1949, 1965, and Antonio Domínguez Ortiz, *Política y Hacienda de Felipe IV*, Madrid, 1960. For the reign of Philip v, reference should be made to Francisco Gallardo Fernández, *Origen, Progresos y Estado de las Rentas de la Corona de España*, Madrid, 1806–1832, and to the classic by Gerónimo de Uztáriz, *Theórica y Práctica de Comercio y de Marina*, Madrid, 1742. The best modern work on Philip v relies heavily on Uztáriz: André Mounier, *Les faits et la doctrine économiques en Espagne sous Philippe V – Gerónimo de Uztáriz (1670–1732)*, Bordeaux, 1919.

province, whether peninsular such as Aragon, or foreign such as Flanders or Milan, was largely in charge of its own expenses and taxation, and the *Consejo de Hacienda* (council of finance) at Madrid was directly responsible for only the realms of Castile and León. However, though it collected only Castilian taxes, the Hacienda was employed to finance all the needs of the empire, so that the cost of imperial policy fell on Castile and León alone. We shall in the next few chapters examine the financial relations between the crown of Castile and the realms of Aragon. It should be noted here that the taxes in the rest of the monarchy were usually consumed in the dominions themselves, and that only a trickle made its way to the peninsula; the only money forthcoming from Italy, for example, being the salaries of the members of the council of Italy. America was the sole dependency to send any income to the Spanish crown, and even this was neither regular nor substantial. In financial matters, therefore, the Hacienda stood alone, and 'Castile bears the weight of the whole monarchy'.[2] There were two opinions among *arbitristas* about this state of affairs. The first view considered that Spain should cease to support an overseas empire which was of no direct benefit to the mother country, and which tied up both troops and money in places as diverse as the Netherlands, Italy and America. The alternative view, of more respectable parentage since the principal *arbitristas* of the seventeenth century as well as the great conde duque de Olivares had held it, considered that the other realms of the monarchy, and more particularly the realms of the crown of Aragon, should take their share of the imperial burden. Melchor de Macanaz, in this as in other respects a follower of traditional views, supported the latter opinion. The monarchy he served, however, did not restrict itself to any one view, and in fact carried out both of the alternatives, first in 1707 by revoking the *fueros* of the crown of Aragon, and then in 1713 by relieving itself of Italy and the Netherlands at Utrecht.

The structure of the Hacienda in the early eighteenth century was determined in 1694, when it became the sole administrator of taxes in Castile and León. The number of ministers on the council was fixed at six in 1691 and raised to eight in 1701. Other members of the council included the president (or 'governor'), a chancellor, a fiscal and two secretaries. The Hacienda was

2 'Descripzion de la Monarchia de España', AE Corr. Pol. (Esp.), 91 f.239.

divided into four sections: the *Sala de Gobierno,* responsible for all administration and the collection of taxes; the *Sala de Justicia,* concerned with judicial business; the *Sala de Millones,* controlling the special taxes known as *millones* (the *sala* included the president, three councillors and the fiscal); and the *Tribunal de la Contaduría Mayor de Cuentas,* with one councillor and four accountants, which did all the work of accounting. The royal treasury was an adjunct of the Hacienda and operated as part of it, usually under the same officials. It was known as the *Tesorería General,* and received and distributed a number of the taxes administered by the Hacienda. In addition, the *Tesorero General,* who was its head, was in charge of the deposit box known as the *Arcas de tres llaves,* so called because only the operation of three keys, held by three different persons, could open it. The president of the Hacienda was the single most important man in the system. For most of the time that Orry exercised influence, the president was the bishop of Gironda[3]. From 1709 to 1713 it was the marqués de Campoflorido.

In 1683 an ambitious attempt had been made to reform the whole structure of taxation, but it failed completely, and subsequent changes were limited to altering the size and functions of the central council alone. There was a reform along these lines in 1691, and on 25 February 1701. No fundamental changes were considered until the comprehensive proposals for reform drawn up by Orry in 1703.[4] Setting aside all his other long-term proposals, Orry was concerned primarily with securing a steady income for the war effort; he therefore suggested the setting up of a special treasury for military finance. In accordance with this proposal, on 2 October 1703 the king set up a *Tesorería Mayor de la Guerra,* which was to receive all money for war from the Hacienda, but which could not make payments except by order of the king or of the minister for war. The *Tesorero Mayor* was thus meant to be a passive instrument and nothing more.[5] The post was allotted to a prominent financier, Juan de Orcasitas y Avellaneda, conde de Moriana. His terms of office were from

[3] Lorenzo Armengual, titular bishop of Gironda, for a time secretary to the archbishop of Saragossa then later his auxiliary bishop. Created bishop of Cadiz at the end of the war.

[4] AE Corr. Pol. (Esp.), 119 *passim.*

[5] Decree of 4 Nov. 1703, AGS, Dirección General del Tesoro, Inventario 4, leg.10; Guerre, A¹ 1786 f.101, Gramont to Chamillart, 15 Aug. 1704.

2 October 1703 to 17 October 1704, from 1 June 1705 to 30 June 1707, and finally from 1 July 1713 to 31 December 1716.

After 1703, then, there were two central treasuries, the Tesorería Mayor and the Tesorería General, each receiving an important portion of Hacienda revenue. This diversity of receipt-houses meant that accounts remained complicated, and it was still impossible to know the precise state of national finance at any given moment. Gradually, however, the system regulated itself. The Tesorería Mayor increased in importance as the War of Succession progressed, and the government found it convenient to enter more and more revenues into the one treasury. On 31 December 1708 a royal decree ordered all the principal revenues of the crown to be paid into the Tesorería Mayor as from 1 January 1709, but there is no evidence of how far this order was complied with.[6] In 1711 the Tesorería Mayor ceased functioning, and all revenues were entered into the Tesorería General alone. On 26 June 1713, as a result of the return of Orry to the direction of finances, the Tesorería Mayor was again established, with the conde de Moriana at its head, and continued in this form until 1718, when an order of 4 July suppressed it and transferred all its functions to the Tesorería General, which now collected all the revenue of the crown.[7] From this outline it will be seen that the war treasury was a particular creation of Orry, and flourished most in periods when he wielded power.

There were corresponding changes in the council of finance itself, motivated by a desire for economy and efficiency. When the royal family returned to Madrid after the first Allied occupation in 1706, all the councils were drastically reduced in size, among them the Hacienda, which was cut from twenty-eight members to only ten.[8] No structural alterations occurred, however, until Orry's return to power in 1713. Then on 10 November that year he and Macanaz published the *nueva planta* or new system, by which all the councils were substantially enlarged. The Hacienda, for instance, was given four presidents instead of one.[9] The purpose of the *nueva planta,* which we have already touched upon, was clearly to introduce greater departmentalisation and greater

---

[6] AGS, Secretaría de Estado leg.7835; Tribunal Mayor de Cuentas leg.1882.

[7] Hacienda, Ordenes Generales de Rentas vol. III ff.277–355.

[8] Amelot to Louis xiv, 5 Oct. 1706, AE Corr. Pol. (Esp.), 161 f.132.

[9] The text of the decree is given in AGS, Dirección General del Tesoro, Inventario 4, leg.10.

dependence on ministerial guidance. But no conspicuous advantages resulted from this reform, and when the French advisers of Philip were expelled in 1715 a decree of 4 August 1715 restored the Hacienda to its form in 1701. Of all the changes in these years, only the institution of the Tesorería Mayor retained some importance, because its development coincided with state centralisation. When the realms of Aragon were brought under the Castilian crown, for example, their revenues also entered into the single Tesorería at Madrid.

It may safely be said that the principal changes in methods of accounting were introduced by the French. For the first time in Spanish history systematic and regular accounting, usually double-entried (as had long been practised), plotted the precise development of government finance. Where entries used to be made in Roman numerals, now all accounts were kept in Arabic numerals. Officials in the Tribunal Mayor de Cuentas began to draw up annual statements, suitably balancing income and expenditure, to cover the terms of office of each royal treasurer. Thanks to this, it has been possible to examine in detail every aspect of royal revenue and expenditure for the whole of the reign of Philip v. The contrast with the preceding reign is striking. Under Charles 11 the confusion of accounts and the irregularity of financial statements make it extremely difficult to arrive at any detailed assessment of the state of the Hacienda. In the eighteenth century, on the other hand, a wealth of sometimes contradictory figures is available to facilitate the study of state finance.

Before discussing the collection and administration of revenues it will be necessary to enter into a brief description of the tax system in Castile. The picture available in 1700 alters radically by 1718, so that a clear distinction must be drawn between the systems in existence at these two dates. The royal taxes, known as the *rentas reales,* may be best analysed in the earlier period along lines adopted by Orry in his 1703 memoir.[10] He considered quite correctly that since no revenue came to the crown from Aragon, Catalonia, Valencia or Navarre, the primary task was to analyse the income from Castile and America, the only two territories to support the treasury. The taxes levied on Castile alone were known

---

[10] A good and very helpful summary of the memoir is given by B. J. Roud, in his Cambridge B. Litt. thesis on finance and administration under Philip v, which he kindly allowed me to consult.

as *rentas provinciales,* and in addition to these there were general taxes, *rentas generales* (particularly customs dues and monopolies), whose very nature meant they extended beyond the frontiers of Castile. These two broad classifications were divided by Orry into four main classes: 1. *Regalías,* old royal taxes granted in perpetuity. 2. *Servicios,* taxes voted by the cortes to assist the crown. The most important of these taxes on consumer goods was the *millones.* 3. *Gracias apostólicas,* or ecclesiastical taxes granted, as the title implies, by the papacy. These had to be re-negotiated regularly and were not perpetual. 4. American taxes, and those due from other realms.

The best known of all taxes classified under the definition of *regalías,* was the *alcabala,* which originated in the fourteenth century and was a tax of about 10 per cent on each sale of any movable or immovable goods. The *alcabala* was estimated to produce one-fifth of the total revenue. The *cientos* were an addition to the *alcabala* and were created in 1639 under Philip IV; originally levied at a rate of 4 per cent on top of the *alcabala* (and therefore named *cuatro unos por ciento*), under Charles II in 1686 they were reduced by half (hence the name *cuatro medios*) to a rate of 2 per cent. From 1705 they were levied again at the old rate. The *aduanas* or customs duties were payable on entry as well as on exit, the rate varying according to the region and the tax-farmer concerned: they brought in about one-tenth of total revenue. The customs dues went under a wide variety of names, depending on the locality, such as *almojarifazgos* for those payable in Andalucia (the duty at Seville was known as the *almojarifazgo mayor*), *puertos secos* for those in Navarre and *puertos altos* for those on the border between Castile and the provinces of Aragon and Valencia. The importance of these duties brings into relief the lack of unity in the peninsula where, as in France, tolls and taxes were payable before goods could be transported from one province to another. The different types of duty which could be charged on the entry of goods was legion: there were the *almojarifazgos,* the *cuatro unos por ciento* of Cadiz, the same of Málaga, the *diezmos de la mar, puertos secos* and *puertos altos, puertos de Portugal, lanas* (on wool), special customs duties in the Canary islands, the *sosa y barrilla de Murcia* (Murcian glass-wort; the tax on this came to 6 reales a *quintal* or about 4 per cent *ad valorem*), taxes on *cacao y chocolate,* the *extracción y regalía de Sevilla,* the same of Málaga, the duty on sugar in Granada, the *renta de la pasa* in Málaga, the *renta de la pimienta,* the tax on *goma y polvos azules,* the tax on paper, and the *alcabalas y cientos del tabaco.*

Other taxes classified among the *regalías* included the salt-tax or *salinas,* a duty of 21 reales on every *fanega* of salt. Salt had been a royal monopoly since the time of Philip 11, and the monopoly was extended to the crown of Aragon after 1707. There were also taxes on mines, which were generally adjudged to be the property of the crown; and on the minting of coin, from which the crown claimed seigniorage. The *media anata* consisted basically of half the first year's salary on any public office, but additional dues made the tax, in Orry's opinion, equivalent to about one-sixth the value of an office. The *papel sellado,* a stamp-tax on paper, which had been a royal monopoly in Castile since 1636 and was to become a monopoly in Aragon after 1707, brought in an annual income similar to that of the *media anata,* namely about one-tenth the yield of the *alcabalas.* A tax on playing-cards, the *renta de naipes,* also brought in a considerable sum. Tobacco, which was a royal monopoly farmed out to local administrators, provided the third greatest source of income to the crown, after the *alcabalas* and the *millones*: the monopoly had existed in Castile since 1636, in Aragon since 1686. The remaining taxes in the category of *regalías* fell on food, there being special impositions on cacao, chocolate and coffee. It should be noted that the kingdom of Granada paid four special taxes levied nowhere else: these were the *renta de la abuela,* a tax on oil, bricks and other commodities; the *renta de la población,* consisting of various taxes originally levied by Philip 11 to pay for the resettlement of the area after the Alpujarra rebellion; the *renta de la seda,* a very heavy tax on silks, equivalent to about 46 per cent of actual value; and the *renta del azúcar* or duty on sugar, on which the many taxes paid amounted to 21 per cent of actual value.

The chief tax among the *servicios* was the *millones,* created in 1588 after the failure of the great Armada, as a temporary imposition on consumer goods such as wine, vinegar, oil, meat, soap and paper. Later the tax became permanent. The principal imposition was the *servicio de 24 millones,* first granted in 1650, which was supposed to produce 24 million ducats in six years, or four million a year. Its actual product was only slightly less than that of the *alcabala.* The rate of tax on each item varied: in the 1720s an *arroba* of wine paid a fixed tax of 64 maravedis, an *arroba* of oil 50 maravedis, and one of vinegar 32. In Madrid there was a special additional consumer tax called the *sisa,* which was equivalent to one-eighth the value of the item taxed. The *millones* were extended considerably when necessary: thus in 1638 the *servicio de ocho mil soldados* was created, whereby the taxes on meat and wine were raised in order to pay for the costs of the war with France. The *servicio ordinario y extraordinario* was a fixed sum of about 150 million maravedis which was apportioned among the population of Castile, generally by households. Granada was the only region exempted from this tax. A further duty of 15 maravedis per thousand (*el quince al millar*) was levied on top of this to cover costs. The *milicias* (suppressed in 1724) and *lanzas* were both commutations of feudal services; the former, of personal service; the latter, of the obligation to supply armed men. In practice both taxes were used to support local militia and other purposes of war. The *servicio y montazgo* was a tax on each sheep at pasture, and was an essential component of the control exercised by the guild of sheep-farmers, the Mesta, over the flocks in Spain. Finally, the *fiel medidor,* a duty first raised in 1642 under Philip IV to pay for the services of a judge of weights and measures, was equivalent to 4 maravedis on each *arroba* of wine, vinegar and oil.

The only other regular taxes to be considered here are those payable by the Church. In general the Spanish clergy were exempt from taxation, though they were liable to the *servicio de 24 millones.* Their freedom from secular taxation, however, was balanced by payment of duties negotiated with the bishops and the Holy See. The four most important clerical impositions were the *tercias reales* or *dos novenos,* a tax originating in the thirteenth century and equivalent to two-ninths of the income from tithes; the *subsidio,* an annual tax on real property; the *excusado,* a sort of tithe; and the *cruzada,* which was originally paid to promote the struggle against the Moors.

America was still an important supplier of bullion to the government, and the royal taxes collected there added up to considerable sums every year. Unfortunately, as we have already seen, the money sent by the treasuries in Lima and Mexico for the crown, seldom corresponded with what reached Spain. Most of the money was invariably eaten up by administrative costs, so that in practice

America had ceased to be a reliable contributor to the Hacienda.

Over the centuries the chief demand made on the *rentas reales* was from *juros*. A *juro* was an annuity paid by the crown in return usually for advances of capital. The principal method of payment was by assigning the revenue from certain taxes or even by alienating the tax. As royal indebtedness increased, so did the complexity of the *juro* commitment. The debts were made hereditary, *por juro de heredad*, whence the name; and the creditors were called *juristas*. By the end of the seventeenth century *juros* were the biggest single liability of the Hacienda.

Not all the taxes noted above reached the Hacienda. The ecclesiastical taxes in particular were not administered by the council nor did they as a rule figure in the accounts. The crown devoted them directly to the upkeep of the Spanish outposts in northern Africa, including Oran and other forts. Similarly, the *lanzas* and *milicias* were usually used to maintain the provincial militia and tended not to figure in the accounts of the Hacienda. In addition to all these, there were the purely municipal taxes, voted and levied by the towns themselves. Though these technically belonged to the crown, apparently nothing reached the Hacienda.

Harassed by inherited debts and overwhelmed by current obligations, the crown in the late seventeenth century came to terms with its creditors in an effort to divide the revenue fairly between past and present claimants. A decree of 6 February 1688[11] decided that the crown would henceforth reserve to itself four million escudos of each year's income, for state expenses. The balance of the revenue would be devoted to the following three purposes: firstly, payment of preferential *juros* or *juros reservados*, that is, those *juros* which the government held to be of primary importance, particularly those held by the Church; secondly, a sum of 500,000 escudos to repay loans from merchant bankers; thirdly, a sum of 200,000 escudos for salaries and pensions payable by the crown. The new system was not always successful, but it was being practised at the time that Orry reviewed the state of the Hacienda.

Thanks to Orry's labours, it is possible to arrive at a presumably exact computation of the revenues entering the Hacienda in 1702–3, and the proportion of this income that went on *juros*.

[11] AGS, Consejo y Juntas de Hacienda leg.1112.

Table 5 (pp. 203–11), which gives revenue in vellon reales, retains the original Spanish name of each tax concerned. From the table it will be seen that *juros* continued to be a permanent and serious liability on government income. To the revenues listed here must be added the income from the clerical taxes. It was estimated at this date that the *cruzada* brought in as much as 2,533,803 escudos (25,338,030 reales) a year, but that previous and current assignations wiped this amount out almost immediately.[12]

The actual revenue of the Hacienda bore little relation to the possible revenue. In other words, only a proportion of the income from taxes ever reached the crown. Exemptions and frauds accounted for much of the deficit; collection, moreover, required an army of tax-collectors and often consumed much of the value of the taxes in costs. Nearly all the *rentas* were contracted and farmed out to individual merchants and financiers who paid the Hacienda a lump sum and in turn collected the taxes through subordinates. This system meant that the government had to estimate the probable income in order to issue a farm, and that the tax-farmers usually made a handsome profit on the transaction. The state therefore suffered in its revenue, and its subjects suffered at the hands of free-enterprise tax-collectors. Clearly the big problem was the lack of an administrative apparatus responsible to the government alone. On occasion the Hacienda resorted to alternative methods of tax-collection. Sometimes it took taxes into 'administration', which meant direct control over levying and collecting. At other times it allowed localities an *encabezamiento*, that is, the government assessed the taxes and local officials collected them, so that no third parties made a profit. However, neither of these methods was ever convincingly successful, so that the crown inevitably reverted to the system of *arrendamientos,* or tax-farming.

The great advantage of *arrendamientos* was that revenue was immediately realisable from the financiers who undertook the farm. Towards the beginning of the reign the chief tax-farmers included Hubert Hubrechtz, who controlled the *millones* of Cuenca and the salt-mines of Galicia and Asturias; Francisco Sánchez de Portal, who controlled the cacao and chocolate monopoly; Francisco Esteban Rodríguez, who controlled the

---

[12] Memorandum by secretary of the *despacho*, the marqués de Ribas, in Guerre, A¹ 1786 f.302. A breakdown of the expenditure of the *cruzada* is given on f.303.

TABLE 5. THE RENTAS REALES IN 1702 (IN VELLON REALES)[13]

Names of farms in Hacienda	Current product	Net product[14]	Settled to crown by 1688 decree[15]	Total juros created	Juros paid currently[16]
Alcabalas y tercias	20,129,024	19,363,136	7,009,637	31,964,868	10,801,218
Quatro medios por ciento	9,808,308	9,332,472	5,359,257	10,983,202	3,241,869
Servicio ord. y extraord. (except Granada)	4,256,246	4,092,257	2,732,437	4,095,597	1,596,018
Papel sellado	1,899,718	1,275,135	762,362	2,174,434	466,306
Rentas de Salinas	9,363,479	9,053,598	3,921,759	9,080,345	3,371,382
Almojarifazgo of Seville and Indies	5,843,225	5,567,726	2,576,088	10,260,318	2,477,600
Diezmos de la mar	2,375,966	2,276,024	1,091,824	3,053,680	1,184,200
Puertos secos	1,012,105	967,876	400,618	1,865,010	475,505
Renta de Lanas	2,823,529	2,715,048	1,459,121	4,342,223	1,152,323
Additional tax on this	794,118	779,370	—	—	779,370
Puertos between Castile and Portugal	555,545	529,141	305,323	1,105,855	216,594
Servicio y montazgo	340,118	323,529	101,323	400,307	198,251
Renta de las Islas de Canaria	588,238	561,465	184,609	659,719	309,266
Alcabalas y cientos	236,447	225,643	78,503	288,076	121,790
Casas de moneda	25,200	25,200	11,996	1,005,051	13,204
Media Annata	1,834,918	1,834,918	678,000	2,280,141	703,501
Alcabala y ciento del Tabaco	493,524	477,615	211,673	468,930	189,155
Sosa y Barilla de Murcia	91,082	86,662	25,853	239,227	43,522
Renta de Naipes	108,088	102,843	42,233	208,885	60,610
New tax on cacao and chocolate	448,529	435,074	—	—	—
Extracto or regalia of Seville	317,647	308,395	112,235	166,070	85,774

TABLE 5. – contd

Names of farms in Hacienda	Current product	Net Product[14]	Settled to crown by 1668 decrees[15]	Total juros created	Juros paid currently[16]
Ibid. of Málaga	123,906	120,296	53,647	76,990	6,394
Quatro uno por ciento of annata of Málaga	65,774	63,858	22,706	20,588	7,206
Ibid. of Cadiz	187,506	183,288	52,971	44,118	15,441
Quinto de la nieve	76,471	73,472	23,837	69,238	49,635
Batiojas de Sevilla	18,052	17,716	9,176	29,412	7,729
Alcazares de Sevilla	146,451	146,451	70,440	203,898	76,011
Seda de Granada	472,353	449,514	81,202	1,269,735	368,313
Abuela de Granada	48,000	45,671	2,941	67,177	13,318
Tercias de Gibraltar	27,061	26,273	11,000	26,381	10,364
Tercias de Jeba y Ardales	20,827	20,221	8,973	28,913	11,247
Tercias de la Palma y Gelbez	25,883	24,627	15,124	21,119	9,503
Alcabalas y cientos de la cerveza de Madrid	4,400	4,400	—	—	—
Ibid. de veridas compustas de Madrid	4,400	4,400	—	—	—
Estanco del Cafe de Sevilla y Cadiz	15,039	15,039	—	—	—
Moneda forera	26,987	26,281	—	—	—
Alcabalas de Señorío de Vizcaya	15,766	15,766	—	15,766	15,766
Herrerías de Vizcaya	5,353	5,353	—	5,353	5,353
Names of farms in Sala de Millones					
Servicios de 24,000 soldados	19,888,690	18,613,411	9,977,310	11,035,286	5,964,150
Servicio de 8,000 soldados	1,800,796	1,695,283	846,735	1,657,291	643,820

Renta del Tabaco	6,861,679	6,655,828	6,227,729	583,870	428,099
Cacao y Chocolate	448,529	435,074	254,794	89,819	33,863
Alzucares de Granada	301,471	292,426	257,713	41,912	34,713
Pasa de Málaga	735,294	713,235	575,206	127,093	119,632
Renta de la nieve	276,471	276,471	217,225	5,693	5,693
Renta del Jabón	448,529	435,074	239,618	117,227	98,044
Renta del Aguardiente	257,353	249,632	196,581	—	—
Renta de Pescados	720,588	599,038	251,439	638,876	340,626
Renta del Papel	205,882	199,706	49,324	196,825	150,382
Renta de Puertos de Portugal	155,882	155,882	142,912	—	—
Total of all farms	96,730,447	91,887,273	46,613,454	101,014,518	35,893,760

[13] Based on the table, drawn up under Orry's supervision, in AE Corr. Pol. (Esp.), 119 ff.53–7. Totals have been corrected where necessary.
[14] This amount is net after payment of administrative dues.
[15] This column includes the crown's four million ducats, together with the 500,000 for debts and 200,000 for mercedes.
[16] This column includes sums paid to juros reservados as well as to other juristas.

saltmines of Old Castile, Murcia, Badajoz and Cuenca; and Juan Goyeneche, who contracted for supplies in Old Castile and Extremadura.[17] During the War of Succession certain taxes were often granted to financiers as payment for their advances towards the cost of campaigns. This alienation of taxes, for a period or in perpetuity, had a long ancestry, for by it the crown always hoped to free itself not only from debt but also from the need to administer yet another tax. The net result, however, was only to diminish the revenue and authority of the crown. No changes were made in the old methods of administration for the duration of the war.

The development of the Hacienda in the present period will be studied for convenience under two heads. In the first place we shall analyse the state of the finances during the war. This will be followed by a consideration of the various reforms and plans for reform introduced before 1715.

As we have seen from table 5, the ordinary income of the Hacienda in 1703 was 96,730,447 reales.[18] Against this we can set the estimates for government expenses in the year 1703–4:

TABLE 6. SPANISH GOVERNMENT EXPENSES 1703–1704 (IN REALES OF VELLON)

Military garrisons in Spain, and other expenses	9,376,051
Garrisons in Africa, Ibiza and Port Mahon	4,395,304
Armaments and quicksilver mines	6,007,263
Military salaries	2,647,973
Salaries of ambassadors and envoys	454,734
Royal household	17,331,987
Repayment of loans from financiers	5,312,164
Salaries of conciliar and judicial officials	7,564,604
Mercedes and gifts	2,054,235
Juristas	34,691,709
Total	89,836,024

These expense estimates are clearly only a peacetime minimum, leaving 6,894,423 reales in credit to the exchequer. Various

17 AGS, Tribunal Mayor de Cuentas leg.1870.
18 The marqués de Ribas gives a conflicting total of 95,013,067 in Guerre, A¹ 1786 f.302. This archival reference is also the source for the data in table 6.

important items such as the maintenance of troops overseas do not figure in the estimate, and since the war had not really begun in the peninsula no serious military obligations had yet arisen. The estimate should therefore be taken as a guide to the proportional disbursement of revenue, rather than as a comprehensive list of obligations.

The Tesorería Mayor de la Guerra was established in 1703. From this date onwards the archives supply us with detailed accounts of the money passing through this part of the Hacienda. Unfortunately, since the Tesorería Mayor collected only a part of the revenue, there is no way of measuring the total income of the crown for the first few months of the treasury's existence. In the Tesorería's first year, Orry planned to enter 65,378,224 reales into its account,[19] but the receipts of the conde de Moriana show that from 2 October 1703 to 17 October 1704 only 46,635,363 reales were entered.[20] The Tesorería was suspended for almost a year after this. When it began functioning again under Moriana from 1 June 1705 to 30 June 1707, the accounts showed that in these two years the sum of 220,557,593 reales[21] had been entered. Since this sum gives an annual average of 105,867,644 reales it would appear that most of the crown's revenue was now being entered in the treasury and, significantly, that it was being devoted to the war.

The increased figures suggest moreover that revenue had been swollen by extra sources of income, achieved by suspending payments of *mercedes* and *juros,* and by imposing new taxes and forced loans. The Tesorería General continued to function side by side with the Tesorería Mayor until March 1706, when the term of office of Diego de Cetina, the treasurer general, came to an end. Since there are no accounts for the Tesorería General until December 1706, it is likely that Moriana acted as the sole treasurer of the crown during these months, and that he received all military and other revenues. It now became official policy to enter all revenue into the Tesorería Mayor, a trend confirmed by the decree of 31 December 1708 which we have already noted. Moriana was succeeded as Tesorero Mayor by the marqués de

---

[19] 'Caudal que se considera para este año de 1704, que debe entrar en la Thesoreria Mayor', Guerre, A¹ 1786 f.307.
[20] AGS, Tribunal Mayor de Cuentas leg.1869, where an erroneous total is given.
[21] *Ibid.*, leg.1871.

H

Campoflorido, a highly successful financier who had held contracts for a large number of taxes, and who held office from 1
July 1707 to 30 June 1709. In these two years the sums entering
the treasury apparently amounted to 302,572,638 reales,[22] which
gives an annual average of 151,286,319 reales.

After Campoflorido's term, the Tesorería Mayor was suppressed, and the Tesorería General continued to function under
Juan Antonio Gutiérrez de Carriazo from July 1709 to 31 December 1711, with exactly the same duties as the Tesorería Mayor.
Gutiérrez put his receipts for the period at 426,904,898 reales,[23] a
yearly average of 170,761,959 reales. For the next two years the
Tesorería General under Manuel González de Arce handled only
a part of the total revenue, amounting to just over a hundred
million reales annually.

The Tesorería Mayor was restored in 1713, when Orry returned to Spain as chief minister of the crown. Moriana was
again appointed treasurer, a post he held from 1 July 1713 to 31
December 1716. This period is probably the most important in
the history of the Hacienda during the war, for the total receipts
now for the first time come to 802,045,877 reales,[24] giving an
annual average income of 229,155,965 reales, which is nearly
twice the total income of only a decade before. There can be
little doubt that this figure represented the total receipts of the
Hacienda, for the decree setting up the Tesorería Mayor on 26
June 1713 made it quite clear that 'all the revenues belonging to
my royal Hacienda should enter into it'.[25] The increase in income
continued to be registered in the accounts of Moriana's successor,
Nicolás de Hinojosa, treasurer from 1 January 1717 to 31 August
1718: his total receipts were 394,022,074 reales,[26] an annual
average of 236,413,244 reales. This increased income can best be
studied in a table showing the part played by the two treasuries.
The two most notable features of table 7 are the growth of the
Tesorería Mayor, of great importance for the centralisation of
revenue and accounting; and the increase in government income.

[22] *Ibid.*, leg.1875.
[23] *Ibid.*, legs.1880–1.
[24] *Ibid.*, leg.1892–5.
[25] Decree of 28 June 1713, AGS, Dirección General del Tesoro, Inventario 4,
leg. 10.
[26] AGS, Tribunal Mayor de Cuentas legs.1903–5. Hinojosa gives an erroneous
total of 393,992,074.

TABLE 7. AVERAGE ANNUAL HACIENDA INCOME 1703–18,
SHOWING TREASURY DISTRIBUTION (IN REALES OF VELLON)

| | INCOME | | DISTRIBUTION | |
Period	Total	Rentas reales	Tesorería General	Tesorería Mayor
1703–4	120,351,097	96,730,447	30,496,818[27]	46,635,363
1705–7			30,496,818	105,867,644
1707–9			1,248,016[28]	151,286,319
1709–11			172,009,975	—
1711–3			112,871,326	—
1713	229,429,103[29]	116,722,543[30]	—	229,155,965
1713–6			—	229,155,965
1717–8			—	236,413,244

The increase in income is a remarkable feature of the war of
the Spanish Succession. Table 7 shows that in 1703 the *rentas
reales* were just over ninety-six million in a total of 120,351,097
reales, and that by the end of the war they were about twenty
millions more in a total income that had almost doubled. This
means that if the normal revenues of Castile had increased by 20
per cent, extraordinary sources of revenue had increased by 350
per cent. What factors contributed to this development? The
only plausible reason for an increase in the *rentas reales* would
seem to be more effective administration, because few large
taxes were added to those in existence. Such 'effective administration' would often mean no more than that the price of the tax-
farms was raised. This was, for example, the case with the new
contracts laid down by a decree of 23 December 1713, which
regulated the rate for the following year,[31] in accordance with the
reforms introduced in 1713.

[27] *Ibid.*, leg.1870.
[28] *Ibid.*, leg.1888.
[29] AN, K.1359 f.35.
[30] *Ibid.* This includes revenue from Aragon and Valencia. Figures in Uztáriz,
Theórica y Práctica, pp. 151–2 and 376, give a total of 116,424,458 reales. The table
in AGS, Guerra Moderna, suplemento leg.252, which excludes Aragon and Valencia, gives a much lower figure.
[31] The price of the *arrendamientos* before 1714 and after 1716 was 2,400 million
maravedís: see Uztáriz, p. 376; and AGS, Dirección General del Tesoro, Inventario
4, leg.10. But for 1714 they were raised to 2,488 millions: see AGS, Contadurías
Generales leg.1724.

Increase in extraordinary revenue is simpler to explain. Apart from Indies silver, the most important voluntary source of money was the financiers. But whereas it has been relatively easy to estimate the volume of money forthcoming from America, it remains extremely difficult to arrive at any precise appraisal of the very considerable help given by financiers and merchants. This brings us to the question of extraordinary taxation and related sources of income.

The government introduced very few new taxes on consumer goods. It was clearly recognised by the Hacienda that enough taxes were already in existence and that taxpayers could not be bled any further, save perhaps in commodities for which demand was inelastic. This saving clause explains the Hacienda decree of 24 December 1703 which reimposed a *millones* tax and one on meat, both being taxes granted by the cortes in 1656 but suspended on 13 February 1686; at the same time a decree dated 26 November 1704 laid an extra tax of two reales on each *fanega* of salt, and reimposed as from 1 January 1705 an extra rate of 2 per cent on the sales tax known as the *cuatro medios por ciento*.[32] On 28 January 1705 the government decreed a tax of one real on every *fanega* of arable land, and two reales on each *fanega* of vineyard or orchard land, with a levy of 5 per cent on pasture land.[33] In 1707 the tax on paper was raised, and as from 1 July 1709 a new tax of two silver reales on each *arroba* of wool was exacted. On 28 July 1709 the price of a pound of tobacco in Madrid was raised by two reales.[34] These appear to be the most important of the new taxes, but they brought in little money compared with the extraordinary impositions levied by the government.

The most significant of all impositions, from a political as well as a financial point of view, was that on 'alienations'. The attack on alienated royal rights (whether public offices or the income from taxes or simply landed estates) was something that had long been urged by Spanish *arbitristas,* and the financial needs of war provided a convenient occasion for the implementation of a

---

[32] Hacienda, Ordenes Generales de Rentas vol. II ff.169–73; AGS, Dirección General del Tesoro, Inventario 4, leg.10, order of 1 December 1704.

[33] J. Canga Argüelles, *Diccionario de Hacienda* (2 vols), Madrid, 1833–4, vol. 2, p. 127. This source, a memorandum dated 15 July 1737, gives details of other extraordinary taxation levied during the war.

[34] Hacienda, Ordenes Generales de Rentas vol. II ff.298–305.

policy favoured by both French and Spaniards. The crown in the seventeenth century had resorted to the alienation of property and the sale of public office as a quick way to realise cash. It now attempted to tax these alienations without seriously trying to reclaim them. The first attack came with a decree dated 10 November 1704, which ordered 5 per cent of the value of all public offices and all alienated property and taxes, to be paid to the crown for a year. Another decree of 21 November 1706 ordered that for the year from July 1706 to July 1707 the income from all alienations, both real and personal, was to be paid to the crown until the titles of present owners had been examined and confirmed: this decree was extended for six months on 27 June 1707 and then again from 3 December 1707 to June 1708. Since taxes had habitually been alienated to pay for *juros*, these decrees in effect suspended all payment of *juros* until further notice. A special body called the *Junta de Incorporación* was set up, and titles had to be presented to it for verification. A decree of 22 June 1708 suspended the imposition on those who had succeeded in getting their titles confirmed; but on 23 October 1709 these people were ordered to pay half the value of the properties for the first six months of 1710, and another decree of 22 December 1710 ordered one third of the value of all alienations to be paid to the crown. This seems to suggest that taxes continued to be levied even after the owners of alienations had been confirmed in their title. This imposition continued in one form or another until it was stopped by the decree of 8 January 1717 which suppressed the junta.[35]

The result of the tax on alienations was encouraging. Between June 1706 and June 1707 the total sum of 5,290,851 reales was entered in the Tesorería Mayor.[36] This was only a sixth of the expected yield, but still a large sum. Although continuous returns are not available, it is certain that considerable yields were registered throughout the period of imposition: thus in the two years 1712 and 1713 the total returns came to 21,000,998 reales.[37]

---

[35] Materials for the study of alienations exist in Faustino Gil Ayuso, *Junta de Incorporaciones: Catálogo de los papeles que se conservan en el Archivo Histórico Nacional*, Madrid, 1934. The manuscript 'Cedulas de la Junta de Incorporacion', BRAH, MS 9–5–1–K–29–654, gives important details of the territorial holdings of the upper aristocracy.

[36] AGS, Tribunal Mayor de Cuentas leg.1871.

[37] *Ibid.*, leg.1891.

Another important source of extraordinary revenue was the series of percentage levies imposed on different sections of the population. At the very beginning of the reign, by a decree of 2 March 1701, a proportion of the salaries of all government officials and office-holders was taken by the state. A decree of 22 March 1702 laid down a scale for the payment of this levy, ranging from eight doblones for the most senior officials to one doblón for the most junior.[38] A subsequent decree of 10 November 1704 ordered the levy for a year of 5 per cent on all salaries paid by the Hacienda, and on alienations.[39] This imposition was renewed by a decree of 8 April 1706, and again by one on 2 July 1707; there may have been an extension in 1708, and there was certainly one on 16 September 1709. Income from this source was not large: the 1702 levy was expected to yield only about 75,000 reales,[40] and for the two years 1705-6 the Tesorería Mayor received only 536,881 reales.[41] Against this must be set the estimate in 1713 that a levy of 10 per cent on salaries, that is double the previous rate, would bring in one million reales.[42]

The other regular or irregular impositions levied during the war may for convenience be taken in chronological order. Among them can be classified those donations given freely by the various provinces of Spain from time to time at the beginning of the war. It is difficult to catalogue these, since they are legion, but one example is typical. In 1702 the realm was asked to make a donation of fealty, and among the offerings were 440,000 reales from Madrid, 30,000 from Asturias, and 15,000 from Toledo; at the same time the Church promised to give 1,293,300 reales.[43] In 1705 a *donativo general* was demanded from all Spain. The total yield in Castile from this free gift was 8,365,424 reales,[44] a fraction of the expected income. Constitutional difficulties arose over the *fueros* of Aragon when the archbishop of Saragossa, the then viceroy of Aragon, was asked for a donation from the province in this year. As we shall see later, severe opposition was

[38] AHN, Consejos suprimidos leg.13222, año 1702, f.9.
[39] AHN, Estado leg.193 f.35.
[40] Blécourt to Louis xiv, 6 Apr. 1702, AE Corr. Pol. (Esp.), 103 f.311.
[41] AGS, Tribunal Mayor de Cuentas leg.1871.
[42] AN, K.1359 f.35.
[43] AE Corr. Pol. (Esp.), 122 ff.115, 120-2. See also the *Gaceta de Madrid* for 7 Nov., 14 Nov., and 21 Nov. 1702, BN, fonds Lorraine 970.
[44] AGS, Tribunal Mayor de Cuentas leg.1871.

aroused in all sections of the Aragonese community. Despite this, thirty-one of the chief nobles and gentry of the realm made a gift of 27,380 reales in coin and several hundred bushels of grain; the amount was small but as a gesture it was no doubt acceptable to Madrid. In addition, the archbishop promised 200,000 reales in silver from the Church.[45]

In April 1706 the kingdom of Navarre made Philip v a generous donation of 450,142 reales, Pamplona alone giving 300,000 of this;[46] and in November the province of Biscay offered a donation of 60,000 reales.[47] Many other cities and towns added to these, in large and small sums, all as part of their patriotic contribution to the nation's defence. Even the grandees played their part, and the sums that twenty of them presented to the crown in April 1706 exceeded 2,000,000 reales.[48] This popular support was a powerful help to the Bourbons.

Not surprisingly there were also cries of dissatisfaction. The decree of 21 November 1706 which levied a tax on alienations, came under bitter attack from the duque de Medinaceli, who on 9 May 1707 published a public protest against the resumption of alienated rights, claiming that this contravened the ancient privileges of his peerage.[49] This document is comparable in importance to the protest made by Arcos in 1701, and no doubt played a vital part in Medinaceli's disillusion with the Habsburg régime.

The year 1707 saw a further call for sacrifices. Letters were sent out in the spring to ask all the clergy of Castile, León, Navarre and the Canaries, together with the four military orders, to contribute to a *donativo* of twenty million reales for the needs of war. By December the following year only 10,288,739 reales of this sum had reached the Tesorería Mayor, and of this 2,451,930 was from the see of Toledo alone.[50] While the ecclesiastical levy

[45] AHN, Estado leg.264 f.14, 23.

[46] *Ibid.*, leg. 286¹ f.9, 'Relacion del donativo'. See also the *Gaceta de Madrid*, 20 Apr. 1706, BN, fonds Lorraine 970: 'el señor Obispo de Pamplona . . . ofreciendo annualmente otros 1,000 doblones por el tiempo que durare la Guerra.'

[47] *Gaceta de Madrid*, 7 Dec. 1706, BN, fonds Lorraine 970.

[48] A list of the contributions is enclosed with the letter from Amelot to Torcy, 21 May 1706, AE Corr. Pol. (Esp.), 159 f.66. The largest amount was from the marqués de Castelrodrigo, who gave 810,296 reales in silver. The duque de Popoli gave a silver dish weighing 36 pounds; the duque de Béjar gave twelve horsed and equipped cavalry soldiers.

[49] AE Corr. Pol. (Esp.), 168 f.34; BN, fonds espagnol 153.

[50] Full documentation on this imposition is in AHN, Estado legs.324, 530.

was being collected, a decree of 18 October 1707 imposed a *donativo voluntario* of forty reales on every household in Castile; the product was to enter the Tesorería Mayor.[51] In 1709, as we have already seen,[52] Philip v approached the financiers of Spain for aid, and obtained sums from all the main ones, including Moriana. On 30 July that same year an order directed to the *corregidors* and other officials imposed another free gift on Castile, at the rate of twelve reales per family.[53] The years 1712 to 1714 witnessed for the first time the imposition of a *capitación*,[54] which despite its name was not a poll tax but a levy on each *vecino* or head of a household. This was levied not only in Castile but also in the realms of Aragon, which had now been united administratively to the Castilian crown. The rate of the imposition in 1712 was 60 reales a household for the upkeep of troops, and in August and September the same year a tax of 40 reales per household, for the payment of officers' salaries, was levied. The income from this came to 8,380,000 reales in Castile and 5,760,000 in Aragon, a total of 14,140,000. A decree of 5 December laid down the rate for the following year, which was to be 40 reales per household in Castile and 100 in Aragon. In all, three impositions appear to have been levied on Castile in 1713, two of 40 reales and one of 60.[55] By a decree of 12 September the rate of impositions in both Castile and Aragon were substantially lowered. The changes in the treasury system after 1711 mean that no comprehensive account of revenue is available for the years 1711 to 1713; as a result, although the Tesorería General registers the income from *donativos* in these years as 8,744,969 reales,[56] it is certain that the yield was very much higher.

There were two unexpected and substantial sources of income. The first of these was the revenue forthcoming from vacant episcopal sees. In the years 1712 and 1713, a total of 3,068,016 reales entered the treasury from this source.[57] A memorandum[58] drawn up in 1714 shows that in 1713 the crown was drawing

[51] AE Corr. Pol. (Esp.), 174 f.51; Guerre, A¹ 2050 f.189.
[52] Above, p. 74.
[53] Hacienda, Consejo de Castilla, impresos vol. 6549 f.11.
[54] J. Canga Argüelles, vol. 1, p. 187; vol. 2, p. 127.
[55] AGS, Guerra Moderna leg.2356 f.6.
[56] AGS, Tribunal Mayor de Cuentas leg.1891.
[57] *Ibid.*
[58] Memorandum of 20 Apr. 1714, 'Vacantes de Obispados, frutos de 1713', AHN, Estado leg.648.

on no less than twelve unoccupied Castilian sees, namely those of
Toledo, Ciudad Rodrigo, Lugo, Palencia, Salamanca, Jaén, Avila,
Soria, Plasencia, Málaga, Sigüenza, and the Canary Islands. Not
all these sees were profitable to the treasury; one, Sigüenza, had
its realisable income in the form of grain, which was used for
the army; and another, the Canaries, had its effective income
assigned to the banker Arther. Only the first six of the bishoprics
were productive, and gave the crown a net annual revenue in
1713 of 1,857,499 reales, of which 1,356,564 came from the
primatial see of Toledo. These details cover only the crown of
Castile. In Navarre, the rich see of Pamplona fell vacant during
the war, and in 1713 was bringing Philip v an annual income of
325,260 reales.[59] Valencia and Saragossa, which for differing
reasons became vacant in 1710, will be discussed later.

The other substantial source of income created by the war, was
the confiscation of the property of traitors in Castile. As we have
seen, the defection of prominent nobles was a help rather than
a hindrance to the Bourbons, since it brought in yet more money
to the war chest. A catalogue of confiscations in Castile in 1706[60]
lists forty-eight people, among them the grandees whose confiscations are detailed in table 1. Apart from these nobles, and
substantial confiscations from three members of the Parada
family and from a certain Joseph de Torres y Morales, the victims
appear to have been persons of only moderate income. The total
annual value of their sequestrated property, both in cash and in
kind, was 853,066 reales of vellon, 23,151 *fanegas* of wheat, 10,267
fanegas of barley, 1,537 *fanegas* of rye, and 2,343 *arrobas* of olive-oil.
The catalogue of confiscations carried out in 1710 is slightly
shorter, listing thirty-two names, among them the nobles already
noted in table 2. From five of these thirty-two, no income at all
was realised, leaving the total annual receipts for the whole
number at 741,896 reales, 6,545 *fanegas* of wheat, 3,679 of barley
and 164 of rye, with 34 *arrobas* of oil. The totals from both periods
come to an annual 1,594,962 reales, 29,696 *fanegas* wheat, 13,946
barley, 1,701 rye and 2,377 *arrobas* oil.

[59] AN, K.1359 f.35.
[60] 'Relacion de los Estados y Haziendas que se recobran y administran por la
Superintendencia de vienes confiscados y sequestrados, y de los valores que por
maior produzen las Rentas de cada una. Hecho en Madrid a 7 de Febrero de 1713',
AHN, Estado leg.2973. This covers the lists for both 1706 and 1710.

This sum was not the maximum annual yield from this source, and covers only those confiscations made after each Allied occupation of Madrid in 1706 and 1710. In the course of the war several other sequestrations were made that do not appear in the lists referred to. A catalogue of confiscations drawn up in 1721[61] details the penalisation of one hundred and twenty-seven people in the kingdom of Castile alone. This number includes nearly all those appearing in the earlier lists. At this date confiscations in Castile from these people were bringing in a total of 2,860,995 reales a year, of which 1,552,044 remained net to the Hacienda after payment of expenses and salaries. Income from these confiscations was used by the Hacienda principally to pay *mercedes*, that is pensions and similar grants. As late as 1721 the government was paying out 284,790 reales annually from the confiscations for *mercedes* in Castile. Similar sums were disbursed in the other realms out of confiscations carried out there. No steps appear to have been taken to exploit confiscations in order to increase the economic potential of the treasury. Nor indeed was it royal policy to hold on to confiscations for ever. Quite frequently a confiscated estate would be handed over to the next-of-kin, no doubt in the belief that relatives should not suffer for the sins of one member of the family. In 1708, for example, the governor of the council of Castile protested against the royal decision to grant the confiscated lands of the traitor conde de Villafranqueza to a cousin of the conde, saying that this would prejudice royal rights.[62] But the crown was unwilling to extend its rights at the expense of the property of its subjects.

The significance of American silver can be plotted graphically, as in figure 1. Here the data given in tables 5 and 7, regarding the volume of silver and the revenue of the crown, are set against each other. The figure verifies the impression that only the Vigo disaster was of any great help to royal finances, and that in other years bullion was of marginal importance only.

This brief survey of extraordinary sources of revenue leaves us yet to consider one factor which is usually cited as the single most important reason for the increase in government income.

[61] AGS, Secretaría de Hacienda 972: this is a folio volume entitled 'Reynado de D. Phelipe Quinto: Bienes confiscados por la Guerra de Succesion.' The statement for Castile is dated 15 July 1721.
[62] AHN, Estado leg.188 f.4.

To what extent did revenues from Aragon and Valencia augment the receipts of the treasury at Madrid? If the annexation of these realms made any initial difference to government income, we should expect the difference to be registered in the Hacienda accounts. Yet in 1713, six years after the abolition of the liberties

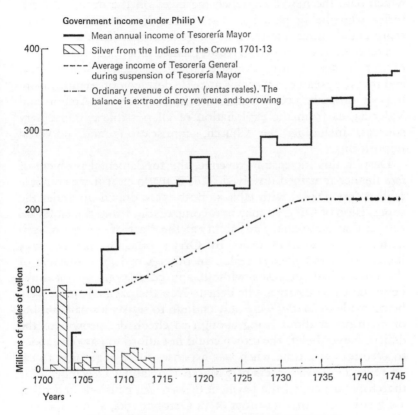

I. GOVERNMENT INCOME UNDER PHILIP V

of Aragon and Valencia, the only income registered in the Hacienda was an annual 2,374,680 reales from Aragon and 2,730,000 reales from Valencia.[63] These sums are important and substantial, but cannot reasonably be considered the principal factor in the recovery of the finances, since neither figure exceeds

[63] AGS, Guerra Moderna, suplemento, leg.252. These figures are higher than those given for the résumé of income in AN, K.1359 f.35, which gives 2,368,125 reales for Aragon and 1,902,015 for Valencia.

1·8 per cent of the total *rentas reales* for 1713, and each is only 0·8 per cent of the year's revenue. The remarkable growth of income during the War of Succession cannot then be identified exclusively or even chiefly with the annexation of the realms of Aragon. This conclusion is valid, however, only until 1718, by which date the new comprehensive taxes on the occupied territories were being paid into the treasury at Madrid until they represented about one-tenth of all government income.

The conclusion we can arrive at, then, is that under the pressure of war financial returns almost doubled between 1703 and 1713, and that the greater part of this increase derived not so much from heavier ordinary taxation or from the revenues of Aragon and Valencia, as from the exploitation of all possible extraordinary sources, including the Church, confiscations and universal impositions.

Despite this increase in revenue, the fundamental problem of *juro* finance remained unsolved. This is made clear if we compare table 8 (pp. 225–7) with table 5. Both were drawn up under the supervision of Orry, so they bear comparison. From the tables we can see that the annual *juro* liability at the start of the reign, estimated at 101,014,518 reales by Orry's officials, had by 1713 increased to 108,786,071 reales. In other words, the revenue of the crown had increased without any corresponding measures being taken to mortgage its debts. Even the payments that were being made to *juristas* were only enough to satisfy a small number of creditors without being enough to check the growth of the deficit. Nevertheless the crown could not afford to pay out money to creditors at a time when war expenses were beginning to eat up revenue. Royal orders of 5 March 1701 and 4 December 1702 therefore suspended the payment of *mercedes*, pensions and other assignations.[64] Another order of 14 October 1704 also suspended all payments out of the Hacienda, making an exception only for debts to financiers; this was followed by a similar order on 23 October 1709, which was renewed on 8 January 1711 and 7 January 1712.[65] The payment of *juros* was affected by all these measures, as well as by the proceedings of the *Junta de Incorporación*. The taxation and suspension of *juros* was a short-term expedient that eased fiscal problems but also postponed any solution for

[64] Canga Argüelles, vol. 2, p. 127.
[65] AGS, Dirección General del Tesoro, Inventario 4, leg.10.

TABLE 8. THE RENTAS REALES IN 1713[66]

Administered by the Hacienda	Current product	Net product	Settled to crown by 1688 decree	Total juros created	Juros paid in 1702
Alcabalas	19,283,462	18,898,583	8,239,239	32,560,683	10,659,343
Tercias	336,043	331,792	152,331	408,262	179,461
Quatro medios por ciento	8,714,346	8,478,040	5,546,810	11,864,382	2,921,230
Servicio ord. y extraord. (except Granada)	3,979,914	3,979,914	2,358,255	4,322,489	1,621,659
Papel sellado	779,002	779,002	485,275	1,919,418	293,728
Rentas de Salinas	7,333,666	7,127,507	3,937,061	9,268,094	3,190,416
Almojarifazgo mayor of Seville and Indies	6,470,588	6,213,896	2,706,127	11,072,191	3,507,770
Diezmos de la Mar	2,247,406	2,153,253	993,509	2,907,646	1,159,744
Puertos secos	342,943	327,964	181,629	1,950,475	146,335
Renta de Lanas	2,823,529	2,715,048	1,572,979	4,658,184	1,142,069
Additional tax on this	750,000	727,596	727,596	—	—
Puertos between Castile and Portugal	603,230	577,200	338,990	1,281,189	238,210
Servicio y montazgo	420,400	400,000	165,076	407,071	234,924
Renta de las Islas de Canarias	588,235	558,749	240,135	657,164	318,614
Alcabalas y cientos de Yerbas de Calatrava, etc.	200,325	191,176	87,566	361,197	103,610
Casas de Moneda	22,080	22,080	10,524	641,599	11,556
Media anata de Mercedes	1,398,988	1,398,988	745,939	2,279,856	653,049
Alcabala y cientos del Tabaco	1,018,323	988,664	828,538	495,752	160,126
Sosa y Barrilla de Murcia	97,449	92,721	47,384	238,965	45,336
Renta de Naipes	106,323	102,843	41,947	208,885	60,897
Nuevo impuesto de Cacao y chocolate	470,588	456,588	456,588	—	—

TABLE 8 – *contd*

Administered by the Hacienda	Current product	Net product	Settled to crown by 1688 decree	Total juros created	Juros paid in 1702
Extracción o regalía de Sevilla	181,765	176,471	90,697	166,082	85,774
Ibid. de Málaga	91,505	88,839	82,445	18,092	6,394
Quatro unos por ciento de la Aduana de Málaga	48,581	47,166	39,960	20,588	7,206
Quinto de la Nieve	70,471	68,418	22,921	53,147	45,497
Bateojas de Sevilla	18,176	17,647	9,706	29,412	7,941
Alcazares de Sevilla	104,786	104,786	58,614	177,236	46,172
Alcabala y cientos de Azucares de Granada	134,519	127,562	68,987	277,455	58,575
Seda de Granada	270,103	256,996	22,961	1,269,741	234,035
Abuela de Granada	52,000	49,477	20,004	67,177	29,473
Población de Granada	797,059	797,059	797,059	—	—
Estanco del Cafe y Te de Cadiz	3,437	3,437	3,437	—	—
Herrerías de Vizcaya	5,353	5,353	5,353	—	—
Administered by Sala de Millones					
Servicio de 24 millones	18,560,120	18,009,572	11,496,125	15,589,466	6,513,447
Servicio de 8,000 soldados	1,728,571	1,677,224	1,018,759	1,674,676	658,466
Renta del Tabaco	14,223,432	13,796,730	13,497,802	629,865	298,928
Renta del Cacao y chocolate	470,588	456,471	416,181	89,525	40,290
Azucares de Granada	369,608	358,908	323,871	42,206	35,037
Pasa de Málaga	735,294	713,235	593,603	127,093	119,632
Renta de la Nieve	284,765	276,471	270,778	5,693	5,693

Renta del Jabón	514,706	499,265	401,221	117,227	98,044
Renta del Aguardiente	213,235	206,838	206,838	—	—
Renta de Pescados	742,206	720,588	278,999	730,964	441,589
Renta del Papel	196,912	191,177	43,432	196,824	147,744
Puertas entre Castilla y Portugal	176,471	171,177	171,177	—	—
Total	97,980,503	95,342,471	59,804,425	108,786,071	35,538,014

Additional income

Rentas de Aragon (excluding tobacco), estimated to be	2,374,680
Rentas de Valencia, *ibid.*	2,730,000
Tax of 6 and 7 reales on *fanega* of salt	5,793,945
Tax on salt of Galicia	2,900,000
Quatro medios por ciento reintroduced from 1 Nov. 1706	8,294,940
New tax on meat, from 1 Dec. 1705	6,522,490
Extra tax on *papel sellado* since 1707	1,314,950
New tax of 2 reales silver on *arroba* of wool, since 1 July 1709	315,000
Income from posts, united to Crown since 1707	1,875,000
Secret expenses incl. *fiel medidor*	1,972,190
Servicio de milicias	3,184,210
Servicio de lanzas	1,500,000
Total	38,777,405

Total income for 1713: *136,757,908 reales*

66 From AGS, Guerra Moderna suplemento leg.252. The division of material is as in table 5.

them. Despite the good intentions of Orry and other reformers, the problem of *juros* was shelved for the duration of the war, and instead efforts were concentrated on building up the stability of receipts in order to meet military commitments.

What proportion of government revenue was spent on the war? We would expect the Tesorería Mayor, which had been set up exclusively to deal with military finances, to provide an answer. However, the Tesorería General still continued to be concerned with some military matters; and the Tesorería Mayor, though specifically concerned with the war, also dealt with various non-military expenses. As table 9 shows, therefore, neither treasury dealt with all military finance during the War of Succession, with the possible exception of the Tesorería General from 1709 to 1711.

TABLE 9. AVERAGE ANNUAL EXPENDITURE OF THE
TREASURIES, 1703–18 (IN REALES OF VELLON)

| Period | Tesorería General | | Tesorería Mayor | |
	Total	Military	Total	Military
1703–4	30,496,818	13,503,594	46,635,363	40,036,813
1705–7	30,496,818	13,503,594	106,084,883[67]	87,932,987
1707–9	1,234,100	42,708	151,289,308[68]	125,447,392
1709–11	172,047,328	159,407,981	—	—
1711–3	112,873,490	101,905,145	—	—
1713–6	—	—	229,238,893[69]	179,940,890
1717–8	—	—	237,867,828	183,491,049

In table 9 and figure 2 civil expenditure consists of the difference between total and military expenditure. The principal civil expenses were household and secret expenditure, *juros* and *mercedes*, and the salaries of government officials and ambassadors. The two largest categories of military expenditure were the payment of wages and the purchase of supplies. Payments made

[67] AGS, Tribunal Mayor de Cuentas legs.1872–1874, give a total expenditure for this period of 220,710,258 reales: the accounts in fact add up to 221,010,174 reales, an average of 106,084,883 reales a year.
[68] This average accepts Moriana's total of 302,578,617 reales, noted above as faulty.
[69] AGS, Tribunal Mayor de Cuentas legs.1896–1902.

through the Tesorería Mayor to these and other items are analysed in tables 10a and 10b.

TABLE 10A. AVERAGE ANNUAL MILITARY EXPENDITURE OF
TESORERIA MAYOR 1703-9 (IN REALES OF VELLON)

	1703-4	1705-7	1707-9
Wages and salaries	24,834,327	37,422,451	54,500,674
Victual supplies	7,156,252	18,848,015	
Uniforms	890,716	4,063,978	62,071,526
Gunpowder and artillery	1,019,554	2,796,459	
Naval	—	793,145	
Other expenses	6,135,964	24,008,939	8,875,192
Average annual total	40,036,813	87,932,987	125,447,392

TABLE 10B. AVERAGE ANNUAL MILITARY EXPENDITURE OF
TESORERIA MAYOR 1713-18 (IN REALES OF VELLON)

	1713-6	1717-8
Wages and salaries	94,432,376	93,300,833
Victual supplies	44,491,430	20,004,450
Uniforms	5,954,664	6,154,198
Gunpowder and artillery		4,108,170
Naval	14,887,610	40,997,195
Other expenses	20,174,810	18,926,202
Average annual total	179,940,890	183,491,048

Although table 10a does not represent the total military expenditure of the crown, it does allow us to see where money was being spent. In table 10b the high costs of the period 1713-6 were caused principally by the siege of Barcelona and the pacification of Catalonia. The lack of figures for armaments is due to the fact that the accounts for this item do not appear to be complete. One interesting feature of the whole period is the lack of any proper expenditure on the navy before 1713. Prior to that date the naval forces of the crown were virtually non-existent; only after Utrecht did Patiño and others begin to lay the foundations of an ambitious naval policy.

Despite the tendency of the figures with which we have been working to show a comfortable balance between income and expenditure, it is certain that the government laboured under serious financial difficulties. Although the level of income was greatly increased by extraordinary taxation, it managed to reach the level of expenditure only through borrowing from financiers. Very little of this borrowing consisted of cash loans; more usually it consisted of material services (such as food supplies) and the extension of credit. As a result, it is impossible to say from the accounts alone how great a debt was owed to merchant bankers by the crown. Quite apart from this, the financial position had

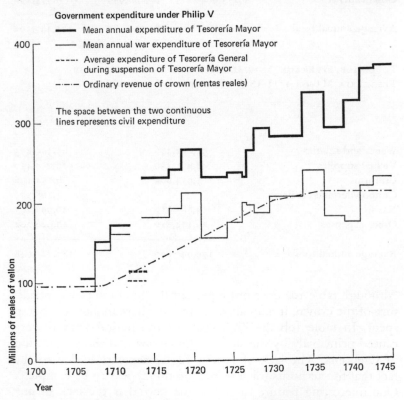

Government expenditure under Philip V

——— Mean annual expenditure of Tesorería Mayor

——— Mean annual war expenditure of Tesorería Mayor

- - - - Average expenditure of Tesorería General during suspension of Tesorería Mayor

–·–·– Ordinary revenue of crown (rentas reales)

The space between the two continuous lines represents civil expenditure

Millions of reales of vellon

Year

2. GOVERNMENT EXPENDITURE UNDER PHILIP V

been seriously aggravated by rising costs. In 1706 the cost of the war to Spain had been estimated at 100,000,000 reales.[70] By 1713 the accumulation of obligations and costs had, if we accept one official estimate,[71] more than doubled the expense, bringing it to a total of 266,007,500 reales, a sum which does not take into consideration any long-term debts such as *juros*. If this estimate is correct, costs exceeded total income by something like thirty-seven million reales. The deficit finance this involved must have appalled even the ablest ministers of the crown.

Of the ministers who attempted to introduce some reform into the Hacienda, two in particular – Orry and Bergeyck – deserve our attention. Orry, as we have seen, was sent into Spain specifically to help reform the finances of the crown. The aim he set himself in 1703 was a fourfold one: to institute a new fiscal system, to recover alienated rights, to shake off the hold of *juristas,* and to ensure an augmented revenue through the new system.[72] For his proposed new system he wrote off any possible income from America or the rest of the Spanish empire, and concentrated instead on Castile, whose taxes he divided into the six categories of his system: 1. The *alcabalas, cuatro medios por ciento, millones,* and municipal taxes or *sisas* were to be abolished

---

[70] Orry to Chamillart, 30 Jan. 1706, Guerre, A¹ 1976 f.75.

[71] 'Resumen General de la Real Hacienda, el año de 1713', 27 Nov. 1712, K.1359 f.35. The obligations may be summarised thus (in reales):

Wages of soldiers for one year	56,966,920
Salaries of all officers	41,944,790
Wages of garrison at Longon	1,497,650
Contracts for food supplies	84,633,350
Contracts for Ceuta and other African forts	6,794,700
Hospitals	5,097,390
Animals, transport, recruits	15,565,450
Provision and cost of armaments	15,212,270
To Tesorería General	8,778,490
Secret expenses	709,600
Salaries of financial officials	1,505,000
To financiers, for loans in 1712	13,301,870
Invalid soldiers	1,200,000
Special costs of royal household	2,500,000
Postage and carriage of letters	380,000
Other extraordinary expenses	3,284,700
Letters to Italy, secret and other extraordinary expenses	6,635,320
Total	266,007,500

[72] AE Corr. Pol. (Esp.), 119 f.33. The details that follow are from subsequent folios of this source.

and replaced by a single tax at a greatly reduced rate. 2. The salt tax (*salinas*) was to be raised from 22 reales to 50 reales a *fanega*. 3. The *aduanas* or customs duties were to be reduced to a single tax farm, with one general tariff. 4. Various taxes and monopolies in the *rentas reales,* such as tobacco, cards, coffee, etc., were to be resumed into a single tax farm. 5. Various alienated taxes, such as rights of postage, minting, etc., were to be reclaimed for the crown as *dominios de la Corona* and administered directly by the Hacienda. 6. An agreement or concordat would be sought with the Church to raise the rate of taxes on the clergy.

Reducing these suggestions to figures, Orry considered that the current revenue of 125,455,000 reales could be raised to about 202,500,000 reales:

	Present income	*Expected income*
New tax	59,750,000	50,000,000
Salt	7,500,000	25,000,000
Customs	18,047,500	32,500,000
Rentas	10,212,500	20,000,000
Dominios	14,570,000	25,000,000
Clergy	15,375,000	50,000,000
	125,455,000	202,500,000

The new tax would also be used to create a fund, whose purpose would be to repay *juristas* the sums due to them. In this way debts would eventually be worked off. Naturally this radical alteration in the tax system would require a complete change in the administrative system. Orry therefore envisaged sweeping changes in the composition of government bodies and councils. Castile would be divided into fourteen regions, each with a receiver-general of finance. Each region would be divided into five *partidos* with a receipt-office in each. The plan goes on to describe in great detail the score of fundamental changes to be introduced into all spheres of administration. Spain was, for example, to be divided into seventeen provinces, each with a royal governor and an intendant. The intendants were to be responsible to the council of Castile and ultimately to a supreme official in charge of all branches of the government, called the *veedor general* or general supervisor.

Orry's plan was no less than a scheme to re-model the entire monarchy. Even the royal household was catered for, and details were given of which officials should be retained and which should not. No other scheme of comparable dimensions exists in the whole history of Spain. Beside Orry's plan all the schemes of the *arbitristas* seem to pale into insignificance. However, Orry had no opportunity to put his plan into practice before 1706, and in that year he was recalled to France. He had to wait till 1713 before Philip v gave him the chance, as chief minister of the Spanish crown, to put into effect a plan drawn up ten years previously.

By 1713, of course, the intendants had been brought into existence by Bergeyck, so Orry concentrated instead on two main tasks: reforming the superior administration, and reorganising the taxes. In the *nueva planta* of 1713 for which he was principally responsible,[73] Orry assumed the post of *veedor general*, which gave him a direct voice in all matters of government. A step towards tax reorganisation was taken by a decree of 26 December 1713, called the *nueva planta de arrendamiento*,[74] which laid down that there was to be only one chief contractor for the farms of each province, so that all the taxes, of whatever kind, came under the control of one man. The contractor could sub-farm at will; the government's sole concern was that he should pay the price of his farm in cash to the chief treasurer in the capital city of the province. In accordance with this decree, in 1714 twenty-one provinces including Madrid but excluding Extremadura (which was at the time administered directly by the Hacienda) were farmed out to individual contractors. The importance of the financiers Goyeneche and Ortega is shown by the fact that these two took over all the *rentas provinciales* in the six provinces of Burgos, Granada, Valladolid, Cuenca, Guadalajara and León, at a total cost of 23,489,682 reales a year.[75] This system continued for the next two years. Meanwhile it was also proposed that there should be some centralisation of the *rentas generales*. A decree of 8 December 1714 ordered that from 1 January 1715 these taxes should be administered as a single farm by a junta in Madrid.[76] The junta was composed of leading ministers of the

73 See above, p. 111, note 94
74 AGS, Dirección General del Tesoro, Inventario 4, leg.10.
75 AGS, Contadurias Generales leg. 1724.
76 Hacienda, Ordenes Generales de Rentas, vol. 2 ff.439–40.

Hacienda, including Orry, the bishop of Gironda, and the marqués de Campoflorido; and of leading financiers such as Jacobo de Flon and Antoine Sartine.[77]

Little progress was made beyond these reforms, which in any case had not been fundamental ones, for they aimed only at centralisation and not at structural changes in the system. Orry's dismissal in 1715 marked the end of experimentation. A decree of 13 April 1716 ordered the junta for the *rentas generales* to be suppressed, and the farming out of the *rentas provinciales* to be resumed.[78] The list of tax-farmers for 1716 consequently shows several contractors, rather than just one, in charge of the taxes of each province.

Very little, then, appears to have been achieved. Yet Orry in 1714 made the incredible claim that he had rescued Philip v from his financial difficulties.

I came here in 1713 [he wrote to Torcy]. I found that there was a deficit of 100 millions [livres] and that 33 millions which we did not have was needed in order to cover the proposed expenditure. What we did was to cut down the expenditure so as to come to the end of the year without drawing on the revenue for 1714. Meanwhile the revenues for 1714 had mounted to 40 millions [livres], so that soon H.M. had reached 1715 without having engaged the slightest part of that year's income.[79]

This claim is highly improbable and may simply be described as untrue. Orry may have made some short-term economies, but he could not possibly have made any serious improvement in the state of the treasury. Already in 1715 the new French ambassador, Saint-Aignan, was reporting to Louis xiv that the Spanish government was in difficulties because of 'the bad condition of the finances of His Catholic Majesty'.[80] Moreover, 1713–4 was the very period that higher costs, in the form of the siege of Barcelona, were pressing on the treasury.

The fact is that despite his great plans and pretensions, Orry was not a man to be trusted in a position of responsibility. All the authorities agree on his amazing capacity for work. In his last days in Spain he seemed capable of anything: 'He passes like

---

[77] Hacienda, Consejo de Castilla impresos, vol. 6549 p. 45.
[78] Hacienda, Ordenes Generales de Rentas, vol. 3 ff.54–5.
[79] Orry to Torcy, 9 Dec. 1714, AE Corr. Pol. (Esp.), 237 f.132.
[80] 19 Aug. 1715, *ibid.*, 242 f.93.

a flash from details of munitions to the ministry of a vast kingdom; in effect he has taken on himself the war, finances, and the marine.'[81] The maréchal de Tessé observed in his memoirs that Orry showed great capabilities and that 'if he had succeeded the king of Spain could have become a powerful monarch'.[82] The duke of Berwick, who saw both his bad and good sides, described him as 'a man of great spirit, very eloquent and infinitely hard-working'.[83] Significantly, however, Berwick goes on to say: 'He excelled above all in the knowledge and administration of finance, and I doubt whether anyone would have succeeded better, had he worked under a suitable man.' Orry, in other words, was an excellent subordinate. As one Spaniard said of him to the French ambassador in 1713: 'You cannot say of Orry that he is all bad or all good. There is no one like him for putting bricks together, but I would never have him for an architect.'[84] The man under whom he worked for several years, Amelot, was in the best position to judge Orry's capabilities.

In the period shortly after his arrival, said the ambassador,[85] Orry had had an inflated view of his importance. 'He rejected suggestions and requests made to him, and gave away employments and gifts without consulting anyone, as though he were absolute master.' Amelot would have to scold him repeatedly, sometimes reducing Orry to tears. Soon however he would revert to his old ways, and have to be reprimanded again, either by Amelot or by Ursins. It was this situation which made both of them favour the recall of Orry in 1706. Nevertheless, they had always lived on good terms with each other. 'I have always got on well with Mr Orry . . . I showed him friendship and confidence, and managed him to some extent.' The difficulty, however, was in Orry's relationship with others, especially Spaniards. 'His haughty, often hard, attitude drove the Spaniards to despair. . . . He had few scruples about defaulting on his word, and

[81] Juan de San Domingo to Torcy, 11 Sept. 1713, AE Corr. Pol. (Esp.), 226 f.100.

[82] Mémoires, vol. 2, p. 166: 'Orry seul avoit commencé de saper par le fondement l'autorité des conseils, et en eut été capable, parce qu'il faisoit signer au roi tout ce qu'il vouloit.' Also in vol. 2, p. 164: 'Cet homme-là eut été pendu, ou grand homme.'

[83] Berwick's Mémoires, cited in Mémoires de Saint-Simon, vol. 13, p. 442. Cf. also Berwick to Chamillart, 4 Mar. 1704, Guerre, A¹ 1787 f.137, speaking of Orry: 'il luy faut un superieur qui luy fasse rendre compte de tout, et sans qui il ne puisse rien faire; moyennant cela Mr Orry est tres utile.'

[84] Quoted in AE Corr. Pol. (Esp.), 220 f.41.

[85] Amelot to Chamillart, 10 Oct. 1706, Guerre, A¹ 1978 f.133.

often gave out as good and done, matters which were only so in his imagination. I refer to the payment of troops, supplies, munitions and other necessities.' In addition he affected a familiarity with Spanish grandees which they found intolerable.

After these criticisms, however, Amelot had little to reproach Orry with. An odd feature of the latter's personal affairs was his general disorderliness. His house was always in a mess, his papers always in confusion, his personal accounts in constant disorder. Yet this was the man who reduced the whole monarchy to a volume of tabulated figures and analysis. For the rest, Amelot found no evidence for any accusations of personal dishonesty against Orry, and had not received a single complaint on this matter. Orry was certainly not out for personal gain, for he had regularly refused to draw any salary from the Spanish crown, and had only begun to draw one in January 1706.

If Amelot's testimony may be accepted, we have in Orry a figure who had the energy and ambition to become a great minister, but in whom few could place any confidence, because of fundamental defects in his character. The criticism that Orry confused fiction with fact is a peculiarly telling one, for many contemporaries were of the same opinion. In autumn 1704, for example, when Orry was claiming that twelve million livres were available for the war in the peninsula, it was pointed out by a French military intendant that most of this sum existed only in his imagination.[86] Similarly in March 1705 the French ambassador delivered a detailed attack on Orry's figures, calling them 'sophistical'.[87] At the same time the secretary of the *despacho*, the marqués de Ribas, accused Orry of confusing some receipts with expenditure, and denounced his figures.[88] Even without crediting the stories told by Saint-Simon about Orry,[89] there is clearly reason here to be wary of Orry's statistics.

[86] 'Les 12 millions qu'Orry pretendoit avoir en poche pour les frais de la guerre n'existent la plus grande partie que dans son imagination,' Ozon to Torcy, 17 Sept. 1704, AE Corr. Pol. (Esp.), 139 f.50.

[87] Gramont to Torcy, 17 Mar. 1705, AE Corr. Pol. (Esp.), 146 f.179.

[88] Gramont to Chamillart, 19 Sept. 1704, Guerre, A¹ 1786 f.182.

[89] For example Saint-Simon says that Orry had told Puységur in 1704 that the forces on the Portuguese frontier were fully equipped, but Puységur on arriving there found conditions quite the opposite. Berwick contradicts this story. See *Mémoires de Saint-Simon*, vol. 12, p. 62–3. But cf. the letter of Tserclaës Tilly to the minister of war, the marqués de Canales, 10 Aug. 1704, from Badajoz, in Guerre, A¹ 1786 f.107. He complained of the wholesale lack of provisions, and observed: 'Estraño que Mr Orry se halle tan poco informado de la falta de todo, que hay aqui,

In conclusion, it may be said that Orry's work in Spain has been generally overestimated by historians,[90] who have been unaware of the significant contributions made by Amelot, by Bergeyck, and by native Spaniards. Orry's personal failings, particularly his temperamental failure to get on with his colleagues, vitiated all his activities, and because of this he never fulfilled his initial promise. Despite this, his achievements are notable. More than anyone else he seems to have been responsible for the introduction of systematic accounting methods into Spanish government finance. He instituted a separate war treasury, attempted to recover alienated property and rights for the crown, and established a permanent personal bodyguard for the king. He was responsible for the various Hacienda reforms of 1713 and 1714, and helped to develop the system of intendants which Bergeyck had instituted in 1711. His colleagues recognised his value though they resented his person, and, as Madame des Ursins confessed on one occasion, 'the king [Louis] knew how necessary it was to send M Orry back to this court. M Amelot felt the same, and I have often heard him tell Their Majesties that he would not have known what to do to get things moving, without Orry.'[91]

Bergeyck's activities were on an altogether smaller scale. He was nevertheless a man of greater eminence than Orry, having in his time been finance minister of the Spanish Netherlands, and his attempts at reform in Spain were far more practical and professional in inspiration. From the time of his arrival in Spain in 1711 he was keenly aware of the almost insurmountable difficulties facing him. In October he discovered that 'all the sources of revenue for this year and the first four months of next year, are completely consumed, and were assigned even before my arrival

---

y que haya informado al Rey y a la Reyna que hay provisiones sobradas en esta Provincia.'

[90] The brief study by François Rousseau, *Un réformateur français en Espagne au XVIIIe siecle*, Corbeil, 1892, is based almost entirely on Baudrillart.

[91] Ursins to Villeroy, 15 Jan. 1707, cited in L. Mandon, *De l'influence française en Espagne sous Philippe V, 1700–1713*, Montpellier et Cette, 1873. After Orry's departure from Spain in 1706, he was replaced by two French civil servants, Quenneville and le Bartz, who were sent expressly for the purpose from France. Le Bartz was to be distinguished as one of the first proponents of a national bank in France, according to a plan of his dated 1710: see Boislisle, *Correspondance*, vol. 3, pp. 648–51 and Paul Harsin, *Crédit public et Banque d'Etat en France du XVI au XVIIIe siècle*, Paris, 1933, p. 46. Quenneville did notable work for the Hacienda; see his memoir in AE Corr. Pol. (Esp.), 194 f.197.

at Corella . . . Thus the king has no resources left for this winter, save in the arrival of the galleons.'[92] On the same day as this, he wrote a letter to Torcy, outlining a new plan of his by which the whole existing tax system would be scrapped. In its stead, he proposed to 'divide all the royal revenue into two sections: one, a general farm of all the taxes by a company; and the other, two impositions to be levied on all the realms in proportion to their capability and the total expenditure of the state'.[93]

In order to carry this plan into effect, Bergeyck required three things: the goodwill of Spaniards, the help of a company of financiers, and administrative officials to superintend the impositions. The first he got from the governor of the council of Castile who, on hearing of the plan, 'embraced and kissed me for joy, and told me that he knew of nothing better or more suited to reestablish the monarchy'.[94] The second he got in the form of assurances from the financiers Goyeneche, Jacobo Flon, Arther and others, who promised to put forward the necessary capital for a company to farm the taxes.[95] The third item involved the establishment of a system of intendants who, as we have already seen, came into being in December 1711. These were the first royal agents in Spanish history to have jurisdiction over all parts of Spain, regardless of *fueros*. Bergeyck was on the threshold of a major change in the fiscal and administrative structure of Spain, and all this had been achieved in the space of four months.

Unfortunately, however, his own indispensability undid him. As the best candidate to speak for Spain at the vitally important peace talks in France,[96] Bergeyck was temporarily relieved of his duties and sent northwards. On his return to Madrid at the end of January 1713 he found most of his work undone. Nevertheless, he pressed forward with a further plan of reform which advanced far beyond his previous proposals and would have revolutionised the tax system in Spain. The basic inspiration for the new plan was in fact an old one: the desire to replace the existing multiplicity of taxes by a single universal tax.[97]

[92] Bergeyck to Vendôme, 19 Oct. 1711, BN, fonds français 14178 f.468.

[93] Bergeyck to Torcy, 19 Oct. 1711, AE Corr. Pol. (Esp.), 209 f.234.

[94] Bergeyck to Philip v, 24 Sept. 1711, AHN, Estado leg.2819.

[95] *Ibid.*

[96] Bergeyck had represented Philip at the previous peace talks in 1709.

[97] A. Matilla Tascón, *La Unica Contribución y el Catastro de La Ensenada*, Madrid, 1947, which discusses Bergeyck on p. 28, outlines precedents for the single tax.

Bergeyck did not go so far as to consider replacing all the taxes of the crown. Those to be abolished were the *alcabalas,* all the *cientos,* the *milicias* and the *fiel medidor,* the *servicio ordinario y extraordinario,* and all the *millones.* Together these taxes had brought in more than half the ordinary revenue of the crown. They were to be replaced by a single tax as from 1 January 1713. Meanwhile the *rentas generales, tercias* and other farmed taxes were to continue as before. It was estimated that the savings from the new system would help to pay off the *juros* speedily. Bergeyck saw no harm in abolishing some of the *rentas provinciales,* since many of them had been alienated and brought little to the treasury. A universal tax, on the other hand, would operate in regions such as Granada, where several of the old taxes did not exist. Administration would be simplified: in the provinces the intendant would control the tax, and in Madrid the organisation would be easier; 'the principal advantage offered by this plan is to have one tax and one official, instead of an infinite number as before.' Old debts from taxpayers would be forgiven, so that the system could start afresh. The advantages of the scheme were obviously legion.[98]

The government was thoroughly convinced by Bergeyck's arguments. The king set up a junta to discuss the issue. It was decided that the kingdom should be consulted, and deputies from the chief cities of Castile and León were invited to register their opinions. The representatives of Toledo, Seville, Granada, Cordoba, Jaén and Murcia gave their firm written support; but the other cities, while agreeing on the theoretical benefits of a single tax, pointed to the very great practical difficulties in-involved.[99] It was now March 1713, barely six weeks since Bergeyck's return to Madrid. Already, however, he had a sense of impending failure. The opposition of the municipalities had in effect put an end to the plan's practicability. By mid-March he had ceased to attend the *despacho,* [100] and when towards the end of the month the financiers let it be known that they could not advance any money until the plan, which threatened their interests

98 'Planta de Bergei, 1713', BNac., MS 1971039 gives the full text of Bergeyck's plan. There is a copy in AN, K.1359 f.37.

99 B Nac., MS 7528.

100 Bourke to Torcy, 13 Mar. 1713, AE Corr. Pol. (Esp.), 221 f.38: 'Il dit a tous ceux qui s'addressent a luy quil ne se melle de rien, et ainsi voila notre forme de gouvernement dans son ancien Etat jusqua une autre saison.'

as tax-farmers, was dropped,[101] all hope collapsed. This was the end of Bergeyck's attempt to reform the tax structure of Spain.

By any standards Bergeyck was one of the most brilliant ministers ever to have wielded authority in Spain. His energy and imagination were unparalleled. A few weeks in the autumn of 1711 were sufficient for him to establish the intendants in Spain; barely a month in 1713 sufficed for him to attempt the introduction of the single universal tax. All his other schemes were conceived and carried out at the same astonishing speed. His active ministry in Spain, both in 1711 and in 1713, totalled no more than six months; yet in that time he overhauled the finances, established the intendants, introduced schemes for reform, established new industries and imported foreign workers, drew up a plan to assure a regular income from the Indies,[102] and initiated the resurrection of the Spanish navy.[103] The factory at Valdemoro remained as a tribute to his achievements long after the grandiose plans of Orry had vanished out of memory. Certainly his work was hurried and often premature: the intendants, for instance, barely maintained their existence until 1718. But for all his deficiencies Bergeyck was the true precursor of Bourbon renewal. When Patiño reestablished the intendants in 1718, and when Ensenada in the next reign instituted the *única contribución,* they could both have acknowledged the Belgian administrator as the true begetter of their reforms. Looking back in 1712 on all the ministers who had served Philip v, Amelot rightly considered that 'only the comte de Bergeyck appeared capable of maintaining the finances and superintending the war'.[104]

Despite heavy commitments and liabilities, the Spanish crown by 1718 was beginning to put its counting-house in order. The increase in income was to be, as figure 1 shows, a permanent phenomenon. The system of *juro* finance, however, with all its attendant evils, persisted in the treasury and frustrated any attempts to reform the structure of taxation. If this period saw no

---

[101] *Ibid.*, 27 Mar. 1713, AE Corr. Pol. (Esp.), 221 f.124.

[102] While waiting to be summoned to the peace conference at the end of 1711, according to the French ambassador, Bergeyck 'travaille . . . a un autre plan pour faire trouver au Roy d'Espagne par le moyen des Indes un revenu fixe qui suplée aux fonds qui luy manqueront du costé de l'Espagne': Bonnac to Louis xiv, 30 Nov. 1711, AE Corr. Pol. (Esp.), 210 f.89.

[103] Discussed below, p. 379.

[104] Amelot to Pontchartrain, 21 Jan. 1712, AE Corr. Pol. (Esp.), 218 f.42.

fundamental changes in the financial machine, it saw at least important administrative reforms which made the machine more efficient. The centralisation of receipt and expenditure in one treasury responsible for the whole peninsula; and the appointment of a number of officials, intendants as well as other subordinates, who could enforce the treasury's policy: offered the best and most effective alternatives to a total displacement of the old system.

10 The Revolt of Aragon

'There was never a land in the world more disquieted and troubled for the sake of justice than this is today.'[1] The contemporary observation referred to Saragossa in 1591, but it may equally well have applied to the city in 1705. A sense of continuity, all too consciously exploited by opponents of Philip v, runs through the great anti-Castilian rebellions of 1591, 1640 and 1705. Of these three years, we know least about the last.[2] Was it 'for the sake of justice' that the eastern realms of Spain rebelled three times in just over a century? Any answer at the moment can only be tentative, since virtually no regional studies exist to supply the necessary historical background.

The kingdom of Aragon, one of the three provinces in the crown of Aragon, was in 1700 still completely independent of the government of Castile, for despite the uprising in 1591 the king had not seriously disturbed the constitutional liberties, the *fueros,* of the realm. The immediate ruler of Aragon[3] in both political and military matters was the viceroy, a post held at this date by the archbishop of Saragossa. The king was under no obligation to choose an Aragonese as viceroy, and royal policy had tended to favour the appointment of Castilians. Charles ii, however, showed himself more favourable to Aragonese pretensions, and the archbishop, one of his nominees, was a native of Aragon. Tenure of viceregal office was generally three years, but the king

---

[1] Quoted in Gregorio Marañón, *Antonio Pérez*, London, 1954, p. 280.

[2] Pierre Vilar, *La Catalogne*, is suggestive but brief. The various works by Pedro Voltes Bou are not illuminating.

[3] The account that follows is based largely on the manuscript 'Noticia de el Govierno de Aragon, formacion de los tribunales, y Magistrados que le exercian, segun los fueros y antigua planta', in AE Corr. Pol. (Esp.) supplément, 9 ff.20-5. Dated 1700, this memoir was in fact drawn up in 1711.

could shorten or extend this at will. Government of the kingdom was exercised, thanks to the traditional *fueros*, principally through autonomous agencies, but this did not mean that the crown had very little authority. On the contrary, the king of Castile did have, in his role as the king of Aragon, a very considerable part in the functioning of government. The cortes of the realm could only meet and be dissolved with the permission of the king, and the king could decide what business had to be set before the cortes for discussion. An even more important feature of royal authority was the power to appoint the principal officials of the realm; thanks to this, it became essential for the ruling circles of Aragon to keep on good terms with the king if they wished to remain in office. Long-standing corruption and alienation of some offices may have made inroads on this particular prerogative, but it seems to have retained some value at the beginning of the eighteenth century.

Directly subordinate to the viceroy in judicial administration came the audiencia of Saragossa, the chief court dispensing royal justice in Aragon. It consisted of two chambers, one for civil pleas, with a regent and four councillors (or *oidores*) sitting on it, and one for criminal pleas, presided over by the same regent but with five councillors. All the councillors of the court had to be natives of Aragon, and all had to have at least six years practice of the law before taking up their posts. The councillors usually held their judicial deliberations in the residence of the viceroy, who had the right to be present on such occasions. Though the councillors, as judges of Aragon, were technically free from all Castilian interference and responsible only to the kingdom, it was apparently not unknown for them to issue judgments in accord with a royal order transmitted through the viceroy. Local justice was administered by a residential judge in each principal city and town. In the case of Saragossa, the residential judge was known as the *zalmedina* (in Castile he would have been roughly equivalent to a *corregidor*). This official was nominated every year by the king from a short list presented by the viceroy: the list featured the most notable citizens of the city. It was the viceroy who was likewise responsible for choosing and nominating the other local judges. The last judicial institution to be touched on here is the office of justiciar (*Justicia*) of Aragon, which played so large a part in the events of 1591. The justiciar's court was in many ways parallel to that of the audiencia,[4] since it too exercised jurisdiction throughout Aragon. Appeals from cases in this court could go to the audiencia, and similarly appeals from the audiencia were entertained in the justiciar's court. At this period the court was headed by the justiciar and five other judges known as 'lieutenants' (*lugartenientes*). The justiciar was in theory nominated by the crown, the lieutenants by the cortes of the realm; in the case of the lieutenants, they were elected by lot in the cortes, after which the king formally nominated them. What made the justiciar's court highly significant was that the king had no constitutional right to remove any of the judges: the justiciar was appointed for life, and the lieutenants enjoyed the same privilege in practice; so that here was a court to which the Aragonese could look in time of trouble, for unlike other judicial bodies it was entirely independent of royal control.

Saragossa was governed in political and economic matters by a so-called consistory (*consistorio*) of five officials (*jurados*), who had extensive administrative powers which were nevertheless limited by royal ordinances regulating the government of the city. The *jurados* were obliged on certain matters to consult a city council of thirty-five members, known as the chapter and council (*Capítulo y Consejo*). Both these councillors and the *jurados* held their posts for a year only. Election was by lot: a number of names approved by the king were put in a bag and drawn according to traditional procedure. At the end of each year of office the councillors of Saragossa were legally obliged to give an account of their stewardship.

Annual election was also the practice with membership of the *diputados,* the deputies who were members of the *Diputación,* the standing committee of the cortes of Aragon. It was the principal duty of the *Diputación* to guard the *fueros* of the realm when the cortes were not in session. There were eight deputies on this body, two from each of the estates or *brazos* of the cortes. Of the two ecclesiastical deputies, one had to be a prelate (bishop, abbot or equivalent) and one a dignitary (such as a canon): these were the only deputies not elected by the usual system of lots. The noble estate was represented by two deputies, while of the two representatives of the gentry (that is, the estate of *caballeros* or

---

[4] See, e.g. John Lynch, *Spain under the Habsburgs* (vol. 1), Blackwell, Oxford 1964, p. 338.

hijos de algo) one had to be a member of a military order and gentle birth was all that was demanded of the other. The fourth estate, the municipalities, was represented by a deputy from the city of Saragossa and one from any other town in the realm. The deputies were elected annually by lot on the third of May.

Besides watching over the *fueros,* the deputies were responsible for the administration of the customs revenues of the kingdom, and for the management of the *peaje* tax and the royal tobacco monopoly: these taxes and their yield are discussed in a later chapter. All other royal taxes were administered by a body known as the *Junta Patrimonial,* on which sat the chief officials of the kingdom, including the viceroy, the regent of the audiencia, and the principal fiscal officers and treasurers, notably the *baile general* and the *maestre racional.* The revenue forthcoming from the royal taxes was, as we shall note later, entirely consumed in Aragon. Those ministers appointed by the king naturally had to be paid by him, so we find the receipts of the treasuries in Saragossa going out in the first place to pay the salaries of all the senior officials of the realm, and in the second place to pay grants and *mercedes* as well as the interest on *censos.*

The total independence of the crown of Aragon from that of Castile was a historical fact that nearly two centuries of Habsburg rule had not altered. If he wished to intervene in Aragonese affairs, the king at Madrid had to accept with good grace the limitations on his authority imposed by the *fueros.* In other respects his authority in the realm was restricted by the feudal structure of jurisdiction and landownership. As table 11 shows (page 246), the crown exercised direct jurisdiction, that is, control over administration and feudal taxation, over only about 20 per cent of the towns and settlements in Aragon. Even this figure is misleading, however, for in most of the districts of the kingdom the crown exercised no jurisdiction whatever, as table 11 shows; and Benavarre was the only region where royal control was paramount.

Despite the obvious interest of this table, it is not very informative, for a mere listing of jurisdictions does not define the comparative influence of the respective estates. The power and wealth of the Aragonese nobility, for example, was certainly more firmly based than their jurisdiction over urban centres might indicate.

I

Here, however, as in most other aspects of Aragonese history, the basic research still remains to be done.

One other statistical aspect of the kingdom may be touched on here, namely the population of Aragon during the war. As we

TABLE 11. JURISDICTIONS IN ARAGON IN 1718[5]

Corregimiento	Royal	Seigneurial	Ecclesiastical[6]	Comunidad, etc.	Total of towns
Saragossa	12	50	16 (3)	18	96
Albarracin	1	6	0	21	28
Alcañiz	0	56[7]	42 (29)	0	98
Barbastro	36	43	37 (20)	53	169
Benavarre	160	4	6	19	189
Borja	2	15	11 (8)	0	28
Calatayud	2	30	7 (2)	55	94
Cinco Villas	19	16	14 (1)	17	66
Daroca	2	1	5 (2)	108	116
Huesca	9	74	35 (12)	11	129
Jaca	48	72	43 (1)	27	190
Tarazona	1	13	11 (2)	0	25
Teruel	1	6	9 (5)	75	91
Total:	293	386	236	404	1319
Percentages:	22·2%	29·2%	17·9%	30·7%	

shall see in the final chapter, little reliance can be placed on population estimates during this period, particularly since such estimates were usually made for tax purposes only and were not meant to be precise computations of the resident population. Of the various military tax-censuses made of Aragon after its occupation by Castilian troops, the most reliable appear to be those made immediately after the occupation in 1711. These first estimates were made with the purpose of levying taxes on the whole population, so that there is less likelihood of privileged

[5] Based on BRAH, MS 9-26-1-4762 (see appendix 3). All settlements listed as having only one *vecino* and/or house have been omitted from this calculation.

[6] Jurisdictions belonging to the Order of Saint John are given in parentheses but are included in the preceding figure.

[7] Included in this figure are thirty towns (including the city of Alcañiz) under the jurisdiction of the Order of Calatrava, and seven under that of the Order of Santiago.

persons having escaped the net. In view of this, we can set down in table 12 the various estimates of population made by the army between 1711 and 1713.

TABLE 12. POPULATION OF ARAGON 1711–3

Corregimiento	1711		1711[8]			1712	1713
			towns	vecinos	deserted towns		
Saragossa	—		91	10,199	3	—	10,437
Albarracin	—		26	1,798	3	—	1,775
Alcañiz	—		111	13,131	—	—	12,603
Barbastro	—		122	5,001	17	—	5,061
Benavarre (Ribagorza)	—		170	2,780	102	—	3,098
Borja	—		29	2,896	—	—	2,586
Calatayud	—		77	7,897	2	—	7,820
Cinco Villas	—		82	4,033	2	—	4,346
Daroca	—		128	9,028	6	—	9,320
Huesca	—		131	4,786	25	—	4,737
Jaca	—		188	3,287	12	—	3,500
Tarazona	—		25	3,516	—	—	2,087
Teruel	—		79	7,811	2	—	7,871
Totals	83,817[9]	1,259	76,145	174		75,244[10]	75,241[11]

At first sight, table 12 suggests a regular fall in the population of Aragon, but this is highly unlikely, at least on the scale indicated by the figures, and there is little doubt that the different results of each census arose solely from differing bases and methods of assessment. A choice of any one of these returns is necessarily arbitrary: I have chosen to work with the figure of 76,145 principally because it carries complementary data on the number of towns assessed, and because it makes an explicit allowance for

[8] These figures for 1711 are enclosed with the letter of Tserclaës Tilly to Grimaldo, 22 Aug. 1711, AHN, Estado leg.416¹. The discrepancy in the number of towns between these figures and those in table 11 is often considerable, but for lack of detail in the 1711 returns, no check can be made.

[9] 'Estado de la imposicion general por via de quartel de Imbierno', AHN, Estado leg.411².

[10] Uztáriz, *Theórica y Practica*, p. 35.

[11] 'Vecindario General de España', BNac., MS.2274 ff.275–302.

depopulated towns. Adopting a multiplier of five[12] to represent five members per household, we can convert 76,145 *vecinos* into a population of 380,725 persons.

It was perhaps inevitable that the succession of a new dynasty to the Spanish throne should arouse a conflict of loyalties among those who had been attached for generations to the House of Austria, and that Aragon should select the opportunity to break away from Castile. Throughout the Spanish dominions there were serious stresses created by the war, which broke up the old Habsburg empire definitively. The pattern of discontent was set early in 1702 by the kingdom of Naples, another province that had distinguished itself by rebelling against Madrid in the seventeenth century. The French ambassador to Spain, who was at the time accompanying Philip v on his tour of Italy, reported of the Neapolitans that 'the emperor has a considerable party there, and the desire to have a king of their own is always uppermost in their minds'.[13] Was particularism then a serious factor? It is one which certainly cannot be ruled out in Catalonia, for instance, where the influential classes wished to assert themselves against the limitations imposed by Castile, and greeted with eagerness a Habsburg pretender who would choose Barcelona as his capital and give them a freedom not allowed by Madrid. The War of Succession sees an ironic repetition of the 1640 crisis, for in 1703 the Methuen treaties made Portugal defect from the French alliance and join England. The defection of Catalonia in 1705 completed the picture. This time the irony was a bitter one, for instead of Castilian troops quartering themselves in Lisbon and Barcelona, we witness Portuguese and Catalan troops quartering themselves in Madrid.

Aided only by France, Castile defended itself tirelessly against the English, Dutch, Germans, Portuguese and Catalans. In these circumstances the fidelity of Castile requires some explanation. The answer is essentially simple. Despite the just claims of other realms to consider themselves part of *España*, Castile had throughout the Habsburg era monopolised the entire machinery of empire, whether in Europe or in America; and the other realms were now attempting to redress the balance. Castile was therefore

[12] For the use of this coefficient, see chapter 14, which also presents a survey of the population of the peninsula.
[13] Marcin to Louis XIV, 27 May 1702, AE Corr. Pol. (Esp.), 104 f.284.

fighting for its own inheritance, and for the moment this was identified with the Bourbon dynasty. Castilian loyalty to Philip was unquestionable. From his accession the young king had promoted the resurgence of his realms, which, thanks to the *fueros,* did not in practice include the crown of Aragon. Philip therefore built up armaments in Castile, but none in Aragon or Valencia. Moreover, in Madrid the Castilians were in touch with Philip, saw him and knew his presence: the same could not be said for the peoples of the other provinces. Philip was a king 'chosen by the Castilians', to quote a Catalan apologist.[14] To his other subjects he was an absentee ruler. Only in Castile, therefore, did the people prove their personal attachment to the king by popular uprisings. During the first Allied occupation of Madrid in 1706, Amelot made a note of some typical examples of fidelity: a convoy of eight hundred soldiers from Portugal was attacked by the people led by their priests, and ninety Portuguese were killed; enemy couriers could not get through the countryside because the peasants captured them and brought their letters to the royal camp; villagers in La Mancha put to flight seven hundred Portuguese troops who were sent to punish them; in occupied Madrid nobody dared cry out 'Viva Carlos III', and instead the populace were forcing Portuguese soldiers to shout 'Viva Felipe Quinto!'[15] These incidents are paralleled nowhere else in the peninsula, except perhaps in Navarre where, according to another letter from Amelot, 'the bishop of Calahorra has mounted a horse at the head of 1,500 clergy of his diocese, all well armed and mounted, to defend the frontier of Navarre'![16] The loyalty of Castilians may have been further affirmed by their sufferings at the hands of Catalans and Portuguese; and by the fact that their enemies were in the company of known Lutheran and Anglican heretics. Little credit for accuracy can be given to the propaganda put out by either side, but there is no reason to discount all the complaints put forward, for example, by the city of Salamanca in 1706, on account of outrages committed during the Allied occupation from 13 to 24 September; or to reject entirely the claim in 1710 that 'there were sold in the streets of

---

[14] Cited in Pierre Vilar, *La Catalogne,* vol. 1, p. 670 fn.8
[15] Amelot to Louis XIV, 29 July 1706, AE Corr. Pol. (Esp.), 160 f.112.
[16] *Ibid.* 3 Aug 1706, AE Corr. Pol. (Esp.), 160 f.151. This exam ple was also followed, by the bishop of Murcia.

Madrid chalices, patens, ciboria and all kinds of sacred vessels and ornaments which the heretics had sacked from neighbouring churches'.[17]

While historians have never doubted the loyalty of Castile, they have also never doubted the disloyalty during this war of Aragon. Aragon and Valencia, it has been claimed, were like Catalonia in rebellion against the crown. Such at least was the excuse given by the Bourbon government at the time for the revocation of the *fueros*. Similarly, the archduke and the English claimed that the provinces were in rebellion, proof positive of the unpopularity of the Bourbons and the fidelity of the people to the House of Austria. Aragon and Valencia were therefore proven rebels and both sides were vindicated. Since, however, there is considerable evidence to doubt the validity of this conclusion, it would be advisable to trace the progress of events in Aragon.

We are not primarily concerned here with the long-term historical reasons for discontent with Castile, such as the imbalance between the imperial roles of Aragon and Castile, or the exclusion of the ruling class of Aragon from their due share of official posts in the government of the monarchy. Substantial research remains to be done before any such explanations become plausible and sufficient. All that can be noted here are the factors which seem to have had a direct share in precipitating discontent in Aragon. The first serious mistake made by Philip v and his advisers was to show excessive concern over the Spanish territories in Italy, at that time threatened by imperialist forces. It was decided to make a royal tour through the Italian possessions in order to bind them more securely to the Bourbon cause. Louis xiv appears not to have been aware of the very real dangers of leaving a newly-acquired kingdom without first making sure of its loyalty. Certainly Philip v carried out all his required duties. He had arrived in Madrid on 18 February 1701. On 8 May he met the deputies of the realm and received their homage in the monastery of San Jerónimo. This meeting is sometimes known as the cortes of Madrid, though in fact it was no cortes at all: instead, it was a vast meeting at which representatives of all the communities in the realm, from the bishops and grandees down to the deputies of each province, and including representatives of the realms of the

[17] NLS, Astorga Collection, G.25 f.3, nos. 6, 10.

crown of Aragon, put in an appearance to affirm loyalty to the king. By the end of August it had been decided that Philip should visit Italy. On 1 September a decree was issued nominating Cardinal Portocarrero of Toledo as governor of Spain during the king's absence. On 5 September Philip left Madrid on his journey to Italy. He had spent seven months in Castile: how long was he going to spend now on his journey across the territory of the crown of Aragon?

There were few or no signs of hostility to Philip on the part of the Aragonese. He was greeted at the frontiers of the kingdom by leading members of the nobility and high dignitaries. The first place at which he arrived in Aragon, on 12 September, was a little town names Ussed. There he was greeted by cries of 'Long live the king of Aragon: long live Philip the Fourth!', since he was the fourth of that name to rule over their realm. On Friday 16 September he entered the city of Saragossa amid great rejoicing. On the twentieth he left the city. If the Aragonese had received so brief a visit, they were at least more fortunate than the Valencians, who never saw Philip at all. It did not occur to the king to make a detour through Valencia: he was too concerned to meet his wife-to-be at Barcelona. Marie Louise of Savoy had been due to arrive at that port by sea, but owing to an attack of sea-sickness she went ashore at Marseilles and made the rest of the journey by land. At Villefranche she was met by the princess des Ursins and together they made their way to Barcelona. Meanwhile Philip had entered the city on 1 October, to a cool reception from the Catalans. Three days later, on the fourth, he swore to maintain the *fueros* of Catalonia. On the twelfth the Catalan cortes met in the monastery of San Francisco, with all the estates present. In an atmosphere of mutual generosity the king confirmed the *fueros,* acceded to all the requests of the deputies, and granted privileges, including fourteen new peerages, to a total of fifty-four persons. The cortes in return granted a *donativo* of 1,500,000 reales and a *servicio*, payable over six years, of twelve millions.[18] Two days after the opening of the cortes the new queen of Spain arrived in Barcelona. This event completed the royal pleasure. When the cortes had completed its sessions the king and queen together brought it formally to a close on 14 January 1702. Finally, on

[18] Danvila y Collado, *El poder civil en España,* vol. 3, pp. 408 ff., gives full details of this and other cortes of the reign.

8 April, Philip left Barcelona for Naples, leaving Spain in the control of his thirteen year-old wife.

Philip's six-month stay in Barcelona was a major gesture to the Catalans, as was his choice of the city to meet his wife (whom he had married by proxy on 11 September), and his generous attitude to the cortes.[19] Yet this generosity was at the expense of similar gestures to Saragossa and Valencia. Moreover, even the Castilians had strongly resented the king's absence: his departure from Madrid provoked hostility and near-riots from the crowds who wished him to remain in the capital. 'L'amour parut aller jusqu'à la fureur, jusqu'à l'idolatrie', observed the French ambassador, Marcin, who witnessed the scenes in Madrid. In Spain as a whole there was regret at the journey, and Portocarrero and other leading Spanish councillors were opposed to it;[20] but the plan was inspired by France, and it was carried through. We find circulating in Madrid at this time a pamphlet, dated 12 February 1702, which expressed Spanish dissatisfaction in moderate but measured terms:

> The absence of His Majesty from Spain is open to irremediable hazards and mischiefs. . . . What greater glory could we Spaniards have than to see our king traversing the whole land with his triumphant banners?[21]

Awareness of a need to accord fair treatment to Saragossa made Marie Louise go directly to the city after her husband's departure for Italy. On 26 April she opened the Aragonese cortes and formally swore to preserve the *fueros*. In return the assembly granted her a *donativo* of 100,000 pesos, to be drawn principally from the tax on tobacco. On 17 June the queen left Saragossa.

After this the province of Aragon remained at peace for a couple of years. As events were to show, this was a peace of preparation. Hostility to Castilians was never far distant, but it was hostility to the French that appears to have been one of the primary factors subverting the loyalties of the population. A distinguished contemporary Aragonese historian referred to the common people at the time as 'naturalmente enemigo de

---

[19] A cynic would comment that Philip's long stay was occasioned only by his desire to have an adequate honeymoon before leaving for Italy.

[20] Baudrillart, *Philippe V et la Cour de France*, vol. 1, pp. 84, 91.

[21] *Copia de Carta que un Cortesano remitió a Barcelona a mano de un Ministro*: 'la ausencia de su Magestad de España esta expuesta a casos y daños irremediables ... Que mayor gloria podiamos tener los Españoles, que ver a nuestro Rey, que con sus triunfantes Estandartes corria toda la tierra?' AE Corr Pol. (Esp.), 102 f.408.

franceses'.[22] We can only guess at the reasons that might justify this statement. Certainly, Aragon appears to have had an honourable history of Francophobia. In the cortes of 1646, to go back no more than half a century, a law was passed forbidding the children of Frenchmen, even if they had been born in Aragon and were married to natives, to hold any public office whatsoever. The motive seems to have been commercial jealousy rather than purely political hostility; the decree was in any case undoubtedly 'dictated more by hatred than by reason'.[23] The consequence was a drastic fall in the number of French traders and financiers, with serious repercussions on the public economy of Aragon. In alarm the authorities pushed through a repeal of the 1646 law in the cortes of 1678, despite the firm opposition of the third estate.[24] Within a few years the French appear once again to have regained control over the commerce of Aragon. This led to further legislation in the cortes of 1686. On this occasion it was decreed that no Frenchman could carry on trade in the province unless he was married to a native of Aragon or of any other part of Spain; and that his employees had to be born within the Spanish empire.[25] If this law was observed, it no doubt had adverse effects on French commercial activity; but it was almost certainly a dead letter by the time of Philip's accession to the throne.

Discontent in Aragon seems, oddly enough, to have been stirred up in a way closely resembling the events of the Pérez affair of 1591. The agent this time was the conde de Cifuentes who, as we have seen, was arrested for treason in 1704 and subsequently escaped to Aragon, where he had both lands and influence. In February 1705 he was hiding in Teruel, in March he ventured into Saragossa, where he found refuge in a convent of the Discalced Carmelites. The viceroy and governor of Aragon at this date was the archbishop of Saragossa, Don Antonio Ibáñez de la Riva Herrera, 'a saintly prelate, but Castilian at heart and governed by Don Lorenzo Armengual, his secretary and later his auxiliary bishop'.[26] The archbishop sent troops to surround the convent when he heard of the fugitive's presence. The events of 1591

---

[22] Conde de Robres, *Historia de las guerras civiles*, p. 249.
[23] Ignacio de Asso, *Historia de la Economía Política de Aragón*, Saragossa, 1798 (new edition 1947), p. 206.
[24] 'No sin resistencia del brazo de los Caballeros y Universidades', *ibid.*, p. 206.
[25] *Ibid* p. 249.
[26] Conde de Robres, p. 249.

were repeated. There were riots in favour of Cifuentes, and the people grew convinced that their ancient liberties were threatened.[27] For the period of about two months that he remained in Saragossa, Cifuentes appears to have been immune from arrest because of his great popularity, which enabled him to publicise even further the alleged evil intentions of the new French-inspired government. The archbishop was unable to lay hands on him, and Cifuentes moved from town to town through Aragon, ending up finally in rebel Barcelona.

For most of 1705 Aragon was only in the background of military operations. The Franco-Spanish forces were concentrated in the south, where the siege of Allied-held Gibraltar occupied them. The Allies, meanwhile, were moving their troops by sea up the Levantine coast. The fall of Barcelona on 9 October created an immense shock, and led to the immediate transference of Bourbon forces from Gibraltar. The French commander, Tessé, reported back to Madrid, then set out for Catalonia. The fall of Valencia city on 16 December completed the collapse in the eastern territories.

The government's immediate concern now was the transport of troops across Aragon to rebel Catalonia. Not since the days of Olivares had Castilian soldiers crossed in such force across Aragonese territory. What was entirely novel, however, was the presence of French troops. It did not need the urgings of Cifuentes to arouse the Aragonese to solicitude for their *fueros,* since it was obvious that the king of Castile had no right to send forces into the realm without formal permission. Troop movements began in November. The Aragonese claimed, and received, the formal payment to which they were entitled, of fifty pesos for each body of troops sent across their land. In return the troops were met at the frontier by an agent (*comisario*) and guided across country to Catalonia. The whole process gave rise to unnecessary provocations. According to Macanaz,[28] several detachments that refused to pay the required fifty pesos were not allowed to enter Aragon. Even troops that did enter were not always taken the shortest or most suitable way by their *comisarios,* with the result that several minor incidents occurred.

[27] *Ibid.,* p. 252. Cf. Fray Nicolás de Jesús Belando, *Historia civil de España desde el año de 1700 hasta el de 1733* (3 vols), Madrid, 1740–4, vol. I, p. 207.

[28] *Discurso jurídico, histórico y político sobre las Regalías de los Señores Reyes de Aragón* (1729), in *Regalías,* p. 140, note 53.

Meanwhile the ruling classes of Aragon were being asked to make a contribution to the needs of the royal treasury. In 1705 a *donativo voluntario* was requested from all the provinces of Spain. The sum realised from Aragon was, as we have already seen,[29] not large. Most of the nobility refused to give any money, and contributed instead in kind. Ministers in Madrid appear to have looked on the small donation as an affront, and to have been unaware of the constitutional difficulties involved in extracting money from a realm that had no obligation to pay taxes to Castile. Aragon, moreover, had not been invaded by enemy troops, so that the *donativo* was clearly intended to aid the troops of Castile alone. Faced by a lack of comprehension in Madrid, the archbishop felt obliged to elucidate matters:

Concerning the *donativo* paid by the nobility [he wrote to the secretary of the *despacho*, Grimaldo, on 26 September], I must inform you that circumstances here cannot be compared to those in other kingdoms. In the first place, according to the *fueros* in Aragon no native, much less any noble, contributes any taxation to the king. Whenever grave emergencies have arisen, it has been usual to ask for a *donativo voluntario* from the towns as well as from individual lords and gentry. This city is doing the same thing, since its payments are in arrears and its income fully pledged, so that for this grant they are now making use of the amounts usually paid by agreement to creditors, who will be reimbursed by a *donativo* from the citizens. And although the sums offered me by the gentry are very small, they are larger and have come more quickly than other *donativos* that have been made in my time.

I must also inform you that all the ancient noble houses of Aragon are at present undergoing litigation, for example the estate of Villahermosa, the condado de Aranda, that of Luna, that of Fuentes, that of Castelflorit, that of San Clemente, and others; in that of Sástago, only a few days ago, a Castilian came in to live on the estates; and the condado of Belchite has a lawsuit with the duque de Hijar. And all the other nobles and gentry who have paid the *donativo* have such low incomes and salaries that they can barely maintain themselves.

You should also bring to the king's attention the fact that the population do not look on this war as one of those waged with fire and blood. The actions of the rebels do not touch their lives or their property. At most, what the rebels do is to try and gain their support for a change of government, by means of insinuations and arguments introduced in various ways, especially through letters, and through friars and clergy, of which breed I now have four in the cells. And

[29] Above, p. 219.

since there are few who are very loyal, many who are indifferent and not a few who are disaffected, it is a miracle of divine providence that serious disturbances [*tumultos escandalosos*] have not occurred in this city and in others of the kingdom. To prevent these I took several precautions (of which I have informed the king) in the winter and summer, and it has caused amazement to the wisest people to see this city in complete peace and tranquillity, and the same for the other cities and towns of Aragon, in spite of the uprisings in Catalonia.[30]

Four days later the archbishop was again forced to impress on Madrid the fact that no more money could be got out of Aragon unless extraordinary measures were adopted.[31] He reminded Grimaldo that

this kingdom of Aragon is so privileged by its *fueros* that no individual pays any tax whatsoever [to the king], nor is there any possibility of the realm making any considerable grant without being assembled in the general cortes.

Even in 1640, he said, referring to the obvious historical parallel, Philip IV had felt the need for a cortes in Saragossa to support his measures in Catalonia.

All that has been possible has been to ask for a *donativo voluntario* from the towns and from several individuals, by means of royal letters which sent officials into the realm (much of the *donativo* being consumed by their expenses). This is the constitution, which cannot be altered without breaking the *fueros*; and if this were attempted there would follow a universal uproar that would be prejudicial at any time but most of all in present circumstances.

The tension reflected so clearly by the archbishop in September was doubly aggravated in the late autumn by the movement of troops, both French and Castilian, into Aragon. At this stage Philip v decided to appoint a Castilian to the viceroyalty of Aragon. The conde de San Esteban de Gormaz, Philip's nominee, arrived in Saragossa to take up his duties in the autumn. Lack of evidence makes it impossible to say what the effect of the new appointment was. The archbishop loyally made way and was subsequently appointed inquisitor general, but it is difficult to imagine general support for an appointment that went against the spirit of the *fueros,* since Charles II had conceded to the Aragonese

---

[30] Archbishop of Saragossa to Grimaldo, 26 Sept. 1705, AHN, Estado leg.264 f.4.
[31] *Ibid.* 30 Sept. 1705, AHN, Estado leg.264 f.6.

the right to have one of their own nation as viceroy. Perhaps the most interesting feature of the appointment is that San Esteban's secretary, already at this period a man of great political promise, was Melchor de Macanaz.

In his new post, Macanaz took part in the secret interception of letters to the leading nobles of Aragon. Correspondence was opened, then re-sealed, and allowed to continue to the recipients. In this way the plans of Cifuentes, and those of the conde de Sástago and the marqués de Coscojuela, both deep in rebel counsels, were carefully watched by the authorities. The threat to the crown came, however, not only from the nobility but also from the populace. This was illustrated clearly by the events of December 28, the feast of the Holy Innocents. Macanaz, who was present throughout, is our principal authority for what transpired.[32]

On the eve of Innocents day a French regiment under the command of Marshal Tessé began to enter Saragossa by the Portillo gate. The troops, like several other regiments currently making their way across the realm, were on their way to deal with enemy forces on the borders between Aragon and Catalonia. Two battalions had entered the city, when suddenly the gates were shut fast by the people and a riot started. The surprised soldiers were set upon and beaten, some murdered, by the populace. Banners were torn down, drums smashed, insignia trampled upon. Cries of 'Death!' and 'Protect our *fueros* and liberties!' could be heard. The French scattered, and Tessé together with his officers had to seek refuge with the viceroy. San Esteban jumped on his horse and rode through the streets in an attempt to pacify the mob. Everywhere he went there were cries of 'Long live our viceroy!' and 'Protect our *fueros* and leave no Frenchman alive!'

The riot in Saragossa might be attributed merely to a momentary crisis in the city itself, but for the fact that similar uprisings occurred at about the same time in different parts of the realm in Huesca, Calatayud, Daroca, in regions adjacent to these, and in several others. According to Macanaz, the French were driven to seek refuge in Fraga, Caspe and other towns not hostile to them, 'while the rest of the kingdom was watered with the blood of the king's troops'. The motives for the uprising are not

---

[32] *Regalías*, pp. 124–6; Modesto Lafuente, *Historia General de España* (30 vols), 2nd edn Madrid, 1869, vol. 18 p. 126.

entirely clear. Cifuentes and his agents may have had a hand in it; alternatively, the riots may have been spontaneous, provoked both by concern for the *fueros* and by hatred for the French. When Macanaz asked the rioters in Saragossa what their grievances were, 'they said that the troops were taking horse and billeting themselves in towns, without any right beyond that conceded them by Philip IV in the cortes of 1646; and that even this right stipulated that the natives were not obliged to supply more than lodging and a simple meal, and horses only from one stopping-place to the next'.

Whatever the origins of the incident, it was clear that Aragon had ceased to be secure for the royal cause. By the end of 1705 the military threat from the Allies had also grown. All the territory between the Rivers Cinca and Segre had fallen to the rebels, and the town of Alcañiz[33] was occupied by Cifuentes. Saragossa was now threatened. The counterattack from Aragon was led by Tserclaës Tilly, who took the main route from Saragossa through Bujaraloz to Fraga, thus pushing the enemy back on Lérida. A subsidiary force under Miguel Pons marched south and garrisoned Caspe and Maella. A line of Bourbon defences through Barbastro, Mequinenza and Maella prepared the way for the march into Catalonia in 1706.

Tessé, now commanding in Aragon, had his base at Caspe. On 12 March the king arrived at the camp, to lead the advance to Barcelona in person. The troops took the main road through Fraga, Cervera and Igualada to the Catalan capital. On 6 April the royalist siege of Barcelona began. As we have already seen, it was raised on 10 May, and, since a direct line of retreat was cut off, the king had to return to Madrid by a route that took him through Perpignan, Narbonne, Carcassonne, Toulouse, Pau, St Jean-Pied-de-Port, Roncesvalles and Pamplona.

The summer of 1706 saw victories on every hand for the Allied forces. The fall of Madrid in June was followed by the proclamation of the archduke in Saragossa on the twenty-ninth of the same month. On 15 July the archduke in person entered Saragossa and was greeted with enthusiasm by the people. His short stay of nine days (he left on the twenty-fourth) completed the process begun

---

[33] 'Fue este Pueblo donde se suscitó la primera chispa de la Rebolución del Reyno de Aragón el año 1705': Juan de Estrada, *Población General de España* (3 vols), Madrid, 1747, vol. 2. p. 451.

by the riots of December. All Frenchmen were expelled from the kingdom by decree, and several were murdered and maltreated in disturbances. The city remained in rebel control for the next eleven months, until the battle of Almansa destroyed Allied power in the eastern territories. A direct result of the battle was Orléans' successful march to Saragossa, which he entered on 26 May 1707.

The return of the capital to Bourbon obedience brought with it, as we shall see, profound constitutional changes. The city fell into enemy hands once again, in 1710 after the Allied victory of Saragossa, and the archduke came to live in it for a brief six days, from 21 to 26 August. But by then Bourbon rule in the province seemed inevitable. The rebel kingdom was subdued, its *fueros* abolished, and Castilians were entrusted with the government.

It remains, nevertheless, extremely difficult to accept the simple, apparently plausible, explanation of the situation which has so far been given. Aragonese discontent with Castile, hatred for the French, and concern for the *fueros,* are in themselves valid factors. Yet there seems to be little doubt that 'looking over the crown of Aragon as a whole, or each of its provinces in particular, the greater part of the prelates and chapters, nobles and gentry, and many municipalities, did not cooperate in the proclamation of the archduke'.[34] The claim comes from a contemporary, and could be written off as special pleading. After all, against it we can balance the claim of another contemporary who was also on the spot, Macanaz, that 'the whole kingdom rebelled'.[35] Yet there is, despite Macanaz, enough evidence to make one doubt whether a revolt did in fact occur in Aragon on such a scale as to warrant condemnation of the whole realm and revocation of its ancient liberties.

Perhaps the most fruitful line of inquiry would be an analysis of the degree of resistance, or of support, offered by the Aragonese to the Allies, since it would be pointless to gauge their loyalty by the amount of love they bore to Castilians or to Frenchmen. What, first of all, were the material factors aiding defection? It is likely that several towns along the Catalan frontier felt they had more in common with the Catalans than with the Castilians. Typical of these was Fraga, of whose citizens a correspondent

---

[34] Conde de Robres, *Historia de las guerras civiles,* p. 371.
[35] *Regalías,* p. 124.

informed the government that 'their commerce being more in Catalonia than in Aragon, they will undoubtedly swing the same way . . . as well as on account of the Catalan language, which they all speak, many inhabitants of the town being Catalan by origin'.[36] Many peasants appear to have supported the rebels, for reasons which remain obscure. When Cifuentes, for instance, was besieging the town of Maella in July 1706, he was accompanied by 250 horse and 400 foot, and by a vast number of 'more than 1,500 peasants, who followed him voluntarily'.[37] Both in town and country, therefore, there were partisans of the archduke. Many remained so, simply because of the readiness of the royalists to treat all Aragonese as rebels. Little allowance was made in Bourbon propaganda for the possibility that some subjects at least might be loyal: all were indiscriminately subjected to taxation, billeting and other vexations. 'Loyal towns, as well as churches and religious communities, are taxed, with the threat that *if they do not pay they will suffer all the rigours of war and be treated as rebels against His Majesty,* a clause which serves not to persuade but to wound'.[38] With grievances like this, pamphleteers could well sneer at the claim that they had been liberated by the French:

> Unos fueron a presidios,
> otros fuimos desterrados,
> millares encarcelados,
> con oprobrios ofendidos:
> viéndonos tan afligidos,
> que mejor trato tendria
> un Christiano en Berberia![39]

Perhaps the most striking feature of the Allied advance into Aragon is the lack of resistance offered by the population. For apologists of Philip v this proved beyond doubt the guilt of the Aragonese. The facts can, however, be read a different way. We

---

[36] D Joseph de Urries to Grimaldo, 23 Sept. 1705, AHN, Estado leg.264 f.68. Fraga, however, remained loyal.

[37] *Miscelenea curiosa, asuntos de España*, vol. 2, no. 19, in the Astorga Collection, NLS, G.25 e.2.

[38] The italics are in the original. D Joseph de Sisson to Grimaldo, 11 July 1707, AHN, Estado leg.320¹.

[39] *Lástimas de los Aragoneses*, Astorga Collection, NLS, G.25 e.3, no. 55. Some went into garrisons, / others of us were exiles, / thousands were imprisoned, / and covered with insults: / seeing how afflicted we are, / how much better would be the treatment / of a Christian in Barbary!

have already seen[40] that there was an almost total lack of military defences in the peninsula. The kingdom of Aragon, no less than other parts of Spain, shared in 'the poor and needy state' of garrisons and armaments. Both in Catalonia and in Aragon, towns and cities fell to the enemy for no other reason than a lack of armaments. The key fortress of Gerona in Catalonia, for example, found in July 1705 that its artillery was insufficient for self-defence, and applied to Barcelona for reinforcements to help the garrison. Before aid could arrive, Barcelona had surrendered to the archduke, and Gerona then decided that capitulation was its only alternative. The governor and bishop went into exile, and the garrison was allowed to march out.[41]

The position of Lérida, the principal city on the route from Barcelona to Saragossa, was also similar. In mid-September of 1705 it found itself virtually defenceless. Very little gunpowder remained in its stores, a great deal having been sent the previous winter to help the city of Tortosa. The citadel had no more than twenty-five soldiers to conduct its defence; the greater part of the city's troops had been previously dispatched to other towns to help. In reply to an urgent message from the bishop of Lérida (Don Francisco de Solís, a firm supporter of Philip v who later in 1706 was appointed viceroy of Catalonia), the archbishop of Saragossa arranged for powder to be sent from Barbastro; but this succour came too late. Personnel required to man the city's guns were too few and inadequate; and in the current military situation there was no help to be expected from any quarter. To make matters worse, people in the town, supplemented by peasants, were growing restive and had lost faith in the city's ability to defend itself. While the lack of defences was a cogent explanation for defeat, the attitude of the populace was sufficient to make defence impossible. Two riots occurred in the first fortnight of September; then on the fifteenth that month a very serious outbreak in the town occurred. Accusing the handful of cavalry in the town under Don Miguel Pons of having fired on them, the rioters demanded their withdrawal, and the authorities had to give way. The departure of the cavalry sealed Lérida's fate. Five days later, on the twentieth, just as the rioters were

[40] Above, p. 57
[41] Pedro Voltes Bou, 'La Entrega de la plaza de Gerona al Archiduque Carlos de Austria', *Anales del Instituto de Estudios Gerundenses*, IV (1949).

demanding that the deputies of the city make their submission to the obviously superior forces of the archduke, the enemy took possession of the town. By the twenty-fourth the citadel had fallen. The conde de San Esteban, writing from near-by Fraga, told the archbishop of Saragossa that the governor of Lérida and the few soldiers with him had borne themselves 'with indescribable valour'.[42]

After Lérida there was virtually nothing to stand in the way of the Allies. Early in September the authorities at Tamarite, just north-west of Lérida, had informed the archbishop of Saragossa that despite their willingness to sacrifice 'our lives in your defence and that of our country, we have a duty to state that this town is exposed and situated in a valley with no defence save what can be managed in hand-to-hand fighting'.[43] When the principal Allied advance into Aragon began in 1706, after the failure of Philip v's siege of Barcelona, Tamarite and other towns in a similar condition were taken effortlessly. The fall of Barbastro on 19 June 1706 left the realm 'without an army or any regular militia'.[44] The main line of the enemy's march had meanwhile proceeded to the capital. There the archbishop's chief concern was the lack of any defence: writing to Madrid, he emphasised 'the necessity of sending some troops as soon as possible, before those of the enemy enter'. At the same time he tried to put a brave face on the fact that there was no help forthcoming, and that the disaffected in the city were painting red and black crosses on the doors of those who supported Philip v – 'and they have even put some on mine'.[45] A month later the Allies entered Saragossa.

Further to the north, the bishop of Lérida had undertaken the defence of Jaca. In August he complained to Madrid that 'Aragon is without any soldiers, . . . but only 2,000 good troops found by the king would win back within a fortnight all we have lost'. The bishop's optimism did not extend to Jaca, which he said contained 'not much more than 200 men capable of bearing

[42] The fall of Lérida may be followed in the letters of the bishop of Lérida and others in AHN, Estado leg. 264 ff.2, 4, 8, 28, 36.

[43] Letter of *Bayle* and *Jurados* of Tamarite to archbishop, 8 Sept. 1705, contained in letter of archbishop to Grimaldo, 11 Sept. 1705, AHN, Estado leg.264 f.28.

[44] Printed memorial of 30 Aug. 1707 from deputies of Aragon, AHN, Estado leg.312.

[45] Archbishop to D Antonio Ybáñes de Bustamante, 4 June 1706, AHN, Estado leg.281[1] f.30.

arms'.[46] There is little doubt that this state of military defence-lessness prevailed throughout Aragon, and was principally responsible for the ease with which the enemy swept over the territory. If the crown is to be blamed in any way, it must be for the total failure to contribute adequate troops to defend the realm. Yet in a sense the fault lies wholly with the Aragonese, who had neglected their own defences and resisted any intervention by Castilians until it was too late. Moreover, they appear to have shown greater sympathy to the Catalans than to the Castilians and French, to judge by the ease with which they persuaded themselves that resistance to the archduke was impracticable.

If the general conclusion to be drawn is that the Aragonese did not put up any substantial resistance, this is still inadequate evidence on which to base a charge of rebellion. Bourbon apologists after the war were quick to point out that the towns which fell so easily to the Allies in 1706 were the very ones that cost much blood and many lives to recover. This argument, as we shall see when we come to the case of Valencia, is a weak one. The sole reason why the Spaniards found it difficult to recapture towns was because the Allies had taken care to fortify them properly, learning in this way from the mistakes of their enemies. Valencia and Aragon, which had a higher proportion of walled cities and citadels than Castile, were correspondingly more difficult to recover once they had been garrisoned.[47]

The fact remains that sections of the population in Aragon did willingly defect to the enemy. Saragossa in particular was riddled with traitors, as the archbishop made plain to his correspondents in Madrid. Macanaz, noting their names down many years later when he was writing his memoirs, recalled the situation in the city when he was accompanying the king through Aragon in 1706, on the way to join Tessé for the siege of Barcelona:

For forty [*sic*] days and nights I could not go to bed, both because of

[46] Bishop to Grimaldo, 11 Aug. and 24 Nov. 1706, AHN, Estado leg.281¹ ff.26, 6.

[47] Juan de Cabrera, *Crisis Política determina el mas florido imperio, y la mejor institución de príncipes*, Madrid, 1719, p. 183, gives an interesting explanation for the failure of the Allies to capture Castile. He says that Peterborough 'hallando los lugares abiertos y sin defensa, y que los pueblos obligados de la fuerça daban la obediencia al señor Archiduque, pero que bolviendo sus tropas las espaldas para pasar adelante, aclamaban a su legítimo dueño y Rey Phelipe Quinto, dixo era impossible la conquista permanente de Castilla por falta de algunas ciudades muradas y fuertes, donde puestas guarniciones mantuviessen en freno y obediencia a los paysanos.'

the preparations being made for the stay of His Majesty and the army as well as because of the continuous disturbances created by the disaffected and the care that was taken to pacify them in a friendly way. ... The situation was so disgraceful that in the audiencia there was hardly anyone to be trusted, except for the *fiscal*, Don José de Rodrigo; in the Church, the archbishop and a very few canons; in the court of the justiciar of Aragon, only Don Miguel de Jaca, the justiciar; in the government of the kingdom, only Don Miguel Francisco Pueyo, who was the governor; among the nobility, the conde de Albatera, the conde de Guara, Don José de Urries y Navarro, the conde de Atares, the conde de Bureta, the conde de San Clemente, the conde de Cobatillas, the marqués de Sierta, the marqués de Tosos, and some gentry, with the magistrate [*Zalmedina*] Don Juan Gerónimo de Blancas; among the deputies of the realm, the marqués de Alcázar and the deputy of Borja. In the city of Saragossa, there was virtually nobody reliable; the captain of the guard, Don Gerónimo Anton, was very disaffected. Of the bishops, those of Huesca and Albarracin were very hostile; of the cities, Teruel, Calatayud and Daroca were not to be trusted; of the towns, only Caspe and Fraga were entirely reliable; Jaca never defected, and Tarazona and Borja stayed loyal to us.[48]

According to Lafuente, who follows Macanaz closely in his account of the events of 1706 in Aragon, Calatayud, Daroca, Teruel, Cantavieja, Alcañiz and other cities defected: 'in short, the whole kingdom rose in rebellion, save for Tarazona and Borja, the fortress of Jaca and the forts of Canfranc and Ainsa'.[49]

Of the groups in the kingdom who were alleged to have taken part in the rebellion, two stand out distinctly: the peasants and the lower clergy. Almost no information is at present available on the role played by the peasantry, though there is every likelihood that, as in Valencia, their protest was aimed more at their seigneurs than at the Bourbon régime. On the clergy we have the archbishop's own word that 'the origin and cause of the sedition and rebellion in this kingdom have been friars and clergy, and particularly village priests [*curas de los pueblos*] who are the only directors of their flocks'. The reference to village priests clearly

[48] Modesto Lafuente, *Historia General de España*, vol. 18, p. 133 note 1. Lafuente drew this quotation and many others from the manuscript memoirs of Macanaz, now in the possession of Don Francisco Maldonado at his home near Salamanca. Excerpts from the first two volumes of this work can be consulted in MS 24 of the library of the University of Valencia. The volumes, which are of the greatest value for Spanish history, were recently rejected for publication by the Real Academia de la Historia.

[49] *Ibid.*, p. 153.

associates the peasants and clergy together as rebels. The archbishop went even further and claimed to have ascertained that 'the greater part of the *curas* of the kingdom have been rebels'.[50] To root them out he was considering means to institute an ecclesiastical visitation of every parish in Aragon. Above all, he went on in his letter to the king's secretary, there was 'the parish priest of the town of Magallón, which has been the most rebellious town in all the kingdom and has remained so throughout the revolt by reason of its site and large population'.[51] This unequivocal identification of the clergy with the rebels (and the archbishop would surely have been among the last to condemn his own priests without adequate proof), together with the significant role of the peasants, points unmistakably to the strong popular roots of the disturbances in Aragon. The well-known combination of priest and peasant, the basis of so many fundamental movements in Spanish history, appears to have been at the heart of the revolt in 1706.

This identification of the 'rebels' in Aragon is necessary to any discussion of the alleged rebellion against Philip v; for if the common people were the main participants in the uprising we are faced with the possibility, all too likely when the situation in Valencia is compared, that what happened in 1706 was not a revolt against Castile in defence of the *fueros,* but a spontaneous movement of social protest sparked off by the Allied invasion of the eastern provinces.[52] This remains for the moment no more than a hypothesis, but is nevertheless consonant with other evidence in both Aragon and Valencia.

It was undoubtedly the activity of the common people, instigated at times by a few members of the upper classes (notably, of course, by Cifuentes), that gave observers such as Macanaz an enduring impression of widespread rebellion. Yet Aragonese nobles such as the conde de Robres were justifiably indignant that the sins of the few rebels should be visited on the faithful

[50] Cf. also the vigorous claim by Amelot to Louis xiv, 14 Oct. 1705, AE Corr. Pol. (Esp.), 148 f.269, that 'les moynes, qui sont un corps considerable en Espagne et surtout a Madrid, sont les plus grands ennemis de Philippe cinq. Il s'est trouvé des gens de leur Robbe dans tous les complots qui ont esté descouverts'. Amelot clearly means the religious orders rather than the parish clergy.

[51] Archbishop to Grimaldo, 6 Sept. 1707, AHN, Estado leg.312. Magallón is situated near Borja, by the Navarrese frontier.

[52] Conde de Robres, *Historia de las guerras civiles,* pp. 371-2, admits that the common people were the principal supporters of the archduke.

many. He himself was one of the many loyal supporters of the régime. In 1706 he was residing in his home town of Huesca, where events gave him ample proof of the unpopularity of French troops, a factor to which he assigned great importance among the causes of the rebellion in Aragon. The advance of the Allies from the south-east threatened Huesca directly, and Robres was thereupon entrusted with the defence of the city. He found the task impossible, both because there were no troops available and because of the popular disturbances. Information filtering northwards from Saragossa indicated that the capital was also suffering from rioting among the populace, who were apparently being encouraged by the conde de Sástago and the marqués de Coscojuela. When news also came that Saragossa had proclaimed Charles III, pressure in Huesca for a similar proclamation became irresistible. Robres excused himself from his obligations by feigning illness, allowed someone else to carry out the unpleasant duty of declaring for the archduke, and went into exile to Castile, where he remained till the recovery of Aragon in 1707.[53]

There were hundreds like Robres, and the archbishop of Saragossa was only too well aware of it. When Bourbon arms conquered Aragon, this prelate acquiesced in all the measures taken by the victorious royalists. But on one point he refused to agree with the government. The decree revoking the *fueros* had stated in justification 'that all the inhabitants of this kingdom committed the crime of rebellion against the king'. This, the archbishop said, was false:[54]

it being certain that nearly all the nobles, gentry and chief persons of this city and of the others in Aragon, have been most loyal, many of them leaving this realm for Castile and Navarre, and others remaining so as not to forsake their wives, children and families, suffering many outrages and being deprived of their property, and those absent suffering total destruction of their goods and income. And some cities have remained most loyal, for example Tarazona, Jaca and Borja; some towns have been sacked and destroyed by the rebels, for example

---

53 *Ibid.*, pp. 301–4.

54 Cf. the opinion of the duc de Gramont in a 1707 memoir on Aragon: 'Il y a peu de villes dans ce Royaume, ou il n'y ayt actuellement un party formé pour le Roy, et surtout dans celles qui confinent la riviere de Cinga [Cinca], qui passe a Fraga, a comencer depuis Govesca [Huesca?] et Balbastro [Barbastro], jusques a la frontiere du royaume de Valence, ou les peuples mieux intentionés qu'ailléurs, attendent l'entrée des troupes du Roy': AE Corr. Pol. (Esp.), 177 f.361.

Maella, Villarroya [de la Sierra], Fraga, Mallén, and Borja; and others
have been maltreated and their property looted, for example the towns
of Tauste, Epila, La Almunia, Jabuenca, Tierga, Trasobares, Aranda
de Xarque, and all the places on the slopes of Mount Moncayo near
Tarazona. It is well known that other towns have been most loyal and
suffered much on that account, as for example the towns of Caspe,
Hijar, Sadaba, Sos, Alcorissa, Albalate del Arzobispo, Urrea de Hijar,
Alloza, Ariño, Mediana, Longares, Ojosnegros, Monreal del Campo,
Bujaraloz, and others in the kingdom.[55]

The archbishop's list, covering many of the principal towns in
Aragon, certainly did not exhaust the number of places whose
fidelity to Philip v was beyond criticism. The king himself had
to make concessions to loyal towns after he had revoked the
fueros of a realm of alleged rebels. The city of Borja, for instance,
in February 1708 had all its privileges confirmed to it, regardless
of the revocation; in addition, it was granted 'in every month a
day of free market in perpetuity, this day to be Thursday of the
first week in the month'. The town of Mora, not among those mentioned by the archbishop, was likewise in May 1708 granted a
confirmation of all its privileges, in gratitude for its loyalty.[56] How
many other towns, whether stubborn in resistance to the archduke or surrendering involuntarily to superior force, could be
numbered among the faithful?

More significant, however, than the counting of towns, is the
counting of heads. There can be no doubt that the ruling classes
in Aragon were almost solidly on the side of the Bourbon
monarchy. A glance at the noble estate of Aragon[57] shows that
barely half a dozen of the titled aristocracy of the realm deserted
to the enemy. Of the 250 or more individuals who suffered confiscation of their property by the Bourbon government after
1707,[58] less than a dozen were titled nobles. Nearly all the higher
aristocracy, most of the upper clergy, and virtually all the senior
administrative officials of Aragon remained loyal to Philip v. In
these circumstances, with probably half the towns of the kingdom
indubitably loyal, with several others overwhelmed only by
superior force, and with the ruling classes as a whole unswerving

[55] Archbishop to Grimaldo, 16 July 1707, AHN, Estado leg.320¹.
[56] Both decrees, dated 23 Feb. and 23 May, in AHN, Consejos leg.18355.
[57] See appendix 4.
[58] For confiscations, see below, p. 356.

in their allegiance, it is rash to talk of 'the revolt of Aragon' without extensive qualification.

The chief rebels are well known. Most of their names appeared in print in 1709 in the *Anales de Cataluña* of the Catalan propagandist Feliu de la Peña.[59] Feliu's list includes the names of fifty-eight clergy, among them Fray Juan Navarro, bishop of Albarracin; Don Martín Vinuales, bishop-elect of Huesca; Don Manuel Marco, abbot-elect of Monte Aragón; several canons and deans; and other ecclesiastics. His list of laymen names a hundred and sixty people, all but thirteen of them with the noble prefix *Don*. The titled rebels in his list are Don Juan de Lanuza, conde de Plasencia; Don Jorge Fernández de Heredía y Hijar, conde de Fuentes; Don Bartolomé Moncayo y Palafox, marqués de Coscojuela; Don Cristobal de Alagón y Córdoba, conde de Sástago, together with his two sons; and Don Antonio de Benavides, marqués de Castropiños. Other rebels not mentioned by Feliu include two of the principal grandees of Aragon, the duque de Hijar and the conde de Luna, who defected subsequently in 1710 and thereupon lost their estates. Among the prominent citizens in the same company were Don Antonio Luzan, governor of Aragon under the archduke, who deserted to Barcelona together with his four children; Don Manuel de Contamina and Don Francisco Edmir, both men of some property; and Don Miguel Antillón, baron of Antillón, another man of property.[60] These names are proportionately far fewer than those of the aristocratic defectors in Castile, yet their significance is in some respects far greater, for names and titles that shed lustre on the revolt against Philip II recur among the defectors of 1706. Over the name of Juan de Lanuza in particular there hangs a historic fatality that may have retained its magic for the rebels. Did the namesake of that young justiciar, who had lost his head on the block in defence of the *fueros* in 1591, feel that there was some continuity between the old cause and his own?

[59] Narciso Feliu de la Peña y Farell, *Anales de Cataluña* (3 vols), Barcelona, 1709, vol. 3, pp. 626-8: 'Relación de los Aragoneses que dexaron el Reyno de Aragón, para seguir al Rey nuestro Señor Carlos III'.

[60] These names are from the confiscation lists in AHN, Estado leg.2973, which also name the conde de las Almunias as a defector: I have been unable to locate any details of this title.

'All these malcontents one sees in the kingdoms of Valencia and of Catalonia,' a correspondent of the French minister of war wrote from Spain in 1705, 'cannot complain of the king, for he demands nothing of them; so that all their grievances arise only from the harshness of their lords who crush them with taxes and tributes'.[1] This observation provides the essential key to an explanation of events in the eastern provinces. There could hardly be rebellion against the king, since he had given little cause for rebellion. As in Aragon, the king of Castile was a distant personage with little direct authority. His representative in the realm, the viceroy, controlled both political and military government, but had necessarily to act within the framework of the *fueros* of Valencia. The crown's influence was felt in two ways only: through the nomination not only of the viceroy but also of a handful of senior officials in the government of Valencia, and through royal jurisdiction over a number of towns in the kingdom.

Writing in 1713, Macanaz estimated that the towns of Valencia 'come to a total of 560, of which only 33 belong to the king and the rest to seigneurs; and even in his jurisdictions the king receives little more than a few general taxes'.[2] Subsequently, in his memoirs, he stated: 'we see that the king has only 73 large and small towns, and that over 300 are seigneurial'.[3] Differences between these two groups of figures probably arise from a differing basis of assessment, but the second figure for royal jurisdictions

---

[1] Bourke to Chamillart, 28 Aug. 1705, Guerre, A¹ 1886 f.295.
[2] *Informe dado al Rey sobre el gobierno antiguo*, in *Regalías*, p. 15.
[3] 'Copia de los Manuscritos de Macanaz', BUV, MS 24, unfolioed. This manuscript consists of passages relevant to Valencia copied from the first two volumes of Macanaz's memoirs.

appears to be more correct. It seems[4] that the king's authority
extended over twelve towns in the district of Valencia, twelve
in Alcira, four in Alcoy, five in Alicante, three in Castellón, none
in Cofrentes, two in Denia, two in Montesa, twelve in Morella,
six in Orihuela, five in Peñiscola, nine in San Felipe (Játiva), and
four in Jijona; a total of seventy-six towns. Royal control of
these towns centred principally on taxation, though the income
from this source as well as from the general taxes in Valencia
appear to have brought little to the crown, since it was diverted
to expenses and to the payment of salaries, particularly those of
the members of the council of Aragon in Madrid. The small
number of towns under royal jurisdiction can lead to somewhat
misleading conclusions about the extent of royal power. The
fact that they included most of the largest towns in the realm
might even signify that the crown played a preponderant role in
Valencia. However, though jurisdiction over large cities may have
involved control over a great part of the population, it also
brought the crown into conflict with municipalities jealous of
their independence. The result was that, as Macanaz observed,
though Valencia and other cities levied taxes on trade, 'all this
taxation was consumed on salaries, entertainments and the repayment of *censos*, so that commerce used to cost as much here as
in Castile, and foodstuffs even more, and the king got nothing
out of all this'.[5]

Administration was for the most part independent of the king,
in Valencia as in Aragon and Catalonia. Justice was dispensed by
an audiencia, which contained three chambers, one for criminal
and two for civil cases. The number of judges sitting on it was
usually fifteen, presided over by a regent who was nominally
deputising for the viceroy. The capital city was governed by a
body known as the council of hundred, which consisted of 112
members of all social classes, the majority representation being
held by members of the guilds (the *gremios*). The executive committee of the council consisted of six councillors or *jurados*, of
whom the two chief members were known as *jurados en cap*. As
guardian of the constitution there existed the *Diputación de la
Generalidad*, consisting of six members (two clergy, two from the

---

[4] The source for this estimate is a typewritten list in the Indice de Cartas Pueblas
of the Archivo del Reino de Valencia in Valencia city, reproduced in appendix 5.

[5] *Regalías*, p. 7.

nobility, and two citizens), who formed a standing commission of the cortes and whose principal task was to see that the *fueros* were observed and the taxes regularly collected. The finances of the realm were controlled by a *baile general,* a *maestre racional,* a fiscal and three other officials, all of whom were technically nominated by the crown.

The soil of Valencia was dominated not by the king but by the great lords and the Church, who together enjoyed authority over most of the towns and over a substantial part of the population. According to Macanaz, the nobles of Valencia were the chief beneficiaries from the various taxes with which the people were burdened: 'the duque del Infantado gets 31,000 *libras* a year from two towns as small as Alberique and Alcocer, and the conde de Cocentaina gets more than 40,000 from one square league of territory'.[6] So far, unfortunately, the territorial structure of landownership in the crown of Aragon remains unstudied. We are left, therefore, to assume that the picture given by Macanaz is valid for the whole of Valencia. A glance at appendix 5 will help to confirm the impression of aristocratic predominance. From it we see not only the restricted authority of the crown, but also the fact that the nobility of Castile exercised considerable jurisdiction in Valencia. The duque de Medinaceli, for instance ('one of the lords who has most estates in this kingdom', to quote a contemporary Valencian writer[7]), seems to have been among the most powerful of the lords in the realm, a circumstance which explains his subsequent opposition in 1707 to the suppression of the *fueros.*

The demographic structure of Valencia likewise remains unknown. At one moment in history, the occasion of the Morisco expulsions in the early seventeenth century, a few reliable details have been made available. But no other contributions to the history of the Valencian population exist. No general censuses of the population of the kingdom in this period are trustworthy, since they were invariably drawn up for specific tax purposes only. Sections of the population not normally liable to taxation could therefore be excluded from the census figures. Examples of this procedure are available in the tax surveys drawn up under

---

[6] 'Copia de los Manuscritos de Macanaz', BUV, MS 24.

[7] 'Orti: Papeles varios', BUV, MS 17: 'Manifiesto de que no huvo Rebelion en Valencia en los sucesos del año 1705 y los siguientes', V, viii.

military supervision in 1709 and 1711. In the former year the returns deliberately excluded all settlements of under eight households, and on this basis a total of 59,427 *vecinos* for thirteen districts or *gobernaciones* in Valencia was reached.[8] In 1711 an even smaller total of 57,656 *vecinos* was achieved.[9] Both these estimates are too low. The most satisfactory surveys of population were in fact made in 1712–4, and it was an estimate for 1713–4 that Uztáriz used as part of his general survey of the population in Spain. The reason for considering these estimates as satisfactory is simply that the government went on using them as the basis for imposing taxes, which indicated that they were not far off the actual taxable population. The authorities were usually quick to revise figures that were overestimates (as the figures for Aragon show), and it was not to their interest to underestimate numbers. The total population for 1712–3 is given as 63,700 *vecinos* and that for 1713–4 as 63,770.[10] The population of Valencia city at the former date was put at 8,290 *vecinos* and at 8,800 for the latter date. Details available for 1712–3 are as follows:

Gobernación	vecinos
Peñiscola	4,103
Morella	5,737
Castellón	4,394
Valencia	18,323
Alcira	4,999
Cofrentes	1,158
Montesa	1,407
San Felipe	5,487
Denia	5,566
Alcoy	3,339
Elche	2,827
Orihuela	4,242
Alicante	2,118
Total	63,700

[8] List included with order of 26 Oct. 1709 by Caetano y Aragón, in AHN, Estado leg.375.

[9] 'Estado de la impossicion general por via de Quartel de Ymbierno', AHN, Estado leg.411².

[10] 1712–3 figures from 'Vecindario general de España', BNac, MS 2274 ff.340–9. Those for 1713–4 from letter of Rodrigo Cavallero to Grimaldo, 29 Oct. 1714, AGS, Guerra Moderna, suplemento, leg.252.

Uztáriz, as we shall see later, adopted a multiplier of five persons per household, to convert *vecinos* into actual population figures. This coefficient may for the moment be taken as an acceptable one. Applying it to the population figures for 1712, we get a total of 318,500 persons. Some historians may consider this figure too high. The eighteenth-century geographer Cavanilles, in a survey of what he regarded as the devastation caused by the War of Succession in Valencia, claimed that 'the damage suffered was so grave that in 1718 there were only 255,080 persons in the kingdom'.[11] A choice between these figures can only be an arbitrary one. It may, however, be possible to establish at least a minimal figure for the population. If we use an even lower coefficient of 4·5, as many historians prefer, and apply this to the deliberate underestimate of the *vecindario* in 1709, we get a figure of 267,421 persons. This suggests that Cavanilles' figure is too low and that a total approaching 300,000 is more probable.

The so-called revolt of Valencia during the war of the Spanish Succession is better documented than the corresponding revolt in Aragon, so that the broad outline of events can be established with some precision.[12] Yet the true circumstances of the rebellion have never been adequately explored. As with Aragon, historians have tended to accept the version given by official Bourbon historiography, while ignoring the case put forward repeatedly, in readily accessible works, by Valencian historians.

It is undeniable that many of the factors making for dissatisfaction in Aragon, also played a part in Valencia. The memory of the independence enjoyed by the realms of Aragon under Charles II did not predispose Valencians to welcome a régime with more absolutist pretensions. Nevertheless they greeted the new king gladly. On 16 February 1701 the deputies of Valencia sent an embassy to Madrid to greet Philip v. Subsequently, when war broke out between the Bourbons and the Allies, Valencians disposed to the House of Austria found the demands of conscience irresistible. 'On Monday, 5 October 1702,' noted a contemporary, 'there set sail fourteen men, partisans of the Empire and opponents of the war, among them Maestro Daniel who was bound for

---

[11] Antonio Josef Cavanilles, *Observaciones sobre la historia natural del reyno de Valencia*, Madrid, 1795–7, p.x.

[12] The only attempt made so far to study events in Valencia, is the inadequate compilation by Pedro Voltes Bou, *La Guerra de Sucesión en Valencia*, Valencia, 1964.

the island of Ibiza'.[13] Others who were not prepared to choose sides so early in the struggle also came out later in support of the archduke. As in Aragon, therefore, a considerable pro-imperial party existed from the very beginning, and accounted for many of the defections that took place.

Hatred of the French community was likewise a very important factor in disturbances in Valencia. Father José Miñana, whose *De bello rustico valentino,* written between 1707 and 1723, is an invaluable contemporary analysis, had no doubt that public hatred of Frenchmen contributed greatly to the rebellion. The motives for this antipathy are explained in his own words. 'Hatred was aggravated,' according to him, 'by traders and the numberless other hosts of French, who carried on contemptible and disgraceful profiteering in several provinces of Spain, with no other aim than to get hold of all the gold and silver and transport it to France.'[14] Dislike of the French and distrust of France is revealed in a report of 1701 from Valencia that 'many secular and regular clergy, in conversation, explain their leaning to the archduke and to the continuation of the House of Austria in these realms . . . by the fear that on the entry of the House of Bourbon they would suffer the harsh and rigorous rule of the Christian King, and by the fact that the French nation is looked on very badly by Valencians'. A subsequent letter expressed the fear of Valencians that the Frenchmen resident in Valencia would now lord it over them.[15] The harsh treatment subsequently meted out by the Allies to the French traders, who were all expelled from Valencia, many of them losing both property and life, is ample proof of their unpopularity.

The total indifference of the crown to Valencia may perhaps be seen as a valid cause for grievance. No attempt at all was made to hold a cortes in the kingdom,[16] so that Valencia alone of the constituent provinces of Aragon was given no opportunity to

---

[13] Quoted in Felipe Mateu y Llopis, *Aportación a la Historia Monetaria del Reino de Valencia en el siglo XVIII,* Valencia, 1955, p. 47.

[14] José Manuel Miñana, *De bello rustico valentino,* translated into Castilian in the *Revue Hispanique,* 55 (1922), pp. 447–617. The quotation is from p. 456 (I, i). The original work is in three books.

[15] Letters of 15 Mar. and 6 Dec. 1701, to the duque de Montalto, in AHN, Estado libro 214.

[16] Ursins to Torcy, 23 May 1702, AE Corr. Pol. (Esp.), 104 f.264: 'Le bruit qui a couru a Madrid que la Reine iroit ensuitte a Valence tenir les estats est sans aucun fondement. Nous n'avons aucun ordre pour cela'.

present its grievances or to see its sovereign in person. There is no way of telling how important the failure to hold a cortes in Valencia may have been: it is never cited as an explicit grievance, and needs to be read into the general complaint made by Valencians that the king had neglected them. It is fair to point out in defence of Philip v and his queen, on the other hand, that the holding of cortes in Barcelona and Aragon had no appreciable effect on the would-be rebels in those territories.

The actual rebellion had its roots not so much in these immediate grievances as in events which had shaken Valencia over a decade previously.[17] The settlement of Christian peasants on land once held by the Moriscos had been part of the effort made in the early seventeenth century by the crown and by the nobility to save the agrarian economy of Valencia. Inevitably this involved the subjection of the peasantry to the great lords, and the rejection of a system of free peasant landholding in favour of a seigneurial régime, where the lords controlled the land, its jurisdiction and its taxes. In the cortes of Valencia the lay and ecclesiastical nobility controlled two of the three estates, the *brazo militar* and the *brazo eclesiástico*. In influence, if not in numbers, they also controlled the *Diputación de la Generalidad*. The majority of the towns were in their hands, and the soil was almost entirely in their control. The repopulation of the kingdom after the expulsions of 1609 could not fail to accord with their interests. The new peasant settlers were given the usufruct of the soil only on the strictest and most onerous terms of servitude and labour obligations.[18]

The seventeenth century consequently saw the Valencian peasantry reduced to servitude and misery. Like the peasantry of Castile, they longed for an end to seigneurial control and looked to the crown for redress.[19] Finally, at the end of the seventeenth century, they burst into revolt. Disturbances centred round the Játiva region, in an area covering the north of the modern district

[17] For most of what follows, I rely on the brilliant but short work by Francisco de P. Momblanch y Gonzálbez, *La segunda Germanía del Reino de Valencia*, Alicante, 1957.

[18] Momblanch, pp. 22–6, gives details of labour obligations in the town of Muro.

[19] Cf. Noel Salomon, *La campagne de Nouvelle Castille à la fin du XVIe siècle*, Paris, 1964, pp. 203–5. Seigneurial oppression, Salomon confirms, inspired the Castilian peasant to make 'tant d'affirmations paysannes de liberté et de fidélité monarchiste'.

of Alicante and the south of the modern district of Valencia. On 9 July 1693 the duque de Gandía imprisoned four of his peasants who had refused to pay their dues as vassals. Almost immediately three hundred or more peasants refused to continue their work, massed together and demanded the release of the four men. A peasant from the town of Rafol de Almunia named Francisco García Menor assumed the leadership of what speedily became a mass uprising consisting of about one thousand peasants. Once the movement had gained a sense of purpose it set about planning a campaign and electing a leader. José Navarro, a surgeon from the town of Muro, was chosen as supreme chief with the title of *General del Eixercit dels Agermanats*. The adoption of the name *Agermanats* (in Castilian, *Germanías* or brotherhoods) was clearly calculated to revive the spirit of the nation-wide insurrections of the 1520s. The rebels marched over the lands of the duchy of Gandía, raising the peasantry as they went, and widened the revolt to take in also the territories of the marqués de Albaida and the conde de Cocentaina. Their purpose was to march northwards out of the noble-controlled *gobernación* of Játiva, and across the River Jùcar into the royal territories in the *gobernación* of Valencia. There they would wait for the king to redress their grievances. Far from the march degenerating into a frenzy of looting and murder, it retained complete order and no banditry or theft was allowed. The hopes for a royal intervention in their cause were soon shattered. On 15 July the peasant army was routed by government troops. It took three weeks for the revolt to die down. The insurrection, however, was never totally extinguished, and among the top leaders only Navarro was captured and executed. García escaped and was condemned in his absence.

The events of 1693 explain the whole course of events in Valencia during the War of Succession. A sullen peasantry, ripe for revolt, became the decisive factor in the war. As a contemporary put it, 'there still remained the hope and desire to gain exemption from taxes if the opportunity should again offer itself'.[20] What occurred in Valencia after 1705, then, was a social revolution deliberately unleashed by the Allies but also carefully exploited by them for political ends.

The prominent part played by the lower clergy in the

[20] Manuscript of Moseu Isidro Planes, 'Satisfacción que dí a un amigo Castellano', etc., in Momblanch, appendix no. 12, pp. 155-8.

disturbances of 1705 may well have owed much to a common class-sympathy originating in 1693 or even before that. No specific reason for clerical attitudes, other than devotion to the House of Austria, is given in any of the available sources. Miñana, a priest himself, confesses that 'the rights of the archduke of Austria first began to be discussed everywhere among the people with the acquiescence of the monks of certain orders and several village priests, and this pestilence was spread in such a way that it finally caught even some of the most prudent people'.[21] It is difficult to comprehend dynastic loyalty of so contagious a nature. It is, on the other hand, clearly noticeable that the disaffected clergy were drawn from the very regions that had been the scene of recent peasant disturbances, and there is ample evidence that priests and people fought side by side in the same cause, which was certainly social justice no less than devotion to an Austrian king.

As late as 1704 the kingdom of Valencia showed no outward sign of wavering in its loyalty to Philip v. On the contrary, in the spring of that year the realm raised at its own expense a *tercio* of six hundred infantry which was put at the disposal of the king. Philip rather unwisely sent it off to help in the defence of Cadiz;[22] unwisely, since the troops would have been better utilised in Valencia. The presence of the English fleet off the Valencian coast in July 1704 should have warned Madrid that the threat to the Levantine coast was no less than the threat to Cadiz. But no steps were taken in this year to defend the eastern coastline adequately. Gifts such as the 500 doblones given in 1704 by the city council of Valencia to the government were no doubt spent on defences elsewhere in the peninsula. Philip v was too wholly preoccupied with the defence of Andalucia and Cadiz, and the Gibraltar campaign, to devote much time to the crown of Aragon. There is no doubt that the government was fully aware of the defenceless state of Valencia. When in 1703 the council of war pointed out the 'defenceless state of the coast of Valencia for defence against an invasion', the council of state agreed that the matter should be passed to the council of Aragon for a decision on what measures to adopt.[23] All the councils knew what was wrong, but none cared to initiate any action.

[21] Miñana, p. 457 (I, i).
[22] 'Orti: papeles varios', I, vi: BUV, MS 17.
[23] *Oficio* of the council of state, 7 Nov. 1703. AHN, Estado leg.681.

K

When the Allied fleet appeared off the Valencian coast in the late summer of 1705, it met few military obstacles. Alicante on 8 August refused entry to the ships, which thereupon proceeded to the coastal town of Altea. Arriving here on the tenth, the Allies took the town without any trouble. They were helped by the town's parish priest, who enlisted the support of the peasantry in accepting the sovereignty of the archduke.²⁴ The main Allied fleet now sailed on to Barcelona, leaving eight warships and three small vessels off Valencia: these continued along the coastline and later helped to reduce the fortress of Denia. The rallying of the peasantry to the side of largely Protestant invaders in the cause of a dynastic struggle, would seem to be inexplicable. Yet the Allied plan was a brilliantly devised one, aimed specifically at winning the peasants over to the imperial cause.

While the fleet was in Altea it set ashore two men who were to play a leading part in the capture of Valencia. One of these was a man named Francisco García de Avila, described as being from Gandía. There seems to be little doubt that this was the same person as the peasant leader of 1693. He began immediately to circulate through the villages and towns on the coast, offering the peasantry freedom from their taxes and service obligations, and promising that the lands of the nobility would be divided up among them. The people responded eagerly to these offers. 'All the peasants living on the coast as far as Denia were encouraged by the false hope that they would soon be relieved of their tribute, and began to rebel'.²⁵ The attempt to stir up the peasantry against their lords was extremely successful. Armies of peasants were soon to be seen throughout Valencia, acting as invaluable auxiliaries to the regular imperialist troops. Nor did the archduke fail to lend substance to the promises made in his name. Several towns were, for their fidelity to his cause, elevated from the status of mere *población* to that of *villa real*. Muro, one of those which benefited in this way, was, in additional recognition of its services, freed entirely from all its seigneurial obligations to its lord, the conde de Cocentaina.²⁶ The grateful town promptly voted a grant of money to help its beneficent new ruler.

²⁴ Miñana, p. 459 (I, ii): 'no faltaron algunos turbulentos campesinos, entre los cuales estaba el Párroco de aquel pueblo, ardiente defensor del partido del Archiduque'.
²⁵ *Ibid.*, p. 461 (I, iii).
²⁶ Momblanch, pp. 84–5.

García's invaluable services to the Habsburg cause were exceeded only by those of Juan Bautista Basset y Ramos, who had been put ashore at Altea together with a handful of companions. A Valencian by birth, and a carpenter by trade, Basset had fled from his native land many years previously after activities which, according to Miñana, had included murder and other crimes. Abroad, he entered the service of the empire, and distinguished himself both in Milan and in Hungary. His military capacities and his origin made him the inevitable choice for leadership of the Allied campaign in Valencia.[27] He appears to have been loved and remembered among his people, and later historians of Valencia treated his reputation with kindness.

The first objective of the invaders was the strategic fortress and town of Denia. A force was sent from Altea by the land route, while the remaining Allied ships invested the town by sea. The land force seems to have consisted principally of a host of peasants led by García, while Basset himself received help from relatives of his among the peasantry. On seeing the impossible odds facing his tiny and under-armed garrison, the commander of the fortress, Pascual de Perellos, fled; and the helpless governor, Felipe Antonio Gavila, was obliged to capitulate on 17 August. 'In this way the fortress and city of Denia was occupied and garrisoned effortlessly, without any resistance from the inhabitants, and even with their full consent.'[28] Denia now became the centre of a propaganda campaign directed at the peasantry. 'To Denia came joyfully the peasants of the whole coastal area, in order to give their allegiance, and General Basset in the name of the archduke gave them patents freeing them from their landlords. This gilded pill was tasted by all the disaffected, and several came even from other parts of Valencia to enjoy the favour, offered by the proclamation, of freedom from taxes'.[29] The towns of Benidorm, Finestrat, Orcheta, Jalon and Relleu, all in the marine peninsula of modern Alicante, now declared for Charles III of Spain.

After this, the capture of the kingdom of Valencia was relatively easy. With only a handful of regular troops at his command, Basset could still conjure allies up out of the soil simply by

[27] Basset later won the enmity of Peterborough, when that noble lord had assumed command of the Allied military effort. He was imprisoned for a period in Tortosa, in 1707, but subsequently released.
[28] Miñana, p. 460 (I, iii).
[29] Manuscript of Isidro Planes, Momblanch, appendix no. 12, pp. 155–8.

declaring the liberation of the peasantry. The support of the rural masses was not by itself enough to guarantee success, but Basset could also rely on one factor which was to be of paramount importance both in Aragon and in Valencia, namely the utter defencelessness of the cities.

The fall of Denia, one of the four chief fortresses of Valencia (the others were Alicante, Peñiscola and Montesa), threw the capital city into confusion. Aware of its own lack of defences, the city on 21 August sent a letter to Philip v asking for the dispatch of four hundred cavalry, which Valencia would maintain at its own expense. The king replied on the 28th, saying that he intended to send 1,800 horse immediately. Meanwhile the rulers of Valencia appear to have taken no steps to form an effective fighting force of their own, and both the viceroy, Antonio Mendoza, marqués de Villagarcía, and the military governor, Juan Castelví, conde de Cervellón, appear to have relied exclusively on help from Madrid. Not until 14 December, when it was far too late, did one noble, the duque de Cansano, succeed in forming two companies of horse and foot.[30]

Meanwhile the threat to Barcelona, which fell to the archduke on 9 October, was beginning to absorb most of Philip v's attention. In these circumstances the defence of Valencia was relegated to second place, and the government ordered the few troops available in Valencia to proceed at once towards Catalonia. This order created consternation in the city council of Valencia. On 13 September they informed the king that 'the concern of all Your Majesty's most faithful subjects was universal, on hearing that Your Majesty had ordered troops to leave this realm and march towards the principality of Catalonia'.[31] Not only had Philip not yet sent the troops he had promised, he was now withdrawing the few available defences remaining to the Valencians. In his original order, Philip had catered for the stay in Valencia of only one regiment, that commanded by the Catalan officer Rafael Nebot.[32] After the protests by Valencia, he consented in a

[30] 'Orti: papeles varios', I, lv: BUV, MS 17.

[31] *Reparos críticos, fundados en hechos verdaderos, contra varios pasages que refiere el Marqués de San Felipe en sus Comentarios de la Guerra de España, que escribió un Valenciano en obsequio de la verdad y lealtad de su Patria*, in Antonio Valladares de Sotomayor, *Semanario Erudito*, Madrid, 1788, vol. 18, pp. 108–9. The authorship of this invaluable contemporary commentary is disputed.

[32] It is a mystery why Nebot was retained as an officer at all. His brother, Juan Nebot, of the town of Brafin near Tarragona, was a lieutenant of cavalry in Catalonia,

letter of 28 September to the retention of two squadrons of cavalry under the marshal Luis de Zúñiga.

Further royal concessions followed when it became obvious that Catalonia was lost and that some attempt should be made to save Valencia. Tortosa fell to the Allied forces in September, to be followed quickly by the fall of Vinaroz. The members of the *Diputación* wrote to Philip on 30 September[33] to point out that the frontier with Catalonia was completely exposed, that the enemy had unimpeded control of the sea and sea coast, and that Valencia was in desperate need of troops. The king replied on 14 October to say that another Valencian cavalry regiment, commanded by Francisco Velasco, marqués de Pozoblanco, could also remain in the realm. The difficulty now was to utilise these few troops in a way that would leave adequate provision for defence, and yet also allow them to repel the invasion from the north. To move towards the Allies might leave the south exposed to possible attack by the sea. The authorities were willing to take the risk, but equally the Valencians were unwilling to be left undefended. On 30 October Villagarcía published an order by the royal commander Tserclaës Tilly for Nebot's regiment, which was stationed near Denia, to march northwards and join that of Pozoblanco near Vinaroz. At the same time the realm was ordered to raise for itself two infantry regiments, each of five hundred men, one of which was to replace Nebot at Denia and the other to serve at Vinaroz. Resentment and anger at this new development, which would have left untrained recruits to guard the heartland of Valencia, became irrepressible. The Valencian authorities wrote to Philip to say that they were going to send a full-scale ambassador to remonstrate with the government. The result of these protests was that Colonel Nebot was allowed to stay at Denia.[34]

The disaffection of the peasantry had by now gained a general hold. Matters worsened critically when in the second week of December Nebot and his regiment rebelled openly against the government and took over the town of Oliva. After this they

---

and as early as 1704 was discovered plotting in the archduke's favour and had to flee the principality. For this see the letter from the viceroy of Catalonia, Francisco de Velasco, to the marqués de Ribas, 10 July 1704, AHN, Estado leg.466. The Nebots were on close terms, and proved valuable friends to the Allies.

[33] Letter of 30 Sept. 1705, AHN, Estado leg.265 f.5.

[34] Royal letter of 4 Nov. 1705, in *Reparos críticos*.

marched against, and easily captured, the town of Játiva. The fate of this impressive fortress was to be of great significance during the war and its aftermath.³⁵ At this time a large town of about two thousand houses and four thousand *vecinos,* with nine monasteries and two nunneries, Játiva with its hill-top fort dominated the region to the south of Valencia city. The town had been at the very centre of the peasant insurrection of 1693, and the parties that had arisen on that occasion were still very much in evidence. The division of factions seems to have been between those who in 1693 had supported the cause of the peasants and of the king, and those who supported the domination of the seigneurs. The former were known in Valencian as *baulets,* the latter as *botiflers.*³⁶ In the new circumstances of 1705 the term *baulets* referred to supporters of the House of Austria which had, through its agents García and Basset, shown itself so eager to support the liberation of the peasantry; and the term *botiflers* referred to adherents of the Bourbon dynasty, consisting for the most part of the ruling classes in Valencia. The persistence of this profound social division in Játiva made the town ill-equipped to present a unified resistance to Nebot's troops. Equally signicant, however, was the fact that the citadel of Játiva was under-manned and virtually weaponless, so that adequate defence was impossible. To add to all this there was treachery within. Many of the clergy spoke up openly for the rebels. Finally, the commander of the cavalry force in the town, a nobleman named Juan Tárrega,³⁷ used his influence to subvert the population and to induce the town to surrender to Nebot. Most of the people greeted the pro-Allied troops favourably, but many of the leading nobles and officials, including the governor, Francisco Rocafull, went into exile. Some murders of Bourbon supporters were committed, thanks to the activities of a one-time bandit named José Marco, who had become notorious under the nickname of

³⁵ Most of what follows is drawn from Carlos Sarthou Carreres, *Datos para la Historia de Játiva* (3 vols), Jativa, 1933-5, esp. vol. 1, pp. 339-45 and vol. 2, pp. 15-18.

³⁶ I have no knowledge of the origin of these names. 'Botiflers' is spelt in Castilian as 'Boutifleros'.

³⁷ There are contradictory accounts of Tárrega. Miñana says he was head of the cavalry. Sarthou and others say he was an exile who entered the town with Nebot. After the recapture of Játiva by royalists, Tárrega (created marqués de Almunia by the archduke) was imprisoned in the citadel of the town, and transferred in 1718 to the citadel in Pamplona.

'Penjadet' and who was now serving as an officer with Nebot.

Rebel successes continued without interruption after this. Nebot succeeded by a ruse in capturing the marshal Luis de Zúñiga, who was thereupon confined in Denia. Then on 12 December the town of Gandía was occupied by Basset. The duque de Gandía, Pascual Francisco Borja, went into exile to Madrid. The town of Alcira was next to fall, taken, says Miñana, by 'treachery'. It was then the turn of Valencia city.

The indecision about defence in the capital led Madrid to send the duque de Cansano out to Valencia, apparently to replace the viceroy Villagarcía. It was Cansano who took the first steps to raise a small force to defend the city. But this was clearly not enough. On Friday 11 December an urgent appeal for help was sent to Philip v.[38] Three days later, on Monday, it was learnt that all the roads to Madrid were cut off and in enemy hands, making it virtually impossible for messages to get through.[39] Nevertheless, two more letters were sent to Madrid. On Tuesday evening the leaders of the nobility met in the house of the duque de Cansano to discuss measures for organising the infantry and cavalry needed for defence. That very day the three estates of the cortes of Valencia sent an appeal to Philip expressing their complete lack of defence.[40] The night of the fifteenth inside Valencia was heavy with fear and apprehension. It was known that Basset's forces were within striking distance. Some time after midnight enemy troops could be seen approaching the walls. They were joined enthusiastically by peasant farmers and their wives from the plains round Valencia. Immediately, the city population became excited, and amid the uproar the gaol in the Serrano tower was seen to be on fire. The prisoners in it had seen their opportunity, fired their cells and made an escape into the already confused

[38] AHN, Estado leg.279 f.26. The nine signatories to the appeal claimed that 'corre gran perill de quedar infructuos nostron bon desig, si vostra Magestat retarda imbiarnos tropas'.

[39] This day by day account is drawn from the splendid manuscript diary of José Vicente Orti y Mayor, 'Diario de lo sucedido en la ciudad de Valencia desde el dia 3 del mes de Octubre del año de 1700 hasta el dia 1° del mes de Setiembre del año de 1715', BUV, MS 460. Only one volume, for the years 1705–9, is in the BUV. The two other volumes are certainly in private hands, but I have been unable to trace them. The author of the diary was nephew to the Joseph Orti mentioned elsewhere in my text.

[40] Letter of 15 Dec. 1705, in Juan Perales, *Décadas de la Historia de la . . . ciudad y Reino de Valencia*, Madrid, 1880, III, iv, p. 875.

night. Villagarcía tried to encourage the city guard and others to put up a semblance of resistance to the enemy, but to no purpose. Some of the city's leaders instead seized the viceroy, took from him the keys to the main gate, and let the enemy in. As Villagarcía explained subsequently in disgust, Valencia fell 'without the slightest hostility being offered the enemy, and without a single shot being fired from the walls'.[41] This was all the more surprising since, according to the same witness, the troops with Basset and Nebot numbered no more than two hundred cavalry from Nebot's regiment and a hundred other soldiers on horseback.[42] These could easily have been repulsed. The decisive factor, however, was that with these men there were also about four hundred peasants, men from the environs of Valencia, with whom the townspeople would obviously have been in sympathy. In these circumstances the Valencians received the enemy without resistance. 'That night the populace, to demonstrate their regard for Basset, who was their hope, wealth and salvation, lit fires in the streets and illuminated their houses with torches.'[43]

The supporters of Basset inside Valencia were, as Miñana makes clear, mainly the peasants and the poor. 'The streets and roads were full of armed peasants and ragged beggars, who ran through the city calling for the death of the nobles and friends of the king.'[44] Several prominent men in the city came out openly in favour of the archduke, but for the most part the upper classes and administrative officials remained faithful to Philip v and preferred to go into exile rather than serve the Austrian pretendant. Imperial support came almost exclusively from the lower levels of society, and Basset's success relied wholly on the sort of peasant aid that had enabled him to capture Valencia.

On 21 December a solemn *Te Deum* and procession to celebrate the new régime was held in the cathedral. 'The crowds and cheering cannot be described, for they were so great as to be scandalous, and hats were even thrown in the air during the procession . . . and the height of irreverence was reached when a Capuchin priest in the course of the procession embraced General Basset as he was

---

[41] Villagarcía to Grimaldo, 17 Dec. 1705, AHN, Estado leg.279 f.23.
[42] Juan de Estrada, *Población General de España*, vol. 3, p. 7, says that 'entró Basset por la Puerta de San Vicente con 500 Patriotas a pie, y 300 en Cavallos y Mulos'.
[43] Miñana, p. 466 (I, v). [44] *Ibid.*, pp. 468–9 (I, viii).

walking between the two *jurados en cap*, the priest kissing the layman's hand.'[45]

The secretary of the *Diputación* of the kingdom of Valencia, Joseph Orti, who was later to maintain against all comers that Valencia had never really defected from its loyalty to Philip v, put forward at the time an interesting case to support his contention.[46] The city had been obliged to surrender, he said, for three main reasons: firstly, there were no adequate defences; secondly, defencelessness and other factors had created fear and confusion among the population; thirdly, events of the night of the fifteenth, such as the gaol catching fire, had demoralised the defenders.[47] While conceding that there was some popular disaffection, Orti belittled its importance, and chose instead to lay the burden of defeat on the viceroy, whom he described as totally incompetent. Valencia, Orti said, was 'surrendered not to the enemy but because of the horror of confusion; the dismay of the defenceless; the invasion by troops; the dereliction of everybody; abandonment by their own leader; the dangers of the night; the fears of the malign; and the security of the loyal'. While not denying that a surrender had taken place, Orti denied that any corporate defection had occurred. 'Valencia surrendered to the archduke: that is so, it cannot be denied. It surrendered: did it therefore commit rebellion? The inference is false.'[48]

If we leave aside for a moment the very important question of the responsibility of the lower classes for the fall of Valencia and other cities, there appears to be every reason to accept the substance of Orti's contention. Like Saragossa, and indeed like most other towns in the crown of Aragon, Valencia was almost defenceless. As a nineteenth-century historian of Valencia points out, 'if the capital of our kingdom opened its gates to the archduke's army, it was because of the lack of resources and the dereliction in which the whole country found itself'.[49] The incompetence of the viceroy[50] appears to be beyond question. But

[45] Orti y Mayor, 'Diario', f.41.
[46] I am attributing to Orti the 'papeles varios' in BUV, MS 17. It also seems likely that Orti was the author of the *Reparos críticos* printed in *Semanario Erudito*.
[47] 'Orti: papeles varios', II, xix, xxix, lxxvii.
[48] *Ibid*. II, xvi-xvii.
[49] Vicente Boix, *Historia de la Ciudad y Reino de Valencia* (2 vols), Valencia, 1845-7, vol. 2, p. 59. See also vol. 2, p. 67.
[50] Amelot to Louis xiv, 8 Nov. 1705, A E Corr. Pol. (Esp.), 149 f.124, confides that he intends to replace Villagarcía because the viceroy is no soldier.

what of the reception accorded to Basset? Did this not involve treason? The fact remains incontestable that if there was treason it was not committed by the upper classes, since the nobility, gentry and administrators of Valencia continued to support Philip v solidly. When the city fell, nearly all the nobility, and all the ministers of the audiencia, with one solitary exception, remained faithful to the Bourbons. On New Year's Day 1706 the viceroy went into exile, to be followed the next day by the archbishop.[51] Scores of the most prominent people in the town followed their example: according to Miñana they came 'both from the nobility and from the people'. 'There remained,' according to Orti, 'an infinite number of the loyal from all classes, of whom many suffered prison, fines, banishment and other penalties.'[52]

The two most prominent noble defectors, those who actually surrendered the city to Basset, were Don Felipe Lino de Castelví, fourth conde de Carlet, and Don Vicente Boil, marqués de la Escala.[53] Few others declared themselves at this early stage. The officials of the audiencia had only one defector: Don Manuel Mercader,[54] created marqués de la Vega by the archduke in August 1707. Three other prominent ministers, Vicente Pascual, Eleuterio Torres and Francisco Faus, also remained in the city, 'either because of poor health,' says Miñana, 'or for other good reasons.' The only other defectors of note were José de Cardona, conde de Cardona, one of the captains of troop in the capital, who was later, in August 1707, to be rewarded by the archduke with a grandeeship; and Vicente Carroz, marqués de Mirasol. All the other leaders of Valencia suffered voluntary or involuntary exile, and many suffered prison.[55] Cansano was not, like Villagarcía,

51 Orti y Mayor, 'Diario', f.44. Orti y Mayor himself was imprisoned in the Serrano tower by the Habsburg party.

52 *Reparos críticos*, p. 128.

53 Boix, vol. 2, p. 72.

54 Feliu de la Peña, *Anales de Cataluña*, vol. 3, pp. 629–31, includes two persons named Manuel Mercader, one the archdeacon of the cathedral, the other the marqués de la Vega: these may be the same person.

55 Miñana, pp. 469–70 (I, viii-ix), lists many of the faithful by name. Exiles included 'el Arzobispo, y el Virrey, José Ferrer, conde de la Almenara. . . . José Castelví con sus parientes, Vicente Mousourin, José Salcedo, Felipe Ripoll, asesor del procurador regio, José Sánchez, Manuel Esteban del Lago, y algunos otros'. Others who proved their loyalty were 'José García Azor, arcediano de Alpuente, diocesis de Segorbe; Pedro José Borrull, eximio jurisconsulto; Pedro Domenech; Vicente y Andrés Monserrat, hermanos; Bruno Salcedo; Francisco Ducals; Francisco

given his freedom, but was sent prisoner to Barcelona. Needless to say, all Frenchmen were expelled from the city, and their property was no doubt confiscated. The tiny number of distinguished adherents to the archduke's cause was as noticeable to contemporaries as it was to subsequent historians of Valencia. Miñana was telling no less than the truth when he reported the unwillingness of the nobility to accept posts of honour under the imperialists who, 'finding hardly anyone in these circumstances to discharge public office in the name of the Austrians, for lack of better men entrusted the posts to obscure people wishing to obtain them'.[56] Support for the rebels was therefore minimal among the upper and middle classes, and it was only a section, perhaps as much as a majority, of the common people that came out in the archduke's favour.

On 2 February English and Catalan troops under the earl of Peterborough entered Valencia and released Basset for work elsewhere. Meanwhile royalist troops had begun to penetrate into Valencia. From Castile along the main road through Requena and Chiva came troops under the new viceroy of Valencia, the duque de Arcos, appointed to replace Villagarcía. With him were the generals Antonio del Valle and the duque de Popoli. At the same time royalist troops under Cristobal Moscoso, conde de las Torres, entered from Aragon and marched down through San Mateo and along the coast. Moscoso's progress was aided by the fact that most of the towns in the north of Valencia had remained faithful to Philip v. One of the exceptions was Villareal de los Infantes, a town which fell on 12 January with the loss of more peasant defenders than of besieging soldiers. The year 1706 was an uneasy one in the kingdom, with substantial numbers of foreign troops fighting for the first time on Valencian territory. Yet no major battles were fought, and most of the campaigns consisted of attempts to capture or to defend fortified cities.

Despuig; Pedro Mayor; Damián Cerdá; Vicente Falco; Blanes y Alfonso Borgoñó'. Among later refugees from the city was the poet Isidro Costa (p. 496: I, xxix). Several individuals were expelled by the Imperial authorities: these apparently included the marqués de Mirasol (p. 496: I, xxix); also Nicolás Castelví, conde de Castella; José Vives, conde de Faura; José Juan, marqués de Centelles and his son; and many others (p. 508: II, v). Other deportees listed in *ibid.*, II, v; II, xviii.

[56] Miñana, p. 496 (I, xxix).

The presence of both Moscoso and Arcos in Valencia made the former automatically subordinate to the latter. This was a position that Moscoso refused to accept. He resigned his command, went to Madrid, and was thereupon appointed viceroy in place of Arcos, who was recalled.[57] The key town and port of Alicante was at this time being besieged by Francisco García and his men. It was relieved temporarily by the timely intervention of the militant bishop of Murcia, Luis de Belluga, who marched to its help at the head of thirteen hundred troops, together with two hundred troops under the governor of Orihuela, the marqués de Rafal. In the very north of Valencia, the coastal fortress of Peñiscola was simultaneously being besieged on the orders of Peterborough by Antonio Mas, a nobleman of the region who had deserted to the archduke. Royalist troops were likewise occupied in sieges: Moscoso, for example, captured the town of Cullera, and was promptly rewarded by Philip v with the title of marqués de Cullera.

In general, the year was favourable to the Allied cause. The two chief blows received by the royalists were the fall of Requena and of Alicante. The capture of Requena by Peterborough on 1 July after a week's stiff resistance, assured the central region of the kingdom to the Allies and cut off the principal route from Castile. A month after this, on 8 August, Alicante fell to the Allies, though its citadel, defended by Irishmen under the able royalist commander Mahony, held out until 4 September.[58] These reverses seemed to point to the imperialists as the eventual victors. The result was a tide of new desertions to the Allied side. Among the Valencian notables to defect now were Juan Pardo, marqués de la Casta; Gaspar de Calatayud, conde de Sirat; José Ceverio y Cardona, conde de Villafranqueza; and Antonio Tomás Cavanilles, conde de Casal.[59]

The relative ease with which Peterborough and Basset took over Valencia contrasts sharply with the great effort subsequently made by Philip v to recover the realm. To Bourbon apologists such as Macanaz, this proved the rebelliousness of the Valencians; but the facts can be interpreted another way. The example of Orihuela is instructive. Jaime Rosel, marqués de Rafal, was

[57] Ibid. p. 485 (I, xx); Mateu y Llopis, Aportación a la Historia Monetaria, p. 55.
[58] Miñana, pp. 518–20 (II, xv) says the siege lasted from 1 Aug. to 10 Sept.
[59] Ibid., p. 515 (II, xiii).

governor of Orihuela at the outbreak of war, and was undoubtedly faithful to the Bourbon cause. At the beginning of the new reign his city sent a loyal address to Philip v:

assuring Your Majesty that you will find in us the greatest example of loyalty, not only to the extinction of our fortune but even to the shedding of our blood and the loss of our lives in the noble defence of Your Majesty's royal crown.[60]

In practice, the city showed its loyalty by sending troops to help in the defence of Alicante. This meant, however, that few troops were left behind to defend the city in an emergency. The city thereupon wrote to Philip on 17 and 18 December with a request for reinforcements. On the 20th came a letter from Basset, demanding the surrender of the city to Charles iii. This was sent at once to Madrid with a further plea for help. No replies were received from Philip except a brief note dated 26 December, confirming Rafal as governor of the city. Throughout that very critical December, Orihuela managed to muddle through without adequate defence. Finally, on 7 January, some help was offered by Luis Belluga, in a letter to his episcopal colleague of Orihuela, José de la Torre. This is no indication that this offer was ever taken up. By March royal reinforcements had still not arrived. It was in this situation that, towards the end of March, the new military governor of Alicante, Marshal Daniel Mahony, ordered Rafal to transfer his city's troops to Villena to help in the defence of that town.[61] Anger at this order, which would have left the city undefended, was widespread in Orihuela. Many of the regular clergy, sympathetic to the cause of Basset and of the peasantry, took the opportunity to inflame the people against the royalists. Mahony unwisely now demanded a subsidy of 500 doblones from the city. When Rafal informed Mahony of the city's refusal to pay, the latter complained to Madrid, whereupon the royal secretary, Grimaldo, wrote a strongly worded rebuke to Rafal. This was too much for the governor, who promptly went out to meet Nebot in the recently captured town of Elche, and offered the submission of himself and his city. Charles iii was accordingly proclaimed publicly, to great popular

---

[60] Alfonso Pardo and Manuel de Villena, marqués de Rafal, *El Marqués de Rafal y el levantamiento de Orihuela en la Guerra de Sucesión, 1706*, Madrid, 1910, p. 9.

[61] *Ibid.*, pp. 34–5, letter from Mahony to Rafal, 26 Mar. 1706.

enthusiasm, while the bishop and other loyalists fled the city.[62]

There seems to be little doubt that the defection of Orihuela owed much to its sense of military insecurity. In all the Valencian cities the lack of adequate defence, whether against a riotous populace within or a menacing foe without, was the determining factor in the 'rebellion'. Valencia was only the largest of the casualties. Vinaroz, which in October 1705 had declared itself 'most faithful and loyal to its king, Philip the Fifth', was obliged to appeal urgently to Villagarcía for help in the form of powder, cannonballs and muskets.[63] Peñiscola, which proved itself faithful to the Bourbon cause, was garrisoned, if we may believe someone who was present, by no more than seventy soldiers.[64] Worst of all was the key fortress of Alicante. The officer in charge of the citadel reported in November 1705 that it was held by only a hundred soldiers, of whom only eight were regular paid militia, leaving the possibility that the other ninety-two irregulars might refuse to serve in an emergency; and this was in a fort capable of holding a garrison of fifteen hundred men. For an adequate defence the fort also needed five hundred flintlocks with bayonets, yet the only firearms on the spot were twenty-one muskets.[65] When the actual siege of Alicante was in progress, according to Miñana, there was a force of only 325 men defending the town, under the command of Mahony. The defenders finally 'surrendered because the enemy's fire was so intense (it is said that they fired 120,000 cannonballs and 6,000 grenades against the city and the citadel) that there was no place left to hide'.[66]

It should not be imagined that the Valencians would have gladly exchanged this defencelessness for occupation by the king's soldiers. To be loyal to the crown was one thing, to have Castilian troops in their homes quite another. There is ample evidence that the royal cavalry at least was universally hated. As we have seen already in the case of Lérida, popular fury was directed first of all at foreign troops, whether Catalan in Aragon or Castilian in

---

[62] Miñana, p. 518 (II, xv). Nebot entered Orihuela on 25 June 1706. The bishop and 'otros muchos honrados de la plebe' left the city in disgust.

[63] Town of Vinaroz to Villagarcía, 5 Oct. 1705, AHN, Estado leg.279 f.15.

[64] 'No teniendo en ella mas que 70 milicianos y sus ofiziales', D. Sancho de Echebarria to Grimaldo, writing from Benicarló, 15 Oct. 1705, ibid., f.19. Another correspondent, D Jaime Antonio Borras, wrote from Peñiscola to Villagarcía: 'No tenemos guarnicion con que dominar el pueblo', 5 Oct. 1705, ibid., f.3.

[65] Villagarcía to Grimaldo, 24 Nov. 1705, ibid., f.46.

[66] Miñana, pp. 520–1 (II, xv).

Valencia. Vinaroz, for example, refused to allow a troop of royal cavalry to enter the town on the grounds that 'they knew they were going to sack the place and cut their throats, and that they would not let them in even if it meant losing their lives'. The reason for this attitude, explained a correspondent to the viceroy, was 'the horror aroused by the royal guards through the disorders they commit when quartered'.[67] Similarly a troop of horse under Antonio de Amezaga had difficulty in entering and securing the loyal town of San Mateo, because the townspeople were afraid of the cavalry.[68] There would appear to be an obvious contradiction here between the constantly reiterated appeal for help, and the hostility to help when it came in the form of cavalry. Yet the Valencians had reason to fear their liberators. We have the word of an indisputably loyal Valencian that, when the troops of Moscoso entered the kingdom:

they began to sack and plunder whatever they could without discrimination, whereupon that part of the realm was finally aroused and arms were taken up not only by those sympathetic to the archduke but also by many loyal people wishing to defend their homes and property.[69]

The irresponsible behaviour of royalist troops in Valencia stands in marked contrast to the exemplary conduct of the Allies. Aided as they were by the mass of the peasantry, the Allies could ill afford to antagonise the local population. There was undoubted persecution of those loyal to Philip v, but even here the Allies made it their task to win over supporters so as not to appear as conquerors but as friends. The conduct of the archduke in Valencia could not be faulted in this respect. Charles entered Valencia city on 30 September 1706 and stayed there till 7 March 1707. In the months before his arrival in the capital, Valencia had suffered growing civil dissension. The imperial party had taken over control of the city from supporters of Philip v, to whom they gave the now common name of *botiflers*. The mood of disaster that had fallen over Valencia was heightened by an annular eclipse of the sun which occurred at 9 a.m. on Wednesday 12 May, and caused consternation in the city. On the following Sunday, at a *Te Deum* being held in the cathedral, cries of 'Death

[67] D Jaime Antonio Borras to Villagarcía, from Peñiscola, 4 Oct. 1705, AHN Estado leg.279 f.3.
[68] Amezaga to Villagarcía, 6 Oct. 1705, *ibid.*, f.15.
[69] *Reparos críticos*, p. 70.

to the *botiflers*!' disrupted the liturgy and scandalised the assembled congregation. It was clear that for many of the common people the revolution had not gone far enough. That evening an official of the Inquisition was conducting the service in the cathedral. A soldier stood up to interrupt his sermon, and cried out before a shocked assembly, '*Botiflers! botiflers!* All the Jesuits are *botiflers*!'[70] The new rulers of Valencia had thus to contend with a radical movement which had adopted tones of anti-clericalism, directed on this occasion against the Jesuits, who were known to be sympathetic to the Bourbon dynasty.

When Charles entered the city he made it his task to create as favourable an impression as possible. That he succeeded is vouched for by every contemporary account available:

> The archduke stayed in Valencia five months, during which time there was no feast-day when he did not personally assist at divine office in the cathedral. When he attended these functions he always went on horseback, so as to be better seen, and during the office he stayed motionless on his knees. His door was open to all who wished to see him at his meals. He held public audience every week, thereby remedying many complaints. And in this way he not only secured the goodwill of sympathisers but even won that of many who had not sympathised before.[71]

His public piety and regular attendance at church were also singled out for attention in the diary kept by Orti y Mayor. Miñana notes that during his stay the archduke occupied himself with nothing but hunting wild-fowl in the lakes and woods near the city;[72] but this in itself is no criticism of Charles, and it is significant that Miñana offers no other criticism of his public conduct.

The behaviour of Charles' followers, Protestant for the most part, may well have given rise to grievances. To be inundated with foreign heretics could not have pleased a city where the Inquisition had always been most active. But Charles firmly repressed any public exercise of the Protestant religion, and the inquisitors seem to have had no complaint. No native Spaniards took the opportunity to embrace heresy. 'After Valencia had been restored to its legitimate sovereign, the Holy Office of the Inquisition celebrated several *autos de fe*, but in none of them did

---

[70] 'Ha Boutifleros, ha Boutifleros; todos los Padres de la Compañía son Boutifleros': Orti y Mayor, 'Diario', ff.111–3.

[71] *Reparos críticos*, pp. 139–40.   [72] Miñana, p. 531 (II, xxvi).

there appear any Valencian, Catalan or Aragonese accused of Lutheranism or Calvinism.'[73] Charles had ordered that the Church and Inquisition be protected inviolate in all their rights, and his instructions to his viceroy of Valencia, the conde de la Corzana, emphasised 'how important it is for God's service and our own that the affairs of the Holy Office of the Inquisition, and its ministers, be cared for as our Catholic zeal has always desired. . . . It is our will that ecclesiastical immunity be preserved.'[74]

During his stay Charles superintended the formation of a new government for the city and for the kingdom. A new municipal council was elected and sworn in;[75] and Charles summoned the three estates of the realm, a step never taken by his Bourbon rival. On 8 December 1706 he was present at the swearing-in of the newly elected members of the cortes.[76] In return he was granted financial help. On 8 February the city added its own contribution with a grant of 50,000 libras. Valencia appears, like Barcelona, to have enjoyed a temporary boom during the Allied occupation. The reason for this seems to have lain exclusively in the import of bullion by the foreign troops (on 12 November the archduke had decreed that Portuguese coin could circulate in Valencia).

That winter [writes Orti] the officials in Valencia laboured a great deal on the needs of the army, and everyone was fully paid, so that the city had never been seen so rich and wealthy. Valencia was flooded by the English with pieces of eight and by the Portuguese with gold and silver coin (which the king [i.e. Philip] later ordered to be collected and devalued) in very substantial quantities, not to mention the good coin that the silversmiths struck.

The ready availability of bullion made it possible for the archduke to issue a number of silver coins during his stay.[77]

It may be that the benefits of the archduke's rule – expulsion of

[73] Reparos críticos, p. 84.

[74] Antonio Rodríguez Villa, Don Diego Hurtado de Mendoza y Sandoval, Conde de la Corzana (1650–1720), doc. XII, pp. 211–8. The good treatment of the Inquisition, may explain the unwillingness in 1709 of the chief inquisitor of Valencia, Diego Múñoz de Baquerizo (later, in 1714, bishop of Segorbe), to prosecute clergy who had been disloyal. He was replaced as judge of a tribunal set up expressly for this purpose. Details in Reparos críticos, p. 175.

[75] Some details in Voltes Bou, La Guerra de Sucesión.

[76] Orti y Mayor, 'Diario', has valuable comments on the proceedings in Valencia at this time.

[77] Mateu y Llopis, p. 67.

French traders, reduction in taxation and abolition of feudal dues, granting of honours to select individuals – helped to win the population over to the side of the Allies and so made the reconquest of Valencia by Philip doubly difficult. There was, however, one elementary feature of the Allied occupation that explains quite simply the difficulty experienced by royal troops. Wherever Bourbon commanders met with severe resistance, it was because the Allies had defenced and garrisoned the town in a way that the previous rulers of Valencia had not done. Denia, the first fortress to fall into Allied hands, and one of the last to be recovered, was at the time of its capture by Spanish troops on 17 November 1708 said to be garrisoned by almost a thousand soldiers, including two Portuguese battalions, one hundred and fifty English soldiers and one cavalry company. The citadel was found to contain fifty pieces of cannon and two thousand barrels of gunpowder.[78] The long siege of Alicante, the last town in Valencia to fall to the royalists, was similarly due to the citadel being held by a strong garrison. Other towns were equally strengthened in resistance by support from foreign troops: among them was Elche, which Berwick ordered to be sacked after its capture.[79] The most outstanding example of defiance came from Játiva.

In a survey written at the end of the war, Melchor de Macanaz claimed that 'there was no town that was not taken by force of arms. The people were so obstinate that Játiva, after a long siege, had to be reduced to ashes. Orihuela, Elche, Alicante and Alcoy cost sieges and much blood. Denia was twice besieged. Tortosa underwent a long blockade and then a siege'.[80] Many towns were, on the contrary, taken without any force of arms; but on Játiva Macanaz appears to have the facts behind him. The fate of this town became in time a symbol of the rebellion of Valencia. Yet it is certain that the chief citizens of Játiva remained loyal to Philip v, and suffered terrorisation or prison as a result. Several were even executed by the occupying authorities.[81] Far from being

[78] *Diario y Relación puntual de la reducción de Denia*, in *Miscelenea curiosa, asuntos de España*, II no. 12, Astorga Collection G. 25e. 2, NLS. Parnell, *The War of the Succession*, p. 259, puts the number of English troops at 427.

[79] Miñana, p. 527 (II, xx). [80] *Regalías*, p. 8.

[81] A lengthy list of victims, both imprisoned and executed, is given by Francisco Xavier Borrull y Vilanova, *Fidelidad de la ciudad y reino de Valencia en tiempo de las guerras civiles que empezaron en el año de 1705*, Valencia 1810, pp. 97–8.

sure of the support of the people of the town, Basset 'ordered the imprisonment of many men of all classes, among them nearly all the nobility who had not fled, and more than 120 priests, most of them friars, for the crime of supporting the king'.[82] Of greater consequence is the fact that he also arranged for Játiva to be properly fortified and garrisoned, since the town's defences were not good. The troops sent in to make up the garrison were English, estimated at seven hundred or so in number, under the command of Lieutenant-Colonel Campbell. Játiva was now adequately prepared to defend itself.

The entry of Charles into Valencia in September 1706 had been the concluding episode of his retreat from Madrid. His army had been pursued up to the frontiers of Valencia by the duke of Berwick, who began a piecemeal attack on the Allied strongholds. On 23 October the town of Elche, defended by four hundred and fifty English soldiers and a large peasant force, but possessing no artillery, was forced to capitulate to French troops after a two-day siege. On the 11th of this month Orhiuela also surrendered, to Spanish troops led by Luis de Belluga, the bishop of Murcia. Cartagena, the home port of Spain's Mediterranean fleet, which had been influenced by the conde de Santa Cruz to adhere to the Allies,[83] was the next large town to be invested by Berwick. Besieged from 11 to 17 November, it eventually gave in to superior artillery fire. Berwick now occupied a line covering the south of Valencia and stretching to the north along the border with Murcia and Castile. The Allies were still on the defensive, but their generals Galway and Das Minas decided to strike at Berwick before the arrival of a French relief force under the duc d'Orléans. Pushing Berwick's main force northward, the Allied generals occupied the key towns of Yecla and Villena in April 1707. On 24 April the Allied army advanced from Villena and camped the night at Caudete. The next morning they pushed forwards to the Castilian town of Almansa. It was there that Berwick met them and crushed them.

Despite the loss of this major battle, the Allies still held all the large towns of Valencia, which they had taken care to fortify. Much blood and effort was to be spent in recovering them for Philip v. Orléans, who arrived at the front the day after the victory

[82] Miñana, p. 511 (II, vii).
[83] Ibid., p. 517 (II, xiv).

automatically superseded Berwick as head of the Bourbon forces. The two commanders moved forward to attack Requena and Valencia, while Lieutenant-General D'Asfeld, a highly efficient soldier of undoubted ability and noted cruelty, who ended his career as a marshal of France, was sent off to attack Játiva and Denia.

Requena was securely garrisoned and defended, yet the town opened its gates to Orléans without a fight, on 2 May. Chiva fell in the same way a few days afterwards. On the sixth, Orléans, then at Cheste, sent a demand for surrender to Valencia. The capital had been evacuated by the conde de la Corzana, who had withdrawn his defence forces further north to Murviedro. Without adequate protection, the city submitted peacefully on 8 May to Orléans. The day after this Orléans left to join the campaign in Navarre, and Berwick resumed full command in Valencia.

The peaceful surrender of Valencia contrasts sharply with the struggle put up by Játiva. D'Asfeld appeared before the town on 5 May with about three thousand five hundred men. The garrison, as we have seen, contained about seven hundred English soldiers as well as Valencian and Catalan troops.[84] When the town refused to surrender, D'Asfeld was obliged to wait for the arrival of artillery and reinforcements sent by Berwick. After a three-week siege the royalists succeeded in storming the town on 24 May. Their losses in this whole operation are estimated by Miñana at five hundred dead and many wounded, a very high casualty rate. The number of rebels killed in the fighting is put by the same author at about two hundred and seventy. The citadel, manned by the English, held out some while after the fall of the town. Finally Campbell capitulated and was allowed to march out with his troops.[85]

The sack of Játiva by D'Asfeld's troops after its capture on 24 May reflected the anger of the French general at the town's stubborn resistance. Berwick, equally incensed, gave the order for the town to be razed to the ground as a warning to other rebels. It was apparently D'Asfeld's troops who carried out the actual destruction of Játiva. The population was methodically evacuated, house by house. There were immediate protests from

---

[84] Miñana, p. 559 (III, v) refers to the Catalans under the name of *ladrones*, bandits. My account of Játiva differs somewhat from that given by Parnell.

[85] Spanish sources date the surrender of the citadel to about 26 May. Parnell says it held out until 12 June.

Church authorities at the violation of ecclesiastical immunity and the seizure of Church buildings and monasteries. A protest sent to the duque de Medinaceli and other interested notables in Madrid produced a reply that the royal decision to destroy Játiva was unalterable.[86] There is some doubt as to the date when the town was put to the torch. It seems most likely that the firing took place on 12 June. According to one account, perhaps the most reliable, the town blazed for eight days; according to another it smouldered up to the end of February 1708.[87] The entire town was not, of course, burned. Several public buildings, including churches, monasteries, and the hospital, and several houses belonging to faithful followers of Philip v, were spared.[88] Whichever way this incident is looked at, it was one of the most regrettable events of the war. D'Asfeld was long to be remembered by historians of Valencia as a man of blood, and the destruction of the town was to remain an emotional barrier between Valencians and the French dynasty of Castile.

The ruthlessness of the foreign[89] generals in Valencia was, it seems, provoked by the stubborn resistance of towns. The little town of Cuarte, for example, was destroyed for having resisted the troops of the new governor of Valencia, the Belgian Antonio del Valle.[90] Yet it would be untrue to attribute the resistance of Játiva to a spirit of rebellion alone. There is no doubt that the presence of an English garrison made all the difference. As the *Gaceta de Madrid* of 24 May 1707 reported at the time: 'Alcira and Játiva are still defending themselves since they have English garrisons. . . . The councillors of these two towns have come to give their obedience, from which it is clear that it is the foreigners alone who are putting up a resistance, with very few of the peasantry.'[91] Similarly, the resistance of other towns owed far

[86] *Reparos críticos*, p. 76.

[87] Lafuente, basing himself on Macanaz, says that Játiva burned from 12 to 20 June; Perales says it burned from 19 June to 1 Mar. 1708. See the discussion, with a description of the sack of Játiva, in Perales, *Décadas*, III, iv, pp. 858–63. Sarthou Carreres, vol. I, pp. 343–5 also goes into the question. Miñana dates the burning from 17 June. Berwick's order for the burning was given on 18 May: see Berwick to Amelot, 21 May 1707, AE Corr. Pol. (Esp.), 176 f.103.

[88] Sarthou Carreres, vol. I, pp. 343–5; Miñana, p. 565 (III, ix), says that only about eighty buildings were left standing.

[89] On the Bourbon side Berwick was English, del Valle was Belgian, Mahony was Irish, Popoli was Italian, D'Asfeld was French: this names but a few.

[90] Perales, *Décadas*, III, iv, p. 846.

[91] Quoted in Borrull y Vilanova, p. 100.

more to the physical presence of foreign defenders than to their stubbornness in rebellion.

For the rest of 1707 the military front moved to Aragon, and Bourbon officials in Valencia attempted to consolidate what they had gained. A few further captures were registered, such as the town of Alcoy, which surrendered on 9 January 1708. The chief obstacles that remained were the forts of Denia and Alicante, and it was against these that D'Asfeld moved in the autumn of 1708. The second siege of Denia, which we have mentioned above, occupied the first two weeks of November. After this the only major town remaining in rebel hands was Alicante, defended by eight hundred foreign troops, mostly English, and Spanish troops numbering over a thousand. The attack on Alicante began on 1 December. Within a few days the English governor, Major-General Richards, realised that the town could not be defended. He surrendered it on the 7th, on condition that the Spanish garrison be allowed out free to march to Catalonia, and that the inhabitants of the town be not treated as rebels. Richards then withdrew with his own forces into the citadel, which he proceeded to defend against D'Asfeld for the next few months. Unable to reduce the citadel with artillery, D'Asfeld decided to mine it. The digging of a shaft under the citadel occupied about three months, after which the French filled a chamber at the end of the shaft with a huge amount of gunpowder, reckoned as 117,600 pounds. D'Asfeld then invited Richards to surrender his post. Three invitations were issued on as many days, but Richards doubted the effectiveness of the threat. On 3 March the mine was finally exploded: it split the hill on one side of the castle and swallowed up Richards together with over fifty officers and soldiers, but did not harm the castle itself. The rest of the garrison held out till the arrival of an English fleet in the port on 15 April. When the fleet found it impossible to help the defenders, terms of surrender were agreed upon, and on 19 April the citadel of Alicante was handed over to the royalists. Valencia had returned to the allegiance of Philip v.

The royalists took care to garrison the towns of Valencia. With troops quartered on the country, with the population forcibly disarmed, and with the ruling classes securely back in power, the kingdom returned to tranquillity. In 1710, after the Allied success at Saragossa, a fleet landed a small force of about three hundred men off the Valencian coast, but del Valle expelled them successfully.[92] 'No one stirred, not the slightest note of sedition sounded through the populous city' of Valencia on this occasion.[93] The only disturbances were those caused by peasant-bandits, an inevitable consequence of war.

Even before the whole of Valencia had been recaptured, the decision was made to revoke the *fueros* of the crown of Aragon. At first there was some disunity of purpose among the Bourbon leaders on this question. On the day that the capital surrendered Orléans on his own initiative as commander-in-chief issued a decree pardoning the Valencians for their act of rebellion.[94] This hasty measure was bitterly resented by the government in Madrid, and, as we have already seen, gave rise to suspicions that Orléans was attempting to win favour in the crown of Aragon for his claims to the Spanish throne. Berwick soon brought a firmer hand into play by ordering, on 12 May 1707, the general disarmament of the population of Valencia, who were required to surrender all their firearms.[95] Just over a fortnight later, on 5 June, Philip v issued a decree which took great pains to qualify the one issued by Orléans, without actually contradicting it. By this new measure it was confirmed that the pardon applied to all Valencians, 'excepting only those who still remain with the enemy, those who remain with arms in their hands, and those who by their rebellion will not have returned in good time to my obedience'.[96]

Even with these exceptions, the pardon was no more than a sham. At no time did the government ever rule out the necessity for severe and radical measures. The *despacho* had for some time been considering what form this should take, and on 4 May they issued a report on the measures to be taken in Valencia.[97] Meanwhile Berwick sent Amelot his own report on the situation:

As to the *fueros* and privileges, I have always been of the opinion that they should be suspended but that nothing be said of their extinction or

[92] Juan de Estrada, *Población General*, vol. 3. p. 15.
[93] Perales, *Décadas*, III, iv., p. 885.
[94] Text of decree in AE Corr. Pol. (Esp.), 172 f.299.
[95] Text of decree in *ibid.*, 172 f.312.
[96] Text of decree in *ibid.*, 173 f.14.
[97] *Consulta* of 4 May 1707, *ibid.*, 172 f.286. The ministers who drew up the report were Amelot, the conde de Frigiliana, the duque de Veraguas, and the duque de San Juan.

abolition. You will have seen that the officials of Valencia have informed His Catholic Majesty that the city and kingdom have decided to make a gift of 30,000 doblones. . . . I have published an order for French and Spanish coinage to have currency here as in Castile, and am arranging for the walls of all the principal towns to be demolished. . . . I have published a very severe order for arms to be handed in. . . . Never has obstinacy like that of Játiva been seen: I have ordered Asfeld to destroy it entirely, to serve as an example.[98]

While Berwick's firmness may have represented a soldier's impatience with the rebels in Valencia, it is not entirely just to attribute a deliberate policy of retribution to the Castilian government. Nor is it fair to blame the revocation of the *fueros* on the French, despite the leading role played by Amelot and others in implementing the eventual decision. Spanish no less than French political theorists had long regarded the *fueros* as a serious obstacle to good and centralised government in the peninsula.

The position of the French was never in doubt. Louis xiv had never been able to understand why the powerful rulers of Spain had tolerated provincialism. Writing to Amelot on the eve of the revocation, he declared that:

I have always been convinced that the best procedure for the king of Spain, after reducing the realms of Aragon and Valencia to his obedience, was to suppress the privileges they enjoyed until their revolt. Maintenance of these privileges has been a perpetual obstacle to royal authority, and a pretext by which these peoples have always been exempt from contributing to the expenses of the state.[99]

Amelot, too, had on his own account been convinced that the division of Spain into autonomous provinces was prejudicial to the state. The evidence of his eyes, even more than any theoretical reasoning, would have led him to this opinion. 'As for the *fueros*,' he wrote early in June 1707 to Orléans, 'it would be dangerous to give the slightest hope of their preservation. The *fueros* are of use only to criminals.'[100] *Les fueros ne sont utiles qu'aux*

[98] Letter of 21 May 1707, *ibid.*, 176 f.103. Cf. Berwick's letter to Chamillart, 3 June 1707, Guerre, A¹ 2049 f.92, informing him that he had ordered Játiva razed, 'et que tous les habitans fussent conduits dans la Manche. J'ay ecrit a Madrid pour qu'on les envoyast aux Indes, car il faut un exemple severe d'une canaille aussy rebelle.'

[99] Louis xiv to Amelot, 27 June 1707, in Girardot, *Correspondance de Louis XIV*.

[100] Amelot to Orléans 8 June 1707, AE Corr. Pol. (Esp.), 176 f.234.

scélérats – the harsh phrase was heavy with retribution. But Amelot was also thinking ahead. We have the testimony of Macanaz that 'the ambassador very much wished to put into effect his idea, for which there is evidence in his letters, that after introducing the new system in its entirety into Valencia, the same would follow in Aragon and Catalonia, and if successful the same system would be imposed on the realms and provinces of Castile'.[101] The suppression of the *fueros*, if we accept this evidence, was to be only the first stage in a reorganisation of the whole of Spain, including Castile.

A plan of this sort was little more than an extension of the proposals of the conde duque de Olivares under Philip IV, and cannot therefore be considered an outrageous novelty. Yet many Spanish historians have approached the revocation as though it were the result of a well-laid French plot to establish royal absolutism in Spain. It is certainly true that from the very first Philip's French advisers had no sympathy whatsoever with the separate existence of Aragon, and would have been only too willing to abolish Aragonese autonomy. But to blame the French alone[102] is to forget that the most prominent *arbitristas* of Castile had long regretted the existence of the *fueros*, and that the chief supporters of the revocation were Spaniards. After the recovery of Aragon for the royalists in 1707 the archbishop of Saragossa wrote to Philip V advising him to 'make a complete change in the political government of Aragon, and establish the laws of Castile there'.[103] The Castilian advisers of the crown were for the most part in favour of such a move. It was at this juncture that Macanaz, then a relatively obscure secretary of the council of Castile, drew up several memoranda which he presented to the government. One of these papers[104] claimed to prove that 'the king of Spain has a right to confiscate all the goods of his subjects in the kingdoms of Valencia and Aragon and in the principality of Catalonia, and that this right extended not only to the goods of the laity but also to those of the clergy and even of the Church'. Another paper suggested a new form of government for Valencia. These writings

[101] 'Copia de los Manuscritos de Macanaz', BUV, MS 24.
[102] Cf. Borrull y Vilanova, p. 17 note 18: 'Qualquiera que lea la historia de aquel tiempo conocerá que Mr Amelot mandaba despoticamente en España en todos asuntos, y que Felipe v hacia lo que el susodicho queria.'
[103] Quoted by Amelot to Orléans, 18 June 1707, AE Corr. Pol. (Esp.), 176 f.279.
[104] *Ibid.*, 159 ff.79–90.

brought him to the attention of Amelot.[105] The government had found their man. In Macanaz, a trained legist capable of dragging in the most obscure but relevant authorities to prove a disputed point, they discovered the necessary apologist for the revocation. In his writings and activities in subsequent years, Macanaz was to prove himself the theoretician and architect of the new régime in the crown of Aragon.

On 29 June 1707 a decree[106] for the abolition of the *fueros* in Aragon and Valencia was issued by the government. It went as follows:

In consideration of the fact that by their rebellion and complete disloyalty to the oath of fidelity they made to me as their rightful king and lord, the realms of Aragon and Valencia and all their inhabitants have forfeited all the *fueros*, privileges, exemptions and liberties which they used to enjoy and which with so liberal a hand had been granted to them both by me and by the kings my predecessors, distinguishing them in this respect from the other realms of this crown and touching me in my absolute dominion over the said two realms of Aragon and Valencia; and since in addition to being comprehended in the other territories which I possess by right in this monarchy, there is now added the fact of the just right of conquest over them which my arms have made in view of their rebellion; and considering also that one of the chief attributes of sovereignty is the imposition and repeal of laws, which with changing times and varying customs I am empowered to alter even without the great and fundamental motives and circumstances present in the case of Aragon and Valencia:

I have judged it convenient for these reasons as well as by my own wish, to reduce all the realms of Spain to uniformity, with the same laws, uses, customs and tribunals, and all to be governed equally by the laws of Castile, which are worthy of praise and admiration throughout the world; and to abolish and repeal entirely (as I now declare abolished and repealed) all the said *fueros*, privileges, practices and customs observed until now in the said kingdoms of Aragon and Valencia, it being my wish that these realms be reduced to the laws of Castile and to the use and practice and form of government obtaining in Castile and in its tribunals, without any differences whatsoever; so that by this means my faithful subjects of Castile may obtain offices and employ-

[105] Bourke to Torcy, 6 June 1707, *ibid.*, 168 f.212: 'J'ay fait connoitre a M Amelot l'auteur du memoire sur la maniere de regler le gouvernement des provinces rebelles, il luy a trouvé beaucoup d'esprit . . . et il m'a paru resolu de l'envoyer a Valence pour y mettre au net l'etat des revenus et des biens confiscables.'

[106] Printed in full in Voltes Bou, *La Guerra de Sucesión*, pp. 76–8.

ment in Aragon and Valencia, just as the Aragonese and Valencians may henceforward obtain them in Castile without any discrimination; so that I may thereby allow Castilians to enjoy further the marks of my gratitude in granting them the highest gifts and graces, so merited by their tested and proven loyalty, while giving to the Aragonese and Valencians similar and equally great proof of my clemency, by making them eligible for that which they were not eligible even amid the great liberty of the *fueros* which they used to enjoy and which are now abolished:

In consequence of which I have resolved that the audiencia of ministers formed for Valencia, and that which I have ordered to be formed for Aragon, be governed and run in every way like the two chanceries of Valladolid and Granada; with literal observance of the same rules, laws, practice, ordinance and customs kept in them, without the least distinction or difference in anything except in the controversies over ecclesiastical jurisdiction and the method of dealing with them; for in this the practice and style heretofore adopted must be observed, in consequence of the agreements reached with the Apostolic See.

With this decree, to resume the words of the conde de Robres, 'arrived the time so desired by the conde duque de Olivares, for the kings of Spain to be independent of all laws save that of their own conscience'.[107] The measure certainly represents one of the most important milestones in Spanish history, and the first real attempt to create a united Spain. What Philip II dared not do in 1591, what Olivares could not do in 1640, had at last been achieved by Philip V.

The great weakness of the decree, however, was that none of the arguments it utilised in favour of the revocation was at all convincing. The crown's sovereignty over Aragon, and its right to alter the ancient laws of the country, were to say the least arguable. The right of conquest, moreover, was a strange one to invoke over what was claimed to be an integral part of Spain. Most important of all, the claim that 'all the inhabitants' of Valencia and Aragon had rebelled was completely false and groundless. The ruling classes of Valencia felt so strongly about this reflection on their loyalty that they sent a strong protest to the crown. Meanwhile in Madrid steps were being taken to dissolve the council of Aragon, which had lost its *raison d'être* with the suppression of the independence of Aragon. The members

[107] Conde de Robres, p. 367.

of the council, in particular its president the conde de Aguilar, were firmly opposed to any move which might deprive them of their salaries. More than this, Aguilar and his fellow peers Montalto, Montellano and Monterey were opposed, now as later, to the abolition of the *fueros*.[108] Macanaz saw that dissolution of the council of Aragon was one sure way of stifling opposition, and impressed on Amelot that this step was absolutely necessary before any progress could be made.[109] The council was therefore abolished on 15 July and its members distributed through the other councils so as not to deprive them of employment or salary.[110] Just a fortnight later Philip v, in response to several protests, issued a new decree revising the judgment he had passed on the loyalty of his subjects in Valencia and Aragon. By this measure, dated 29 July, he recognised that:

many of the towns, cities and villages, and other public and private settlements, both ecclesiastical and secular; as well as most of the nobles, gentry, ancient nobility, *hidalgos* and distinguished citizens have been most true and loyal, suffering the loss of their property and other persecutions and travails that their constant and proven fidelity has undergone; and, since this is well known, in no circumstances can it be held reasonable for my royal decision to single out or punish as delinquents those I recognise to be loyal. But in order to clarify this distinction, I hereby declare that the greater part of the nobility, and other good subjects in the population, and many and entire towns in both realms, have preserved their loyalty pure and blameless, and only those unable to defend themselves have given way to the irresistible force of enemy arms.[111]

As an earnest of his good intentions, therefore, the king reserved many of the local laws of Aragon and Valencia, but stipulated that public law was to remain that of Castile. In the following year he made further concessions to vested interests: a decree of 7 March 1708 reaffirmed the rights of the Order of Calatrava in Aragon

---

[108] Amelot to Louis xiv, 14 Jan. 1709, AE Corr. Pol. (Esp.), 189 f.38 singles out these nobles as forming a cabal to work for the restoration of the *fueros*.

[109] 'Fui consultado por Monsieur Amelot, y le envié un papel algo dilatado haciéndole ver que convenía quitar enteramente el Consejo de Aragón', *Regalías*, p.9.

[110] 'Relacion de todos los officiales y dependientes del Consejo de Aragon,' AHN, Estado leg.320¹. The total number of councillors and employees came to about fifty. Their distribution through the other councils is listed in AHN, Consejos suprimidos leg.18190.

[111] Quoted in full in Borrull y Vilanova.

and Valencia, and a decree of 5 November 1708 guaranteed the Church possession of its property, 'because these jurisdictions and property belong to the Church, which is not judged to be guilty of rebellion, and cannot therefore lose what is its own through crimes committed by its individual members'. This latter decree was to have some bearing on the activities of Macanaz in Valencia.

The admission made in the July 29 decree really destroyed the whole excuse for the revocation of the *fueros*. Once the crown had conceded the fact that nearly all the upper classes and the clergy, and many cities and towns, had supported the Bourbons, it became ridiculous to talk of the 'rebellion of Valencia'. This must have been basically the view of two of the chief citizens of Valencia, Pedro Luis Blanquer, the *jurado en cap,* and Joseph Orti, the secretary of the *Diputación,* who drew up an appeal for the restoration of the *fueros,* and were promptly incarcerated in the Serrano tower, then transferred two days later to the citadel of Pamplona.[112] The common people had of course supported the Allies, but no government of the day would have accepted them as the spokesmen for Valencia.

The list of towns honoured by Philip for their fidelity is impressive enough.[113] 'In recognition of the fidelity and services of the town of Morella in the kingdom of Valencia,' runs a royal order of 27 February 1712, 'I have conceded it a day of free market every week.' The town also acquired the title of *siempre fidelísima.* 'To the town of Benasal,' says an order of 22 May 1709, 'I have conceded the title of *fidelísima,* and permission to add a fleur-de-lis to its coat of arms.' 'In recognition of what the town of Carcagente has done and suffered,' runs an order of 18 May 1708, 'I have decided to concede it confirmation of all its prerogatives and privileges in so far as they do not contradict the new system of Castilian laws; remission of all the taxes it owes me; permission to have a wheat granary; one free fair every year for eight days from the feast of Saint Bartholomew; and that it should exercise its own jurisdiction; and that Castellón de Játiva, whose well-known rebellion merits deprivation of the jurisdiction it formerly held, should be its village.' 'In recognition,' states an order of

---

[112] Orti y Mayor, 'Diario', f.246 vo, under Monday 12 Sept. 1707, the day of the incarceration in the Serrano tower.
[113] All the following examples come from AHN, Consejos suprimidos leg.18355.

23 May 1713, 'of the proved zeal and fidelity of the town of Elda in the kingdom of Valencia, and the special services it has rendered, and how much it suffered during the disturbances in that realm, I have conceded it the title of *fidelísima* and the use of a fleur-de-lis on its arms in memory of its loyalty; and, at the same time, confirmation of all the ancient privileges in use until the disturbances, in so far as they do not contradict the new system of Castilian laws.'

Similar decrees were issued for other Valencian towns. Javea, a town near Denia, was on 12 September 1709 awarded the title of *fidelísima,* the right to add a fleur-de-lis to its arms, and confirmation of its privileges. Jana was on 24 March the same year declared *fidelísima,* granted a fleur-de-lis, the right to have its own oil-press for the use of its inhabitants, and an annual fair for the week from 28 October to 4 November. Almenara was on 13 December 1708 granted confirmation of its privileges, the title of *fidelísima,* a fleur-de-lis, and a free market for one day each week, without prejudice to the rights of the conde de Almenara, who controlled its jurisdiction. The town of Cheste, just north of Chelva, was on 25 February 1708 confirmed in its privileges and granted a free fair for a week every year, from 8 September onwards. The town of Siete Aguas was likewise in 1708 confirmed in its privileges.

The whole region of central Alicante was honoured by an order of 27 May 1708 by which, 'in recognition of the singular fidelity, love and zeal of the towns in the region of Castalla, namely Castalla, Biar, Onil, Ibi and Tibi, as well as Petrel, Monnabar and Bañeres, and in recognition of what they and their inhabitants have suffered in my service, I have decided to grant them the title of 'noble, faithful and loyal' (*noble, fiel y leal*) and that each may add an insignia to their arms; also confirmation of the permission granted them by my generals to carry arms; confirmation of all their privileges; and that in respect of their proximity to the city of Alicante, and the fact that it is they that come to the aid of the city in any emergency, their inhabitants may take their wares into Alicante on paying the same duties as the inhabitants of the city, and that this should be carried out even though the people of these towns have until now been prohibited from taking their fruits into the said city.' The town of Jijona was particularly honoured by an order of 22 May the same year, by which the king granted it 'confirmation of all its privileges; the title of "city", and of "most loyal and faithful" (*muy leal y fidelísima*); it may add a fleur-de-lis to its arms; it may become chief town of the places in the region of Castalla; it may use weapons, its inhabitants not being prohibited by the laws'; and many other favours.

Several other large towns were also honoured for their fidelity. An order of 26 May 1709 granted the towns of Murviedro (the modern Sagunto), Nules, Puzol and Fuente de la Higuera the title of *muy leal* and the addition of a fleur-de-lis to their arms. Nules was also granted a free fair each year. The city of Peñíscola was honoured on 31 May the same year by several concessions, and a decree of 27 September granted noble rank to all those who were members of the town council during its siege by the Allies.[114] The list of faithful towns certainly does not stop here.[115]

Turning from the faithful to the disloyal, we find the list of bodily defectors to the Austrian cause to be short but distinguished. In his catalogue of defectors Feliu de la Peña lists three hundred and three laymen and ninety-two clergy. Of the laymen, about one third do not have the title of *Don*. Perales, drawing in part directly on Feliu, restricts his list of defectors to ninety-seven clergy 'and many others, without counting the religious from all orders', and one hundred and seventy-two laymen.[116]

The noble defectors, as in Aragon, amounted to no more than a fraction of the first estate in Valencia. Don José Folch de Cardona, conde de Cardona, was the most prominent of them, since he belonged to the most distinguished family in the realm. The archduke chose him for a while to be his puppet viceroy of Valencia. Other noble defectors not so far named were Don Joseph Boil, marqués de Boil; and Don Francisco Coloma, conde de Elda. Don Juan de Castelví, conde de Cervellón, appears in no list of bodily defectors but was clearly one, since both his property and that of his wife was confiscated to the government. Another name appearing on the confiscation lists, but not in that of defectors, is the marqués de Villasor.

For all their eminence, the rebel nobility were not so influential in the archduke's cause as the clergy were. Miñana's evidence as to the activity of the lower clergy on the rebel side can be

---

[114] Vicente Gascón Pelegrí, *La región valenciana en la Guerra de Sucesión*, Valencia, 1956, p. 165 note 1.

[115] Borrull y Vilanova, pp. 79 ff. claims that several other towns were faithful, including Elche, Cocentaina, Alcoy, San Mateo, Carlet, Alcudia, etc.

[116] Feliu de la Peña, *Anales*, vol. 3. pp. 629–31; Perales, *Décadas*, III, iv, pp. 871–3.

corroborated from other sources. In Orihuela, 'the greater part of the religious orders, which were very popular in the city, looked favourably on the Austrian cause'.[117] In Játiva it was notorious that the clergy had been prominent among the agitators, because of which the king's Jesuit confessor, Father Robinet, was adamant that they should not be allowed back into the city.[118] As we have seen, the allegiance of the clergy appears to have been governed by class sympathy rather than by any other factor. The only ecclesiastical defector of note in 1707 appears to have been the bishop of Segorbe. A later defector was the archbishop of Valencia, Fray Antonio Folch de Cardona; in 1707 his loyalty was unquestioned, but in 1710 he fled to the enemy after several disputes in which Macanaz played a principal part.

The events of 1706 and 1707 in Valencia were more complex than in any of the other 'rebel' provinces. In the first place, there were repercussions from the class struggle of the previous decade, so that the disruption in the realm in 1706 occurred almost exclusively among the lower orders. The nobles, upper clergy and bourgeoisie for the most part saw little to sympathise with in the aims of the ragged, plundering peasants. In the second place, there was a deliberate attempt by the Allies to exploit the social disturbances for their own ends, and in this they were aided by a handful of disgruntled nobles and commoners who felt that they had nothing to hope for from a French-inspired dynasty. The official Bourbon historiography has very largely succeeded in obscuring these two features of the Valencian situation, in an attempt to justify the suppression of the *fueros* on the grounds that the whole realm was in rebellion. The whole realm was incontrovertibly rebellious, but the rebellion was in fact aimed not against Philip v so much as against the landlords of Valencia; against, that is, those very nobles whose pretensions were a threat no less to the peasantry than to the ideals of Bourbon absolutism.

[117] Alfonso Pardo and Manuel de Villena, *El Marqués de Rafal* p. 40.
[118] Robinet to Grimaldo, 24 Aug. 1709, AHN, Estado leg.367: 'Los Religiosos . . . no deben ser admitidos . . . por haver sido la mayor parte de ellos rebeldes.'

12 The Reform of Valencia

It was on the feast day of Our Lady of the Forsaken, patroness of the city of Valencia, that the forces of Marshal Antonio del Valle entered the place. That day, Saturday 8 May 1707, their protectress seemed indeed to have abandoned the Valencians. The Bourbon troops entered in the afternoon, but remained encamped outside the walls during the ensuing night so as to avoid any clashes with the population. On the 10th Berwick entered the city, and the following day he gave thanks for its liberation in a solemn *Te Deum* at the cathedral. Though Valencia surrendered as peacefully to the royalists as it had done to the rebels, there was little hope of leniency from the king. The pardon which the duc d'Orléans published on 8 May was implicitly repudiated a few weeks later by Philip himself. The commencement of a policy of reprisals was signalled first by Berwick's decree for the disarmament of the whole population, and then by the sack of Játiva, whose inhabitants were resettled in Valencia and La Mancha.

Since Valencia was the first of the 'rebel' provinces to be recovered for the Bourbon cause, it earned the undivided attention of the most accomplished administrators of the crown. Even before the suppression of the *fueros*, the liberties of Valencia were pointedly disregarded. A royal decree of 30 May[1] named six provisional *jurados* for the capital city. At the same time it was ordered that a junta to deal with confiscations be set up, to be composed of four officials from the audiencia. For the audiencia itself it was ordered that the regent should be a Castilian, and that the eight posts in the two civil chambers, and the four posts in

[1] 'Resumen de las resoluciones que ultimam^te ha sido servido tomar S.M. en orden a la Planta del nuevo gobierno del Reyno de Valencia', AHN, Consejos suprimidos leg.18190.

L

the criminal chamber, be divided equally between six Valencians and six Castilians.

On Sunday 5 June the formal election of the new officials in the city took place.[2] The six new *jurados* were as follows: *jurado en cap* of the nobility, the conde de Castella; *jurado en cap* of the citizens, Pedro Luis Blanquer; the other *jurados* being Don Juan Ruiz de Corella, Juan Bautista Bordes, Claudio Bonavida and Miguel Pons. As *racional* or financial officer Doctor Gerónimo Lop was chosen, and as syndic Isidro Costa. At the same time the members of the *Diputación* were nominated: the six members of this body were Canon Gerónimo Frigola, delegated by the archbishop, the conde de la Real, Pedro Luis Blanquer, Don Gerónimo Valterra, Don Joseph de Cardona y Pertuja, and a certain Bochoni. The syndic of the *Diputación* was to be Don Joseph de Castelví, and the assessor Doctor Juan Bautista Borrull. All these elections were necessary to the functioning of the new Bourbon régime, but significantly they took place under new rules. The tenure of the new *jurados* and deputies was no longer to be constitutionally regulated as before, one year in office for the *jurados*, three for the deputies. Instead, all were to hold their posts at the pleasure of the king. How serious a threat to liberty the king's pleasure might be, was clearly demonstrated in September, when, as we have seen, the *jurado en cap* was hustled into prison for having demanded the restoration of the *fueros*.

In Madrid, meanwhile, far-reaching suggestions for the re-organisation of Valencia were being considered. Names proposed for posts in the audiencia of Valencia included prominent administrators from the chief cities of Castile, among them the alcalde of Seville, Don Rodrigo Cavallero y Llanes.[3] Already, however, one name had emerged as the pace-setter for all the reforms being proposed. This was Melchor de Macanaz. Immediately after the battle of Almansa, he had, as we have seen, drawn up detailed memoranda on the future government of the crown of Aragon. It was on the basis of these writings that Amelot decided that Macanaz would be the best agent to supervise changes in finance and administration in Valencia. It was to Valencia, accordingly,

---

[2] Orti y Mayor, 'Diario', f.224.

[3] The other ministers are detailed in a memoir entitled 'Ministros que se proponen para yr a Balencia a servir en aquella Audᵃ': AHN, Estado leg.3201.

that Macanaz went in June 1707. He was, as he pointed out later,[4] 'the first [Castilian] minister to enter this realm'.

Macanaz was instructed first of all to study the finances of Valencia and to send back accounts of the fiscal system. This he did, only to discover that the committee set up in Madrid to examine his reports was taking unnecessarily long to arrive at a proper analysis preparatory to drawing up a plan of reform. Impatient of delay, Amelot prevailed on Philip to appoint a special superintendent of finance for Valencia, with powers to act on Macanaz's memoranda and to bring Valencia more closely into line with the Castilian tax system.[5] This superintendent, Juan Pérez de la Puente, had in fact been nominated in June and arrived in Valencia on Tuesday 30 August in the company of several other ministers.[6] Macanaz and Amelot between themselves were responsible for the suppression of the council of Aragon, in circumstances discussed above. With the abolition of this council there were no further constitutional barriers to freedom of action in Valencia.

With Macanaz the real history of Castilian government in Valencia begins, for it was his work above all that established royal power firmly in this province. This is not to exaggerate his actual success, for many of his more radical proposals were, no doubt wisely, rejected by the authorities. He proposed,[7] for instance, that the reformed audiencia of Valencia should be drastically reduced in power, and should not even have the functions normally assigned to the audiencias of Castile. The number of ministers on it should be reduced to eight, four of them Castilian and four Valencian, while the regent and fiscal should both be Castilians. They should be allowed to exercise some judicial functions, but most of their time should be spent in codifying the laws of Valencia, some of which should be formally accepted as part of the constitution of Valencia, leaving all other aspects of the constitution to be governed by the laws of Castile. Instead of accepting these proposals, the government sent a much larger number of ministers to sit on the audiencia, which was thereupon

[4] Letter to Grimaldo, 2 July 1709, ibid., leg.367. He left Madrid on 20 June and entered Valencia on the 24th.

[5] Regalías, p. 8.

[6] Orti y Mayor's 'Diario' also informs us that Rodrigo Cavallero arrived in Valencia on Saturday 23 July, and that Pedro Larreategui y Colón arrived on Monday 1 August.

[7] Regalías, p. 9.

termed a chancery. The first president of the chancery was Pedro Colón, and the first meeting of this body took place on 13 August. Valencia thereby became the first kingdom in Aragon to experience Bourbon control in government.[8]

Macanaz's initial preoccupations seem to have been with municipal government. He was 'ordered to alter Valencia city to the Castilian pattern, and to send a plan with a proposal of those who were to make up the city council, and this I did and the city remained modelled on that of Seville'.[9] The task may not have been performed by Macanaz alone, and it is likely that Cavallero, with his personal experience of Seville, also contributed his help. The most delicate of all the tasks entrusted to Macanaz was the reconstruction of Játiva. The suggestion to rebuild Játiva as a new town with a new name, seems to have come from Toby Bourke.[10] If the idea was Bourke's, the constructive plans owed their existence to Macanaz, for in September we find him sending a copy of his proposals through Bourke to the French foreign minister Torcy.[11] The Spanish government finally approved the plan, and on 27 November Philip v issued a decree to Macanaz, directing him to rebuild the town under the new name of San Felipe, and to resettle all loyal members of the old population, who were to be compensated for loss of goods out of the possessions of rebels.[12] The difficulties which Macanaz was subsequently to encounter in Valencia arose principally out of his activities in San Felipe.

His chief work remained that of supervising confiscations in the province. A royal decree of 5 October empowered him to 'exercise jurisdiction over the confiscation of goods belonging to rebels in our kingdom of Valencia', and allowed appeal from his decisions only to the council in Madrid.[13] His salary in this occupation was fixed at 1,500 reales a month.[14] By the spring of 1708 Macanaz's other colleagues had also taken up their effective posts. Cavallero, now a member of the chancery, was entrusted early in 1708 with

[8] Further details of changes are given in Perales, *Décadas*, III, iv, pp. 879 ff.

[9] *Regalías*, p. 8.

[10] Bourke to Grimaldo, 19 Mar. 1714, AHN, Estado leg.456, claimed he was 'le premier qui ay donné l'idée et le plan de l'etablissement de la ditte colonie'.

[11] Bourke to Torcy, 12 Sept. 1707, AE Corr. Pol. (Esp.), 170 f.52.

[12] Text of decree in Lafuente, *Historia General de España*, vol. 18, p. 204 note 1.

[13] Text in Lafuente, vol. 18, p. 202, note 3.

[14] By decree of 22 Nov. See letter of Pedrajas to Grimaldo, 23 July 1709, AHN, Estado leg.367.

the administration of the tobacco monopoly in Valencia. With the appointment of Antonio del Valle as *corregidor* of the city of Valencia on 24 June 1708, the ministers principally responsible for the reformation of Valencia were in their appointed roles.

Though the city and realm of Valencia had now been allotted civil administrators, the whole region still continued in practice to be under military occupation. This dual control inevitably gave rise to conflicts of jurisdiction, of which the most significant occurred in the summer of 1708. D'Asfeld was at this period commander of the forces in Valencia, a position he held until his departure for France on 2 July 1709, when he was replaced by Don Francisco Caetano y Aragón. In this position D'Asfeld had inevitably to intervene in the political and fiscal measures being undertaken. When, however, he nominated the new *corregidores* for the chief towns of Valencia, his action was countermanded by Pedro Colón, as president of the chancery, on instructions from Madrid.[15] Colón's complaint was that the appointments were derogatory to the civil jurisdiction of the chancery. The conflict of words that ensued was settled temporarily by a royal instruction of 17 September, which ordered:

that the chancery of Valencia and its ministers abstain completely from political and administrative government, and meet as a body only to deal with criminal matters . . . and deal with the expedition of civil pleas, particularly concerning *mayorazgos* and other similar matters, refraining completely from everything else that touches government, which is to be controlled by the commandant-general, the chevalier D'Asfeld, governing the kingdom in every way as though there were no chancery.[16]

In this controversy Macanaz took sides against the chancery, which seemed to him to be exceeding its powers. The conflict was not merely one of jurisdictions: it also involved a clash of personalities. For Macanaz the only efficient administrators in Valencia were Antonio del Valle, the *corregidor* of the city, and the military intendant Joseph de Pedrajas.[17] The work of the

[15] D'Asfeld to Grimaldo, 28 Aug. 1708, AHN, Estado leg. 346.
[16] AHN, Estado leg. 346.
[17] Cf. Macanaz, *Regalías*, p. 7: 'Luego que la capital se restituyó a la obediencia del Rey, se gobernó por un Comandante que lo fue D. Antonio del Valle, con su Auditor. Para las tropas y finanzas hubo un Comisario ordenador que hoy es alla Superintendente de Rentas Reales, y se llama D. José de Pedrajas, que entró con el ejercito de ordenador del y Comisario de las Guardias Walonas.'

ministers of the chancery, on the other hand, 'was quite the opposite of what was desired', with the result that 'what had until then been governed by Don Antonio del Valle and Don José de Pedrajas with the greatest ability and good service, was henceforward full of complaints, vexations, quarrels and confusion'.[18] Macanaz's chief enemies appear to have been the president of the chancery, Pedro Colón; and Rodrigo Cavallero who was, according to Macanaz, the chief calumniator of Valle and Pedrajas. The conflict between these men was to emerge into the open over Macanaz's controversial activity in the resettlement of Játiva.

Empowered as he was to rebuild Játiva as the new town of San Felipe, Macanaz felt himself justified in taking all necessary steps to punish rebels and to ensure that they should not return to a town that he intended to make solidly royalist. With this in mind, he proceeded to confiscate the property of rebel clergy in San Felipe. Immediately the chapter of Valencia cathedral protested to the papal nuncio, who replied affirming his complete sympathy with their viewpoint.[19] A quarrel over ecclesiastical jurisdiction was clearly in the making. In the spring of 1708 the archbishop of Valencia returned from Castile to his see, and the government, anxious to avoid a clash, issued him with an instruction on the question of San Felipe.[20] The instructions were obviously too diplomatic, for they failed to clarify the respective spheres of ecclesiastical and secular authority. On 11 March 1708 the papal nuncio protested to the king against Macanaz's contraventions of ecclesiastical immunity, and on 3 May sent another protest in the same vein.[21] A reply from the government stated that the king had ordered Macanaz to withdraw his measures. Macanaz, true to his principles, delayed their repeal. The archbishop of Valencia now stepped in. In letters of 3 July and 7 and 21 August, he accused Macanaz of seizing ecclesiastical property and of

[18] *Regalías*, p. 10.

[19] *Reparos críticos*, pp. 166–7, letter from chapter of 27 Dec. 1707, and from nuncio 4 Jan. 1708.

[20] 'Instruzon que a de observar el Sr Arzobisp de Vala conferme alamte de S.M. en lo tocante a la nueva poblacion de la Ziudad de Sn Phe, por lo tocante a su ministerio y jurisdizon', enclosed with letter of Macanaz to Grimaldo, 31 Dec. 1709, AHN, Estado leg.375.

[21] Much of what follows is drawn from the 'Resumen sobre los procedimientos de Don Melchor Macanaz', AHN, Estado leg.350, printed in Voltes Bou, *La Guerra de Sucesión en Valencia*, doc. VII, pp. 185–9.

forcing all transactions to be made on the newly-introduced stamped paper of Castile. Cardinal Portocarrero also made some representations against Macanaz. Both the archbishop and the nuncio, meanwhile, placed Macanaz under excommunication. In view of this, the council of Castile formed a special junta to discuss the issues involved. Its judgment, in a *consulta* of 19 September, tended naturally to favour Macanaz, but it was also decided that concessions should be made to archiepiscopal jurisdiction over Church property. All the relevant papers were thereupon passed to Father Pierre Robinet, the king's Jesuit confessor, who usually had the last word in such matters. Robinet, in an advice he issued on 24 September, suggested that the archbishop and nuncio be told that the king was about to make a decision, and that the two chief authorities in Valencia, D'Asfeld and del Valle, be approached for a decision as to whether Macanaz should be retained in his post.

The mediatory tone adopted by Robinet was only a cover for his actual support of Macanaz. To choose D'Asfeld and del Valle for a decision was to choose two notorious supporters of royal power and of Macanaz. D'Asfeld replied:

that although he had been sure of the correct conduct of Don Melchor the good opinion he had of him was now further strengthened; and, that the king should be very attentive to such a zealous, hard-working truthful and disinterested minister as he was.

Del Valle blamed himself, not Macanaz, for the delay in decreeing repeal of Macanaz's measures; and said that the latter was:

so active and hard-working that he gets through more pleas in a day than the courts do in one month; that it was true that he only used stamped paper [*papel sellado*], but this was the practice of the chancery and other courts; and that he was poorer now than when he first went there.

Macanaz was, as a consequence, retained in his post, and events moved towards a compromise. On 12 November he reported to the archbishop to receive absolution and release from the penalties of excommunication.

The quarrels of 1708 were no more than a minor prelude to those of the following year. That there was no real agreement between the sides is demonstrated by a letter written by Joseph de Grimaldo to D'Asfeld a week after Macanaz's absolution.[22] 'Although they may be clergy,' wrote the king's secretary, 'accused persons must also be convicted by a secular judge when it concerns land and property, and ecclesiastics cannot interfere in such cases; and all that the archbishop might do against this would be flagrant usurpation of royal jurisdiction.' Macanaz was equally convinced that ecclesiastics were subject to the secular power in many important aspects of their activity, and proceeded to demonstrate this in his attitude to the clergy of San Felipe. Fully aware that many of the clergy, particularly the religious orders, in Játiva had been opponents of the royalists, Macanaz refused to allow any religious to return to the town or to recover their property. When the ecclesiastical authorities protested, Macanaz referred the issue to Grimaldo, who in turn asked Robinet for his opinion.

The royal confessor's advice[23] was in every way a confirmation of Macanaz's position:

It seems to me that since His Majesty has not yet arrived at a decision on the return of the religious communities of Játiva to the city of San Felipe, they ought not to be admitted in without a special order from His Majesty. Nor is it suitable that they should be, since the greater part of them have been rebels, and some of those whom the governor has allowed to enter are malignants, as is confirmed by their scandalous operations. . . . My advice is that without a special order from His Majesty, the governor should not allow any residence to the said religious, and should arrange for those who are there without special licence to leave immediately.

This letter was typical of subsequent, more powerful, efforts by Robinet to rally support for his headstrong friend in Valencia. Already, however, Macanaz was fighting on two fronts, both against the ecclesiastical authorities and against the officials of the chancery. At the end of June he had asked Grimaldo[24] for permission to leave Valencia for a while 'to cure myself of the colic which I have suffered for some time'. At the same time he complained that most of the documentation relative to his work on

---

[22] Letter of 18 Nov. 1708, AHN, Estado leg.350, printed in Voltes Bou, doc. VIII, pp. 189–90.
[23] Dated 24 Aug. 1709 and enclosed with the letter of Macanaz to Grimaldo, 20 July 1709, in AHN, Estado leg.367.
[24] Macanaz to Grimaldo, 2 July 1709, *ibid.*, leg.367.

confiscations had been taken over by Rodrigo de Cepeda, of the chancery, 'with the result that I find myself without activity, occupation or favour, though I was the first minister to come into this kingdom. . . . I hope that you will put my case before the king and ask him to grant me some of the favours that other ministers who came to this realm have merited, and that I be given some post in which I can serve him.' Behind this letter lay a growing rift between Macanaz and the ministers of the chancery. The conflict had its partisans even in Madrid, where a special report on Macanaz's administration of confiscations was drawn up for the Hacienda by a certain Juan Fernández de Caceres. Both the report, and the *consulta* on it issued by the Hacienda, were strongly critical of the arbitrary procedure adopted in Valencia by Macanaz.[25]

On 21 December a messenger from the archbishop's court in Valencia came to Macanaz and informed him that he had been placed under excommunication. Among the reasons for this action given by the archbishop in the letters of excommunication, it was claimed :

that he exceeded his powers in the decree published for the formation of the town of San Felipe; that he exceeded his powers in refusing satisfaction to those clergy who have claims to *censos* and other dues out of confiscated property; that he has not given back the revenue of the college in San Felipe; that he has kept the revenue of the ecclesiastical communities that were in San Felipe; that he refuses to let them return to found monasteries . . .

and other similar grievances. On the 24th Macanaz wrote an angry letter to Grimaldo, enclosing with it a memorandum for the king in which he said that:

it is very obvious that the archbishop's plan is to attempt to return to the disputes of 1708, and to usurp from Your Majesty all the jurisdiction that the kings your predecessors have held in this kingdom for many centuries.

Macanaz thereby identified his own cause with that of the *regalías* of the crown, a position which automatically gained the king's support. It was not enough, however, simply to defend

<hr>

[25] *Consulta* of Hacienda, 22 Nov. 1709, AHN, Consejos suprimidos leg.6805 f. 219.

himself: he must go over to the offensive, and present the archbishop as an enemy of royal power:

In this realm [he wrote in his memorandum] the ministers of Your Majesty cannot be proceeded against even if they exceed their jurisdiction and touch on ecclesiastical persons and causes, since the punishment of such excesses belongs to Your Majesty in virtue of agreement with the Apostolic See.

It was left to Father Robinet to press the case against the archbishop with greater effectiveness than Macanaz could ever have managed. On the 31st of that month, Robinet wrote to Grimaldo to urge him to take strong action against the clergy who had proceeded against Macanaz: such clergy, he emphasised, were defending 'false rights in favour of the Church against royal jurisdiction'. Three weeks later, on 22 January 1710, the royal confessor informed the marqués de Mejorada that both the inquisitor general and the bishop of Lèrida supported his point of view.[26]

Events moved towards a climax in the early months of 1710. The officials of the chancery now entered the lists against Macanaz. Aware that the latter could hardly hold his ground in Valencia, Antonio del Valle sent him, apparently at the very end of 1709, to Madrid, so that he could state his case there in person.[27] Once at Madrid, Macanaz could rely on the good offices of the king's confessor. Robinet's vigorous intervention on Macanaz's behalf, and his exhaustive correspondence with Mejorada[28] and others on this affair, may have had more than political ideology or personal friendship behind it. To read the correspondence leads one to an unverifiable suspicion that the confessor was hunting the archbishop. Whatever motives may have been involved, the victory of Macanaz was assured. On the political plane, the government could not afford to give in to his detractors. In March the president (Colón) and the *fiscal* of the chancery were recalled to Madrid,

---

[26] The documentation used in this paragraph is from AHN, Estado leg.375. The memoranda by Macanaz are enclosed in his letters of 24 Dec. and 31 Dec. 1709 to Grimaldo. The bishop of Lérida cited by Robinet was the notorious regalist Francisco de Solis.

[27] According to Orti y Mayor's diary, f.300 vo, Macanaz also went to Madrid in April 1709. The entry under Tuesday 9 Apr. 1709 reads: 'Se fue a Madrid el cavallero D'Asfelt, llevandose consigno a Dⁿ Melchor Rafael de Macanaz, que iva llamado'.

[28] Particularly in AHN, Estado legs.380 and 390. Robinet to Mejorada, 29 Mar. 1710, encloses a list of accusations against Pedro Colón, Cavallero and others.

and it was made known that Macanaz's policy in San Felipe had the government's approval. Triumphant over the chancery, Macanaz had only to bide his time to wait for his triumph over the archbishop. The latter, disillusioned by the attitude of officials in Madrid, began to correspond secretly with Barcelona, from where he received letters through the medium of fishing boats. Macanaz arranged for three of these letters to be intercepted and sent them to Madrid to be deciphered.[29] They definitely incriminated the archbishop, who did not wait for further developments. In November, he deserted to the Allies, and all his property was confiscated to the crown.

Robinet and Macanaz had one last victory over the hapless archbishop. When plans were agreed on for the foundation of the new Royal Library, the first of the great cultural achievements of Philip v's reign, it was decided that the prelate's collection of books should form its basis. Macanaz thereupon arranged for the transfer of the whole archiepiscopal library to Madrid, at the wish of Father Robinet, who in 1713 became the first director of the Biblioteca Real. The other works incorporated into the library included a magnificent collection of books brought by Philip from France, as well as thousands of volumes seized from the shelves of rebels absent in enemy territory.[30]

Macanaz did not return to Valencia after 1710. He remained in the royal entourage and helped to organise food supplies for the defeated royalist troops after the battle of Saragossa. Thereafter his administrative duties centred on Aragon. He still retained some functions in Valencia, however. A royal decree issued in Saragossa on 22 April 1711 declared that 'notwithstanding the duties with which I have entrusted D Melchor Rafael Macanaz, it is my royal will that . . . the finance and reconstruction of the new city of San Felipe remain under his command'.[31] He also

---

[29] The paper entitled 'Empeños con el Arzobispo de Valencia', in 'Copia de los Manuscritos de Macanaz', BUV, MS 24, deals briefly with the author's clashes with Cardona.

[30] Robinet to Grimaldo, 6 July 1712, AHN, Estado leg.413, claims that he was principally responsible for the idea of establishing a royal library, and refers to 'mi representacion al Rey a favor de la libreria Real'. Belando, however, in his *Historia Civil de España*, vol 3, p. 98, says that the marqués de Villena 'la propuso al Rey'. Villena promoted the foundation of the Real Academia Española (*ibid.*, vol. 3, pp. 56–7). Belando is the authority for saying that other rebels besides the archbishop suffered loss of books.

[31] Carlos Sarthou Carreres, *Datos para la Historia de Játiva*, vol. 2, p. 18.

continued to draw an income from confiscations which had been assigned to him in San Felipe, so that for both professional and personal reasons he continued to maintain an interest in his previous post.

After this lengthy attention to a man who by any standards must rank high among the founders of Bourbon Spain, we must look briefly at the other men who helped to reorganise government in Valencia. The most remarkable of them, in view of his subsequent lifetime of service to the crown, was Rodrigo Cavallero. No details of his personal life have yet emerged, but there is enough evidence of his activity in public life to distinguish him as one of the foremost administrators of Philip v. A personal enemy of Macanaz, his first field of distinctive service was Valencia. Thereafter he served in all the principal intendancies of Spain, and notably in Catalonia, until called to share in the actual management of government in Madrid. Whatever partisan criticism Macanaz may have levelled at him, the reproach of inefficiency would have been the least plausible. A memoir drawn up by Cavallero in 1709, in the form of a letter to Francisco Caetano y Aragón, the new military commandant in Valencia, shows that he was no less concerned than Macanaz to extend Castilian forms of government over the eastern territories of the peninsula.[32] He reaffirmed the validity of the verse by Francisco de Quevedo, in which the poet had presented the standard complaint of *arbitristas* that Castile, alone of all the provinces of the monarchy, was bearing the whole weight of taxation to maintain the empire:

> En Valencia y Aragón
> No hay quien te tribute un Real.
> Cataluña y Portugal
> Son de la misma opinión.
> Solo Castilla y León
> Y el noble Reino Andaluz
> Llevan a cuestas la Cruz.
> Católica Magestad,

[32] The original plan is given as a letter from Cavallero to Caetano, 23 Nov. 1709 AHN, Estado leg.375. There is a copy, entitled 'Projet de D Rodrigo Cavallero pour etablir un nouvel ordre dans le gouvernement du Royaume de Valence', in. AN Aff. Etr., B^III 325 f.155. The text is also printed in Voltes Bou, doc. XI, pp. 205–11.

Ten de nosotros piedad.
Pues no te sirven los otros
Asi como nosotros.[32a]

The newly conquered provinces, then, must play their proper part in financing the monarchy. This would become possible only if all remnants of the old *fueros* were totally destroyed, in order to facilitate the unrestricted entry of Castilian forms of taxation. Cavallero saw clearly that an indefinite continuation of military rule was undesirable, for the simple reason that the military governors in existence were 'politically incapable of introducing and carrying out the orders and rules that lead to a new judicial administration and to the necessary introduction of royal taxation'. The administrative officials he proposed to introduce were very much like the still unknown office of intendant: these men, Cavallero suggested, were to govern both civil and military matters, and to be *corregidores* of the towns. They would prevent the division of authority that now existed between the army and the civil officers, and would thereby prove more efficient and more economical. As for the administration of the taxes, which was his principal theme, Cavallero suggested that this come under the control of the president of the chancery. The president would subdelegate four officials, all Castilians, to control four distinct spheres of taxation: one would control the customs duties, another the state monopolies such as salt, another the *alcabalas,* and a fourth the seigneurial taxes such as the *tercios diezmos.* The four administrators and the president would meet one day a week to discuss business: they should draw no salaries, but be paid a percentage of the tax returns.

From his arrival in 1707 up to the year 1711, Cavallero was concerned principally in the administration of the tobacco monopoly, which is discussed below. During that period the superintendant of the finances in Valencia was Juan Pérez de la Puente, an administrator whose work Macanaz criticised very strongly. Puente remained in Valancia until April 1711, when he was recalled to Madrid to serve as a councillor of the Hacienda. His place was taken[33] by Joseph Pedrajas. Pedrajas, who was

---

[32a] In Valencia and Aragon / no tribute is paid to you. / Catalonia and Portugal / are in the same state. / Only Castile and León / and the noble realm of Andalucia / bear the cross (i.e. a coin stamped with a cross) on their shoulders. / Catholic Majesty, / have mercy on us. / Since the others do not serve you / as we do.

[33] Decree of 16 Apr. 1711, AGS, Guerra Moderna leg.1576.

subsequently to distinguish himself as one of the most prominent intendants of the crown, had served in Valencia since February 1706 as one of the army treasurers. His control of the finances in Valencia lasted only two years, until 1713, when Cavallero took over his functions.

When Bergeyck instituted the intendants in December 1711, it was Cavallero who was chosen to occupy this post in Valencia. Cavallero's initial difficulties were no doubt typical of those experienced by intendants elsewhere in Spain. Despite the great powers to which his office entitled him[34] he was, in practice, restricted almost exclusively to military duties. A month after his appointment to the intendancy, he was informed that nearly all the finances were to remain indefinitely under the control of Pedrajas.[35] Other functions which he theoretically exercised, in justice and in police, were likewise denied him, and continued to be controlled by the chancery. But these drawbacks did not detract from the very important work which Cavallero undertook in Valencia. A subsequent royal order gave him control over the finances with effect from 1 July 1713,[36] thereby replacing Pedrajas, and from this date Cavallero seems to have had much more extensive authority over administrative questions. We find him paying for the construction of the main hospital in Valencia city out of ecclesiastical confiscations, paying official salaries out of confiscations, and directing the restoration of roads in the province. His tenure of the intendancy of Valencia, from 1711 to 1718, was probably one of the most formative periods in the history of the kingdom, for it saw the definitive establishment of Castilian norms of government.[37]

As in Aragon, what mattered most to the crown was finance, and all administrative changes were directed towards eliciting further contributions from Valencia. The original commission given to Macanaz was to examine the state of taxation in the realm,

[34] His ordinances, for example, began thus: 'D Rodrigo Cavallero y Llanes, Cavallero del Abito de Santiago, Regidor perpetuo de la Ciudad de Cadiz, del Consejo de su Magestad, y Superintendente de le Justicia, Policia, Guerra y Hazienda en este Reyno de Valencia, y Juez Conservador de la Nacion Francesa . . .' (this is taken from an order of 3 Feb. 1712 in AHN, Estado leg.417). Other points relative to Cavallero and the intendants are discussed in my article noted above, p. 115 fn. 104.

[35] Cavallero to Grimaldo 12 Jan. 1712, AHN, Estado leg. 417.

[36] Ibid., 9 July 1713, ibid., leg.430².

[37] Cavallero's work can be studied in the papers of the intendancy, Serie G¹, in the Archivo del Ayuntamiento de Valencia.

and his reports formed the basis on which Puente was to work as superintendant of finances. Of the later reports available to us, the most satisfactory are those drawn up at the end of his term of office by Joseph Pedrajas. Our assessment of the finances of Valencia will be based largely on these latter.

The principal taxes collected in Valencia on the eve of 1707 were the *baylias*, the *tercios diezmos*, and the *generalidades*. In addition, income was forthcoming from the salt tax, and from the tobacco monopoly.[38] The *baylias* were various taxes from mills, pasture, *censos* and other sources, which the crown received from forty of the principal cities and towns that fell under royal jurisdiction. The *tercios diezmos*, likewise a traditional tax, were equivalent to one third of the tithe of agricultural produce ('fruits and harvests') collected in twenty-four towns under royal jurisdiction. The customs duties or *generalidades* were first ordered to be collected in Valencia in 1376, and it was out of the income from these taxes that grants or *servicios* were voted to the crown. The *generalidades* were divided into old (*derechos antiguos*) and new taxes (*derechos nuevos*): the old taxes comprised the *general de la mercadería*, which was a general customs tax on the frontiers of the realm, and the *general del corte*, a tax on all the textiles cut and sold in the capital city and in the realm. The newer customs duties were levied on the exit and entry of salt, ice and playing-cards. Their rate appears to have been very low, generally 2·5 per cent. After the revocation of the *fueros* the rate, and therefore the yield, was raised. Before 1707 very little was received by the crown from either the salt or the tobacco monopolies.

After 1707 the introduction of the standard Castilian taxes, in particular the *alcabala* and *papel sellado*, followed. Their relative importance, and the difference they made to government revenue, may be gauged from table 13 (page 324) which shows revenue from 1707 to 1712.

The *rentas reales* represented ordinary taxation, which obviously increased very appreciably after 1707. A more rounded figure of all the taxes suffered by Valencians is gained if we look at the

---

[38] Most of the detailed information on these taxes is taken here from the memoranda by Pedrajas in AHN, Estado leg.400, dated 21 Aug. 1711. One of these memoranda is printed in Voltes Bou, doc.X, pp. 192–205. Information on the *generalidades* is taken from BUV, MS 803 folio 12, on 'Resumen de los ingresos de las Generalidades por derechos viejos y nuevos en los años desde 1706 a 1715'.

TABLE 13. NET VALUE OF *rentas reales* IN VALENCIA 1707–12 IN REALES OF VELLON[39]

	1707	1708	1709	1710	1711	1712
Baylías y tercios diezmos	396,540	335,490	430,575	370,295	435,255	427,815
Customs	101,295	1,200,000	304,350	478,205	991,995	1,239,720
Salt	—	—	77,370	302,925	323,295	476,880
Alcabalas y cientos	588,555	3,604,965	2,623,065	2,528,385	2,701,065	2,412,165
Stamped paper	12,165	90,660	91,500	67,440	93,825	89,520
Fines on smuggling	—	—	7,740	61,770	114,900	157,710
Tobacco[40]	—	550,400	832,630	1,172,977	960,743	1,042,163
Total	1,098,555	5,781,515	4,367,230	4,981,997	5,621,078	5,845,973

[39] This table is based on that of Pedrajas, dated 19 June 1713, in AHN, Estado leg.429. The lack of figures in 1707 and 1708 means that some taxes had not begun to be properly administered. By 'net value' is meant the value after deducting all expenses of officials.

[40] Tobacco was administered separately from the other taxes, but is included here for convenience.

estimate of income for the financial year 1712–13, as drawn up by Pedrajas:[41]

	Income		*Expenditure*	
	pesos			*pesos*
Baylias	6,844			
Tercios diezmos	24,810			
Customs	60,000			
Salinas	22,000			
Papel Sellado	5,000			
Alcabalas y cientos	6,000			
Tobacco	95,397			
Mint (for this year)	30,000			
Confiscations (remnant)	15,991			
60 per cent on confiscations	22,000			
Imposition for governors' salaries	21,333⅓			
Winter-quartering	300,000			
Total	609,375⅓			
			Expenses and Salaries	71,442
			To *asentistas*	92,400⅓
	163,842⅓			163,842⅓
Balance, for war purposes	445,533			

It is not certain what proportion of this revenue actually went to the Hacienda in Madrid. The treasury returns for 1713, as we have seen,[42] indicate that 2,730,000 reales were to be received from Valencia. The transfer of money to Madrid would in any event have been a more or less fictional exercise, since the cash was needed on the spot, in Valencia, to finance the operations of the army.

We are now in a position to look briefly at each of the new taxes contained in the table above. The *salinas* were an old source of income, but began to be fiscally profitable only after 1707.

---

[41] AHN, Estado leg.400. Pedrajas gives his statement in 'pesos', but since the peso is equivalent to the Valencian libra, the estimate can be read equally as 'libras'.

[42] Above, p. 223.

The main sources of salt were salt-lakes in the vicinity of Alicante, and it was only when this city was recovered in 1709 that the tax could begin to operate. The *salina* of La Mata, a large lake near the port of Santa Pola, was the chief supplier of Valencia and other cities. Other local *salinas* existed at Orihuela and at Sal de Ventura. The king possessed three in the realm, at Calpe, Manuel and Elda. The only other *salina* of importance was a small one at Cofrentes, the property of the duque de Gandía.[43] The administrator appointed to control the salt-tax in 1709 was Don Felipe Bolifon, formerly director of the customs-office at Alicante.

Introduction of *papel sellado* was a simple matter that needed no great administrative effort. The introduction of *alcabalas,* on the other hand, gave rise to profound difficulties. Administration of this tax was entrusted to Pérez de la Puente, who made a limited exaction in 1707 and then introduced the tax fully in 1708. He proceeded by way of *encabezamiento,* that is, he apportioned a lump sum among the localities which were to pay the tax, and each locality had to decide on its own method of raising the required sum. The standard rate of taxation adopted was 14 per cent on all commercial transactions. The reaction to the tax in Valencia city is described thus by Macanaz:

From the moment it was decreed, the price of all commodities rose, and when supplies came from outside they were registered at the gates and had to pay duty at the rate of 14 per cent, without any exception for coal, eggs, vegetables or other minor items, so that from that time the food-sellers stopped coming in, and the city found itself in great need of supplies, resulting in innumerable complaints and great disorder.[44]

In addition to this, Valencia and other cities found themselves so committed to paying other taxes whose rates were not being upgraded, that they protested their inability to pay what was required of them. As a result, the full amount of the 1708 *alcabala* was not received, and there was little likelihood that the tax would be successful in subsequent years. After 1708, then, Puente did not attempt to issue further *encabezamientos,* and, as Pedrajas observed in 1713, 'this tax has never been properly established or collected, and for the last three years it has been neglected'. The principal reason for the failure of the *alcabala* in Valencia

---

[43] *Regalias,* p.6.   [44] *Ibid.,* p. 9.

appears therefore to have been the inability of the townships to bear the burden of this tax on top of all the other demands made by the occupying forces of Castile. The Valencians, Pedrajas pointed out, were opposed to the tax ('siendo cosa nueva para ellos y que aborrecen'), and any attempt to multiply the officials needed for it would only eat up the proceeds in administrative costs. Despite this unfortunate situation, the *alcabala,* as table 13 shows, appears to have been quite remunerative in the first five years of its existence. It was not until 1713 that Pedrajas decided to drop any further attempts to impose it. In that year Macanaz urged the government to suspend the tax entirely, and to introduce in its place a capitation tax, of which more hereafter.

The enforcement of the royal tobacco monopoly in Valencia was one of the most successful of the new fiscal measures. Although the monopoly had long existed in theory, the crown had received nothing from it in Valencia prior to 1707. Control of its manufacture and distribution had fallen almost entirely into private hands, and tobacco was even being smuggled into Castile and Andalucia, where it posed a threat to the royal monopoly shops (*estancos*). To redress this situation, and to threaten the rights of individual property-owners and seigneurs in Valencia, seemed an almost impossible task. Yet Rodrigo Cavallero, who was appointed administrator of tobacco in Valencia, did not hesitate. In his own words:

I shut my eyes to everything, armed only with my duty, and ordered the destruction of 143 tobacco-mills in the kingdom and the uprooting of the plants, and established (as are now established in all the cities and townships) the king's *estanco*. By the mercy of God, not a single death or wound occurred during all this; nor did the lords who claimed to possess this right in their territories show a single privilege to support them.[45]

Thanks to Cavallero's work, the yield from the monopoly grew to 1,272,834 reales in 1709, 1,430,963 in 1710, 1,393,884 in 1711, and 1,397,318 in 1712.[46] The net sums left from these gross figures, after deducting salaries and other expenses, are incorporated into table 13.

The mint in Valencia was under the direction of Pedrajas, who

45 From Cavallero's letter to Caetano of 23 Nov. 1709, cited above.
46 Statement included in letter of Cavallero to Grimaldo, 13 June 1713, AHN, Estado leg.430².

seems to have been directly responsible for the monetary measures taken after the recovery of the kingdom. There were two main aims to be kept in view, firstly to ensure that only legal currency remained in circulation, and secondly to extract some profit from the minting of new coin. On 5 October 1707 Philip v ordered the chancery of Valencia to gather up all Allied coin, and to supervise the minting of a coinage equivalent to that of Castile. Between 1707 and 1713 Pedrajas supervised three such mintings, coin in gold, silver and copper being issued. Coins minted by the archduke, and those circulated by the Portuguese, were gathered up, re-stamped and reissued. The profit made by the crown from the last of the three mintings was 30 per cent, so that out of an issue of 100,000 pesos the government benefited to the extent of 30,000, as shown in the table drawn up by Pedrajas.

Probably the most interesting of all the casual sources of revenue was that from confiscations. Macanaz was the minister first appointed to superintend this question, and he found himself involved in administering confiscations throughout the realm but particularly also in San Felipe. No thoroughly systematic analysis of confiscations in Valencia is available: according to Macanaz, this was because of the confusion created by those who were in charge before his arrival. We can, nevertheless, draw up a tentative list of some of those who suffered loss of their property as a result of their rebellion (table 14).

The full confiscation lists for Valencia in 1713 indicate that somewhere in the region of a hundred persons were penalised by the loss of part or all of their property, which was worth 14,498 libras 14s 5d gross, and 4,340 libras 15s 11d net. Very little was obtained from the confiscations from noble families, on which so many obligations had to be met that little or nothing remained to the crown. Very much more, on the other hand, was realisable from the property of ordinary citizens: from those who suffered confiscations in Denia, for instance, bringing in a net sum of 800 libras annually to the treasury, or those in Alicante who equally contributed a net toral of 1,133 libras in confiscations.

The extent and significance of confiscations in Valencia may be appraised to some extent in the light of three memoranda drawn up by Macanaz in 1708.[47] The first of these statements gives an

---

[47] The three memoranda are enclosed with his letter of 13 June 1708 to Grimaldo, AHN, Estado leg.331.

TABLE 14. ANNUAL VALUE OF PRINCIPAL CONFISCATIONS IN
VALENCIA IN 1713[48] (IN LIBRAS)

	Annual income £ s. d.			Expenses £ s. d.			Obligations £ s. d.			Liquid to crown £ s. d.		
Conde del Casal, and wife	1516	0	0	1298	6	0	217	14	0			
Conde de Villafranqueza, and family	453	15	10	276	15	8	177	0	2			
Marqués de Boil, and son	2449	5	4	1416	6	7	1032	8	9			
Conde de Cervellón, and wife	3487	0	7	768	0	0	2719	0	7			
Marqués de la Casta	94	9	0				94	9	0			
Marqués de Villasor	100	0	0							100	0	0
Conde de Fuentes	8	11	11							8	11	11
D Luis Desplugues y March	1225	0	0	206	0	0				1019	0	0
Joseph Vicente Torres, and family	409	1	10	405	10	0				3	11	10
D Manuel Mercader	204	0	0	204	0	0						
D Pedro Valterra, and mother	274	3	6	274	3	6						
D Francisco Carroz	100	0	0	80	0	0				20	0	0
D Pedro Richauri	162	6	8							162	6	8

[48] 'Resumen Gen¹ del producto de los bienes confiscados y sequestrados existentes en la ciudad y Reyno de Valencia', AHN, Estado leg.2973. This list includes some of the chief ministers of the archduke's régime in Valencia. The figures for income should be compared with the following figures, for 1717, for the seven nobles named (source: AGS, Secretaría de Hacienda leg.972).

	Annual income	Expenses	Remainder
Conde del Casal	1480	889	591
Conde de Villafranqueza	931	498	433
Marqués de Boil	2411	1617	794
Conde de Cervellón	2017	716	1301
Marqués de la Casta	456	4	452
Marqués de Villasor	250	100	150
Conde de Fuentes	—	—	—

For purposes of converting Valencian currency into Castilian, 1 libra or pound = 15 reales = 1 peso.

account of the value of property restored to faithful adherents of the king in San Felipe, during the first six months of 1708: the total comes to 1,341,122 pesos, a figure which is not very illuminating unless set beside other data not yet available. The second statement lists the *mercedes* in the form of money granted by the king up to the middle of 1708. The most important recipients appear to have been the hospital in Valencia, which received a gift of 12,000 pesos, and the new hospital in San Felipe, which received an annuity of 23,000 pesos. A clearer picture of the monetary *mercedes* granted out of confiscations in Valencia is received if we examine the list of grants operative in 1717. At that date[49] annuities totalling 460,850 reales were being granted out of confiscations. Those benefiting from this included Toby Bourke, who was granted an annuity of 30,000 reales on 28 November 1707; the príncipe de Santo Buono, who received one of 105,000 on 25 July 1708; the duque de Atri, who received one of 135,000, the money being situated on the lands of the conde de Elda; and the Inquisition of Valencia, which received an annuity of 51,000 reales. Over and above these annuities, however, a lump sum of 15,164,238 reales was granted out of confiscations from the town of Játiva, in the form of non-recurring *mercedes*. The largest sum in this category, 70,000 ducats of *plata doble,* was paid on 18 January 1708 to the families of seventy-two French traders in Valencia, as compensation for their losses in the war. Other prominent recipients of these non-recurring *mercedes* included the duque de Cansano, 20,000 ducats; the marqués de Santelmo, 20,000; the marqués de Argensola, 12,000; Don Francisco Caetano y Aragón, 12,000; the marqués de Sardeñola, 15,000; and Macanaz, 15,000. Italian, Irish and other non-peninsular soldiers serving Philip v appear prominently in the list.

The third of Macanaz's three memoranda gives details of the lands granted by the king as *mercedes*. From 18 January to 13 June 1708 the crown redistributed 15,058,350 reales worth of land in Valencia. A large proportion of this went to Italian nobles who had been dispossessed of their lands in Italy for their loyalty to Philip v. Nobles receiving land included the marqués de Camporeal, with 27,500 pesos worth; while the duque de Cansano was due to receive 27,500 pesos, the marqués Pisanelli 13,750 pesos, and the marqués de Sardeñola 20,625 pesos. Macanaz

49 Details from AGS, Secretaría de Hacienda leg.972.

himself received 20,625 pesos of land, and Bourke received 43,585 pesos. French traders were granted land worth 137,500 pesos. Irish soldiers of fortune also received their share, as in the case of Tom Cavanagh and Walter Stapleton, who each received land worth 5,500 pesos. The greatest of the soldiers of fortune serving in Spain, James FitzJames, duke of Berwick, was granted the towns of Liria and Jérica, with ownership of all confiscated property therein, and the title of the former town.

These few details tend to indicate that confiscations in Valencia were very limited in extent. The small total for revenue from this source in 1713, the unassuming figure for *mercedes* in 1717, and the moderate land grants recorded for 1708, the year when in fact most assignations from confiscations were made, show that the crown was not excessively punitive in its chastisement of rebels. As late as 1722, it was estimated that income from confiscations in Valencia totalled only 207,690 reales, leaving the small sum of 71,610 reales liquid to the Hacienda.[50] The conquest of Valencia therefore seems to have been attended by no wholesale confiscations or annexations of property. If the crown extended its authority, it was through fiscal and jurisdictional measures, not through the seizure of land or goods. Nor did the crown take the opportunity to redistribute the property of traitors among more faithful adherents. The only extensive changes in landownership occurred in the territory of Játiva-San Felipe. Elsewhere the government could hardly penalise whole cities or families for the sins of a few. Even those lands that were confiscated were often returned to their owners later, particularly when these were prominent nobles: examples of this will be touched on in a later chapter. On the whole, then, the war led to no significant changes in the social or economic structure of Valencia.

One distinguished victim of confiscations should be discussed here. Fray Antonio Folch de Cardona, archbishop of Valencia, fled from his see in 1710, as we have already seen.[51] On being approached about the archbishop's property, Father Robinet advised in favour of its sequestration, which was accordingly decreed on 21 November 1710. The unhappy prelate died in

[50] 'Reyno de Valencia. Contaduría General de Bienes Confiscados', 17 Sept. 1722, AGS, Secretaría de Hacienda leg.972.

[51] Documentation in this paragraph is from AGS, Secretaría de Hacienda leg.65, which includes a 1725 'Resumen del producto de la Mitra de Valencia segun las Relaciones remitidas por la Intendencia de aquel Reyno con carta de 7 agosto 1725'.

exile in Vienna on 21 July 1724. During the intervening period the Spanish government enjoyed the revenues from his vacant see. According to a statement drawn up by the intendant of Valencia in 1725, the revenue received by the crown from November 1710 to July 1724 came to a total of 929,952 libras 16 sueldos (or 13,949,292 reales in Castilian money). This was an average of about a million reales each year.

The administration of confiscations, after the departure of Macanaz from Valencia, was assigned to Juan Fernández de Caceres for a while,[52] and then to Don Damián Cerdá. The archiepiscopal confiscations, however, were kept out of Cerdá's hands and retained in those of Pedrajas. It might be thought that the *mercedes* granted by the king were full and free gifts. Though this was the theory, in practice Philip reserved the right to tax the gifts he had made. Accordingly, in September 1709 the king decreed a tax of 80 per cent on the value of all confiscations gifted in Valencia. One of the recipients of *mercedes*, Toby Bourke, reacted in the following way in a letter to Torcy:[53]

A decree has been issued enjoining all those to whom the king of Spain has given confiscated lands in the kingdom of Valencia, to pay 80 per cent of the fruit of those lands. This measure will reduce to beggary numerous officers and many widows and orphans whose fathers and husbands died in this war in the service of the Catholic King. No benefit will come of it, for those to whom the lands, which were deserted and left fallow, were given, will not for several years be able to recover the money which they have used for cultivation and renovation. And after all these expenses, they must give one half of the fruits to the labourer who works the lands, and are required to pay the 80 per cent out of the other half, without deducting costs. . . . Such are the expedients that the *junta de medios* [committee of means] proposes to the Catholic King in order to pay the troops, but one cannot expect better from a bunch of civil servants [*togados*] . . . Through this decree I stand to lose all that the king of Spain has given me in confiscations.

A month later Bourke informed Torcy that 'the new proprietors refuse to till or sow their lands for the coming year',[54] so as to have nothing with which to pay the tax. In these circumstances the returns were bound to be disappointing. Don Rodrigo de

[52] Damián Cerdá to Mejorada, 22 July 1711, AHN, Estado leg.400.
[53] Bourke to Torcy, 21 Oct. 1709, AE Corr. Pol. (Esp.), 193 f.160.
[54] *Ibid.*, 3 Nov. 1709, *ibid.*, f.226.

Cepeda, *oidor* of the chancery, who was given the task of administering the imposition, reported in February 1711 that only 360,660
reales had so far been received in the war treasury.[55] The president
of the Hacienda, the marqués de Campoflorido, thereupon advised
the king to reduce the rate of the tax to 60 per cent, since the
higher rate was self-defeating.[56] It was at this rate that it brought
in 22,000 pesos to the treasury of Valencia in 1713.

The imposition levied for salaries of governors was applied
to the military governors of Valencia, Alcira, Denia, Orihuela,
Peñiscola, Morella, Alcoy, Castellón, San Felipe, Jijona, Cofrentes
and Montesa. The tax was collected throughout the realm. Its
total value was small compared with that of the next tax to be
discussed here, the annual extraordinary imposition whose proceeds were meant to cover the cost of winter-quartering the army
in Valencia. This imposition was the most burdensome of all
the new taxes payable by the kingdom. It was not formally levied
in 1707 and 1708, when alternative arrangements were made. On
15 May 1707, for example, Berwick informed the Valencian
authorities that the whole realm was to contribute to a free gift
of 50,000 doblones (three million reales). This sum was duly
paid. A similar sum seems to have been demanded in 1708, to
cover the costs of the military occupation, but I have not encountered any detail of the figure involved.[57] For the rest of the
war, the winter-quarter levy was intended to cover troop expenses for an average of six months. For the winter of 1709–10,
Francisco Caetano y Aragón ordered the levy to be made on all
settlements of over eight houses, at a rate of fifteen reales per
month. The figure given for the total number of households
or *vecinos* liable to the tax was 59,427, and the estimated income
to be expected was 1,333,860 reales a month.[58] In fact, the actual
revenue collected in the Tesorería Mayor at Madrid for the period
1 November 1709 to 30 April 1710 seems to have amounted to
only 6,000,589 reales, in addition to contributions in the form of
grain.[59] This represents even less than the sum expected for five

[55] Cepeda to Grimaldo, 18 Feb. 1711, AHN, Estado leg.412.
[56] Campoflorido to Grimaldo, 24 Feb. 1711, *ibid.*
[57] We find the city of Valencia, in a letter of 8 Jan. 1708 to Berwick, AHN,
Estado leg.345, forwarding the sum of 170,000 pesos 'por este año por razon del
encabezamiento y su particular contribuzion'. The sum may well have been part
of the 1708 contribution.
[58] Order of 26 Oct. 1709 by Caetano y Aragón, AHN, Estado leg.375.
[59] AGS, Tribunal Mayor de Cuentas leg.1881.

months of winter-quartering. The winter-quarter levy of 1710-1, brought in as little as in the previous year. This time the number of *vecinos* taxed was 54,740, but the revenue at the same rate of imposition, came to 7,389,900 reales.[60] The authorities now began to have serious doubts about the rate as well as the manner of imposition of this tax. It was clear that many towns could not afford to pay the required rate, and that some concessions would have to be made in order to collect the estimated amounts. Reform was, however, postponed for nearly five years.

The imposition levied in 1711-2 was for a five-month period only, from November to the end of the following March. The estimated revenue was to be somewhere between eight and nine million reales,[61] but by the middle of March only about five and a half million had been received. There is no definite indication as to whether the balance of the tax was eventually collected. Financial straits made it necessary to impose the next levy, the fourth in the series, for a period of seven months, from the beginning of October 1712 to the end of April 1713. The revenue expected was 11,531,200 reales.[62] For the imposition in 1713-4 no details are available. The sixth levy suffered by Valencia was for the six months from September 1714 to February 1715. The rate of imposition was to be ten pesos or 150 reales per *vecino*. Since the total income was expected to be 638,300 pesos or 9,574,500 reales, it may be surmised that the number of tax-paying *vecinos* was put at 63,830.[63]

The next imposition to be levied in Valencia took on a new character, and must therefore be discussed separately from the levies made for purposes of winter-quartering. The need for systematisation of taxation had been felt ever since the failure of the Castilian taxes to strike root in Valencia. There now appeared to be at least three tax systems in existence, each of

---

[60] AHN, Estado leg.430¹, memoir on the *cuartel de invierno*. The figure is given as 492,660 pesos.

[61] Cavallero to Grimaldo, 15 Mar. 1712, AHN Estado leg.417, in a statement of the 'Repartimiento del quartel de Ibierno deste año de 1712', puts the estimated revenue at 9,296,100. Later, however, in a memoir enclosed with his letter of 13 June 1713 to Grimaldo, *ibid.*, leg.430², Cavallero estimated the yield as 8,648,400 reales, a figure which accords with that of 8,640,000 given in Canga Argüelles, *Diccionario de Hacienda*, vol. 2, p. 127.

[62] AHN, Estado leg.430², AGS, Guerra Moderna leg.2356 f.21.

[63] Statement included in letter of Cavallero to Grimaldo, 1 Oct. 1715, AGS, Guerra Moderna leg.1612.

them requiring separate administration: first, there were the military impositions; secondly, there were the civil taxes; and thirdly, there were the royal monopolies. With the appointment of an intendant after 1711, and the possibility that this might help to unify the administration of Valencia, hopes arose that some simplification of the tax structure might follow. Macanaz in 1713 echoed these hopes when he presented his memoir on the government of the crown of Aragon to the king. His words speak for themselves:[64]

The *alcabalas* and *cientos* have not fared well since their introduction for lack of substance in the towns, and because of this there has been imposed by way of winter-quartering a large contribution which has regularly exceeded 500,000 pesos, and for which a check has been made on the state of the towns, their produce, trade and number of vecinos, so that the levy has become a kind of poll-tax [*capitación*]. It would be fitting if in future the *alcabalas* and *cientos* were abolished, and in their place were substituted a tax by the name of poll-tax or *taille* or maintenance levy [*tributo y alojamiento*], equivalent not only to what the *alcabalas* and *cientos* are worth but also to the difference in value between their import and that of the winter-quartering. This sort of tribute is easy to put into practice . . . and does not need any new tax.

Here then for the first time is a statement of a plan that was to be carried out after the expulsion of Macanaz from Spain. *Arbitristas* before him had long suggested the substitution of one for many taxes. The originality of Macanaz's suggestion lay in his proposal to suspend the operation of Castilian taxes in Valencia, and to introduce in their place a single tax that was to be their equal in value.

When the alteration eventually came, it was effected so informally as to be unremarkable. The author of the measure remains unknown. It may well have been Macanaz, who had been dismissed from office only a month previously, but of this there is no proof. On 4 March 1715 it was decided that the levy in Valencia for that year be equivalent to, and a substitute for, the Castilian taxes in existence. A subsequent order of 21 March decided that the income from this 'equivalent' tax should be used only for military purposes.[65] From this time the *equivalente,* as it was known in Valencia, came into existence. It marked no obvious new departure since, like the winter-quartering levy, it was

[64] *Regalías,* pp. 12–13.
[65] Canga Argüelles, vol. 1, p. 267. Ct. Carrera Pujal, vol. 5, p. 448, who says, wrongly I believe, that the *equivalente* was introduced in 1714.

merely compensating for the deficiencies of the Castilian taxes in the realm. In practice, however, the *equivalente* set an important precedent to be followed subsequently by both Aragon and Catalonia. For 1716, the first year in which the tax was imposed, no details of its rate or collection are available. If we take the 1717 rate as a guide, however, we can probably presume that in 1716, as in 1717,[66] the sum levied was ten million reales. The repartition of this ten million among the thirteen *partidos* of Valencia in 1717 was as follows:

gobernaciones	libras valencianas
Valencia	203,439 : 13 : 4
Alcira	59,581
Denia	62,193
San Felipe	62,388
Montesa	15,239
Cofrentes	7,478
Elche	26,230
Alicante	22,920
Orihuela	44,676
Castellón de la Plana	45,921
Peñiscola	40,411
Morella	40,344
Alcoy	35,846
Total	666,666 : 13 : 4

This table bears comparison with one reproduced on a previous page giving the global population of Valencia. Its publication by Cavallero in November 1716 brought protests from Valencia. On 2 February the *procuradores* or representatives of the towns of Valencia issued a printed memorial asking for a lowering of the rate of the *equivalente*.[67] In the memorial they stated that they had sent two protests to the intendant in December, and were now appealing to the king. Economic difficulties in the province, they said, had made even the payment of standard taxes impossible. Payment of *alcabalas* had been remitted in 1708 for a period of

---

[66] The 'repartimiento del million de excudos de vellon por el equivalente de rentas y derechos provinciales para el año proximo de 1717' is detailed in the letter of Cavallero to Miguel Fernández Durán, 29 Dec. 1716, AGS, Guerra Moderna leg.1617.

[67] AGS, Secretaría de Estado leg.7840.

eight months, several people had been granted remissions up to
1710, and in 1716 only one half of the *equivalente* due had in fact
been collected. In these circumstances, the *procuradores* asked for
suspension of the *equivalente* in 1717 and for remission of that
still due for 1716. Though this request was not granted, a substantial concession was made by the government, in that the rate
of the imposition was ordered to be reduced by 40 per cent. Even
with the reduction, moderation had to be exercised in administering the tax if adequate returns were to be realised. As Luis
Antonio Mergelina, who replaced Cavallero as intendant of
Valencia in January 1718, observed of the *equivalente* to his
superiors: 'the prudence I have exercised is such that its current
rate does not come to half what the *alcabalas* could produce in a
benign administration.' The rate envisaged by Mergelina for the
equivalente of 1718, 7,800,000 reales,[68] was no doubt a moderate
one, but subsequent experience was to cause even this demand to
be reduced. For the rest of the reign the *equivalente* remained the
principal source of royal revenue in Valencia. The only notable
change in the tax system at this period occurred with the royal
decree of 26 October 1718[69] which suppressed throughout
Valencia all the customs duties known as *derechos antiguos,* and
ordered the continuation only of the *derechos nuevos.* By 1725, to
select an arbitrary date, the kingdom of Valencia was contributing 13,238,884 reales annually to the Hacienda. This was made
up as follows:[70]

Credit receipts	21,871
Equivalente for 1724	7,750,000
Customs	2,084,536
Salinas	665,210
Tobacco	2,359,113
Cloths	150,194
Papel sellado	207,960
Total	13,238,884 reales

[68] Mergelina to Fernández Durán, 1 Mar. 1718, AGS, Guerra Moderna leg.1629,
gives estimates for the *equivalente* of 1718. Canga Argüelles, vol. 1, p. 267, gives the
figure of 7,762, 800 reales for the imposition of 1718.
[69] Hacienda, Ordenes Generales de Rentas, vol. 3, ff.384–5. Only a proportion of
this sum reached the royal treasury, the balance being spent in Valencia.
[70] AGS, Guerra Moderna leg.2362.

The Bourbon achievement in Valencia, though documented here principally in the field of finance, of course went far beyond this. The whole constitutional and fiscal autonomy of the realm was broken down. The institutional changes within the realm were not, however, as far-reaching as the alterations that took place in commercial life. The customs barriers between the different kingdoms of the peninsula were an obvious hindrance to commercial advance, however profitable they may have been to regional exchequers. On 25 January 1708, therefore, the king decreed the abolition of the so-called *puertos secos*, a customs due of about 16 per cent, on Valencia's border with Castile and Aragon, and declared that all commerce should be regulated on an equal and free basis. A later decree of 14 August 1711 reduced the Valencia port customs duties from 22½ to 15 per cent. When the war was over and Catalonia had been reduced to obedience, the king reissued the decree on 19 November 1714, in the following terms:[71]

Since it is my principal concern to contribute as much as I can to the common good of my subjects and especially to that which promotes the liberty and growth of trade between the provinces, so that when some are flourishing they may succour the needs of others, aiding each other without the impediments and inconveniences experienced in the past; I have resolved that the *puerto secos* between Castile, Aragon, Valencia and Catalonia be totally abolished, and that those two kingdoms and the principality be considered as provinces united to Castile, with trade continuing between them freely and without any impediment.

Writing towards the end of the reign of Philip v, the *arbitrista* Bernardo de Ulloa saw in this decree a measure which signally benefited the industry and trade of Valencia.

Through the decision of His Majesty to abolish the *puerto secos* between Castile and Valencia [wrote Ulloa], not only has there occurred an abundant and cheap supply of bread and meat, but also the free exit to Castile and Andalucia of rice, fruits and cloths, as a result of which the factory-looms have increased in number.[72]

Perhaps the most significant political step taken by the monarchy, however, was the decision to equalise the coinage of Castile and Valencia. On 22 August 1707 the council of Castile ordered

---

[71] Hacienda, Ordenes Generales de Rentas, vol. 2, f.423.

[72] *Restablecimiento de las Fábricas y Comercio español* (2 vols), Madrid, 1740, vol. 1, p. 123.

a new *junta* to be set up to examine this question. The principal members appointed to the new body were the Valencian administrators Macanaz, Cavallero, Puente and Cepeda.[73] On 5 October that year the king ordered the Valencian chancery to gather up all Allied coin still in circulation, and to mint new money conforming to the weight and content of Castilian coinage.[74] This directive appears not to have been put into practice until 1718, when coins were struck simultaneously in Aragon, Catalonia, Valencia and Castile.[75] After this date unity of coinage confirmed the transformation of the ancient kingdom of Valencia into a province of the Spanish crown.

It would be pointless to pretend that the Valencians were pleased with their new status. Very few of the middle or upper urban classes had been rebels, and the realm as a whole had been more loyal than seditious. Yet it was now occupied by a foreign army, subjected to foreign laws, forced to obey foreign officials and to use a foreign currency. The discontent and resentment aroused by the suppression of the *fueros*, or rather by the excuse given for the suppression, were never to be allayed. In February 1714 we find the new governor of Valencia, the marqués de Villadarias, reporting to Grimaldo that 'the obstinate demand of the Catalans for the restoration of their *fueros* finds acceptance in the kingdom of Valencia, whose people clamour with equal persistence for their privileges'.[76] The occupying army was not apparently a large one. According to a contemporary Valencian, the writer Isidro Planes, the Bourbon troops in the realm in 1712 totalled no more than 16,453, consisting of 6,191 cavalry and 10,262 infantry.[77] But though the kingdom may not have been physically repressed, the heavy hand of Castile lay over every aspect of public life. The ministers of the king, nearly all of them Castilians, directed everyday affairs with a thoroughness and efficiency unknown before 1707. 'God look with merciful eyes on this kingdom and deliver us from such evil ministers,' wrote

[73] Mateu y Llopis, *Aportación a la Historia Monetaria*, p. 89.
[74] *Ibid.*, p. 79.
[75] Hamilton, *War and Prices*, p. 42.
[76] Villadarias to Grimaldo, 19 Feb. 1714, AHN, Estado, leg.456.
[77] 'Sucessos fatales de esta Ciudad y Reyno de Valencia; o Puntual Diario de lo sucedido en los años de el Señor de 1712–1715', BUV, MS 456 f.12 vo. This is only the fourth volume of this valuable work by Planes; the other volumes are missing.

Planes in one commentary on the activities of Rodrigo Cavallero.[78] Yet Cavallero was one of the most honest and selfless of all the officials called to serve in Valencia. The complaints may have been justified more with respect to the inevitable high-handedness of administrators in a hostile country.

Steps were taken to assure the realm against further disorders. With a few deliberate exceptions, the whole population was disarmed. To make up for this enforced defencelessness, regiments of militia were formed by a regulation issued on 28 September 1711.[79] Their primary duty was to guard the coastline, from which the most serious threat was likely to come. The Allied fleet was still active, and pirates were beginning their depredations. In all this activity the authorities seem to have underestimated the power of the common people to reassert themselves. Then in June 1715 Don Sancho de Echevarría, the governor of Peñiscola, a city honoured by the king for its fidelity, reported increased dissatisfaction among his people.[80] The trouble was caused by excessive taxes. When Echevarría heard the complaints, he proceeded to levy a reduced rate of tax on the grain harvest. This was not enough for some peasants, and the day after Echevarría's measure a man got up publicly to say that the people would pay only at gun-point. When the governor ordered his arrest, a riot broke out in the city. The populace proceeded to take over the whole of Peñiscola, threatening death to all the town councillors and the army officers. At least one councillor was killed in the disturbances. In a successful attempt to pacify the rioters, the governor went out to them and promised, in the king's name, pardon for their actions and freedom from current taxes. This seems to have brought the disturbances to an end. Fearful of the possibility that other similar events might recur in a realm so recently pacified by royal troops, the government took a soft line. The king decided to keep the promises made in his name, until such time as the ringleaders in Peñiscola could be singled out and punished. The crisis passed, and Valencia remained quiescent.

[78] *Ibid.*, f.13 vo.
[79] BUV, MS 803 f.25: 'Reglamento de las Milicias del Reino de Valencia.'
[80] Details on Peñiscola are from the section in AGS, Guerra Moderna leg.1813, on 'el tumulto de Peñiscola, Junio de 1715'.

13   The Reform of Aragon

The recovery of Aragon followed almost automatically from the royalist victory at Almansa. The duc d'Orléans entered Saragossa on 26 May 1707 and proceeded to take over government of the city and of the realm. On 14 November the city of Lérida capitulated to royal forces, thereby securing the Catalan frontier. The decree abolishing the *fueros* laid the basis for the exercise of Philip v's authority, and almost the first steps taken by the new rulers of Aragon were directed towards the raising of taxes, finance being the most pressing problem. A few administrative changes were effected, but the real effort was expended on the military campaigns. No radical steps were taken to establish royal authority in 1707. The changes that were instituted were confined mainly to the city of Saragossa. The failure to proceed further may have been partly caused by a lack of suitable personnel, since the most important officials, like Macanaz, had been sent to Valencia.

On the entry of Orléans, no move was made to introduce any administrative innovations. In effect, the duke simply confirmed the old government of the country, in accordance with a *consulta* of the council of Aragon issued on 4 June, with which Philip v concurred.[1] Eight deputies were accordingly nominated, two from each of the four estates of the realm, and in addition some secretarial officials were appointed. The nomination was clearly done without any proper consultation, for the archbishop of Saragossa immediately pointed out that of the eight named, no less than five were rebels who had now fled to Catalonia. The three loyal deputies, the baron de Letosa, Don Bruno la Balsa, and

[1] 'Resumen de las resoluciones q. ultimam^te se ha ser^do S.M. tomar tocante al nuevo gobierno de Aragon', no date, but certainly June 1707: AHN, Consejos suprimidos leg.18190.

M

Don Gaspar de Segovia, were consequently supplemented by five more nominees. In the city of Saragossa there were likewise no changes made. The council of Aragon, with the king's approval, decided that the five *jurados* of the city should continue in office with all their administrative personnel, but that no decision should be taken about the thirty city councillors. Without waiting for Philip's decision, Orléans on his own initiative not only nominated five new *jurados*, but also arranged for the continuation in office of the councillors and other minor officials of the city, a *fait accompli* which the government had to accept. All other senior officials, including the justiciar and the *zalmedina* (or *corregidor*), were confirmed in office.

Orléans' personal part in nominating the governing officials of Aragon may help to explain his subsequent opposition to the repeal of the *fueros*. When the decree of 29 June was issued it automatically abolished the whole constitution of Aragon, and with it much of the goodwill Orléans had won in that realm. The imposition of new taxes, to be discussed below, was probably the most unpopular of all the new measures. The most visible sign of Castilian rule, however, was the establishment that year, 1707, of a chancery to administer justice in Aragon. This body, modelled on the chanceries of Castile, was similar in form to that set up at the same date in Valencia.[2] Two other important steps in the city of Saragossa itself marked the initiation of the new system. On 27 August a *corregidor* on the Castilian pattern was appointed to the Aragonese capital. The nominee was Juan Gerónimo de Blancas, at the time a prisoner in Barcelona. A temporary replacement in the person of the conde de Montemar, military commander of the city, carried out the functions of office until Blancas was freed in November 1712 and took up his post.[3] Then on 15 December 1707 a royal order created a new *ayuntamiento* or city council. Twenty-four councillors or *regidores* were named, and it was ordered 'that the government, practice and style used heretofore in the city are to cease, and there are to be established in it the same rules, without any variation, as are observed and kept in the other realms of Castile'.[4]

[2] Macanaz, *Regalías*, p. 21.

[3] *Recopilación de todas las cédulas y órdenes reales que desde el año 1708 se han dirigido a la Ciudad de Zaragoza*, Saragossa, 1730, pp. 32–3, 36–7. I have consulted the copy of this work in the Astorga Collection of the NLS.

[4] *Ibid.*, pp. 1–2. I have been unable to consult detailed sources for changes in

On 25 February 1708 Berwick arrived in Saragossa to help with the pacification of the realm, and left shortly after in March to go to France. No measures of any importance seem to have been taken this year apart from a reorganisation, decreed on 30 November, of the city government of Saragossa.[5] Extensive fiscal changes occurred, but the complete overhaul of the administrative system had to wait till after the Bourbon victory at Villaviciosa on 10 December 1710, which reversed Philip's earlier defeat at Saragossa on 20 August the same year. The delay in the reorganisation of Aragon, despite the suppression of the *fueros* in 1707, is proved by the continuation in office of Don Antonio Gabin, last justiciar of Aragon, who was issuing orders in this capacity as late as November 1710.[6]

After the defeat at Saragossa, Melchor de Macanaz had been entrusted by Philip v with the task of ensuring food supplies for the retreating army.[7] Macanaz's invaluable work in Valencia and his wide administrative experience, made him the obvious choice for the tasks ahead in Aragon. On 1 February 1711 a royal order nominated him to control the finances of that realm,[8] and on 11 February he was named intendant general of Aragon.[9] On 3 April a royal decree reformed the whole administrative structure of the realm from top to bottom. The importance of this measure, which was addressed in the first instance to the principe de Tsercla̓es Tilly, commander of the troops in Aragon, merits a lengthy quotation of the text:[10]

I have decided that for the moment and as a temporary measure, there should be in this realm of Aragon a commandant general, to whose care should fall its military, political, economic and administrative government, wherefore I have been pleased to elect and nominate you,

---

Saragossa, such as the *Compendio de las Reales Cédulas, Cartas y Provisiones dirigidas a la Ciudad de Zaragoza desde el año de 1707 haste el de 1713*, of Diego Franca de Villalba, of which there is apparently a copy in the University of Saragossa.

[5] Carrera Pujal, *Historia de la Economía Española*, vol. 5, p. 361.

[6] See the note on 'El último Justicia de Aragón en 1710', in the *Boletín de la Real Academia de la Historia*, XIV (1889), p. 433.

[7] *Regalías*, p. xv.

[8] 'Minuta del Despacho', dated Feb. 1711, AHN, Estado leg.410[1]. Macanaz was appointed 'por Ministro de Finanzas en el Reyno de Aragon para que desde primero deeste presente mes, corra a buestra direczion la Administrazion, venefizio y cobranza de todas las que antes administraba D. Thomas Moreno Pacheco'.

[9] *Regalías*, p. 201.

[10] I quote from the copy in AE Corr. Pol. (Esp.), 211 f.156.

the Principe Tserclaës de Tilly. At the same time I have decided that there be an audiencia, with two chambers, one for civil matters, with four ministers; and the other for criminal matters; together with a fiscal, who would assist in both chambers; and the necessary subordinates. And that there also be a regent to rule this audiencia, which I wish to be composed of persons chosen by me without restriction of province, country or origin; and in consequence of this I nominate as regent of this audiencia Don Francisco de Aperregui, the most senior *oidor* of the council of Navarre; for the civil chamber, Don Manuel de Fuentes y Peralta, Don Joseph de Castro y Azaujo, Don Gil Custudio de Lissa y Guebara, and Don Jaime Ric y Veyan; and for the criminal chamber, Don Agustín de Montiano, Don Lorenzo de Medina, Don Diego de Barbastro, Don Ignacio de Segovia, and Don Joseph Agustín Camargo; and as fiscal, Don Joseph Rodrigo y Villalpando. In the criminal chamber, pleas are to be judged and determined according to the custom and laws of Castile . . . and in the civil chamber, civil pleas are to be judged according to the municipal laws of this realm of Aragon, since it is my will that the said municipal laws be observed for all cases between private individuals. [And in those cases] where I intervene against one of my subjects . . . judgment is to be . . . according to the laws of Castile. The commandant general of the realm is to preside over the said audiencia. Appeals in the third instance, of both civil and criminal cases, are to be allowed to the council of Castile. [Salaries] are to be paid in the way they were before 1705.

For the levy, administration and collection of all that belongs to the royal revenue, there is to be an administrator, for which I have nominated Don Melchor Macanaz. A chamber is to be established with the name of the junta, or tribunal, of the Royal Exchequer. [*Junta, o Tribunal del Real Erario.* Eight persons were to compose this tribunal]: two from the clergy, of whom one should be a bishop, abbot or *comendador*, and the other a canon of one of the churches of the realm; two from the upper nobility; two from the gentry estate [*estado de Hijosdalgo*], and two citizens of Saragossa or another of the cities in the realm. [The bishop of Huesca was named as one of the ecclesiastical members].

I have also resolved that this kingdom be divided into districts or *partidos*, and that in each there should be a military governor, whom I shall nominate, subordinate in all matters to the commandant general; and that the problems and measures arising in matters of government be communicated to me through the commandant general and the governors of the districts, each of whom has to care for the political and economic government of his district; and that appeals in these matters should be allowed to the council of war.

[The salaries of the commandant general and the governors were to come from the Tesorería Mayor de la Guerra, but each district in Aragon was to pay a special half-yearly tax towards this, which would be entered in the said Tesorería].

Touching the municipal government of the cities, towns and places of this realm, the election and nomination of justices, judges and their subordinates is my responsibility, depending on the number of persons available; the same applies to the nomination of the *corregidor* or *alcalde* and his subordinates, who, in the exercise of their office and in the administration of justice, are to observe the same rules and laws as are stated and regulated for the two chambers of the audiencia.

In what touches the Church, I have no intention of prejudicing it, nor on the other hand of diminishing my *regalías* in any way. I therefore resolve that all ecclesiastical matters, and any rights of the crown [*regalías*], which were formerly administered by the justiciar of Aragon and his court, shall hereafter be administered by the regent and ministers of the audiencia, or by persons whom I may in future deputise for this.

From this decree it will be seen that the chancery set up in 1707 had now been altered to an audiencia, a relative reduction in status. At the same time, Macanaz's powers as intendant had been implicitly suspended, and he was now to share control of the financial administration with a special tribunal.

Macanaz strongly resented the duty of conferring with a tribunal which might not agree with his policies, and decided to ignore its existence, with the result that in May the ministers of the *Junta del Real Erario* sent a petition to Philip v, complaining that 'the duties of this office, such as tax-farming, commissioning, examination of frauds, and others, are being exercised privately by Don Melchor Macanaz, without the tribunal receiving any business in which the ministers Your Majesty has appointed may employ themselves'.[11] The next month Tserclaës Tilly himself wrote to support the ministers of the tribunal, whose complaints were justified by the terms of the decree of 3 April.[12] Since it was obvious that Macanaz was exceeding his powers, the king issued a resolution on 26 June, ordering the 3 April decree to be observed without any modification. According to his own account, written many years later, Macanaz considered that the king's resolution 'left me without the slightest room for movement,

---

[11] AHN, Estado leg.416¹.
[12] Tserclaës Tilly to Grimaldo, 23 June 1711, *ibid.*

whereas I had thought that I would have all the authority of an intendant, and they (the ministers) would be concerned only with the taxation'.[13] On 28 June he wrote a long and argumentative letter[14] to the king's secretary, Grimaldo, complaining that

the decree of the 26th of this month lays down that the minister who controls finances is entitled only to administer and to collect the taxes; but without jurisdiction, which has to be exercised by the *Junta del Real Erario*; but the point arises that neither in the twenty-one provinces of Castile nor in the kingdom of Valencia is there an administrator general who does not have first instance for the remedy of frauds and other crimes touching good administration.

With this letter Macanaz sent a memoir of 'Reflections on the decree which His Majesty issued at Corella on the 26th of this month, on the finances of Aragon and their jurisdiction'. A week later, still bitter at the turn of events, he wrote to tell Grimaldo that the tribunal had now commenced operating according to the terms of the decree of 26 June:

So that I do not consume my salary in idleness [he ended], it would be as well for His Majesty to see if there is anywhere else that I can be of more use to his service.

The tribunal, in other words, had now usurped his functions, 'without leaving me anything to do'.[15]

This threat to resign from his duties in Aragon brought a quick reaction from Madrid. A decision on the dispute was sought from the marqués de Campoflorido, at the time president of the Hacienda. Well aware of Macanaz's brilliant services to the crown, Campoflorido could ill afford to lose his talents. He therefore directed Grimaldo to 'tell him to continue in the direction of the finances there with the same powers and jurisdiction as are held by the superintendants of finance in Castile'.[16] The king accordingly issued a decision in favour of Macanaz on 3 August. When Philip sent the text of his decree to the members of the tribunal, they refused to accept it as it stood. Macanaz, in an attempt to justify the king's new decision, drew up a memoir 'to resolve the objections that some ministers of the *Real Erario*

[13] *Discurso jurídico, histórico*, in *Regalías*, p. 184.
[14] AHN, Estado leg.416¹; also printed in *Regalías*, p. 185.
[15] Macanaz to Grimaldo, 5 July 1711, AHN, Estado leg.416¹.
[16] Campoflorido to Grimaldo, 24 July 1711, *ibid*.

have raised against His Majesty's decision'.[17] In view, however, of the very firm regalist and anti-*fuero* viewpoint taken by Macanaz, the ministers were hardly mollified. Instead, they decided to dissolve the tribunal voluntarily, in protest. As Macanaz put it, 'they resolved to stay at home and not to meet again, leaving me, as intendant general, to take care of everything; which I did without much difficulty'.[18]

The administrative history of Aragon under the new Bourbon régime remains a little-known subject. It is safe to assume, at least during the period of Macanaz's office, that the intendant was the key to the most important developments in the realm, for the simple reason that financial affairs were the chief preoccupation of the Castilian government. Moreover, as Macanaz claims, Philip v 'gave him *carte blanche* to put into effect what he thought most convenient for the service of His Majesty',[19] and it is unlikely that he was moderate in his exercise of authority.

A short digression on Macanaz is in place here. In September 1711 he was offered the post of president of the Hacienda, to replace Campoflorido, but was unwilling to take up the task of overhauling the finances at such a critical moment in the war. Campoflorido remained in the post, and Bergeyck took over the superintendance of the finances. When Bergeyck eventually left the country in January 1712 to go to Utrecht as plenipotentiary for Spain, Macanaz was offered his post, but was reluctant to accept responsibility for some extraordinary taxation proposed by the government, and returned to Aragon. Control of the finances was assumed by the new president of the Hacienda, Lorenzo Armengual, titular bishop of Gironda and former auxiliary to the archbishop of Saragossa.[20] It was in the summer of 1712 that Macanaz was called to Madrid on a delicate mission. On 22 April 1709 Philip v had expelled the papal nuncio from Spain and broken off diplomatic relations with Rome, because of the support given by the pope to the archduke. With the approach of peace, negotiations were opened through the papal nuncio in Paris, Cardinal Aldobrandi, and it was suggested that Macanaz

[17] This memoir is enclosed in the letter from Macanaz to Grimaldo, 16 Aug. 1711, *ibid*.

[18] *Regalías*, p. 198.

[19] *Ibid.*, p. xvi.

[20] *Ibid.*, p. xvii. At the end of the war Armengual was made bishop of Cadiz.

should be sent as the Spanish representative. He arrived in Madrid on 22 June 1712 but decided not to accept the mission, and his place was taken by one of the members of the audiencia of Saragossa, José Rodrigo Villalpando, later to become marqués de Compuesta. Philip wished to keep Macanaz in the capital, and appointed him fiscal general of the council of Castile, a post equivalent to that of attorney general of the crown.

In Aragon, his duties as intendant were taken over by Balthasar Patiño, marqués de Castelar, with effect from 1 July 1713. The duties of Castelar at this period were principally military, and it was only on 14 August 1718 that his post as intendant was supplemented by that of *corregidor* of Saragossa, to bring his functions into line with those of the other intendants in Spain. Macanaz, during his short tenure of power, and Castelar, during a much longer term of office, together consolidated the exercise of the crown's authority in the kingdom of Aragon. The sum total of administrative and institutional change seems, however, to have been very little. The new officials in Aragon, including the intendant and the personnel of the audiencia, appear to have served rather to facilitate Castilian control over the affairs of the province, than to reform and centralise the administration. Perhaps the most significant constitutional result of the suppression of the *fueros* was the demise of the cortes of Aragon, a subject which is touched on in the final chapter. But the Aragonese municipalities (with the exception of Saragossa), the Church, the structure of land and society, continued largely unchanged. The particular attention paid both in Aragon and Valencia to the reform of the chanceries shows that the king was concerned to consolidate his jurisdiction in these realms. Beyond that, however, the only sector to feel the full weight of innovation was that of public finance.

The emphasis on finance was to be expected in view of the needs of the monarchy and the demands of war. Before 1707 not a penny reached the crown from Aragon, and this in spite of the fact that the crown had substantial fiscal rights in the kingdom. The royal taxes, the *rentas reales,* were derived in Aragon from two treasuries of receipt, the *tesorería general* and the *bailía general.* The annual income before 1707 totalled about 388,125 reales, of which half was spent on salaries in the two treasuries and half on *mercedes* and other grants.

Nothing remained for the crown. Such was the estimate made by the new Castilian superintendant-general of the finances of Aragon, Thomás Moreno Pacheco, who arrived in Saragossa on 27 August 1707.[21] With his arrival several fundamental changes were made in the tax system. The central administration of all taxes was taken over by the Hacienda, and new Castilian taxes were introduced. The first of these taxes seems to have been that on official stamped paper (*papel sellado*), for which Moreno issued orders in October.[22] In the same month a special tribunal to administer, at least temporarily, the finances of both Aragon and Valencia, was set up by the bishop of Gironda in Madrid.[23]

To take over the entire fiscal system of Aragon was no easy task. In the first place a decision had to be made whether to continue or to suppress the existing tax structure. The very many minor taxes current in Aragon (the *hueste,* similar to the *milicias* in Castile; the *peaje,* a tax of 5 per cent similar to the *alcabala*; the *merinaje,* a tax similar to the Castilian *servicio y montazgo*; the *truedos,* a seigneurial due not paralleled in Castile; and several others)[24] were not likely to be profitable to the crown even if their whole basis of assessment and collection was reformed. The most promising procedure appeared to be to continue only the most fruitful of the current taxes, such as the customs duties or *generalidades,* and to introduce some key Castilian taxes such as the *alcabala.* At the same time those sources of revenue which were obvious royal monopolies, such as salt and tobacco, could be taken over and administered by the crown. After a decision had been taken along these lines, the next great difficulty would be the manner of administration to be adopted. Policy decisions would inevitably delay the imposition of taxes, and therefore the income from them. Even by May 1708 no income had been realised from the *papel sellado* tax, introduced the previous October, because of disagreement over the rate of assessment. Delays of this sort were aggravated by the continued presence of war in Aragon,

[21] *Consulta* of 20 Sept. 1707 on the finances, Moreno to Philip v, B Nac., MS 6753, pp. 53–61. The tax details are also given in Moreno's 'Primera notizia que dho Señor Superintendente embio a Md el dia 6 de Sepre de 1707', *ibid.,* p. 48.

[22] Moreno to the *jurados* of Saragossa, 10 Oct. 1707, *ibid.,* pp. 83–5.

[23] Royal order to Gironda, 31 Oct. 1707, *ibid.,* p. 115.

[24] A detailed list of all the taxes of Aragon prior to 1707 is given in the letter of Moreno to Gironda, 15 Nov. 1707, *ibid.,* pp. 121–38; and by Macanaz in *Regalías,* pp. 66 ff.

since no secure machinery for a new tax system could be devised so long as the fortunes of battle threatened to undo the gains already made.

A royal *cédula* of 23 December 1707, resuming an earlier order of 3 December, addressed to Moreno Pacheco, directed him to begin 'collection of all the salt taxes in the realm of Aragon, under the same prices, duties and regulations as are observed in the *salinas* of these my realms of Castile'.[25] There were in Aragon at this time twenty-nine productive *salinas*, two of them being salt-mines, and the rest salt-lakes. All of them save the two of Remolinos and Castellar were in private hands, being 'alienated and usurped' from the crown, according to Macanaz.[26] Initial reorganisation had not, by June 1708, resulted in any income to the crown, although the price of salt officially laid down – six reales a *fanega*, of which four reales went to the king – should have shown a handsome profit. Further changes in the *salinas* seemed to be indispensable. In 1709 a Frenchman by the name of Mariet made a survey on behalf of the government,[27] and came to the conclusion that in order to run the system economically only eight of the *salinas* should continue to be worked, and the rest should be closed down, with due compensation to the owners. In consequence of these recommendations, it was ordered that the *salinas* of Castellar, Remolinos, Monte de Sástago, Nabal, Peralta de la sal, Arcon, Ojosnegros and Armillas, all of them salt-lakes, should stay open, and all the others were closed. The salt-works at the lakes were to come under the direct control of the Hacienda. For the rest of the reign of Philip v, no further administrative changes were made. The financial position, however, was not entirely resolved. In four of the *salinas* (Peralta, Nabal, Sástago and Ojosnegros) the salt-works remained under private control, resulting in some monetary loss to the Hacienda, which also suffered considerably from the obligation to pay compensation to the owners of the closed mines.[28]

As regards the customs duties (*generalidades*), Moreno was ordered to take over their administration by a royal *cédula* of

[25] B Nac., MS 6753, pp. 199-200.
[26] Macanaz, *Regalías*, p. 18. A complete list of the *salinas* is given by Moreno to Gironda, 8 May 1708, B Nac., MS 6753, pp. 451-60.
[27] Macanaz, *Regalías*, p. 19.
[28] Report of D Julián de Canaveras, 31 July 1734, AGS, Secretaría de Hacienda, leg.86.

21 November 1707.[29] The customs used to be administered solely by the *Diputación del Reino*, and consisted of a flat rate of 10 per cent on goods and merchandise entering and leaving the country. Their annual value was estimated by Moreno to be 1,218,750 reales, but the actual current value was at least a third lower, because of the interruption of trade by the war. The tobacco tax-farm, which also used to be under the control of the *Diputación*, was worth about 307,500 reales a year. Neither the customs nor the tobacco tax were profitable as they stood, since two-thirds of their revenue went on the payment of salaries, and one-third on paying off *censos* (municipal bonds). On 17 December 1707 Moreno was directed to take over nominal control of the tobacco administration, which, however, continued to remain in the hands of Aragonese officials. It was not until January 1708 that the council of Castile ordered Moreno to take the tobacco administration fully under government control, on the lines already adopted in Valencia.[30]

The one important tax innovation in Aragon was the *alcabala*. Almost from the first, Moreno had been convinced that the introduction of this tax would produce speedy and beneficial results. The government agreed, and by an order of 3 December and a *cédula* of 10 December 1707[31] Philip v resolved on 'the imposition of 14 per cent on all that is bought, exchanged and sold', in Aragon. The money forthcoming from this did not actually depend on receipts from the tax. Instead, as in Castile, an assessment of the income was made, and the weight of the tax was distributed by localities. Ignacio de Asso seems to be mistaken in asserting that the *alcabala* was imposed in an arbitrary fashion.[32] On the contrary, a financial estimate sent by Moreno to the duke of Berwick in February 1708[33] suggests that the tax was being imposed on a carefully apportioned basis. The rate of 14 per cent was very soon considered by Madrid to be too high, and an order sent to Moreno on 4 January had it reduced generally to about 5 per cent.[34] In Saragossa the city council petitioned the king to suspend collection of the tax, even at the reduced rate of

[29] B Nac., MS 6753 pp. 155–6.
[30] For all this, see *ibid.*, pp. 191, 253–5, 257–60, 423–30.
[31] *Ibid.*, pp. 175–7.
[32] *Historia de la Economía Política de Aragón*, p. 310.
[33] B Nac., MS 6753, pp. 279–83.
[34] *Ibid.*, p. 229.

5 per cent. This the king was unwilling to do, but he did make one concession in an order of 18 May 1708,[35] which declared that for a period of six months no *alcabalas* need be paid on the fruits of personal labour, a grant intended primarily to benefit peasant-farmers and artisans, whose contribution to the economic recovery of Aragon was indispensable. Whatever the actual rate of imposition, the *alcabala* did not come up to expectations. According to Macanaz, the first year's returns amounted to something less than 250,000 pesos, a figure which the authorities found to be disappointing. The decision was therefore taken to suspend the *alcabala* and to resort to a direct tax, imposed and collected by the army, to finance the cost of winter-quartering.[36] This was the end of the first and only attempt to levy the *alcabala* in Aragon.

Between 1709, when the *alcabalas* were suspended, and 1711, when Macanaz arrived in Saragossa, no alterations of any moment occurred in Aragon. Military events occupied most of the interlude. After the royal victory at Villaviciosa, as we have seen, an entirely new system of government was introduced under the aegis of Melchor de Macanaz.

The next few pages give a short survey of the financial history of Aragon during, and after, the intendancy of Macanaz. The sources of revenue which principally concerned the government were, if we follow some resolutions passed by the *despacho* in February 1711, four in number:[37] '1. Tobacco will come under the superintendancy general of tobaccos in Castile, and orders are to be given to the superintendant to delegate to Don Melchor Macanaz their supervision in Aragon. 2. Orders are to be given to bring from Madrid at once and without delay the necessary stamped paper (*papel sellado*). 3. Confiscations are to be united to the finances and to come under the same minister. 4. The number of *salinas,* the price of salt and the payment to owners of the *salinas,* are to be according to the orders formerly given to Don Thomás Moreno'.

The innovations of 1707, with the one exception of the *alcabala,* were clearly to be carried on. It was Macanaz's task to assess and administer the available revenues. He sent to his

[35] *Recopilación de todas las cédulas,* p. 300.
[36] *Regalías,* p. 20.
[37] Resolutions of 20 Feb. 1711, in AHN, Estado leg.410[1].

superiors in Madrid two analyses of the income to be expected
in Aragon, both of them differing substantially in detail. The
second and last of these fiscal statements, drawn up in August
1711, is the one we shall adopt here.[38] It is reproduced in table
15. It will be seen from the table that in addition to the usual
taxes, which we have already touched on, revenue was forthcoming
from the mint, from the archiepiscopal see, and from confiscations.
Each of these sources will be discussed below.

TABLE 15. ESTIMATED ROYAL INCOME AND EXPENDITURE IN
ARAGON 1711–2

	Income (in reales of *plata doble*)
Customs duties	750,000
Stamped paper (*papel sellado*)	40,000
Salt tax (*salinas*)	400,000
Tobacco tax	442,648
Rights of the *Bailía* and *Tesorería*	64,000
Censos due to the Hacienda	3,000
Censos from the Condado de Ribagorza	9,500
Profit from the mint (non-recurring)	496,936
Revenue from the vacant see of Saragossa	375,000
Ecclesiastical and secular confiscations, estimated at	276,540

	Expenditure
Costs of administration	228,419
Costs of justice	204,587
Wages, pensions, etc.	932,761
Non-recurring grants	372,959

Totals	1,738,726	2,857,624
		1,738,726
Balance, liquid to the king		1,118,898

[38] The first statement, 'Relazion del valor que en este año se considera pueden y
deven tener las rentas', was sent by Macanaz to José Grimaldo on 29 May 1711:
AHN, Estado leg.399 f.37. Other correspondence on this memoir is in *ibid.*, leg.397
f.86. The August memoir, 'Resumen de las Rentas R^a y derechos q pertenezen a
S. Md^d en el reino de Aragon; su valor de un año (por presupuesto)', is in *ibid.*,
leg. 416^1.

This table was in a sense epoch-making, for it assessed the first reliable income ever to be received by the Castilian crown from the kingdom of Aragon. It is likely that the sum given as liquid for the king was actually received by the Hacienda, for, as we have seen, in 1713 the income from Aragon entering the national treasury was put at 2,374,680 reales vellon,[39] which is very close to the figure for 1711.[40] These figures, for both 1711 and 1713, show that Aragon was at last beginning to contribute to the financial needs of the Spanish monarchy.

The monetary history of Aragon in this period has not so far been studied by historians, with the result that little is known of the operations of coinage under Philip v. In 1706 the legal currency given to French coinage in Aragon helped to make up for a serious deficit of specie. By the time that the royalists took over the kingdom, French, Austrian and native coinage were circulating freely and confusingly on the market.

When the *fueros* were abolished in 1707 [writes Ignacio de Asso, the only authority to have discussed the subject], several coins of small value in comparison with the Aragonese pound [the *libra jaquesa*] were introduced; so that by 1709 one found 46,418 reales of French coins in small denomination, not to mention other coins which could not be estimated. By a royal *cedula* issued on 26 November 1709 Philip v granted the city of Saragossa the right to mint small change, which it began to do on 1 January 1710. On 20 January 1712 the same grant was entended, to coin 50,000 marks in addition to the 200,000 agreed on by contract; and on 23 February 1713 Don Pedro Melchor de Alegre, *alcaide* of the mint, was granted a penny for every mark that had been minted.[41]

The precise significance of all this remains unclear, as do the circumstances in which the mint was able to make a profit of nearly half a million silver reales for the king.

The revenue from the see of Saragossa was not easily obtained, and Macanaz played a crucial part in the question. In September 1710 the archbishop, Antonio Ibáñez de la Riba Herrera, had died. As soon as Macanaz began work in Aragon, he arranged to have the income of the vacant see diverted to royal use. On 5 May 1711, however, Grimaldo informed Macanaz that the king had decided not to make use of the revenues of the see in view of

[39] See above, p. 223.
[40] The *real de plata doble* was equivalent to 1.8 reales of vellon.
[41] Asso, p. 283.

representations made to him, the king, that he had no right to them. Macanaz wrote back immediately, enclosing a learned discourse in which he claimed to prove that the *regalías* of the crown extended to the revenues of vacant sees.[42] Pope Alexander II, he claimed, had granted ecclesiastical revenues in Aragon to King Sancho; and Urban II had in 1095 done the same for King Pedro. In 1118 King Alonso had founded the archiepiscopal see of Saragossa, which was therefore by implication his own property, and taken in conjunction with the fact that the papacy had granted the Aragonese crown fiscal privileges relative to the see in 1134, it followed that 'today the mitre of Saragossa possesses no revenue that is not derived from royal gift'. Macanaz then went on, in an ingenious passage, to prove the complete rights of the crown over Church revenues:

by the said bull of Urban II, His Majesty is obliged to give to the bishops of this realm and that of Valencia, only what is necessary for the upkeep of the churches and the maintenance of their persons, without being obliged to give this revenue in the form of tithes and other rights, but in any form that pleases the crown. For this reason, the tithes and other ecclesiastical revenues of this realm and of Valencia belong to the royal patrimony and not to that of the Church.

In other words, the crown had a full right to the tithes provided that alternative financial support was granted to the Church. The crown, he claimed in a further explanatory letter to Grimaldo,[43] claimed the right to enjoy the revenues, but only temporarily, 'as an administrator, or as a good father of the flock'.

The most interesting of all the sources of revenue indicated is undoubtedly that of confiscations. By 1711 only a handful of the principal rebels in Aragon had been penalised with the loss of their goods, and even this punishment was inflicted only on the prominent few who had defected bodily to the enemy. The income from confiscations in this year was certainly just over a quarter of a million silver reales, with some discrepancy between the figures given by Macanaz and those given by the secretary of the *Real Erario*, Antonio de Horbegozo y Landaeta. According to the latter,[44] the annual value of confiscations in 1711 from the estate

---

[42] Macanaz's discourse on this subject is included with his letter of 6 May to Grimaldo, AHN, Estado leg.399 f.6.

[43] Macanaz to Grimaldo, 8 May 1711, *ibid.*,

[44] List, dated 18 Aug. 1711, of 'Confiscaciones de la maior entidad hechas a personas secueares ausented en el dominio enemigo': AHN, Estado leg.416¹.

of six leading delinquents was 258,000 silver reales, and assignations on this came to a total of 118,649 reales, of which 57,200 was assigned to the Inquisition of Aragon and 54,929 to the general hospital in Saragossa. A more satisfying and complete picture of the state of confiscations emerges from the lists drawn up in 1713.[45] According to the account made at this date, the annual value of confiscations from over two hundred and fifty individuals in Aragon came to 575,990 silver reales, of which 335,984 remained liquid to the Hacienda after meeting assignations and administrative expenses. Table 16 gives details of the most important of the confiscations carried out in Aragon.

TABLE 16. ANNUAL VALUE OF PRINCIPAL CONFISCATIONS IN ARAGON IN 1713 (IN REALES OF *plata doble*)

	Annual income	Expenses	Assignations	Liquid to Crown
Hijar estates	98,000	22,400	—	75,600
Condado de Fuentes y Marquesado de Mora	68,000	18,724	—	49,276
Marquesado de Coscojuela	67,952	13,223	54,729	—
Condado de Sástago[46]	42,000	12,000	30,000	—
Conde de Elda[47]	5,022	7,280	—	—
Condado de Plascencia	60,019	9,542	50,477	—
Marqués de Villafranca	24,000	870	—	23,130
Marqués de Castropiños	42,500	6,050	—	36,450
Don Francisco Edmir	12,580	—	—	12,580
Don Manuel de Contamina	12,600	—	—	12,600
Don Antonio Luzan and family	9,892	1,242	—	8,650
Don Antonio Bardaxi and family	4,680	417	—	4,263
Conde de las Almunias	2,590	—	—	2,590

[45] 'Resumen suzinto de las Haciendas sequestradas en el Reino de Aragon a personas difidentes', AHN, Estado leg.2973.

[46] The conde de Sástago, who also features in table 1, was penalised principally in Aragon and only secondarily in Castile. All his estates in Aragon were assigned to the conde de Peralada, who, with his sister, had been granted revenue from several confiscations in Aragon: see AHN, Estado leg.188 f.7.

[47] The conde de Elda, who also features in table 1, is penalised here only for his estates in Aragon.

Unfortunately, no details are available of exactly what estates were included in these confiscations, nor of what impact the confiscations might have had on the noble families concerned. There is no doubt, however, that the burden served only to aggravate the position of the Aragonese aristocracy, who were already, as the archbishop had pointed out in 1705,[48] toiling under the weight of litigation. At least one estate which should have appeared in the confiscation lists because of the owner's defection, did not do so because of litigation: this was the condado de Luna.[49]

The total income from confiscations in Aragon seems to have declined after the end of the war, when a statement of their value in 1720 put the annual revenue at 221,700 reales of *plata doble* (or 415,687 reales of vellon), with the net sum to the Hacienda at 101,821 reales of *plata doble* (or 190,914 reales of vellon).[50] On the distribution of income from confiscations, little information exists, but the above account states that an annual sum of 468,130 vellon reales was set aside in Aragon every year for the granting of *mercedes*.

Our survey so far of the income received by the crown in Aragon has dealt only with civil taxation. It remains to be stressed, therefore, that from the moment of the recovery of Aragon in 1707 the people of this province were also obliged to contribute towards heavy military taxation. Even before the abolition of the *fueros,* the duc d'Orléans in June 1707 had imposed a contribution of 8,567,940 reales on Aragon, to be paid by everyone including the clergy. 2,912,700 reales of the total was payable by the district of Saragossa, and 2,233,740 by the Church.[51] It was the method

---

[48] See above, p. 255.

[49] The Luna estate was said in 1709 to have an annual income of 2,306 escudos 7 reales of *plata doble*, 2495 *cahices* of wheat and 150 of rye. Its obligations included 4,513 escudos, and the upkeep of several churches. Both the estates of Luna and of the condado de Castelflorit were taken into administration by the Hacienda in 1707. For these see the letter of the conde de Gerena to Grimaldo, 26 Feb. 1709, AHN, Estado leg.369 f.47.

[50] 'Reyno de Aragon. Contaduria Gral. de Bienes Confiscados. Relazion de los valores liquidos que se considera tienen annualmente todos los bienes y rentas confiscadas . . . por presupuesto del que tubieron en el año de 1720', drawn up in Madrid, 17 Sept. 1722: AGS, Secretaría de Hacienda leg.972. In this account the condado de Elda produced 10,360 silver reales annually (with a net 4,100 to the Crown); the Fuentes and Mora estates 89,545 annually (with 47,806 net); the Luna estates gave half their income, i.e. 58,888 annually (net 32,253) to the crown; and the barony of Antillon produced 10,032 reales annually (with 7,887 net).

[51] 7 June 1707: 'Razon de la Imposicion en dinero puesta por orden de . . . Orleans sobre la Ciudad de Zaragoza, las otras Ciudades, Villas, Lugares, Aldeas y todo el

used in collecting this imposition that provoked the severe criticisms of Joseph de Sisson, quoted above.[52] The tax was certainly unpopular, and the returns were slow: two months after its imposition, less than one-tenth of the total had come in. In the following year a similar contribution of 9,442,980 reales was demanded from the kingdom.[53] The year after this, 1709, saw a fundamental change in the method of taxation. The *alcabalas* had been suspended because of their failure to bring in the required amount of money, and it therefore became necessary to make up for the loss of revenue in some other way. The simplest solution at hand was to increase the military imposition. As a result, 1709 saw the levying of an enormous contribution to finance the winter-quartering of the troops. The imposition, which was probably about twelve million reales, is strongly criticised by Ignacio de Asso, who claims that it 'consumed both public and private money and ended by causing the alientation of much property and the ruin of several towns, without any benefit or utility to the royal Hacienda, since even in 1717 considerable arrears were still being owed'. In addition to this swollen imposition, the tax on salt was raised, as Asso points out, from one silver real per *arroba* to four.[54]

Between 1709 and the end of the war, then, the people of Aragon were obliged to suffer a heavy winter tax devoted to the upkeep of the Bourbon troops. Many loyal towns and cities were exempted from this, as from all extraordinary taxation, from 1706 to 1714,[55] so that not all Aragonese suffered equally. The rate of the tax varied from year to year. For the winter quarters that lasted from November 1710 to April 1711, the sum levied appears to have been in the region of twelve millions: the total actually collected, however, was only 10,280,025 reales.[56] In the winter of 1711–2 the sum expected was 838,170 pesos

---

clero del Reyno de Aragon, en forma de Contribucion, que se ha de recibir por el señor Tifaine, Thesorero del Ejercito,' AE Corr. Pol. (Esp.), 176 ff.197–232.

[52] See p. 260 note 38.

[53] A table of the imposition, dated 4 Oct. 1708 and signed Tiffaine du Marais, treasurer of the army of Orléans, is in AN, KK 536.

[54] Asso, p. 310.

[55] The exempted towns were Borja, Jaca, Tarazona, Fraga 'y otras diferentes villas y lugares', Juan Antonio Diaz de Arze, intendant of Aragon, to Philip v, 26 July 1735, AGS, Secretaría de Hacienda leg.536.

[56] Tserclaës Tilly to Grimaldo, 22 Aug. 1711, AHN, Estado leg.416[1].

(12,572,550 reales).[57] A decree of 5 December 1712[58] continued the latter rate for the winter of 1712–3, but for 1713–4 it seems to have been reduced. For the six winter months of 1714–5 the contribution imposed on Aragon by the marqués de Castelar came to 11,286,150 vellon reales, of which a large proportion, no less than 3,268,475 reales, was still unrealised by the end of 1715.[59]

The introduction of the new 'single tax' into Aragon is a subject that carries us outside the time limits imposed on this study, but a few words on it are essential. The *única contribución*, as it eventually came to be known, was apparently introduced in 1718. If this date is correct, it means that Aragon followed well after both Valencia and Catalonia in accepting the new system. It can, however, be seriously doubted whether the single tax was adopted so late, and there is evidence that it came into operation as early as 1714.[60] In 1718, at any rate, a single annual tax of eight million reales was imposed on Aragon, by way of an equivalent to all the taxes normally levied in Castile. A census was carried out at the same time to determine whether the province could afford to pay. When it was discovered that only 44,696 households out of the whole population would be capable of paying the tax, the rate was lowered by a decree of 20 January 1718 to five million reales,[61] at which level it remained for most of the reign of Philip v. The *única contribución* was the last of the several stages through which fiscal experimentation in Aragon had passed: first there had been the unsuccessful attempt to introduce Castilian taxes such as the *alcabala*; then there had been the resort to heavy military impositions; and finally a single tax had been adopted as the best way of consolidating a fiscal system on a non-military basis.

What emerges from this account is that the chief contribution of Aragon (as of Valencia) to the treasury after 1707 lay not in the new Castilian taxes nor in the confirmation of the royal monopoly on salt and tobacco, but in the heavy military impositions suffered

[57] *Ibid.*, to Philip v, 1 Dec. 1711, *ibid.*, leg.411³.

[58] Canga Argüelles, *Diccionario de Hacienda*, vol. 2, p. 127.

[59] Castelar to Grimaldo, 1 Oct. 1715, AGS, Guerra Moderna leg.1612.

[60] Diaz de Arze to Philip v, 26 July 1735, cited above, claims that in 1714 'se empezó a practicar en este Reino el repartimiento de la Contribucion, que en los principios se le cargaron 800,000 escudos, y desde el año de 1717 se le baxaron a 500,000'.

[61] Asso, p. 310.

by the province until the introduction of the *única contribución*. Though not much money reached the Hacienda from Aragon, a substantial financial burden had in reality been lifted from the government's shoulders, for its troops were managing to live to a great extent off the income from the eastern provinces. The *única contribución* was not, of course, a substitute for all the existing taxes in Aragon: in practice, it was only a substitute for the military impositions, since the state monopolies of tobacco, salt, stamped paper and other items continued to exist as taxes independent of the so-called 'single tax'. What now appeared as civil taxation was in effect no more than a continuation of the old military taxes, and inevitably most of the money raised in Aragon was spent anyway on the upkeep of the army.

For the rest, Aragon shared with Valencia the effect of the other steps taken by Philip v to give a greater unity to the various provinces of the peninsula. The abolition of customs barriers between Castile and the crown of Aragon, and the move to standardise Spanish coinage, would certainly have been regarded by the bourgeoisie of Barcelona, Valencia and Saragossa as further evidence of the commercial ambitions of the Castilians and their allies the French. Any programme to unify the Spanish peninsula was, and is, bound to be denounced by the peripheral provinces as a programme of Castilianisation. By 1715 not much had been achieved towards this end in Aragon where, as we have seen, most of the significant changes were fiscal in nature. But the work achieved, particularly under the aegis of Macanaz, laid the foundations for the great labour of consolidation carried out in Aragon under Macanaz's heirs, the marqués de Castelar and his successors in the intendancy of Saragossa.

14 Conclusion: the Consequences of the War

The war of the Spanish Succession was one of the most significant in all Spanish history. Viewed in either its military or its political aspects, it had a profound impact on the development of the monarchy. We remain, however, curiously ignorant of the material consequences of the war. Was it a disaster or was it, as some have maintained, beneficial? It is scarcely possible to arrive at a fully satisfactory conclusion in our present state of knowledge, and in some respects it may not be possible ever to do so. There remain nevertheless a few general indications which can be set down without too much controversy.

The trials of the war period derived as much from natural disasters as from the passage of troops. Spain, like its ally France, suffered particularly badly from the crisis year of 1709. In the peninsula the whole period 1708 to 1711 was extremely critical. The harvest of 1708 was very poor, particularly in Andalucia,[1] and the Spanish authorities had to appeal to France for permission to import grain across the land frontier. In the spring of 1709 came heavy rains which swamped any future crops, and thereby introduced the year of great famine. Murcia, La Mancha and Andalucia in particular were starving throughout the first half of 1709. Seville suffered flooding in the winter of 1708–9, and famine in the spring: it was consequently exempted from the payment of some taxes for two years. The hunger, misery and death experienced in this city reached unimaginable proportions.[2] A *fanega* of wheat there cost 120 reales in March 1709, over four times the

[1] Amelot to Louis XIV, 13 Aug. 1708: 'La récolte a esté cette année fort mauvaise en Andalousie, et les grains y sont fort chers', AE Corr. Pol. (Esp.), 181 f.206. Miguel de Zabala y Auñón, *Representación al Rey N. Señor D. Phelipe V, dirigida al más seguro aumento del real erario*, Madrid, 1732, refers to '1708, que fue de los años mas fatales que hemos conocido'.

[2] Domínguez Ortiz, *Sociedad española en el siglo XVIII*, p. 260 note 5.

price of wheat in New Castile. The harvest of 1709 was slightly better in Andalucia, but worse in Aragon, Valencia and parts of Castile. By a decree of 24 October 1709 Philip v opened the ports of Spain to all ships, enemy or neutral, which could bring grain to the peninsula, granting them permission to introduce into Spain all hitherto forbidden goods except the silks and woollens of England and Holland. This last proviso was removed when it was found that the articles were being smuggled in anyway.[3] Prices continued to be high throughout Spain in 1710, and arrangements were made for grain to be imported from abroad and from France.[4] After 1711 the situation improved, as can be seen from the price indices noted below. The difficult situation around 1709 goes some way towards explaining the political crisis and military failures of that period, and the subsequent reverses in 1710. It was not war, but the climate, that brought the spectre of famine to Spain in those years.

A military conflict that preyed over the same land for over a decade, with several major battles, innumerable sieges, and extensive occupations of territory, must certainly have had a severe impact on the civil population. This would seem to be a reasonable conclusion. Yet our present knowledge suggests that the war had no substantial effect on the population, or on population growth. It is true that Ignacio de Asso claims that 'the most fatal blow, which profoundly injured our industry and population, came from the impact of the War of Succession. It is impossible to describe the degree of misery caused by hostilities and by the licence of the troops, and by the demands made on the country by the commissaries and contractors supplying food to the army'.[5] But the evidence indicates that, quite apart from the inevitable sum of human misery caused by the war, little depopulation of any significance took place. It is particularly important to bear in mind the character of the war, if we are to assess its impact. A high proportion, almost certainly a majority, of the soldiers

[3] Decree of 24 Oct. 1709 and *cédula* of 13 Nov. 1709, AN Aff. Etr., B^III 325 ff.152-4.

[4] Details of grain and flour imports from France in 1710 and 1711 are in AE Corr. Pol. (Esp.), 205ff. 192-7. In July 1710 the government issued twelve passports allowing enemy ships to enter Spanish ports with grain; these went to six English, three Dutch and three Hamburg vessels: Grimaldo to Blécourt, 2 July 1710, AN Aff. Etr. B^III 360.

[5] Asso, p. 207.

fighting in the peninsula were foreign. With the exception of Catalan auxiliaries, nearly all the Allied troops were non-Spanish; and a high but indeterminate proportion of the Bourbon troops was French. The direct victims of battles were consequently more likely to be foreign. As for civilian casualties, both sides usually tried to avoid them. The archduke was particularly concerned to win over the native population, especially the lower classes, and it would have been impolitic of him to sanction needless plundering and brutality. The Bourbons were less careful of life when recovering the crown of Aragon, as shown by the reputation for cruelty which D'Asfeld won in Valencia; but in Castile at least they would not have victimised their own people. For both sides a war of attrition was out of the question.[6] They wanted neither wealth nor land, but the hearts of the people. It is not extravagant to surmise that in these circumstances the loss of life would have been kept to a minimum. Even Catalonia, which probably suffered the most material damage from the war, since the Bourbon troops did not hesitate to treat the whole population as confirmed rebels, experienced no more than demographic stagnation in this period.[7] An additional consideration of some importance is that epidemics and plagues, which were the principal agents of mortality in most wars of the time, seem to have been inconspicuous during the War of Succession in Spain. The authorities were not called upon to defend public health until 1720, when there was a danger of the epidemic then raging in France reaching the shores of Spain.

Law and order collapsed in several parts of Spain as a result of the war. Troops resorted to looting during the war when they were not paid.[8] Fragments of information available to us, suggest that in the five years or so after Utrecht there was a general increase in banditry and piracy. At sea there was renewed activity on the part of Algerian or other north African corsairs, who were

[6] Cf. the opinion of the archbishop of Saragossa in 1705: 'the population do not look on this war as one of those waged with fire and blood. The actions of the rebels do not touch their lives or their property'; cited above, p. 255.

[7] J. Nadal and E. Giralt, *La Population Catalane de 1553 à 1717*, Paris, 1960, p. 23.

[8] Cf. Père Labat's description of the situation around Cadiz in 1706: 'Les pluies rendirent les chemins impracticables, et les troupes qui se repandaient de toutes parts, pillant tout ce qu'elles trouvaient, sous prétexte qu'elles n'étaient pas payées firent disparaitre le peu de sûreté qu'il y a pour les voyageurs dans ce pays–là.' *Voyage du P. Labat en Espagne 1705–6*, Paris, 1927, p. 78.

undoubtedly encouraged by the military success of the Arabs during the war, in which they had captured Masalquivir. Many of the 'bandits' and 'pirates' may in fact have been no more than partisans of the archduke continuing the war on a private footing. This is the opinion of Miñana who, commenting on the state of Valencia after the war, says that 'at this time various bands of robbers occupied the roads, seriously threatening the city, since they intercepted the transport of food supplies. All those peasants who had been ruined and remained in revolt, with no fear that their lot could get worse, had taken up arms and posted themselves along the roads in order to plunder.' The bandits were particularly common towards Catalonia, in the region of Tarragona where there were no soldiers and where 'they cruelly harassed those who had in any way shown their loyalty to the king'. Thanks to the lack of weapons among a population which had been effectively disarmed, the bandits even terrorised well-populated towns. 'No less concern', adds Miñana, 'was caused in Valencia by pirates marauding in all the ports and along the coast.'[9] The whole Levant coast was infested by them, and inevitably it was Catalonia, the traditional home of banditry, that suffered the worst. For some time after the subjugation of the principality, the Castilian troops were too busy to deal with them. The pirates who, according to a report by the council of war, were Catalan, Valencian and Majorcan by origin, conducted their attacks principally from the sea, but also made raids inland whenever this was possible. It was not until March 1716 that the Principe Pio, marqués de Castelrodrigo, who was military commandant of Catalonia, took steps to counterattack with a naval force.[10] At the same time it became necessary to act against the north African pirates, who on one occasion in the summer of 1716 made an attack on the coast between Tarragona and Tortosa and sailed away with thirty or more Spanish slaves.[11] It was not only the eastern provinces that suffered banditry, however. All the roads of Old Castile were infested with robbers in the years 1717 to 1719 at least, and it seems likely that this phenomenon can be dated back even earlier to the years after the war. From

[9] Miñana, pp. 567 (III, xiii), 581 (III, xxviii), 586 (III, xxxi).

[10] Details in the letter of Principe Pio to Miguel Fernández Durán, 7 Mar. 1716, AGS, Guerra Moderna leg.1614; and the *consulta* of the council of war, 16 Mar. 1716, *ibid.*, leg.1578.

[11] Principe Pio to Duran, 18 July 1716, *ibid.*, leg.1819.

León, Salamanca, Valladolid and other cities in this area the authorities poured out identical complaints of robberies and outrages. Instructions were accordingly sent out in 1719 to the five intendants of Old Castile, to organise armed patrols to wipe out the bandits.[12] There is no record of how successful these efforts may have been.

Violence and disaster are the accompaniment of any war, but to prove their impact on the population of a country we need firm statistics. These are sadly lacking for Spain in this period. There is no possible way of comparing figures for Spanish population before and after the war. Data for the end of the seventeenth century are available, but not always reliable. The same applies to the early eighteenth century. In some circumstances it would still be possible to compare the two sets of data, but in the present case this is impossible, since each set was drawn up on a quite different basis of reckoning.[13] At best, we can examine estimates made of the population of Spain after the war. The standard estimate is that of Gerónimo de Uztáriz, a government official who had intimate knowledge of the way in which assessments of population were made at the time.[14] Since Uztáriz's figures are seldom quoted in detail, his whole analysis is reproduced here:

Year of estimate	Province	Vecinos
1723	City of Madrid, excluding convents, etc.	30,000
1710+	*Partido* of Madrid	7,680
1710+	Kingdom of Toledo (and part of La Mancha)	42,987
1710+	Province of: Guadalajara	16,974
1710+	Cuenca (and part of La Mancha)	40,603
1710+	Soria	18,068
1710+	Segovia	16,687
1710+	Avila	10,061

[12] José Rodrigo to the five intendants of Old Castile, 15 Nov. 1719, AGS, Secretaria de Gracia y Justicia leg.1. This *legajo* contains letters about banditry from the intendants.

[13] The figures given by Tomás González, and those given by myself (*Econ. Hist. Rev.* XVII, i, 1964) were drawn up for civil taxation purposes. The figures given by Uztáriz were for military taxation, and moreover tended to count *vecinos utiles* rather than *vecinos*.

[14] *Theórica y Práctica de Comercio y de Marina*, p. 35. Of other printed sources on population in this period, Juan de Estrada, *Población General de España* (3 vols), Madrid, 1747, is very interesting, sometimes useful, but usually unreliable.

Year of estimate	Province	Vecinos
1710+	Valladolid	26,939
1710+	Palencia	14,581
1712	Salamanca	19,344
1717	Toro	5,525
1714	Zamora	7,336
1710+	Burgos	49,282
1710+	Kingdom of León	28,556
1710+	Principality of Asturias	30,524
1717	Kingdom of Galicia	118,680
1716	Province of Extremadura[15]	60,393
1712+	City of Seville (13,600) and	
1712+	Kingdom of Seville (68,244)	81,844
1712+	Kingdom of: Córdoba	39,702
1712+	Jaén	30,157
1712+	Granada	78,728
1678	Navarre	35,987
1678	Basque provinces (Vizcaya, Guipuzcoa, Alava)	35,987
1717	Principality of Catalonia	103,360
1712	Kingdom of: Aragon	75,244
1714	Valencia	63,770
1713	Murcia	30,494
	Mallorca, Ibiza, etc., and African forts	21,110
	Total	**1,140,103**

Uztáriz assumed that all the above figures were underestimates, since they were almost without exception made solely for tax purposes during wartime, which meant that they omitted all military personnel, all ecclesiastics and the nomadic population. From his own experience he also felt that administrators tended to underestimate their census figures. With these factors in mind, Uztáriz added a number of checks to his estimate. He added about a quarter of a million to his total to make up for administrative errors, making a new total of 1,425,000 *vecinos*. To this he added a figure of 36,000 for military personnel, 14,000 for shepherds and other nomads, and 50,000 for clergy. From this new total of 1,525,000 he subtracted 25,000 as a check against error. The result

[15] An impressively detailed, and apparently highly reliable census of the *partidos* of Plasencia and Caceres in the province of Extremadura, dated 1709, is given in AGS, Guerra Moderna leg.3771.

was 1,500,000 *vecinos* which, using a multiplier of five persons per household,[16] gave a figure for Spanish population of 7,500,000.

This figure must be approached with extreme caution. Uztáriz undoubtedly used the most reliable information to hand. For Aragon and Valencia, the areas we have already discussed, he appears to have made the most judicious choice from a range of varying population returns. But the defects in his estimate are serious. The system of checks he used is so arbitrary as to vitiate all statistical accuracy. Even his basic figures, however, are questionable. The principal source he used is still available in manuscript form.[17] The population returns given in this source represent that part of the population liable to taxation for military purposes, and do not therefore pretend to measure the whole population. To complicate matters, the population unit usually adopted is not the *vecino* or head of the household, but the *vecino util*, which appears to cover only those *vecinos* capable of contributing to taxes. Being aware of this, Uztáriz appears to have modified the census figures even *before* applying his checks. Thus where Madrid is originally estimated to have 24,344 *vecinos* in 1723, Uztáriz scales the figure up to a round 30,000. León, estimated to have 25,556 *vecinos*, is scaled up to 28,556.[18] This procedure, which was no doubt justified but nevertheless wholly arbitrary, was applied by Uztáriz to nearly all his original data. In short, Uztáriz gives us an estimate of the population of Spain arrived at by a combination of arbitrary reckoning and inspired guesswork, rather than by a convincing analysis of statistics.

Uztáriz, as we have noted, considered that all the original

---

[16] Other contemporaries used smaller multipliers: cf. an Aragonese official named Colomo writing to José Campillo on 12 Aug. 1741, AGS, Secretaría de Hacienda leg.537: 'Es constante entre los que estamos practicos en los vecindarios, que a cada vezino se le deve reputar quando no cinco personas, por lo menos quatro, entre criados y hijos.'

[17] 'Vecindario General de España', B Nac., MS 2274.

[18] Some other differences between the manuscript and Uztáriz are:

	MS	Uztáriz
Kingdom of Toledo	37,987	42,987
Province of: Guadalajara	14,974	16,974
Cuenca	31,603	40,603
Avila	9,061	10,061
Principality of Asturias	20,524	30,524
Kingdom of: Córdoba	36,702	39,702
Jaén	22,157	30,157
Granada	73,728	78,728

population figures available to him were underestimates, and it was on this basis that he proceeded to inflate his statistics. There is reason, however, to believe that many of the original figures were more reliable than this, and that the use of a coefficient of five persons per *vecino* was enough to regulate most deficiencies in the data. As Domínguez Ortiz has argued,[19] five is a satisfactory, perhaps even a generous, multiplier to use in converting *vecinos*. When applied to the data for Valencia, for instance, this multiplier produces a plausible population figure; whereas the inflation of the basic data by something like 25 per cent, which is what Uztáriz's checks amount to, produces a figure for which there is no evidence in any census of Valencia. Similarly, the figures for Galicia and Extremadura, both fairly reliable in themselves, cease to be so when subjected to Uztáriz's calculations. The manuscript figure for Extremadura attributes to it 54,393 *vecinos* in 1717, a figure which is somewhat lower than the figure of about 56,390 *vecinos* estimated by the army tax-collectors in 1713.[20] Uztáriz's figure exceeds both these by about 10 per cent; his addition of another 25 per cent gives Extremadura a population comparable to that of Aragon, a completely inadmissible figure for one of the most war-torn of all the provinces of Spain and the one to have suffered most from depopulation in conflicts with Portugal.

Not all Uztáriz's figures are overestimates. His readjustments to the low returns based on *vecinos utiles* may be very close to the true population figures. Based as they are, however, on arbitrary calculations, they cannot be relied on too closely. Does this mean that all Uztáriz's data must be rejected, and that a general assessment of population at the beginning of the eighteenth century is impossible? The answer must be in the affirmative. Yet Uztáriz cannot be rejected completely. He was an experienced administrator, not careless in his use of statistics. His inclination to blow up available figures was a move in the right direction, since all so-called censuses made in this period tended to be severe underestimates. It seems most likely that his final population figure of 7,500,000 is too high, but that research will eventually come close to this estimate.

[19] *La Sociedad Española en el Siglo XVII*, p. 61. Domínguez Ortiz shows that the sixteenth-century coefficient varied between four and five persons per *vecino*.

[20] The 1713 figure is derived from the 'Repartimiento de 10 reales por vecino' levied on Extremadura that year: the yield came to 563,896 reales: AGS, Guerra Moderna leg.2356 f.25.

To measure the extent of depopulation caused by war calls for more detailed sources than those used by Uztáriz. Unfortunately, the archives contain no documentation for the period of the war which would enable a satisfactory assessment to be made. It may, however, be significant that even in the post-war period when towns in Castile complained to the Hacienda of a decline in population, nowhere do we find any attribution of such decline to the 1702–14 conflict. Some towns continued to shrink during these years; the city of Salamanca, for instance, claimed to have fallen from 3,766 *vecinos* in 1693 to 2,250 in 1732,[21] but at no time did it blame this contraction on the war.

In the kingdom of Aragon we do have some information, not exact but useful as an indicator, on the number of households deserted at the end of the war.[22] Details are available for only a few of the districts in the kingdom, and approximate estimates for these are given below.

Corregimiento or district	Number of towns	Inhabited houses	Ruined houses
Saragossa	96	11,303	399
*Albarracin	27	1,232	256
Barbastro	169	4,832	888
*Benavarre	188	2,138	108
*Calatayud	93	4,765	2,197
Huesca	129	2,881	358
*Jaca	189	1,741	640
Teruel	91	5,775	1,927

While the survey of ruined and uninhabited houses would almost certainly be limited to those that had fallen into this state not too long before 1718, and would therefore refer to the War of Succession (as the eighteenth-century editor of these returns surmised), it would be unwise to rule out the possibility that some of the ruins were of longer standing. A look at some of the chief cities involved should be interesting:

---

[21] Salamanca to the Hacienda, 7 June 1732, AGS, Secretaría de Hacienda leg.85.
[22] Source is BRAH, MS 9–26–1–4762. See appendix 3. Since the figures have no statistical accuracy, I have refrained from expressing the number of ruined houses as a proportion of the inhabited houses, as this would mislead the reader.

* The capital city is excluded in these districts.

City	Inhabited houses	Ruined houses
Saragossa	4,273	218
Barbastro	598	64
Huesca	722	61
Tarazona	842	187 and one entire suburb
Teruel	611	191

These figures, if truly representative of the toll of war, show a rate of destruction in the general region of 10 per cent. If this rate were also equivalent to the loss of population, we would be faced with a very serious situation. As it is, the figures represent only the destruction of houses and not of people. Since it would be absurd to claim that the one took place without also involving the other, there can be little doubt that some depopulation did take place, though perhaps in the form of migration and not in straightforward loss of life. Like all wars, the War of Succession caused movements of population. Peasants and villagers fled from unfriendly armies and from army tax-collectors; citizens moved out when cities were occupied and troops billeted in private houses. The dominant trend during the war was for refugees to move from the rural areas into the towns. Between 1713 and 1714 Valencia city grew from 8,290 households to 8,800 households, according to two consecutive censuses.[23] In this it was typical of other cities and towns that had suffered an influx of population, though the figures for Aragonese towns given above suggest that immigrants were never in a position to settle down and redress the loss of urban population. The refugee problem was perhaps worst in 1708 and 1709, when the failure of the harvests drove peasants into the cities for food, thus causing supply difficulties in the cities and, more seriously, suspension of work on the soil. The king accordingly issued an order to restrict this on 3 July 1709, in view of the 'news that many and diverse people, with the excuse that the climate is unproductive, and in order to be free of taxes and royal contributions, have left the villages where they had their homes and introduced themselves into the larger cities and towns of the kingdom'.[24] Prohibition

[23] Cavallero to Grimaldo, 29 Oct. 1714, AGS, Guerra Moderna, suplemento, leg.252.
[24] Hacienda, Consejo de Castilla, impresos, vol. 6549 f.8.

of movement from one's domicile was difficult to enforce, particularly in wartime, and it is unlikely that this order met with any response. The demands of military tax-collectors merely aggravated the flight from the land. In October 1715 we find the intendant of Catalonia reporting that people were fleeing from the principality to the more inaccessible regions of Rossellón and Cerdaña, and 'the cause of this is attributed by the natives to the impossibility of paying the heavy contribution, and because they have lost this year's harvest through lack of rain. To this is added the treatment which they claim to have received from the troops.'[25]

If we look at the movement of prices in the peninsula during the war years, a picture emerges which seems far from disastrous. The Spain inherited by Philip v was, as we have already observed, on the first steps towards economic recovery. The monetary stability towards which the measures of 1680 and 1686 aspired soon became an accomplished fact. Drastic deflation helped to dampen down speculation and strengthened the position of Spanish currency. Our comparison of the exchange rates between Spain and France has shown that by the early 1700s Spain was able to hold its own in international finance. It is not surprising, then, that one historian can refer to 'monetary stability and a movement of prices which, between 1686 and 1714, make the worst military and political events coincide with a time of calm and economic recovery'.[26] This assertion raises again the paradox discussed by Jovellanos,[27] namely that an apparently destructive war brought with it some economic regeneration. It also raises the question whether the movement of prices bears any relationship to the events of the war.

The long-term trend in Spanish prices, as established by Hamilton, shows a slow rise in the price of commodities from the mid-1680s into the first half of the eighteenth century. This trend is interrupted by a sudden down-swing in the decade 1710–20. The whole reign of Philip v experienced two cyclic fluctuations which appear to coincide with the wars of the Spanish Succession and the Austrian Succession, the peak year in each case being 1710 and 1741, when the index numbers stood at 19·9 and 25·6 points

[25] Nicolás Hinojosa to Grimaldo, 6 Oct. 1715, AGS, Guerra Moderna leg.1811.
[26] Vilar, La Catalogne, vol. 1, p. 671.
[27] Cf. the quotation on p. 195 note 112.

respectively above the 1721–30 average. This movement cannot be considered extreme, and justifies Hamilton's conclusion that 'it would be difficult to find a fifty-year period of more stable prices (cyclically or secularly) in the history of any country' other than Spain between 1700 and 1750.[28]

The short-term movement shows interesting contrasts within the peninsula. Catalonia experienced severe inflation, and it was only outside Catalonia that the war did not have a drastic effect on prices. The comparison may be made by consulting figure 3, and tables 17 and 18 which give the index numbers for prices in New Castile and Catalonia respectively.[29]

TABLE 17. INDEX NUMBERS OF COMMODITY PRICES IN NEW CASTILE, 1699–1718 (BASE 100 = 1675–84)

	Wheat	Barley	Oil	Sugar	Wine	Char-coal	Fire-wood	Index
1699	96·4	67·8	88·6	65·8	85·4	72·1	55·4	75·9
1700	62·0	50·8	84·8	63·2	80·9	87·9	46·9	68·0
1701	51·5	42·3	70·1	75·2	71·1	91·3	57·5	65·5
1702	52·6	50·8	77·6	81·6	67·6	88·7	64·2	69·0
1703	49·8	50·8	72·0	77·7	72·9	74·4	66·6	66·3
1704	48 2	42·3	63·6	96·5	72·0	67·6	63·9	64·8
1705	49·0	35·3	50·9	96·5	71·1	78·5	46·9	61·1
1706	91·4	56·5	52·2	82·5	78·2	76·6	73·3	72·9
1707	68·2	50·8	56·2	76·2	78·4	64·8	76·6	67·3
1708	86·8	73·4	57·1	75·7	80·9	78·1	63·7	73·6
1709	93·1	73·4	57·7	89·4	85·4	64·8	68·2	76·0
1710	126·4	86·1	56·1	80·2	94·3	67·6	57·5	81·1
1711	104·9	45·2	62·9	80·3	92·5	71·0	74·4	75·8
1712	68·2	31·0	77·4	79·1	85·4	81·1	63·9	69·4
1713	70·9	63·8	71·7	84·9	81·8	65·3	77·0	73·6
1714	59·8	53·6	84·1	81·4	70·9	67·6	59·2	68·0
1715	58·2	64·9	90·1	86·9	85·4	69·5	67·6	74·6
1716	45·7	45·2	70·1	81·1	88·7	71·0	68·9	67·2
1717	44·9	33·9	68·6	78·6	60·8	81·1	55·3	60·4
1718	61·5	50·8	50·0	77·9	50·3	57·4	62·5	58·6

[28] Hamilton, p. 150.

[29] Castilian prices calculated from Hamilton. Catalan prices taken from Vilar, vol. 1, pp. 694, 700. The base period 1675–84, used by Vilar, has also been used for Castile to facilitate comparison. The general index in table 18 is mine.

TABLE 18. INDEX NUMBERS OF COMMODITY PRICES IN
BARCELONA, 1707–18 (BASE 100 = 1675–84)

	Wheat	Barley	Oil	Sugar	Wine	Char-coal	Fire-wood	Index
1707	—	—	83·7	—	135·7	130·6	—	116·6
1708	120·5	136·5	83·7	86·5	155·3	147·9	117·3	121·1
1709	166·8	175·7	91·9	91·4	157·7	160·3	131·3	139·3
1710	136·6	156·6	143·0	101·7	202·2	159·4	140·8	148·6
1711	134·7	139·6	153·8	116·9	210·0	144·2	140·8	148·5
1712	127·3	145·5	160·0	104·4	220·8	165·9	140·8	152·1
1713	119·8	116·8	149·5	120·8	165·6	152·0	124·4	121·2
1714	177·5	138·4	177·1	138·0	—	—	187·7	163·7
1715	135·4	115·5	162·8	127·3	157·3	131·3	134·9	137·7
1716	109·7	108·8	158·7	124·7	127·1	—	137·3	127·7
1717	87·4	111·1	151·0	118·4	100·4	103·6	114·4	112·3
1718	88·8	104·0	107·3	119·9	99·6	104·4	105·6	104·2

The peak for prices in New Castile was reached, as we have seen, in 1710. Hamilton considers that for this 'the war was not directly responsible',[30] a conclusion which is quite justified in view of the agrarian crisis. In Old Castile and Andalucia the movement was parallel to that in New Castile, the documentation for the rise in all three regions pointing principally to bad weather and poor harvests. Closer examination of table 17 may conceivably raise doubts. Here we see that the two sharpest rises occurred in 1706 and 1710, precisely the two years of military and political crisis, when the Allies succeeded in capturing Madrid. It would be unwise to deny that these events had some effect on the price of consumables. But the root cause of the rise was certainly the weather. It was a poor harvest in 1705 that led to the grain scarcity in 1706,[31] and 1710, one of the great hunger years of the war, was only an aftermath of the disastrous rains of 1709. It would not be too fanciful to assume that the scarcity of food contributed

[30] Hamilton, p. 142.
[31] 1706 may also have been a year of drought and poor harvest, if the hot weather noted in Languedoc by E. Le Roy Ladurie, Les paysans de Languedoc (2 vols), Paris, 1966, vol. 1, p. 33, was common to all southern Europe. 1707 was in any case a year of poor harvest in Aragon, due no doubt to the heat.

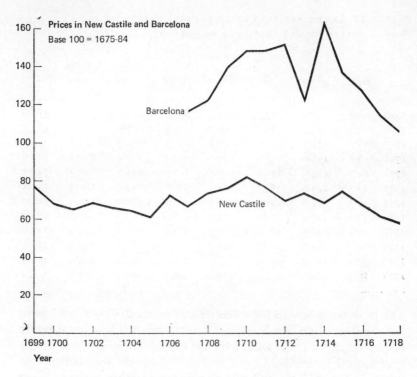

3. PRICES IN NEW CASTILE AND BARCELONA

in some measure to the embarrassment and defeat of the Bourbon armies.

Only in Valencia does Hamilton claim that the war raised prices decisively. Here the price index, with 1721–30 as the base period, rose from 104·3 in 1706 to 119·5 in 1707, reaching a peak of 122·7 in 1710 and falling to 107·1 in 1715.[32] Taking all the regions studied by Hamilton, we find that commodity prices from 1706 to 1710 rose 7·6 per cent in Andalucia, 12·8 per cent in New Castile, 14 per cent in Old Castile, and no less than 22·4 per cent in Valencia.[33] A clue to the situation in Valencia is given by the date of the upswing, 1707. It was in that year that Philip v recovered the kingdom and initiated a radical political and monetary reform,

[32] *Ibid.*, p. 138.
[33] *Ibid,,* p. 146.

so that the rise in prices may be explained not merely by the weather but perhaps more convincingly by the dislocation brought about in an occupied territory. Had Hamilton studied prices in Aragon for this period, he would no doubt have found similar conditions prevailing.[34] In general, it appears that the Mediterranean littoral suffered more in terms of price inflation than the centre of the peninsula. Valencia's case was exceeded only by that of Catalonia. Prices in Barcelona were of crisis proportions. Vilar calculates that if the five-year period 1701-5 is taken as equivalent to 100·4, in 1708 the index rises to 118·3, in 1709 to 142·7 and in 1712 to 151·2.[35] Throughout the peninsula the main rise seems on this showing to have been concentrated around 1710-2.

Price movements thus demonstrate the absence of any serious economic crisis precipitated by the war.[36] The one exception to this is Catalonia. The ruin caused there was clearly substantial.[37] Yet even in these circumstances progress was not ruled out. In Barcelona the importers of wheat, producers of wine, and makers of ships, prospered despite the difficulties of the many who could not benefit from inflation. In Vilar's words, 'the presence of the court and of troops, the influx of money, the rise in prices, were more than ever before a stimulant to the economy'.[38] The picture closely resembles that of Valencia under the same archiducal régime. This interpretation of a tragic period in the history of the Catalan nation is highly significant, for it coincides with the views put forward by Jovellanos and Campomanes. Was the war, which had so mild an effect on Castile and so profound an effect on the Levant coast, directly beneficial to both these regions and to Spain as a whole?

As with many wars, there were some undeniable advantages. According to Jovellanos and Campomanes, the chief benefits were as follows: an increase in the volume and circulation of

---

[34] For prices in Aragon see Ignacio de Asso, p. 286; also Thomás Anzano, *Reflexiones económico – políticas sobre las causas de la alteración de precios que ha padecido Aragón*, Saragossa, 1768.

[35] Vilar, vol. 1, p. 694. This index covers eight commodities.

[36] It should be remembered that the general trend ignores local variations. Appendix 6 shows by reference to prices in 1719 how wide the variations could be in a normal year.

[37] Cf. Juan Mercader, 'Una visión pesimista de la Economía catalana después de la Guerra de Sucesión', *Estudios de Historia Moderna*, V (1955).

[38] Pierre Vilar, *Le Manual de la Companya Nova de Gibraltar*, Paris, 1963, p. 80.

bullion, a revival of finance and banking, growth of cloth-production, and an impetus to military activity and the war industry. Each of these points deserves a brief discussion.

We have already noted the theories of the two eighteenth-century statesmen on the circulation of bullion. Some regions certainly benefited substantially from the Portuguese and English silver that flowed into Spain. But it is doubtful if the country as a whole benefited to any extent, and even in Barcelona and in Valencia the temporary boom enjoyed under Allied occupation appears to have come to an end when the royalists took over. In Bourbon areas, our survey has shown that Spain tended to suffer rather than to benefit from the movement of precious metal. How, in these circumstances, could there have been a revival of banking? It is possible that the business promoted by the war increased the volume of financial transactions in the peninsula, and led to a greater rationalisation of credit facilities. But this subject, and indeed the whole subject of the rise of modern banking in Spain, is one that still awaits its historian.

In cloth production, efforts were made during the war to improve both the quality and the quantity of native textiles, particularly after the optimistic report drawn up by Gaspar Naranjo at the beginning of the reign. Both Orry and Naranjo, as we have seen in an earlier chapter, were responsible for placing large orders for textiles with Spanish firms. In 1705 the junta of commerce was reestablished in Madrid as part of a serious effort to promote the manufacture and export of cloth. Protectionist legislation, beyond the mere manipulation of customs duties, was employed to encourage native production: thus shortly after the end of the war we find a decree of 20 October 1719 ordering that only Spanish cloth be used for military uniforms.[39] Protection seems to have helped Valencia. Bernardo de Ulloa observes that the new tax régime in that kingdom was favourable to textile production, and that whereas the number of looms in Valencia just before 1718 did not exceed eight hundred, by 1725 there were as many as two thousand.[40] In Castile, however, most enterprises were unsuccessful in the long run. One luxury industry, that of silk (which admittedly may have received little

[39] A. Matilla Tascón, *Catálogo de la Colección de Ordenes Generales de Rentas*, Madrid, 1950, I, no. 626.
[40] *Restablecimiento de las Fábricas*, pp. 127–8.

stimulus during the war), continued its decline well into the eighteenth century. The president of the chancery of Granada complained that the number of looms in his city had declined from 6,800 in 1684 to under a third of that figure in 1714. Complaints like this may be found in many memorials of the time. The junta of commerce was generally unable to help. When in 1707 it recommended granting a subsidy of 22,000 reales to Gabriel Pérez de las Cuebas, a woollen manufacturer of Toledo, the council of the Hacienda refused to pay the grant, 'because of the pressing needs of the defence of these realms'.[41] It seems evident in the light of this incident that government policy, or at least the priorities adopted by the government, can be blamed for failures to encourage textile production. An index of this failure is provided by the records of the royal manufactory of cloths at Segovia, which show annual output rising from 3,078 pieces in 1700 to 4,294 pieces in 1703, but declining thereafter to 2,749 in 1717.[42] The table of production from 1699 to 1720 is as follows:

Year	pieces	Year	pieces
1699	2,976	1710	3,200
1700	3,078	1711	3,329
1701	3,751	1712	3,612
1702	4,177	1713	3,417
1703	4,294	1714	3,220
1704	4,215	1715	2,763
1705	4,124	1716	2,900
1706	3,258	1717	2,749
1707	3,975	1718	3,346
1708	3,381	1719	3,529
1709	3,197	1720	3,073

It is difficult to say without further research whether these setbacks were balanced by successful enterprises elsewhere. The probability is that little substantial advance was made. Bergeyck's scheme at Valdemoro was one of the few to emerge on the credit side. Philip v's most ambitious enterprise, a new woollen factory at Guadalajara which was promoted and controlled by the government and manned by Dutch workers, proved a failure. From

[41] *Consulta* of the Hacienda, 9 June 1707, AHN, Archivo Antiguo del Consejo leg.7223. I owe this reference to Mr William Callahan.

[42] The figures are given in *Actas y memorias de la Real Sociedad Económica de los Amigos del País de la provincia de Segovia* (4 vols), Segovia, 1785–93, vol. I, pp. 1–54.

1718 to 1724 the losses incurred by this factory totalled twelve million reales. When Gerónimo de Uztáriz visited the site on Patiño's orders in 1727, he confirmed the low quality of textiles produced there.[43] With a few significant exceptions,[44] therefore, it might appear that Spain had not begun to recover from its industrial inactivity. When the junta of commerce issued a *consulta* on manufactures on 30 September 1721,[45] it entitled the survey 'Decadencia de el comercio en España', a revealing pointer to the pessimism of officials. Such pessimism does not seem entirely justified. Both Valdemoro and Guadalajara were a step in the right direction. During the war, moreover, Spaniards had benefited from the services of several foreign artisans and entrepreneurs, despite the attempts of France to keep them out of the country. One such entrepreneur was Toussaint Percherot, who together with some French compatriots invested his money in the establishment of paper mills at Arco, near Segovia, and at Talamanca, just north of Madrid.[46]

Advance in the war industries also gives us reason to discount contemporary pessimism. The creation of royal guards and of a permanent standing army, called for support from industry in the form of uniforms and weapons. In the early period the Spaniards had to rely heavily on France. But native production of gunpowder and manufacture of artillery soon picked up. Later in the reign a decree of 20 November 1738 forbade the Spanish army to use any weapons other than those produced in Spain.[47] This seems to suggest that the country was by then self-sufficient in armaments, quite a different situation from that which existed at the beginning of the reign. The claim of Campomanes that

[43] AGS, Secretaría de Hacienda leg. 759 f.16.

[44] Partyet in his memoir of 17 May 1715 on Spanish manufactures, AE Mém. et Doc. (Esp.), 32 f.69, discusses one successful silk manufacturer who owed nothing to French help: 'J'ay examiné avec attention la fabrique de Madrid, elle est dans la Calle de l'Espejo ... le maitre de cette manufacture s'apelle François Vasquez, natif de Seville. Il m'a dit qu'il y avoit 7 ans qu'il estoit icy, qu'il avoit enfin obtenu du Roy Catholique par l'attention de la junte du commerce, et surtout par le zele et la vigilance du feu comte de Torrehermosa, plusieurs privileges pour faire fleurir sa fabrique'. Vázquez was exempted from virtually all taxes, and accorded other privileges besides. All his workers were native: 'pas un François ny etranger, tous Espagnols'. He had left Seville, where silks were poor. The Madrid silks were bettered only by those of Valencia.

[45] AE Mém. et Doc. (Esp.), 252 f.94.

[46] See Partyet's memoir, cited above.

[47] Matilla Tascón, *Catálogo de la Colección de Ordenes Generales de Rentas*, I, no. 626.

'for the first time, Spanish troops began to be dressed and armed with manufactures of Spain',[48] appears to be wholly justified.

Consequent to this military expansion was an increase in the size of the Spanish navy. Shipbuilding had never really picked up during the war. Piecemeal organisational changes had occurred,[49] but it was left to Bergeyck to concern himself seriously with naval recovery. His interest in the navy was profound. The French ambassador reported in April 1713 that 'though the comte de Bergeyck is waiting for the conclusion of peace in order to work seriously on the formation of a Spanish naval fleet, he has already begun to speak of it as a design he will not hesitate to carry out'.[50] Bergeyck's own communications to Pontchartrain speak of a plan which, like his scheme for intendants, was intended to draw extensively on French experience:[51]

The king has decided to establish a navy and shipyard in Biscay, and another in Andalucia at Cadiz. . . . His Majesty has decided on the building this year of six vessels of sixty cannon, but I do not dare assure Your Excellency that this will happen, principally because of the lack of the necessary materials. His Majesty has entrusted this manufacture [in Biscay] to Don Antonio Gastanera, whom I do not know but who has a great reputation and general approval. The king has not yet named any captain or other naval officer, because I know none, but I have been led to hope that some can be found in Biscay for these six vessels. . . . No building has been arranged this year for Andalucia.

I have spoken not only to the marquis de Bonnac and to the chevalier Nangy but also to several ministers at this court, about help that the king was hoping for from his friendship with His Most Christian Majesty, in the form of French naval officers to form the Spanish marine, and a small naval militia. Without this help one could not succeed in forming a navy in Spain. I have revealed only to the king the plan that I communicated to Your Excellency. It has become more necessary to keep it secret because of the jealous attitude of the English ministry.

As to sails and rigging for the six vessels being built in Spain, it is to the king's interest to have them bought where they are the best quality and the best price. It is just to choose France.

[48] *Discurso sobre la Educación Popular*, p. 420.
[49] E.g. the 19 June 1705 Order of Marine dividing the personnel of the navy into corps and ranks, text in AN Aff. Etr., B[III] 324 f.46.
[50] Bonnac to Pontchartrain, 6 Apr. 1713, AN Aff. Etr., B[I] 776.
[51] Bergeyck to same, 3 Apr. 1713, *ibid.*

The supersession of Bergeyck in the Spanish government obliged him to fight for the survival of his various plans for finance and the navy. It was subsequently pointed out to him by Bernardo Tinajero de la Escalera, secretary of the council of the Indies, that it might well be more economic to have the vessels built in Havana rather than in Spain. Bergeyck immediately deferred to this plan. At this juncture Orry arrived to take over the administration. He proposed an alternative plan which Bergeyck was obliged to accept. The Belgian informed Pontchartrain, no doubt with his tongue in his cheek, that he was 'delighted that so intelligent and hardworking a minister as [Orry] has come here'. Orry proposed not to wait for ships to be built in Spain or in America, but to buy twenty fully-fitted vessels from France and to begin the base at Cadiz with them.[52] After haggling over terms and prices, purchase of these vessels was eventually begun. In February 1714 Philip v created a new naval officer corps by abolishing all the old profusion of titles by which commanders of the various fleets were known, and instituting in their place a standard superior rank of Captain General of the Sea.[53] The admirals employed in the Atlantic crossing, men such as Pedro de los Ríos and Andrés de Pez, were appointed to the new rank, and were expected to share command of the newly instituted navy with a number of French officers appointed at the same time. It is not known whether these schemes of 1713-4 were successful. The real beginnings of the Spanish navy must in any case be credited not to Bergeyck or to Orry, but to Patiño, whose work as first naval intendant of Cadiz, from January 1717 onwards, alone made possible the several successful naval expeditions that took place under Philip v. The rise of the Spanish navy from the time of the War of Succession, is clearly illustrated by table 10 (page 229), which shows annual expenditure on it rising from 793,145 reales in 1705 to 14,887,610 in 1713 and 40,997,195 in 1717.

At this point we may dispose briefly of the question whether the war benefited Spain. The traumatic experience of foreign, even heretical, troops overrunning their hitherto inviolate ter-

---

[52] The details here are drawn particularly from the letters written to Pontchartrain by Bonnac, 17 Apr. 1713, by Bergeyck, 12 June 1713 and by Orry, 14 Aug. 1713, in *ibid.*

[53] Orry to Pontchartrain, 12 Feb. 1714, *ibid.*

ritory; of their king being twice forced to flee his capital; of the widely-hated French being everywhere accepted as necessary allies; may well have shaken Spaniards out of a stupor. The campaigns in themselves were not savage and reckless of Spanish lives or of the economy, so that Spanish administrators were not awakened out of one nightmare only to be plunged into another. The relatively mild impact of the war made it possible for a drastic reassessment to be made of the priorities facing Spain, and these priorities – government finance, army reorganisation, industrial advancement, political unification – were pursued vigorously wherever circumstances made it possible. Success did not come readily, but it was pursued with a spirit of enterprise, and under favourable administrative conditions, that had been lacking under the later Habsburgs. To this extent, no doubt, the war was beneficial, and the eventual benefits far exceeded in volume the damage caused to Spanish population, agriculture and commerce by a decade or more of civil conflict.

The part played by France in Spanish regeneration was highly equivocal. The French had little respect for the Spaniards, were as a rule willing to help them only if it aided the war effort, and were primarily interested in the opportunities for exploitation offered both in the peninsula and in America. Men, money and advice were certainly poured into Spain, but not out of pure altruism. One could go further and describe the pattern as a classic example of imperialist intervention. But French imperialism and exploitation must here be set firmly in perspective. No attempt was ever made to dominate the peninsula, and there was little concerted attempt to bleed it of its resources.[54] Louis XIV seems to have been genuinely concerned to have a fairly strong and friendly, though not unduly independent, Spain in his orbit. He therefore placed considerable restrictions on French intervention. Immigration into the peninsula was kept within limits, and in Madrid the wielding of political influence was entrusted

[54] Louis XIV's aims in the peninsula may be contrasted with those of Napoleon: the latter was a true chauvinist and imperialist, such as Louis never became. It is also instructive to see how Napoleon and his apologists, like the apologists for Philip V, tried to perpetuate the legend of Spanish decadence so as to boost the new French régime: e.g. Napoleon to Joachim, grand-duc de Berg, 24 May 1808: 'Je désire . . . des mémoires qui me fassent connaître le désordre et le délabrement dans les différentes branches de l'administration. Ces pièces me sont nécessaires pour publier un jour et faire voir dans quel etat de décadence etait tombée l'Espagne', *Correspondance de Napoléon I* (32 vols), Paris, 1858–70, vol. 17, p. 221.

to no more than a handful of French administrative and diplomatic officers. The main reason for this restraint was to convince both the Allies and Spaniards that France did not intend to take over the country. The French military presence in Spain was never an essential principle of French policy: troops were readily withdrawn in 1709 and at the end of the war. Frenchmen after 1715 remained preponderant only in those regions where their commitments had always lain, in the commercial centres at Cadiz, Valencia and elsewhere.

It is not easy to determine the importance of the French contribution to a renewal of Spanish power under Philip v. The achievement of people like Amelot and Orry is indisputable. Far less significant, however, is the role of the French circle at court with its petty factions and its self-appointed *éminences grises*. A reader of Baudrillart's account of the activities of the Spanish court and administration would be forgiven for thinking that French influence was all-pervasive and decisive in the years before Utrecht. The nature of Baudrillart's sources – almost exclusively the French archives – explains the bias of his narrative. A survey conducted from the other side reveals a somewhat different picture. Spaniards of the time, grandees no less than minor officials, had absolute personal devotion to Philip v and great admiration for Louis xiv, France and things French. But they hated Frenchmen as a whole, despised the French circle at court, distrusted French commercial and political policy, and (with the notable exception of Amelot) resented all French diplomats and ministers in Spain. Can it be said that, even in spite of these circumstances, the machinery and philosophy of French absolutism prevailed and took root in Spain?

I have suggested elsewhere[55] that the dominant radical tendencies of the reign were more native than French. This conclusion is also valid for the years of the War of Succession. The foreign reforms that eventually came to stay, such as the intendants, were acceptable precisely because they were consonant with Spanish practice and aspirations. It was Amelot who diminished the power of the councils and abolished the *fueros,* but these as well as other changes had long been supported by the *arbitristas* of Castile. Much of the effective work, then, was done by foreign advisers, by Amelot, Orry and Bergeyck. But the administration

[55] See the article on Macanaz cited above, p.48 note 13.

of their policies was certainly not carried out by Francophile Spaniards. One would search in vain among the administrators of the crown for an *afrancesado* of the type known under the Napoleonic régime in Spain. The most notorious of the early Bourbon reformers, Macanaz, has traditionally been described as a Francophile by Spanish historians; nothing could be further from the truth. In policy and personnel the Bourbon régime in Spain was Spanish and not French. This is not to detract from the fact that nearly all the practical aid received by the new dynasty at its inception was French: it adopted French weapons, French uniforms, French styles of dress, French administrative methods, and much besides. What it did not adopt was the theory and practice of French absolutism.

It is but a step from this to say, justly, that the dynastic change in 1700 brought no fundamental alteration in the structure of Spain as a whole. The accession of a new monarch could not by itself break continuity with Habsburg Spain and inaugurate a new era. The norms of political and public life continued as they were before 1700. The exercise in economic reform represented by the establishment of the junta of commerce in 1705 was itself an assertion of continuity, since the junta had been created originally in 1679. French ways made no impact on the religious habits of Spaniards, and Philip v found he had to conform to the practices of the Inquisition. Most significant of all, the social structure remained unaltered. The political decline of the old aristocracy and their ejection from the councils had little effect on their standing in public life. The political results cannot of course be minimised. The caste system of the grandees, first challenged during the war, was largely swept away in the course of the century. Leadership of the fortunes of the monarchy began to be assumed by men of lesser status, and the chief ministers of Spain after 1715 were for the most part officials who had been rewarded for good service in the War of Succession and who did not rely on titles or blood for preferment. But the removal of the grandees from power did not dispossess them of authority or influence. There was no decline in the importance of the nobility in public life, and they continued to dominate the economic life of Spain through their landed wealth and private territorial jurisdiction. In this respect, the efforts of the *junta de incorporación* must be considered a failure. Yet the activities of the *junta* are significant. In so far as it attempted to levy taxes on alienations rather than actually to revoke the alienations, it was conforming to the policy of Philip v, who wished to deprive the nobles of political power alone and was willing to tax their wealth but not deprive them of it.

The innate respect which the monarchy held for the aristocracy explains the fact that the annexation of Aragon and Valencia had few serious consequences for the nobility of those realms. Sanctions undertaken against rebel nobles appear to have been half-hearted. When lands in Valencia and Aragon were confiscated, no one of consequence in Madrid was willing to accept them as grants because of the widespread belief that they would be returned to their owners on the conclusion of peace.[56] This fear was to be justified. Only rarely did it prove impossible to return a noble's property: where, for instance, a defector's estates were overburdened by debts, they could not possibly be given back, and invariably fell into the hands of creditors. The conde de Cifuentes was one who suffered in this way. As his son-in-law the conde de Siruela, captain general of Aragon, reported in 1734, Cifuentes' creditors had become 'the true owners of his property'. Where debts did not preclude restoration, innocent parties frequently managed to recover the family fortune, since it was manifestly unfair to penalise a whole house for the sins of one member. One beneficiary from this sort of consideration was the condesa de Sástago, who together with her son the marqués de Aguilar was allowed to return to Saragossa from Barcelona in 1714. Most of the family property was returned to her, but her husband had to continue to live in exile.[57]

The noble exiles had for the most part gone to serve the Habsburgs in Italy or in Vienna. Their return, and in most cases the restoration of their property, was made possible by the Treaty of Vienna, signed in April 1725 by Spain and the Empire. Article nine of the treaty stipulated pardon for all defectors, recognition of the honours granted them by the archduke, and recovery of their homes and fortunes. Among those to benefit from this was the marqués de Rafal, who had for part of his exile, from 1709 to 1712, served as viceroy of Mallorca for the archduke. His property

[56] Bourke to Chamillart, 18 July 1707, Guerre, A¹ 2049 f.199.
[57] The cases of Cifuentes and Sástago are documented in AGS, Secretaría de Hacienda leg.66.

was returned to him by a royal order of 31 October 1725, and in 1726 he came back to his native Orihuela. A variety of reasons seem to have prevented other nobles from returning at the same time. The family of the conde de la Corzana (who had died in Vienna in 1720) did not return to Spain until 1738, and then only after the intervention of the marqués de la Ensenada. The principal grandeeships granted by the emperor and recognised by Philip v in accordance with the Treaty of Vienna, were as follows: grandees of the first class, the conde de Sástago, title recognised 15 December 1726; the conde de Cervellón, recognised 21 January 1727; the conde de Cardona, recognised 28 October 1727; the conde de Cifuentes, recognised 23 January 1727. Grandees of the second class, with the dates of their recognition, were as follows: Luc de Spinola, conde de Siruela, 15 December 1726; the marqués de Valparaiso, 18 December 1727; the conde de Fuentes, 18 December 1727; and the marqués de Scipion de Santa Cruz, 25 May 1728.[58] The Treaty of Vienna wiped out the antagonisms of the War of Succession and reconciled the higher aristocracy to the Bourbon régime. For the rest, the nobility of Aragon and Valencia were not seriously affected by the revocation of the *fueros*. They remained indifferent to the abolition of regional autonomy in the field of public law, because their own seigneurial rights were generally untouched. Higher taxation would have affected them only indirectly. The control of the land remained, as before, very much in their hands.

All this is enough to show that the war of the Spanish Succession witnessed no revolutionary social change. Indeed, in view of the many radical measures that had to be taken to meet the challenge of war, it is surprising that there were so few outstandingly successful reforms. The war itself no doubt inhibited any development of the reforms it had stimulated. Finance has been the main theme of the present survey, and it is disappointing after analysing the history of the Hacienda to find that no lasting changes were made in the machinery of taxation. In Castile the complex array of old taxes continued as before to be farmed out at considerable loss to both government and taxpayer. Only the crown of Aragon was fortunate enough to escape the Castilian system by accepting a single comprehensive tax, which still left it less heavily taxed

[58] Details from 'Relacion de los Grandes de España', AHN, Consejos suprimidos leg.5240.

than Castile. The many plans put forward in Castile for reform of the system were all rejected. In 1711 a certain Juan de Saa proposed a scheme to abolish the *millones* and replace them by a single tax. His plan was highly recommended by the financier Juan de Goyeneche and by the intendants Moreno Pacheco and Pedrajas. Macanaz even wrote a personal letter to the king in praise of Saa's plan.[59] But this failed just as the proposals of Orry and Bergeyck were to fail. Financiers, tax-farmers and officials all concurred in rejecting any reform that threatened their interests. *Juro* finance continued to be the order of the day. The situation remained unchanged throughout the reign of Philip v, and it was only in 1749 that Ensenada began his revolutionary attempt to uproot the whole traditional structure in favour of a comprehensive universal tax.

In the administrative field there appeared to be a comparable lack of development. The intendants were by no means a successful innovation, and even after 1718, when Patiño reestablished them, their continued existence was not assured. The various conciliar reforms of the French epoch were all undone in 1715. It seemed as though the clock was to turn back to 1700. But the pause in reform was only momentary. Looking back from the later years of the reign, it is possible to see the war period as the wellspring of reforms of extraordinary importance. The eighteenth century cannot really be understood without reference to the early years of Philip v. The abolition of Orry's measures in 1715 was therefore no more than a symbolic break, for the war and its attendant reforms were to influence subsequent development. Beginning his reign with war, Philip made war the basis of his finances, his administration and his foreign policy. The greater part of Hacienda expenditure throughout the reign went, as figure 2 (p. 230) shows, on war commitments. The stress laid on the creation of an army, and the military bias of administration which came to be based on intendants, led to the greater social importance of the officer class, whose self-conscious antics in the nineteenth and twentieth centuries can be traced back ultimately to the reign of the first Bourbon. The renewal of the military ethos for the first time since the sixteenth century shaped the whole political history of modern Spain. It is possible that Philip v

[59] Robinet to Campoflorido, 9 May 1711, AHN, Estado leg.410²; Macanaz to Philip v, 17 Apr. 1711, *ibid.*

aspired 'to rebuild the empire of his predecessors piece by piece'.[60] Whatever his motives, the series of wars from 1717 to 1720, in 1727, from 1732 to 1735 and from 1739 to the end of the reign, show an inordinate desire to use war as an instrument of policy. These wars were in any case made possible only because the Spanish crown emerged stronger and wealthier from the War of Succession than when the new dynasty came to power.

The newly acquired strength of the crown can be observed in three principal spheres: in the Church, in administration and in constitutional government. In ecclesiastical affairs, the war period witnessed the consolidation of 'regalism' in Spain. Both the word and the doctrines associated with it were popularised by Macanaz, particularly in his celebrated memoir of 1713 to the council of Castile. In its essentials regalism meant little more than a continuation of the firm ecclesiastical policy associated with, for instance, Philip II. Under Philip V, however, it was somewhat more than this. Thanks to Macanaz's writings, regalism meant an assertion, based on juridical right and historical precedent, of royal supremacy over both Church and Inquisition in Spain. Regalism as a doctrine came into existence during the War of Succession, when the episcopacy of Spain became divided between those who did and those who did not support this view of the crown's powers. Among those who were ardent and total regalists the figure of Francisco de Solís stands out.[61] Philip appointed Solís to the see of Lérida in August 1701. There he distinguished himself, as we have seen in passing, by his devotion to the Bourbon cause, a devotion which gained him for a while the vice-royalty of Catalonia. In 1709 he led the clerical party supporting the suspension of diplomatic relations with Rome, an event which will occupy us presently. It was in that year that he published his notorious regalist tract *On the abuses of the Roman Court in what touches the royal rights of His Catholic Majesty and the jurisdiction of bishops* [*Sobre los abusos de la Corte Romana, por lo tocante a las Regalías de S. M. Católica, y jurisdicción que reside en los Obispos*].[62] Delighted with this tract, Philip V immediately nominated Solís to the see of Avila, which had been vacant since 1705. There was considerable

[60] Antonio Bethencourt, *Patiño en la política internacional de Felipe V*, Valladolid, 1954, p. 23.

[61] J. Fernández Alonso, 'Francisco de Solís, obispo intruso de Avila (1709)', *Hispania Sacra*, XIII, 25 (1960).

[62] Printed in *Semanario Erudito*, vol. 9, pp. 206–86.

opposition to this appointment within Spain, especially from the immensely loyal but firmly papalist bishop of Murcia, Luis Belluga. Rome naturally refused to countenance the appointment, and it was not until Solís wrote a personal letter to the pope in June 1710, confirming his allegiance to the Holy See, that he was accepted as lawful bishop of Avila. Belluga's outstanding loyalty to Rome on this and subsequent occasions eventually earned him the red hat. The Solís affair was only one of the several questions over which the Spanish bishops differed. The other incidents we can touch on briefly are the break with Rome in 1709, and the clash between the crown and the inquisitor general in 1705 and 1714.

On 22 April 1709 a royal decree broke off diplomatic relations with Rome and ordered the expulsion of the papal nuncio from Spain. Philip's official reason for this was that Clement XI had been supporting the archduke. While this may have been true, in reality a wide variety of factors had together contributed to the split. Perhaps the most important bone of contention was Naples. Though Philip had inherited Naples and Sicily with the rest of the monarchy, his formal tenure of these territories derived from the papacy, and as late as 1705 the pope had still not agreed to invest him with their possession. The pope's distrust of Spain, as well as a desire not to offend the Empire, seem to have been the operative motives. Action taken by the viceroy of Naples in 1705 against a few treasonable clergy, aggravated papal antipathy. In Spain itself there were several causes for dissension. The most notable of these was the affair of the inquisitor general Mendoza, who is discussed below. When Mendoza appealed to Rome against the king, Philip promptly prohibited all appeals to Rome and banned the reception of papal decrees in Spain. In the years after this both sides had good reason to be offended over the issue of clerical taxation. Philip V quite naturally wished his own clergy to contribute as often and as generously as possible. The pope for his part was reluctant to surrender clerical privileges of exemption, nor was he willing to allow too much extraordinary taxation for fear he might appear to be supporting the Bourbons. In 1706 he issued a rebuke to the see of Toledo for advancing money to the crown, and in 1707 his legate censured the archbishop of Saragossa for the same reason. The disputes gradually mounted in volume. Some were settled amicably, like the affair of the incarcerated bishops. The pope had objected to the continued imprisonment in Spain of the bishops of Segovia and Barcelona: in 1706 Philip gave way and allowed them to pass into exile and be kept under papal supervision at Avignon. This incident was one of the many in which Louis xiv managed to arrange a compromise between the interests of Spain and the Holy See. Well aware of the pope's considerable influence, Louis was unwilling to allow any rupture between his grandson and Rome. His letters to Amelot reveal a constant anxiety to keep the two powers on speaking terms at least; he was strongly opposed to the withdrawal of Philip's ambassador to Rome in 1708, and to the eventual break in 1709.[63]

While Philip's firm attitude to the papacy was fundamentally a continuation of the strong policies of Charles v and Philip 11, his clashes with the Inquisition were a relatively new departure in Spanish history. Not even Philip 11 had dared to cross the Holy Office. Philip did so on two occasions within the space of ten years. On the first occasion he intervened against the inquisitor general Balthasar de Mendoza, bishop of Segovia, over a domestic quarrel in the Inquisition.[64] The king was further incensed against Mendoza when he proved to be a partisan of the Austrian cause, and confined him to his see of Segovia. Mendoza made the mistake of appealing to Rome, which brought about his arrest, and dismissal in March 1705 from the post of inquisitor general. An obscure prelate, the bishop of Ceuta, was appointed to the Inquisition in his place. Philip's next clash occurred over the December 1713 memorandum drawn up by Macanaz.[65] Like the tract drawn up by Solís in 1709, Macanaz's document was strongly regalist and virtually schismatic, since it called for a severe limitation on papal authority in Spain. The inquisitor general at this time was an Italian, Cardinal Giudice,[66] a confirmed enemy of Macanaz. On 31 July 1714 he issued a condemnation of

[63] See for example the letters from Louis xiv to Amelot dated 26 Sept. 1706, 9 Apr. 1708 ('Toute rupture avec la cour de Rome ne peut jamais produire aucune utilité'), 16 Apr. 1708, 22 Apr. 1709: in Girardot, *Correspondance de Louis XIV*.

[64] The background to this case is discussed in H. C. Lea, *A History of the Inquisition of Spain* (4 vols), New York, 1906–8, vol. 2, pp. 168–78.

[65] For this see the article on Macanaz cited above, p. 48 note 13; and Henry Kamen, *The Spanish Inquisition*, London, 1965, pp. 240–2.

[66] The bishop of Ceuta, Vidal Marin, was succeeded as inquisitor general by the archbishop of Saragossa. On the death of the latter in Sept. 1710 the post was given to Giudice through the influence of Medinaceli.

the author and contents of the memorandum. This was a direct challenge to Philip, who had personally authorised the document. He immediately ordered the resignation of Giudice and the suspension of all censures against Macanaz. At the same time he asked Macanaz and a colleague to examine the archives of the Inquisition with a view to reforming the tribunal and subordinating it completely to the crown. This work was never completed, for the fall of Macanaz and his friends from power early in 1715 brought the Italians, and with them Giudice, back into control.

In all these ecclesiastical quarrels the king enhanced his position by acting firmly. The refusal to compromise with Rome or with the Inquisition, and the apparent willingness to go as far as schism and direct control over the Holy Office, showed that 'regalism' was not an empty doctrine but a very conscious code of action. Philip's attitude gave to the crown a strength in spiritual affairs⁶⁷ that it had lacked since the sixteenth century.

In administrative matters we have already seen the crown resuming the initiative. True, the war witnessed only the beginnings of important new changes, but they were significant enough. Despite the lack of tax reforms, alterations in accounting and organisation made the central treasury well equipped to deal with the finances of the monarchy. Despite the lack of reform in the whole system of office-holding, a more compact executive structure at the top enabled work to be dealt with more efficiently in the reformed councils and in the bureaux of the secretaries of state. The system of intendants was the most promising of all the new developments. They were intended in the long run to be the nucleus of an efficient liaison between central and local government, and if at the beginning they were confined largely to military duties, this did not diminish their importance. Their first duty was to administer the army, but they gradually took over other functions outside the military sphere and soon began to act as a civil authority through their general assumption of the post of *corregidor*. At every level of administration, therefore, the crown could look forward to an era of expanding activity.

Most significant of all, Spain had been constitutionally unified, while constitutional government had been for all practical purposes abolished. The Basque provinces and Navarre still retained

⁶⁷ Only five Spanish prelates opposed the break with Rome in 1709: the archbishops of Santiago, Toledo, Seville and Granada, and the bishop of Murcia.

their autonomy, but Castile and Aragon, the largest kingdoms of the peninsula, were now one. Barcelona, Saragossa and Valencia were in future to be ruled from Madrid. From the point of view of parliamentary government, this was no gain at all. The cortes in the crown of Aragon had been thriving: in Castile it was virtually dead. The meetings of the Castilian cortes during the reign of Philip were of no constitutional importance. The cortes of 1701 was summoned solely to swear allegiance to Philip. That of 1709, which opened on 7 April, was summoned merely to take an oath of allegiance to the heir, the principe Luis. By this time the crown of Aragon had lost its autonomy, and Philip required the realms of Aragon and Valencia to send their parliamentary representatives to attend the 1709 Castilian cortes. Sixteen cities, eight from each kingdom, were thus entitled to sit in an assembly which never discussed their affairs. The next cortes held in Madrid sat from 6 October 1712 to 10 June 1713. Its only business was to assent to two acts concerning the crown: firstly, on 9 November, the king renounced his rights of succession to the French throne; secondly, on 10 May, the king issued a pragmatic excluding all female heirs from the throne. The cortes was summoned only once again before 1746, and that was in 1724, to swear allegiance to the Infante Fernando. Parliamentary government was dead, and by implication the voice of the municipalities of Spain was totally extinguished.[68] Absolutism had triumphed in Spain. It should be remembered, however, that the decline of parliamentary government in Castile derived from the middle of the seventeenth century, so that we cannot speak of Philip v introducing a new trend or a new philosophy of Bourbon absolutism. What was novel was the destruction of representative institutions where they had flourished most, in Aragon, yet even that, as we have already seen, must be explained more in terms of the aspirations of Castilian statesmen than in terms of the introduction of French authoritarian government.

In both ecclesiastical and civil affairs there was a restoration of initiative to an invigorated and centralised state, and it is principally in the increase of state power that Bourbon Spain represents an improvement on the Spain of the Habsburgs. Shorn at Utrecht of the burden of Italy and the Netherlands, the country could

---

[68] 'El estado llano, en su doble manifestación del municipio y de las Cortes, quedó anulado como fuerza política': Danvila y Collado, *El poder civil*, vol. 3, p. 409.

devote itself to internal recuperation and external resurgence.

The long climb out of decline was slow but purposeful. Spaniards towards the end of the war, many of them full of hope in their new king, began to reassess the reasons why Spain had fallen so low among nations. Among the many themes they developed there is one in particular which recurs constantly in their writings. An example may be cited in a pamphlet of 1714 entitled *Reply of a friend to one who asks when there will be an end to our ills in Spain.*[69] The writer says:

> Many talented pens have wearied themselves outlining the root of our ills; some say the cause is the union with Austria and with the Low Countries, that graveyard of Spaniards and ruin of their treasure; others prove it to be the conquest of America, which has taken our sons and wearied our bodies in extracting its riches; others identify it with the expulsion of the Moriscos, who supported our agriculture, that producer of soldiers and population . . .
>
> But the principal reason for our lament is the innate hostility with which all foreigners have always looked on Spain.

Another pamphlet of the same year, without a title and in the form of an anonymous letter, blamed foreign advisers (excepting only Amelot) for the evils suffered by the country since 1700.[70] Such xenophobia was nothing new, for Spaniards had long resented their foreign exploiters. But the sentiment was almost certainly aggravated by the experience of the 1702–14 war. The French in particular emerged rather badly, as our evidence has already shown. Père Labat, passing through Spain in 1706, testified that they were everywhere exceedingly unpopular, both for their trade to America and for their activities in the peninsula, and that the name *gavache* continued to be applied to them.[71] The struggle against French commercial privileges which occupied Alberoni and other ministers of the crown, and the split which developed between the Bourbons when the regency came to power in France, strengthened the hostility of Spaniards. Ironically, it was Macanaz, the collaborator of the French

---

[69] *Respuesta de un amigo a otro que le pregunta por el fin que vendrán a tener nuestros males en España*, B Nac., MS 10818/7, printed by V. Palacio Atard in *Anuario de la Historia del Derecho Español*, XVIII (1947).

[70] AE Corr. Pol. (Esp.), 229 f.113.

[71] *Voyage du P. Labat*, p. 88: 'Le nom de *gavache*, dont les Espagnols se servent pour indiquer ceux qu'ils meprisent, et surtout les François, signifie un homme de néant, un gueux, un lache.'

ministers of Philip v, who distinguished himself by his distrust of France. His suspicions were aroused as early as 1706, when Philip v, in his retreat from the siege of Barcelona, was forced to return to Castile through France. On that occasion Macanaz claimed that the French government had plotted to keep Philip in France against his will until he agreed to a division of the monarchy.[72] Subsequent events did nothing to lessen his firm belief that France wished to ruin Spain. Louis xiv's pressure on Philip to divide the monarchy, even to forsake the throne, was proof enough. French commercial ambitions put the issue beyond dispute. Many years later Macanaz informed José Carvajal, chief minister of Spain, that 'since the year 1701 the French government has used every means to destroy Spain; and Cardinal Fleury used to say that he would not be content until he saw it reduced to being a province of France'.[73]

The reference to Macanaz brings us to one of his writings which epitomises the theme of xenophobia. His *Males, daños y perjuicios que han ocasionado a la España, a su Iglesia, y a su Rey, los Extrangeros que han tenido manejo en el Ministerio Español* [*The evils, harm and prejudice which foreigners who have held office in the government have caused to Spain, its Church and its king*][74] was written in exile as a commentary on the *Historia civil de España* of Nicolàs de Jesús Belando. It is a sweeping attack on the preponderance first of French then of Italian ministers in the Spanish government since the accession of Philip v. To a student of Spanish history Macanaz's rage seems fully justified, since Spanish antipathy to both French and Italians was of long standing, and it is ironic that they should have been the dominant influence in a régime that was otherwise thoroughly acceptable to most Spaniards.

Though the war ended on a note of disillusion with foreigners,

---

[72] 'Don Melchor de Macanaz atribuye a los franceses un designio siniestro . . . el de arruinar la España', Lafuente, *Historia General de España*, vol. 18, p. 134 note 1.

[73] Macanaz to Carvajal, 17 July 1747, AGS, Estado leg.4695. In his *Varias notas al Teatro Crítico del Eruditísimo Feyjoo*, written in 1758 and printed in *Semanario Erudito*, vol. 7, pp. 205–80; vol. 8, pp. 1–135, Macanaz has some interesting comments to make on the Ninth Discourse. He says (vol. 7, p. 229) of 'los Ministros de Francia' that 'queriendo ellos sujetar a los Españoles, entretienen la guerra con la multitud de tratados engañosos y artificiales que han hecho, ya con unas, ya con otras potencias, desde el año de 1701 acá, sin haber tenido en todos ellos otra mira que la de acabar con la España'. One wonders if Amelot is included in this condemnation.

[74] B Nac., MS 2768.

there was one saving feature. The remarkable success of the English, who had annexed Gibraltar and Minorca and secured the Asiento at Utrecht, began to arouse the admiration of Spaniards. Britain was fated to be the country's principal enemy for the next half century, but on the Spanish side the enmity was accompanied by emulation. English naval strength was to be the chief cause of the great expansion in Spanish naval power, while English commercial success (particularly the use of trading companies) provoked writers to urge a policy of commercial expansion on their government. Macanaz was among the few who went so far as to try to secure a rapprochement between the two countries.[75] English cultural leadership inevitably struck echoes within Spain, where English books in French translation, 'English thought through a French pen' as he put it, became the inspiration of the Benedictine monk Feijóo, commonly regarded as the father of the Spanish Enlightenment.

In the end, however, it was the Spaniards themselves who took in hand the regeneration of their country. Spanish administrators, entrepreneurs and generals, together helped to rescue the state, industry and the military machine from nearly a century of decadence. Though the retrograde prejudices of Old Spain, typified in the rekindling of the fires of the Inquisition barely half a dozen years after the war, continued as strongly in force as ever, there were glimpses of a new dawn. Young nobles of eminence, like the duque de Osuna,[76] devoted their energies to a serious analysis of Spanish economic conditions; while others of noble but less distinguished birth spent their career in the administrative service as intendants of the crown. The war, which had brought so much misery to Europe, was both to them and to Spain a beginning of hope.

Spanish resurgence, however, did not carry with it any immediate solution to the profound fissures in the life of the state and of the people. The destruction of Aragonese autonomy brought no nearer the day when Spain might become a moral as well as a physical unity: on the contrary, the circumstances, method and consequences of the abolition of the *fueros* only

[75] See p. 711 of the article cited above, p. 48 note 13.

[76] L. Zumalacarregui, 'El proyecto del Duque de Osuna para la reconstrucción económica de España en el siglo XVIII', *Anales de Economía*, VII, 28 (1947). The plan was drawn up by Osuna, then aged thirty-four, in 1712 when he was ambassador in Paris.

helped to convince a later generation that greater justice could be found in a federal structure for Spain. External resurgence was principally a diversion of Spanish resources to further the interests of expansionism in the western Mediterranean. At home the priorities were placed on those industries and enterprises that served this outwardly orientated policy. Within the country the disputes that had emerged during the war and been tidied away at the peace, went without remedy; the cause of constitutionalism, of disengagement from empire and economic retrenchment at home, the cause of the commercial bourgeoisie of Catalonia no less than that of the Levant peasantry: these quarrels were submerged, to surface again in the late nineteenth century. It is one of the ironies of history that the Bourbon dynasty, which established itself over a prostrate popular movement (in Valencia and Aragon), a moribund constitutionalism (in Castile) and a defeated provincialism (in Catalonia), should owe its eventual fall in the twentieth century to a revival of these three factors which the administrators of Philip v thought they had eliminated for ever.

Appendix 1
Measures and money

The different units of weight and measure used in this book will cause less confusion in the reader's mind if reference is made to the details given below. I have limited myself to defining only those units that appear in the text.

Measures
Liquid measures have been expressed in *arrobas*. The *arroba* was not standardised and varied according to region and liquid; used of water or wine, for example, it expressed a weight equivalent to 34 pounds (*libras*).

The basic commercial dry weight used in this book is also the *arroba*, which measured wool, tobacco and other items. It equalled 25 pounds (*libras*). Four *arrobas* were equivalent to a *quintal* or hundredweight.

Grain measures have been expressed in *fanegas*, each *fanega* being equivalent to about 1½ bushels. Used of cacao, the *fanega* expressed a weight of 116 pounds. (The *fanega* was also used as a surface area measure; when this was the case, it normally equalled about 1·6 acres.) Other grain measures used are the *carga* (4 *fanegas*), and the *cahiz* (12 *fanegas*). It should be noted that in Aragon a *cahiz* was equal to only 3½ Castilian *fanegas*.

Money
Wherever possible I have converted all units of currency to the *real* of *vellón*, the most common unit of account in Castile at the time. Because they occur so frequently, names of coins are not hereafter or in the text printed in italics. The real was worth 3·2d of English money in 1734 and 2·4d in 1826.

The main Castilian moneys used in this book, and their values, are:

1 real	=	34 maravedis
10 reales	=	1 escudo (crown)
11 reales	=	1 ducado (ducat)
15 reales	=	1 peso
60 reales	=	1 doblon (doubloon)

The equivalence between Castilian and Aragonese money is:

1	Castilian doblón	=	3·19 Aragonese pounds (*libras jaquesas*)
5	Castilian doblones	=	16 Aragonese pounds
1·87	reales of vellon	=	1 real of *plata doble* (i.e. silver) of Aragon

The equivalence between Castilian and Valencian money is:

1	Castilian peso	=	1 Valencian pound (*libra valenciana*)
256	Castilian reales	=	17 Valencian pounds

Both the Aragonese and Valencian pounds were subdivided into shillings (*sueldos*) and pence (*dineros*).

French money played a fundamental role in the war. The normal equivalence accepted with Castilian money was:

1	livre tournois	=	5 reales of vellon

The French called the doblon a *pistole* or *louis d'or*, and the peso an *écu* or *piastre*.

Appendix 2
Spanish-American shipping

Table 3 on p. 178 has given a breakdown of Spanish–American shipping in terms of vessels and tonnage for the years 1701–15. The details are drawn principally from the register of arrivals and departures in AGI Contratación, libro 2901. The table should not be considered absolutely reliable, for the following reasons:

1. The *libro de registros,* the register-book at Seville, is incomplete. It generally gives details only of vessels arriving at or departing from the Seville–San Lucar–Cadiz complex, that is of ships actually registered with the authorities, and fails to take account of the movement of vessels to and from other parts of Spain. If we followed the register alone we would get substantial errors. Thus in 1706 only one ship, of 91 *toneladas,* is registered as arriving from America. Yet, as we know, the Basque ship *Rosario* arrived in March from America; a vessel of 289 *toneladas,* it had sailed from Cadiz on 21 February 1702. This makes a considerable difference to the 1706 tonnage. Vessels not featuring in the *libro de registros* generally arrived on the Galician and Basque coasts, or in France. Thus in 1709 we have the Basque ship *San Antonio de Padua* arriving in Brest. This does not appear in the register nor, since its tonnage is unknown, in table 3. Again, in 1710 we have a Spanish vessel arriving at Redondela from Vera Cruz: this appears neither in the register nor in table 3. There was clearly, then, a volume of Spanish–American shipping of which the register did not, and could not, take account.

2. The calculation of tonnage is not always reliable. In over 90 per cent of the ships listed, tonnage is given. For the few ships with no given tonnage, and for the warships, I have had to arrive at estimates. I am not here concerned with the relationship

between tonnage and freight, or with whether tonnage figures
have any bearing on the volume of merchandise.

3. The list of ships must, from one point of view, necessarily be
incomplete. Do we, for example, include the tonnage of all
ships that left port, or only the tonnage of ships that arrived at
their destination? If we include all departures, as with the four
ships registered as having left in 1704, we make an error of 50
per cent, since two of the four vessels (145 out of 323 *toneladas*)
were captured the day afterwards and never crossed the Atlantic.
Similarly, if we include in our assessment the tonnage figures for
the Vigo fleet of 1702, we are in effect counting merchandise that
did not exist, since most of it perished in Vigo Bay. If we omit
the Vigo fleet, on the other hand, our tonnage assessment for the
1702 arrivals sinks from 4,379 to 558 *toneladas*. To take another
point relevant to the completeness of the list, should we include
in our count foreign vessels sailing with the Spanish ships?
Technically, they are not part of the Spanish–American traffic.
Of the twenty-five ships sailing from Cadiz in 1708, and returning
in 1710, six were French. If we exclude them, the total tonnage
figures for 1708 fall by a third. If we include them, on the other
hand, we must by the same token include the large French
fleet that came to Vigo with the Spanish vessels. In short, a basic
choice arises: either we measure the total traffic between Spain
and America, regardless of the nationality of ships; or we measure
only the volume of Spanish shipping. In table 3 I have compromised on the two points I have raised by including all departures,
regardless of arrival; and the French ships of 1708 and 1710, but
not those at Vigo.

4. Finally, table 3 should not be used as an index of commercial
activity. It is some guide, of course, to the naval and commercial
activity of Spain during the War of Succession. But it is no guide
at all to the commercial life of the Atlantic or of Latin America,
for the simple reason that the volume of commerce carried on by
the English, French and Dutch far exceeded that carried on from
Spain. During the War of Succession, as chapter 7 suggests,
French shipping to South America was demonstrably greater
than Spanish: on this showing the movement of the port of
Saint-Malo could well shed more light on the Atlantic trade than
the movement of the ports of Seville and Cadiz.

Appendix 3
The population of Aragon in 1718

The library of the Real Academia de la Historia, Madrid, contains a manuscript volume, number 9-26-1-4762, giving details of the population of Aragon in the eighteenth century. The whole account is preceded by a preface dated 7 July 1778. Data are given for 1718, from a census made of all the *corregimientos* of Aragon with a view to imposing military taxation, almost certainly the *única contribución*. The assessment appears to have been made not according to *vecinos,* i.e. heads of households, but *vecinos utiles,* i.e. households which were not exempt from taxation and whose economic position made them capable of paying the tax. By this definition, a list of *vecinos utiles* represents not the actual population of the realm but only the tax-paying population; so that the figures given in the 1718 data are not useful as an estimate of the population of Aragon, which we have already estimated according to the censuses that preceded the *única contribución.* The profound variation even in figures for *vecinos utiles* is shown by the following comparison between the figures for 1717 and 1722 (taken from 'Vecindario General de Espana', B Nac. MS 227 f.253-74 and 304-5) and those for 1718:

	1717	1718	1722
Saragossa	9,201	7,946	9,072
Huesca	3,036	2,954	2,973
Alcañiz	7,243	7,259	7,224
Teruel	4,173	4,132	4,173
Borja	1,759	1,355	1,759
Cinco Villas	2,178	1,858	2,178
Daroca	4,815	4,264	4,551
Albarracin	1,190	928	1,171
Calatayud	3,832	4,245	3,815
Tarazona	1,863	1,057	1,485

	1717	*1718*	*1722*
Barbastro	4,523	4,332	4,522
Jaca	1,886	1,833	1,886
Benavarre	2,576	2,533	2,572
	48,275	44,696	47,381

The usefulness of the 1718 returns, then, lies less in its population data than in other directions.

The returns give the lordship or *señorío* of each settlement in Aragon, and an analysis of this has been given in chapter 10. The total number of towns was arrived at by including only settlements of more than one *vecino* or one house.

The 1718 population of the city of Saragossa is given as 2,595 *vecinos utiles*. Other figures differ from this. Those in the 1713 census (B Nac., MS2274 f.275) give the city 2,491; in the 1716 census (*ibid.*, f.253) the city was assessed at 3,525, and in 1723 a new assessment put the figure at 2,575 'vezinos capazes de contribuir' (letter of 17 Dec. 1726 from city of Saragossa to the Hacienda, AGS Secretaría de Hacienda, leg.536). No obvious balance can be struck between these figures, but it is interesting to note that the *vecindario* given for 1723 is equivalent, according to the returns of the census, to a total city population of 30,039 persons. This puts the equivalence of *vecino util* to persons at 1:11·6, an equivalence which seems excessively high and is certainly not generally valid.

In two of the *corregimientos* of Aragon, the manuscript gives parallel returns for 1646 and 1718. While it is certain that the two censuses were carried out on a different basis, it may not be without interest to compare the returns in order to assess any variation in population. In the two *corregimientos* concerned, Saragossa and Alcañiz, figures have been utilised only for towns that gave returns in both years.

	1646	*1718*	*Variation*
Saragossa	5,588	2,595	− 53·6%
Most other towns	5,916	4,439	− 25 %
Alcañiz	875	482	− 45 %
Most other towns	8,036	6,778	− 15·7%

The population in *vecinos utiles* of other chief towns in Aragon in

1718 is given as follows: Barbastro 408; Benavarre 144; Borja
134; Calatayud 577, with 651 inhabited houses; Sos 134, with
104 inhabited houses; Ejea 215; Tauste 165; Uncastillo 104;
Daroca 268, with 410 inhabited houses; Huesca 655; Jaca 246;
Tarazona 320; Teruel 364.

Appendix 4
The nobility of Aragon and Valencia

The following list is taken from AHN Consejos suprimidos leg.5240 no. 10, from a manuscript entitled 'Relaciones de los Grandes titulos y Dignidades de la Corona de Aragón, Valencia y Cathaluña'. Though not dated, the paper belongs to a date just after the War of Succession. This list has been printed in Antonio Domínguez Ortiz, *La Sociedad española en el siglo XVII,* p. 357, but with a few variations and without some of the accompanying detail. A comparison of the list with appendix 5 will show to what extent the urban centres, if not the countryside, of Valencia was under the control of Castilian rather than Valencian nobles.

NOBILITY OF ARAGON

Grandees

Duque de Villahermosa en Valencia y Conde de Luna en Aragón	estos estados estan en pleyto.
Duque de Yxar	D Fernando Pinateli.
Conde de Aranda	este estado está en pleyto.
Marqués de Camarara en Cathaluña y Conde de Ricla en Aragón	D Balthasar de los Cobos.
Conde de Peralada en Cathaluña y de Albatera en Valencia	D Guillen de Rocafull: reside en Aragon y está casado con hija de la Marquesa de la Viluena.

Títulos

Marquesa de la Vilueña	Da Juana Rocafull.
Marqués de Coscojuela	D Bartolomé de Moncayo: está con los enemigos.
M de Villaverde y Conde de Morata	D Joseph Sanz de Cortes.
M de Ariza	D Juan de Palafox.
M de Cañizares de Navarrens	D Joseph de Bardaxi.

M de Barboles y Conde de Contamina	estos estados estan en pleyto.
M de Torres	D Pedro Bolea y Abarca.
M de Ariño	este estado está en pleyto.
M de Lazan	D Bernabe de Rebolledo y Palafox.
Ma de Osera	Da Maria Villalpando: viuda del Conde de Montijo en Castilla.
M de Villalva	D Manuel de Villanueva.
M de Boil	D Joseph Boil: está con los enemigos.
M de la Torrecilla	D Felix Salabert.
M de San Martin	D Alexandro de Tudela.
M de Valdeolivo	D Rodrigo Pujadas.
M. de Santa Coloma	D Antonio de la Torre.
M de Campo Real	D Fernando de Sada.
M de Vallestar	D Felix Costa.
M de Villasegura	D Antonio Blanco.
M de Villafranca de Ebro	D Juan Miguel Iñiguez.
M de Tosos	D Juan de Afanza.
M de Lierta	D Joseph Fonbuena.
M del Risco	D Juan Luys Lopez.
M de Castro Piños	D Antonio de Benavides: está con los enemigos
M de Miana	D Thomas de Pomar.
M de Selva Real	D Manuel Monter.
Conde de Fuentes y Marqués de Mora	D Jorge de Yxar: está con los enemigos
C de Robres	D Augustin Pons.
C de Belchite y de Aliaga	D Pedro Luys de Yxar.
C de San Clemente y Marqués de Eguaras	D Dionisio de Eguaras.
C de Montenegro y de Montoro	D Juan de Espuch.
C de Peñaflorida	[no name given]
C de Atares y del Villar	D Joseph Sanz de Latras.
C de Plasencia	D Juan de Lanuza: está con los enemigos.
C de Fuenclara	D Joseph Cebrian.
C de Torres Secas	D Alonso de Villalpando.
C de la Rosa	D Juan Abarca.
C de Bureta	D Mathias Marin.
C de Berbedel	D Antonio de Urrea.
C de Guara	D Juan de Azlor.

o

C de Sobradiel — D Mathias Cabero.

C de Sástago — D. Christoval de Cordova: está con los enemigos.

C de la Torre de San Braulio — D [no name] de Pomar y Carnicer.

C de Castelflorid — esta en pleyto.

NOBILITY OF VALENCIA

Grandees

Duque de Segorve, Marqués de Denia — D Luis de la Zerda y Aragón [= the Duque de Medinaceli].

Duque de Gandia, Marqués de Lombay, Conde de Oliva, Conde de Villalonga — D Pasqual Francisco de Borja.

Marqués de Elche — D Joachin Ponce de León [= the Duque de Arcos].

Duque de Liria — D Jacobo Fitz James [= the Duke of Berwick]

Conde de Cozentayna — D Francisco de Benavides Ruiz de Corella.

Conde de Albatera — D Guillem de Rocaful.

Duque de Villahermosa — Hay pleito pendiente en el Consejo entre Da Francisca de Gurrea y Aragon, el Marqués de Cabrega, D Diego y D Antonio Juan Gurrea y Aragón, el Marqués de Albayda, D Miguel Juan de Ardena, el Marqués de Coscojuela y el Conde de Barnuis.

Títulos

Marquesa de Benavides — Da Maria Francisca Belvis, viuda.

Marqués de Albayda, Conde de Buñol — D Jimen Milan de Aragón.

M de Villatorcas — D Joseph de Castelvi y Alagon.

Marquesa de Rafal — Da Gerónyma Rocamora. que pasó con su marido a los enemigos.

Marqués de Dos Aguas — D Xiner Rabaza de Perellos.

M de Llanzol — D Francisco Llanzol de Romani.

Marquesa de Castelnovo — Da Theresa Folch de Cardona y Milan.

M de Malferit — D Jacinto Roca.

M de Navarres	D Joseph Bermudez de Castro Urries Gurrea y Aragon.
M de Colomer	D Francisco Colomer.
Marquesa del Bosque	Da Maria Luisa Martínez de Vera y Bosdi.
M de la Torre de Carruz	D Joseph Miralles.
Marquesa de Llaneras y Condesa de Olocau	Da Maria de Villaragut Chiriroga Hurtado de Mendoza.
M de Almonacir y Conde de Pavia	Es de una administracion y obra pia dexada por Da Cathalina Artal de Aragón, que está a cargo del Marqués de Castelrodrigo y otros administradores.
M de Belgida	D Joseph Vicente Belvis.
M de Noguera	D Joseph Coloma: está en Francia desterrado.
M de la Casta y Conde de Alacuas	D Juan Pardo de la Casta: que pasó a los enemigos.
M del Rafol	D Antonio Armunia.
M de la Escala	D Vicente Buyl de la Escala.
M de Mirasol	D Vicente Carroz.
M de Castelfort	D Chrisostomo Peris.
M de Guadaleste	Hay pleyto pendiente en el Consejo entre el Marqués de Ariza y D Joseph de Cardona que se pasó a los enemigos.
M de Cullera	D Christoval de Moscoso.
Conde de Albalat	D Joseph Sorell y Roca.
C del Real y C de Villamonte	D Ximen Perez de Calatayud.
C de Almenara	D Joseph Proxita y Ferrer.
C de Villanueva	D Joseph Valterra y Blanes.
C de Cervellón	D Juan de Castelvi.
C de Sirat	D Gaspar de Calatayud, que se pasó a los enemigos.
C de Elda y C de Ana	D Francisco Coloma, se pasó a los enemigos.
C del Casal	D Antonio Thomas Cavanillas se pasó a los enemigos.
C de Villafranqueza	D Joseph Ceverio y Cardona, se pasó a los enemigos.
C de Faura	D Joseph Ribes de Cañamar.
C de Sumacarcel	D Christoval Crespi de Valdaura.

C de la Alcudia y C de Gestalgar — D Joseph Dixar Escriva y Mompalan.

C de Sellet — D Juan Luys Marradas.

C de Parsent — D Joseph Sernesio.

C de Carlet — D Phelipe Lins de Castelvi.

C de Penalva — D Luis Juan de Torres.

C de Castella — D Nicolas de Castelvi.

C de Sinarcas y Vizconde de Chelva — Hay pleito pendiente en el Consejo entre partes de Da Lucrecia Ladron de Villanova, Duquesa de Linares viuda, Da Angela y Da Vitoria Ladron de Villanova, el Conde de Real, el Conde de Sellent, D Luys Carroz, y los hijos de D Jayme Valenciano y de la dha Da Vitoria.

Condado de la Granja — Se litiga en el Consejo entre el Colegio de la Compañia de Jesus de la Ciudad de Orihuela, y D Gerónymo Rocamora y Cascañte de la misma ciudad.

Appendix 5
Jurisdiction of the principal towns in Valencia

The towns noted here include the chief towns under noble jurisdiction in Valencia, but a list of complete jurisdictions is given only in the case of the crown: for the rest, the list should suffice to illustrate the preponderant power of the nobility. Details are drawn from a typewritten list in the *Indice de Cartas Pueblas* of the Archivo General del Reino of Valencia: the list refers to the mid-eighteenth century, when there would have been little change from the situation prevailing during the War of Succession.

GOBERNACION DE VALENCIA:
The king: Ademuz, Alpuente, Aras del Puente, Castielfabit, Foyos, La Yesa, Meliana, Murviedro, Puebla de Farnals, Puebla de San Miguel, Titaguas, Valencia (including Alboraya, Grao de Valencia, Masarrochos, Vistabella).

Others: *Duque de Villahermosa:* Chelva, Benageber, Domeno, Pedralba and Bugarra, Sinarcas, Tuejar. *Duque de Medinaceli:* Benaguacil, Chiva, Godelleta, Puebla de Vallbona, Segorbe. *Marqués de Dos Aguas:* Betera, Chirivella, Dos Aguas, Masamagrell, Masanasa. *Marqués de Monfredi:* Alacuas. *Monastery of Valdecristo:* Alcublas, Altura. *Monastery of Poblet:* Aldaya, Cuarte. *Duke of Berwick:* Barracas, Liria, Jérica. *Encomienda del Infante Don Luis:* Begis. *Order of Montesa:* Borboto, Carpesa, Moncada. *Marqués de Albayda:* Buñol. *Marquesa de la Mina:* Catarroja. *Baron de Cheste:* Chestalcamp. *Order of Santiago:* Museros. *Order of St John:* Picana, Torrente. *See of Valencia:* Puzol, Villar. *Duque de Gandia:* Villamarchante.

GOBERNACION DE ALCIRA:
The king: Alcira, Moncada, Resalan, Algemesi, Almusafes, Cargagente, Cogullada, Corvera, Fortaln, Polina, Riola, Guadasuar.

Others: *Duque de Villahermosa:* Monserrat, Real. *Duque de Gandía:* Alfarbe, Catadan, Llombay. *Marqués de Belgida:* Albalat, Pardines, Ribera, Turis. *Duque del Infantado:* Alberique, Alcocer. *Conde de Carlet:* Alcudia de Carlet, Carlet. *Marqués de Dos Aguas:* Picasent. *Conde del Casal:* Alginet. *Order of Montesa:* Montroy, Silla, Sueca. *Conde de las Torres:* Cullera.

GOBERNACION DE ALCOY:
The king: Alcoy, Bañeres, Penaguila, Villajoyosa.

Others: *Duque de Santistéban:* Cocentaina, Muro. *Conde de Cirat:* Agres. *Conde de Montealegre:* Benidorm. *Conde de Puñonrostro:* Relleu. *Order of Montesa:* Lorcha. *Order of Santiago:* Orcheta.

GOBERNACION DE ALICANTE:
The king: Alicante, Monfort, Muchamiel, San Juan, Benimagrell.

Others: *Conde de Villafranqueza:* Villafranqueza.

GOBERNACION DE CASTELLON:
The king: Castellón de la Plana, Burriana, Villarreal.

Others: *Duque de Villahermosa:* Artana. *Duque de Medinaceli:* Ahin, Alcudia de Veo, Eslida, Fondiguilla de Castro, Suera alta y baja, Vall de Uzo o del Duque, Veo, Zeldo. *See of Tortosa:* Almazora. *Conde de Almenara:* Almenara, Chilches, Llosa de Almenara, Quart. *Marqués de Nules:* Mascarell, Moncofar, Nules. *Marqués de Ariza:* Bechi. *Duque de Montellano:* Soneja.

GOBERNACION DE COFRENTES:
The king: nothing.

Others: *Duque de Gandía:* Cofrentes, Jarafuel, Teresa, Jalance, Zarra. *Duque del Infantado:* Ayora. *Conde de Carlet:* Tous. *Marqués de Cañizar:* Navarres.

GOBERNACION DE DENIA:
The king: Callosa de Ensarria, Tárbena.

Others: *Duque de Medinaceli:* Denia, Beniarjó, Benitachel, Bercher, Javea. *Duque de Gandía:* Almoynes, Alqueria de la Condesa, Beniopa, Benipeixcar, Fuente de Encarroz, Gandia, Miramar, Murla, Orba, Pego, Potrias, Rafelcofer, Real de Gandia, Vall de Guart, Valles de Ebro, Villalonga and Alburquerque. *Marqués de Ariza:* Altea, Beniarda, Benimantell, Benisa, Calpe, Ondara, Teulada. *Marqués de Peñafiel:* Belreguart, Oliva. *Conde de Carlet:* Gata. *Conde de Montealegre:* Nucia, Polop. *Duque de*

Villahermosa: Vall de Gallinera. *Conde de Alcudia:* Jalo. *Conde de Puñonrostro:* Pilas.

GOBERNACION DE MONTESA:
The king: Agullente, Alfafara.

Others: *Order of Montesa:* Montesa, Vallada. *Conde de Puñonrostro:* Anna, Enguera. *Marqués de Bélgida:* Chella. *Marqués de Dos Aguas:* Fuente la Higuera. *Marqués de la Romana:* Mogente. *Conde de Sumacarcer:* Sumacarcer.

GOBERNACION DE MORELLA:
The king: Morella, Castellfort, Cati, Forcall, Gaibiel, La Mata, Olocau, Palanques, Portell, Sinetorres, Vallibona, Villafranca.

Others: *Duque de Villahermosa:* Castillo de Benimalefa, Ludiente, Puebla de Arenoso, Sucayna, Torrechiva, Villahermosa. *Order of Montesa:* Albocacer, Ares del Maestre, Adzaneta, Benafigos, Benasal, Cuevas de Mosquera, Culla, Villanueva de Alcolea. *Monastery of San Miguel de los Reyes:* Candiel, Toro, Viver. *Conde de Salduena:* Castellnovo. *Conde de Aranda:* Cortes de Arenoso, Lucena y Figueroles, Useras. *Conde de la Villanueva:* Montan. *Duke of Berwick:* Pina. *Marqués de Castelrodrigo:* Vall de Almonacir. *City of Morella:* Zurita.

GOBERNACION DE ORIHUELA:
The king: Orihuela, Almoradi, Callosa de Segura, Catral, Guardamar, Benicofar.

Others: *Marqués de Rafal:* Beniferri, Granja, Rafal. *Marqués de Dos Arguas:* Albatera, La Daya. *Duque de Arcos:* Aspe, Crevillente. *Marqués de Melgarejo)* Cocs. *Conde de Puñonrostro:* Elda, Petrel. *Duque de Hijar:* Monóvar. *Marqués de la Romana:* Novelda. *Chapter of Orihuela cathedral:* Bigastro.

GOBERNACION DE PEÑISCOLA:
The king: Peñiscola, Artesa, Onda, Tales, Villafames.

Others: *Order of Montesa:* Alcala de Chisvert, Benicarló, Calix, Canet lo Roch, Cervera, Chert, Jana and Carrascal, Rosell, San Mateo, Sarratella, Torre de Endomench, Trayguera, Vinaroz. *Duque de Villahermosa:* Espadilla, Vallat. *Conde de Aranda:* Alcora. *Marqués de Boil:* Borriol. *See of Tortosa:* Cabanes, Torreblanca. *Duque de Medinaceli:* Fansara.

GOBERNACION DE SAN FELIPE:
The king: San Felipe, Benigamin, Bocayrente, Enova, Callosa, Mantaverner, Olleria, Onteniente, Villanueva de Castellón.

Others: *Marqués de Dos Aguas:* Benicolet, Luchente and Pinet, Quatretonda. *Duque de Gandía:* Ayelo de Rugat, Castellón del Duque, Puebla del Duque, Jaraco, Jereza. *Marqués de Albayda:* Albayda, Atzaneta, Palomar. *Marqués de Malferit:* Ayelo de Malferit. *Monastery of Valdigna:* Benifairo de Valdigna, Simat, Tabernes de Valdigna. *City of San Felipe:* Canals. *Conde de Olocau:* Genoves. *Duque de Medinaceli:* Palma and Ador.

GOBERNACION DE JIJONA:

The king: Jijona, Torre Manzanes, Biar, Ibi.

Others: *Marqués de Dos Aguas:* Castalla, Onil, Tibi. *Duque de Arcos:* Elche and its suburb San Juan. *Conde de Puñonrostro:* Salinas.

Appendix 6
Grain prices in Spain in 1719

The following table is based on information in AGS Guerra Moderna, leg.2358, where the contents of the *legajo* are described as 'Correspondencia sobre los precios de granos en todo el Reyno'. The information consists of reports made to the government by the intendants of the whole realm, on the price of cereals in the late summer of 1719. With the exception of reports from Seville and Navarre in November, all the correspondence is dated between July and October. The prices quoted here in reales are for a *fanega* of best grain in each case. The year 1719 was a moderately good one. The range of prices quoted is interesting testimony to the significant market variations within the peninsula.

City	Date	Wheat	Rye	Barley	Remarks
Avila[1]	23 July	6–8		3	
Avila	6 Aug.	8		3	
Avila	17 Sept.	7	4	3	
Barcelona	29 July	30		15	
Burgos	25 Aug.	11		5	
Caller	8 July	8		5½	
La Coruña	13 Aug.	14	8		
Lugo	13 Aug.	13½	10	7	
Orense	13 Aug.	18		9	
Ciudad Real	25 Aug.	11–12		3½–4	
frontiers of Valencia	25 Aug.	15		6	
Cuenca	19 Aug.	15		6	
Requena	19 Aug.	26		8	
estado de Jorquera	19 Aug.	22		10	

[1] The Avila report, from Pedro Estefanía to Miguel Fernández Durán, says under 23 July of the wheat and barley that 'de uno ni otro ay compradores algunos'. In August: 'sin que haia quien quiera comprarlo.' In September: 'no ay quien saque ni compre.'

City	*Date*	*Wheat*	*Rye*	*Barley*	*Remarks*
Granada	25 July	12–15		8–9	
Guadalajara	25 Aug.	10–14		4–5	
Huete	25 Aug.	12		4	
Sigüenza	25 Aug.	8–11		4–5	
Soria	25 Aug.	10–15		7	
León	27 July.	6½–10		3¾–4	
Málaga	8 Aug.	14–16		8–8½	imported grain
Málaga	8 Aug.	13–13½		7	home grain
Málaga	8 Aug.	12		6–7	countryside price
Málaga	17 Oct.	15½–17		8–9	imported grain
Málaga	17 Oct.	14–15		8½	home grain
Málaga	17 Oct.	12–15		7½	countryside price
Mérida	2 Sept.	8–9		4–4½	
Plasencia	2 Sept.	10–11		5–6	
Trujillo	2 Sept	12½–13		5–5¾	
Badajoz	2 Sept	9		5	
Villanueva	2 Sept	12		4	
Molina	4 Aug	9½–10		6½–7	
Murcia	1 Aug	26–27		9½–10	prices due to drought
Murcia	5 Sept.	23–27		9–10	
Palencia	4 Aug.	6½–6¾		3¼–3½	
Palencia	18 Aug.	6½–12		3–5½	
Palencia	31 Oct.	7½–15½		3¾–5¾	
Pamplona	8 Nov.	6½		4	
Segovia	22 July	9		4	
Seville	5 Sept.	10½–13		6¼–7	
Seville	7 Nov.	10–14		6–6¾	
Toro	7 Aug.	6–6½		13½ (per *carga* = c.6 bushels)	
Valladolid	2 Sept.	5–8		2½–3	countryside price
Zamora	17 Aug.	6–7		11–12 (per *carga*)	
Zamora	7 Sept.	6–8		3	
Zaragoza	5 Aug.	22		11	
Alcañiz	5 Aug.	27		11¼	
Jaca	5 Aug.	20		9	
Barbastro	5 Aug.	23½		11⅔	

Appendix 7
The writings of Melchor de Macanaz

The great importance of Macanaz makes it all the more surprising that a biography of him has never been attempted. In this appendix I wish to indicate where his principal writings (nearly all in manuscript) may be consulted. There are two serious omissions from my list. I cannot give any reference to the valuable Macanaz papers in the possession of Don Francisco Maldonado. Nor is it possible to list every one of the hundreds of letters from Macanaz scattered through the official correspondence of the period.

PRINTED WRITINGS

1. *Regalías de los Señores Reyes de Aragón*, Madrid, 1879. This volume, edited by Joaquin Maldonado Macanaz, is prefaced by an autobiographical account of Macanaz, dated Paris 7 Jan. 1739. The introduction contains a valuable analysis of the writings of Macanaz, together with a list of his alleged writings published up to 1879. Tracts included in the volume are the *Informe dado al Rey sobre el gobierno antiguo de Aragón,* dated Madrid 27 May 1713; the *Regalías, Intereses y Derechos que por la rebelión de los tres reinos han recaido en la Corona de Castilla,* written after Utrecht; and the *Discurso jurídico, histórico y político sobre las Regalías de los Señores Reyes de Aragón,* written in 1729, which forms the bulk of the book.

2. *Semanario Erudito*, Madrid, 1788. In this series Valladares de Sotomayor published several works attributed to Macanaz. The most important are the *Representación que hice y remití desde Lieja, Semanario,* vol. 7, pp. 158–204, *Varias Notas al Teatro Crítico del Eruditísimo Feyjoo,* vol. 7, pp. 205–80; vol. 8, pp. 1–135, *Manifiesto y Cotejo* (subtitled *Declaración a la Europa en 28 de Julio de 1748),* vol. 7, pp. 103–32. Others are printed in vol. 7, pp. 132–8;

vol. 8, pp. 136–60, 161–71, 217–38; vol. 9, pp. 3–142. The authenticity of some of these is discussed by Joaquin Maldonado in his introduction to the *Regalías*.

3. The Biblioteca Nacional in Madrid has three small printed volumes by Macanaz. The first, entitled *Obras Escogidas,* Madrid, 1847, was later exposed as apocryphal by Joaquin Maldonado. The other two, *Discúrsos políticos y Testamento de España,* Madrid, 1883?, and *Auxilios para bien gobernar una monarquía católica,* Madrid, 1789, appear to be genuine.

MANUSCRIPT WRITINGS

1. The biggest single collection of writings attributed to Macanaz is in the manuscript section of the Biblioteca Nacional, Madrid. Unfortunately, almost none of the manuscripts is in Macanaz's own hand, so that their authenticity needs checking. The manuscripts I have examined are the following:

767: original autograph letters dated 1722, and copy of a memoir against Giudice.

1060: extract from the Dec. 1713 memoir.

2768: a large volume, this is the 'Males, daños y perjuicios que han ocasionado a la España'. In form, it is a commentary on the *Historia civil de España* of Belando.

5958: imperfect copy of 'Defensa crítica de la Inquisición.

6932: same as in 10738.

10313: includes 'Sobre excesos de la Dataría Romana', dated Madrid 2 July 1714.

10624: 'Reflexiones críticas' on the History of France of the abbé du Bos.

10655: copy of 'Defensa crítica de la Inquisición'.

10701: the same.

10738: writings relevant to diplomacy in 1746–7.

10744: two writings on monarchy, and the 'Notas al Teatro Crítico'.

10745: eight writings, including a commentary on Voltaire.

10754: copy of 'Proyecto sobre la reduccion de Censos y Juros' and of the 'Auxilios para governar'.

10785: copy of the memoir in 767.

10818[31]: copy of letter about Peace of Breda.

10855: three copies of the Dec. 1713 memoir, and other writings.

10865: text of the work published in 1847 as *Obras Escogidas*.

10904: includes the 'Cathálogo de las Obras' of Macanaz undertaken in 1744 by the Spanish ambassador in Paris. The estimated total of his output to that date was 201 folio volumes.

10910: 'Proyecto sobre la reducción de Censos y Juros.'

10911: copy of Dec. 1713 memoir, and the 'Manifiesto y Cotejo'.

10932: at folio 72, copy of a memorial to Ferdinand VI.

10936: f.1–162 has a copy of a 'Defensa que hizo Dn Melchor de Macanaz', which ends: 'Lo firmé en Madrid a 8 de Diz^e de 1717.' Macanaz was not in Madrid in 1717.

10945: copy of 'Auxilios para governar'.

10992: copy of Dec. 1713 memoir.

11029: at folio 275, there is a paper entitled 'Fragmentos históricos de la vida de Dn Melchor Rafael de Macanaz', dated Valencia 31 May 1788. It has several factual errors.

11064: several memoirs.

11073: copies of 'Testamento de España', 'Declaracion a la Europa', and the important 'Disertacion de Macanaz contra Alberoni'.

19330: at p. 386, text of memorial accompanying Dec. 1713 memoir.

20710: 'Representacion echa al Rey en justificacion del escrito de 55 articulos.'

2. The library of the Real Academia de la Historia, Madrid, has valuable originals and copies of works by Macanaz, all in manuscript. References are:

9-28-3-C-97: 'Memorial que Dn Melchor de Macanaz, Fiscal General del Reyno, dio al Rey Nro. señor Dn Phelipe 5. Acompañando las proposiciones que de su Real Orden dispuso sobre negocios de Roma.' A copy.

9-12-2-250-251-252: 'La Francia contra la Francia y Schisma del Jansenismo.' These are the last three volumes of a work in eight volumes, and are in original autograph. Each volume consists of over three hundred folio pages. The work is a detailed attack on Jansenism and Quietism.

9-31-7-7064: 'Reflexiones y avisos para el Govierno de la Monarquia de España.' Macanaz is referred to as 'oy relegado en la Ciudad de Segovia'. Copy.

Est. 23. gr. 1ª.A.nº 15: 'Memorias Políticas, históricas y Gubernativas de España y Francia ... recogidas o compuestas y notadas por Dⁿ Melchor Macanaz. En Paris año de 1729.' This is a massive volume of four hundred folio pages, consisting of various collected papers, many printed. The title page and index is in Macanaz's hand. The volume is of great interest, includes some minor tracts by Macanaz, and gives evidence of his friendship with the abbé de Vayrac.

9-9-6-1510: 'Curiel contra Macanaz.' Contains documents illustrating the quarrel between Curiel and Macanaz. Late eighteenth-century script.

9-28-8-5724: A collection of documents apparently made by Macanaz, but none of the papers appears to be in the original.

9-27-4-5214: Folios 169-83 give details of the early life of Macanaz, as set down in the late eighteenth century by Juan Sempere y Guarinos.

3. Instituto de Valencia de Don Juan, Madrid. The library here has a manuscript copy, not in Macanaz's hand, of the *Nuevo Sistema Económico para el perfecto gobierno de la América*. It is dated 1719, and explicitly attributed to Macanaz. This attribution is startling, for the work is usually supposed to have been written very much later by José Campillo, though no one has proved Campillo's authorship. Needless to say, the *Nuevo Sistema* is a work of great importance.

4. In the Archivo General de Simancas, section Secretaría de Estado, some of the *legajos* are devoted to Macanaz's diplomatic work for Spain.

leg.4690: this includes various letters, dated 1717 to 1723, from Macanaz and his brother Antonio, on persecution by the Inquisition, salary, etc. It also includes Macanaz's correspondence in 1724 from Fontainebleau, Versailles and Paris, with the Spanish court, on diplomatic matters.

leg.4691: correspondence in 1725 and 1726 with the marqués de Grimaldo and the marqués de la Paz. The letters were written from Versailles, Bordeaux, Cambrai, Brussels and Liége; in all these places he was on diplomatic missions for Spain.

leg.4692: correspondence in 1727 and 1728 with la Paz. Diplomatic business took him from Liége (where he spent all of 1726 and most of 1727) to Paris and Soissons.

leg.4693: correspondence in 1729 and 1730 with la Paz, all from Paris. Virtually nothing for the year 1731.

leg.4694: various correspondence for the years 1743-8, with copy of the order freeing him from prison in 1760.

leg.4965: various letters beginning in the 1720s and going through to 1748.

5. MS 24 of the library of the University of Valencia is titled 'Copia de los Manuscritos de Macanaz'. This is the only text of his memoirs available, apart from the original volumes in the possession of Don Francisco Maldonado. Joaquin Maldonado Macanaz lent the first two of these original volumes to the University in the nineteenth century, and a diligent copyist took the opportunity to transcribe those sections that concerned Valencia. The result is an extremely valuable document. It should be noted that only one historian has ever read the whole text of Macanaz's manuscript memoirs and incorporated it into his work: this was Modesto Lafuente, whose *Historia General de España* contains for that reason one of the most outstanding surveys of the early Bourbon period.

Sources

Paris

1. ARCHIVES DU MINISTÈRE DES AFFAIRES ENTRANGÈRES

When Napoleon occupied Spain, he arranged for the transportation of a proportion of the Spanish archives to Paris. Most of the papers have since been returned, but a substantial proportion relating *inter alia* to the War of Succession remains in the French diplomatic archives. The result is that the Spanish archives contain absolutely nothing on state business in the war period, and Franco-Spanish diplomacy can be studied only in the documentation held by the French government. The Foreign Ministry archives are for this reason the richest source on the war, and all students of early Bourbon Spain must begin their researches here. In the section *Correspondance Politique (Espagne)* I have consulted over 140 volumes, namely 87–99, 102–111, 114–120, 122–125, 136–243. In the useful section of *Mémoires et Documents (Espagne)*, I have consulted volumes 32, 92, 97, 101–102, 153, 238, 241, 250 and 252.

2. ARCHIVES NATIONALES

The most relevant documentation here is in the section *Affaires Etrangères*, formerly housed in the Foreign Ministry. In this I have looked particularly at the series B^I and B^{III}, which consist of consular correspondence, together with useful material on commerce and economic policy. Sections K and KK hold varia. I have consulted, in series B^I, bundles 208, 214–221, 455–456, 769–778; in series B^{III}, bundles 323–326, 360–361, 364, 374; in section K, bundle 1359; in KK, bundle 536.

3. BIBLIOTHÈQUE NATIONALE

The documentation on Philip v in the manuscript room is dispersed and not significant. I have consulted, in the *fonds français*, papers 7800, 14178,21438, and 21769; in the *fonds Espagne*, papers 153, 270, 378; and in the *fonds Lorraine*, paper 970.

4. DÉPÔT GÉNÉRAL DE LA GUERRE, VINCENNES

The documentation in this former military fortress, which now houses among other things the War Archives, constitutes the richest single source for a proper study of the military aspects of the War of Succession. I have used it principally for the light it throws on French policy and on internal events in Spain, and have ignored the exhaustive materials available for a study of the peninsular campaign. In the relevant section, *Série A¹*, I have consulted 41 volumes, namely 1695–1696, 1786–1789, 1791, 1793, 1883–1888, 1891–1892, 1976–1979, 1981–1985, 2048–2054, 2104–2105, 2177–2178, 2180, 2253–2255, 2328–2329, 2332, 2404.

Spain

I. ARCHIVO GENERAL DE SIMANCAS

This magnificent archive is, unfortunately, poorly stocked on the reign of Philip v, partly because some of the documentation is in Madrid, partly because of the Napoleonic marauders, and partly because much of the source-material seems to have perished. As a result, Spanish sources alone do not allow us to build up an adequate picture of the reign of Philip v. The sections I have examined are as follows:

Consejo y Juntas de Hacienda. This section, extremely valuable for social and economic history, runs chronologically up to 1700, and then ceases to exist for the reign of Philip v. I have used nearly two hundred of the bundles (*legajos*) as a basis for a study of the reign of Charles 11.

Contadurías Generales. This was one of the accounting agencies of the exchequer. I have consulted *legajos* 173–176, 187–191, 198, 591–593, 1724, 1792–1795, 2698.

Dirección General del Tesoro. This section contains information on the administration of finances. It is catalogued by inventories, of which I have used the following: Inventario 4, legs.10, 13, 18, 94–95, 173, 184; Inventario 7, legs.1, 3; Inventario 16, guión 5, leg.3; Inventario 16, guión 19, legs.1¹⁻², 2¹⁻⁴; Inventario 16, guión 21, legs.2–3, 6; Inventario 24, legs.267, 271, 554–557.

Guerra Moderna. Disappointingly, there is virtually nothing here on the actual War of Succession, and the earliest *legajos* tend to deal only with the siege of Barcelona. I have, however, consulted fifty-nine *legajos* of the later years of the reign, which have supplied useful material. Those consulted were 1558–1559, 1576–1579, 1590–1592, 1594, 1598, 1601, 1606, 1610, 1612–1614, 1616–1617, 1622, 1624, 1629, 1632–1633, 1636, 1638–1639, 1642, 1647–1648, 1811, 1813, 1815, 1818, 1819–1820, 2352–2358, 2362–2363, 2369, 2371–2373, 2389, 3771, 3788, 3873, 3875, 3877–3878, 3883, 3886, 3888. There is a *suplemento* to this section, from which *legajos* 252, 463, 588² have been consulted.

Secretaría de Estado. This section usually deals with the foreign affairs of Castile. I have not found it very useful, save for the documentation on Macanaz (see appendix 7). *Legajos* consulted, apart from those on Macanaz, were 4301–4309, 7584–7586, 7593–7594, 7832–7841.

Secretaría de Gracia y Justicia. Of the papers of this administrative department I consulted only legs.1–3, 45, 85, 348–349, 362. None of these was very helpful, except for 348, which contained a wealth of information on the history of the intendants.

Secretaría de Hacienda. This section, which has documentation on financial administration, contains nothing on the period of the war. I nevertheless consulted twenty-seven *legajos* which gave some useful general data: 1–3, 65–67, 84–88, 90–91, 94, 221, 396–399, 424, 536–537, 550, 563, 565, 576, 972.

Tribunal Mayor de Cuentas. These papers give detailed accounts of income and expenditure from the beginning of the reign. I have consulted seventy-two *legajos:* 551, 1869–1889, 1891–1893, 1895–1905, 1910–1922, 1928–1931, 1937–1946, 1950, 1952–1953, 1955–1956, 1961, 1964, 1977–1987, 1994–1995, 1997–2004, 2011.

2. ARCHIVO HISTÓRICO NACIONAL, MADRID

These archives supplement the documentation at Simancas. Sections consulted here were:

Consejos suprimidos. This consists of various papers of the Councils. I have used *legajos* 6802–6808, 13222–13225, 18184, 18190, 18201, 18309, 18355, 18448.

Estado. This section is fundamental to a study of the War of Succession, and contains the only continuous documentation on the period 1700–15 in any of the central Spanish archives. Though 'Estado', that is 'State', papers were usually concerned with foreign policy, much of the material in this collection is devoted exclusively to internal affairs. The documentation on the war is mainly military in character. I have consulted one hundred and thirty-eight of the *legajos*, namely 188, 190, 193, 195, 260, 262–265, 269–273, 276, 278–283, 286, 312, 317, 319–320, 324, 331, 337, 342-343, 345–346, 348, 352–353, 358, 361, 365, 367, 369–370, 373, 375, 378–380, 382–383, 390, 394, 397, 399–400, 403, 406, 409, 410–413, 416–420, 423, 425–427, 429–434, 436, 439–440, 442, 444, 446–447, 449–450, 453, 456, 458, 465–466, 491, 496, 508, 513, 523–524, 530–532, 596, 648, 664, 681, 736, 744, 758, 802, 812, 816, 914, 917, 1417, 1603–1604, 1606, 2313, 2327, 2460, 2484, 2530, 2574, 2819–2820, 2898, 2902, 2973, 2975, 2989, 3028¹, 3302, 3304, 3329, 3355, 3359, 3469, 3486, 4004. In addition *libro* 214 was consulted.

3. ARCHIVO GENERAL DE INDIAS, SEVILLE

Contratación. In this section, I consulted in particular *libro* 2901, for details of ships and cargos reaching Spain during the war. I also looked at *libro* 2900, and legs.1265–1270, 1968–1969.

Contaduría. Valuable but incomplete details on bullion were obtained here. The *legajos* used were 3, 170, 175, 229, 578, 582, 784, 802, 892, 999, 1762.

Indiferente. This section, which includes several *legajos* on the Vigo disaster, proved to be extremely informative. I consulted legs.2530, 2632–2634, 2714, 2716, 2720–2721, 2745, 2751, 2755–2756.

4. ARCHIVO DEL MINISTERIO DE HACIENDA, MADRID

I originally consulted this archive when it was housed in the Ministry of Finance in Madrid. It has since been transferred to the Archivo Histórico Nacional. The references I give may not therefore be those under which the material is now catalogued. Documents consulted for this study were in the section Consejo de Hacienda, Registro de Consultas, vols 7999–8000; and in Consejo de Castilla, impresos, vol. 6549.

5. BIBLIOTECA NACIONAL, MADRID

The manuscript section of the Biblioteca Nacional was consulted mainly for documents on Macanaz. These are discussed in appendix 7. Other MS documents of particular value were 2274, ('Vecindario General de España'), 7528 (on the *única contribución*), 1971O[39] ('Planta de Bergei 1713'), 6753, 5805, 6952, 10618.

6. BIBLIOTECA DE LA REAL ACADEMIA DE LA HISTORIA, MADRID

The documents concerning Macanaz consulted here are discussed in appendix 7. Other useful documents were 9-5-1-K-29-654 ('Cédulas de la Junta de Incorporación'), Est.24.gr.5ª.B.no.128 (on the finances), 9-29-6-5982 ('Miscelenea Histórica'), 9-26-1-4762 (population of Aragon).

7. BIBLIOTECA DE LA UNIVERSIDAD DE VALENCIA

The library of Valencia University contains extremely valuable manuscript diaries which have so far remained totally neglected. MS 456, 'Sucessos fatales de esta Ciudad y Reyno de Valencia; o Puntual Diario de lo sucedido en los años de el Señor de 1712–1715', is the fourth volume of a work from which the first three volumes are missing or mislaid. The author, Isidro Planes (whose name is not given), offers a closely detailed diary of both local and national events, with a comment on the state of the weather for each day. MS 460, 'Diario de lo sucedido en la ciudad de Valencia desde el dia 3 del mes de Octubre del año de 1700 hasta el dia 1º del mes de Setiembre del año de 1715', by Josef Vicente Orti y Mayor, would have been an even more valuable commentary, since the author was a public figure; however, the volume in the library covers only the years 1705–9. The other papers consulted here were MSS 17 ('Orti: papeles varios'), 24 ('Copia de los Manuscritos de Macanaz'), 166 and 803.

England

BRITISH MUSEUM, LONDON

The following papers were consulted in the manuscript room:
Additional MS 21,449; 21,536–21,537; 28,476–28,479.
Egerton MS 2055; 2084; 16,520.

Bibliographical Note

Some of the more useful works on the period covered by this book have been indicated in the footnotes, and I have not thought it necessary to add a detailed bibliography. An extensive list covering hundreds of books and articles, few of them useful or significant, may be found in A. Ballesteros y Beretta, *Historia de España y su Influencia en la Historia Universal*, Barcelona, 1929, vols 5 and 6; in B. Sánchez Alonso, *Fuentes de la Historia Española e Hispanoamericana* (3rd edn), Madrid, 1952, vol. 2; and in the relevant volumes of the *Indice Histórico Español*. Despite these writings, early Bourbon Spain remains unexplored in nearly every important respect.

There is, for example, no good military history of the war. In English, Parnell's book (page 10 note 2) is the best, though still quite inadequate. No good account exists in Spanish, apart from the contemporary memoirs of San Felipe (page 10 note 2). Yet the archives possess all the material required for a solid analysis of the military campaigns.

The political history of Castile is excellently studied in Baudrillart's fundamental book (page 42 note 1). No Spanish historian has attempted to survey the politics of the War of Succession, and the best accounts available in Spanish are still those given by contemporaries such as San Felipe and Nicolás de Jesús Belando (page 254 note 27). The most significant history of the war period may well prove to be that given by Macanaz in his unpublished manuscript memoirs. The political history of the crown of Aragon is entirely unwritten, though the contemporary writings of men such as Feliu de la Peña (page 268 note 59) and the conde de Robres (page 95 note 39) provide a useful beginning. Needless to say, there is nothing of value in print on the social and economic history of the war period, with the notable exception of the contribution made by Pierre Vilar in his outstanding study of eighteenth-century Catalonia. Mounier's useful study of Uztáriz (page 199 note 1) deals mainly with finance; it has interesting but imprecise data on the economy of the country.

Index

The following pages include an author index, giving name of author, short title of work, and reference to the first footnote citing the work in full.